THE FIRST DECADE

The First Decade

The Hong Kong SAR in Retrospective and Introspective Perspectives

Edited by

Yue-man Yeung

The Chinese University Press

The First Decade: The Hong Kong SAR in Retrospective and Introspective Perspectives
Edited by Yue-man Yeung

ISBN 978–962–996–357–6

THE CHINESE UNIVERSITY PRESS
The Chinese University of Hong Kong
SHA TIN, N.T., HONG KONG
Fax: +852 2603 6692
      +852 2603 7355
E-mail: cup@cuhk.edu.hk
Web-site: www.chineseupress.com

Printed in Hong Kong

Contents

Part I: Hong Kong as Seen from Without

Part II: Hong Kong as Seen from Within

Part III: Summary and Conclusions

List of Figures and Tables

Figures

Tables

Foreword

Lawrence J. Lau
President and Vice-Chancellor
The Chinese University of Hong Kong

The end of a territory's colonial status usually comes through independence via peaceful or other means, after which the new nation strikes out on its own. It is very rare for a colonial territory to be returned to the sovereign country from which it was taken. The reversion of sovereignty over Hong Kong from the United Kingdom to China in 1997, after 156 years of colonial rule, is thus an exceptional case. Similarly, Macao was returned to China by Portugal in 1999, after an even longer period of colonial rule. Both colonial territories were handed back to China amicably and smoothly, with plenty of lead time and preparation and amid the full glare of global scrutiny and publicity.

In the lead up to Hong Kong's handover in 1997, the Western press, politicians, and political commentators were hardly optimistic about its future. What was involved was the return of a tiny but vibrant city famous for its freewheeling style of capitalism to a rapidly rising communist power, whose handling of the Tian'anmen incident had not been forgotten in the West. Indeed, many predicted a dire future for Hong Kong, with *Fortune* magazine even pronouncing the death of Hong Kong in a 1995 special issue. Ten years have elapsed since Hong Kong began its existence as a Special Administrative Region (SAR) within the People's Republic of China, under the "one country, two systems (capitalist and socialist)" formula.

How has Hong Kong fared since the handover? Has the novel political and economic formula of "one country, two systems," buttressed by the Basic Law, worked? These are questions well worth the effort of rigorous and penetrating scrutiny, and Professor Yue-man Yeung has assembled a group of scholars of a calibre equal to the task.

On the whole, the transition from British to Chinese sovereignty must be considered a success. Life has continued with little change. The central government has generally bent over backwards not to interfere in Hong Kong's affairs. The rule of law, the independence of the judiciary, and the civil liberties that Hong Kong people enjoyed under British colonial rule have all remained intact. The economic system is as free as ever. Even the Falun Gong, a religious cult that has been outlawed on the Mainland, has been allowed to continue to operate in Hong Kong. Finally, the citizens of Hong Kong arguably have more say than they did before 1997, and the Hong Kong government has become much more responsive to them. This brings us to the question: Why do the people seem to be so dissatisfied?

While the exodus of Hong Kong people to Canada, the United States, and Australia between 1989 and 1997 was motivated more by political than economic jitters, it was the poor performance of the Hong Kong economy, due to a series of crises largely beyond the control of Hong Kong, that turned the citizens of Hong Kong against the government. It began with the collapse of the Thai baht on 2 July 1997, which triggered a financial crisis in Asia and led to the bursting of the real estate bubble. This was followed by the avian flu crisis, and culminated in the SARS (severe acute respiratory syndrome) nightmare in 2003. With real estate prices falling and unemployment rising, the Hong Kong economy reached rock bottom in mid-2003, which undoubtedly was a major factor in the massive march against the Hong Kong government that took place on 1 July 2003.

I took up the Presidency of the University in mid-2004, at a time when, fortuitously, Hong Kong's fortunes began to turn, largely because of the economic boom in Mainland China and the launching of the Individual Visit Scheme. By the tenth anniversary of the handover, Hong Kong's economy has mostly recovered from its downturn, and in some areas has reached historic highs. The Hong Kong stock market, for instance, has broken many records, but many sectors of the economy and society are confronting new challenges that they have never experienced before.

I believe it is fair to say that China has so far exercised less political control over Hong Kong than the United Kingdom used to do. However, economically, Hong Kong has become much more dependent on China than it had ever been on the United Kingdom. One country is here, and is here to stay; the challenge is how to make the "two systems" work in a way that will benefit both China and Hong Kong, not only in the present, but also over the long term. What stands in the way is insufficient trust — with each side worrying not about what the other side will or can do, but what it might do. The solution is for the people of both China and Hong Kong to begin thinking not only of their own respective interests but also of the interests of the other side. Only win-win strategies can be successful and sustainable in the long run. The synergy between China and Hong Kong under "one country, two systems" is indeed open for both to explore and create for the benefit of both.

This book is comprised of comprehensive and analytical essays that are strong stand-alone pieces, which together tell a compelling story of how well Hong Kong has weathered many storms and survived as a new entity and city within China. The British colonial legacies of the rule of law, an independent judiciary, human rights, an efficient and clean civil service, and strong institutions have stood Hong Kong in good stead in the first decade after 1997. These are indeed the very qualities that set Hong Kong apart from other Chinese cities that are vying to find a niche in the new global economy. Deng Xiaoping's vision of "one country, two systems" has, over the past ten years, proven to be workable. It is up to Hong Kong and its people to demonstrate to the motherland and the world that this political design can be further fine-tuned and improved to the satisfaction of all concerned. Hong Kong will have, within the "one country, two systems" arrangement, the ability and determination to stay a distinctive world city in China and Asia. Given the Hong Kong people's pragmatism and will to succeed, and the willingness of the central government to extend support to Hong Kong, all augurs well for the Hong Kong SAR in the next decade and beyond.

Preface

The idea of organizing an international conference to mark the tenth anniversary of the founding of the Hong Kong Special Administrative Region (SAR) in 2007 sprang from a suggestion from the Vice-Chancellor, Professor Lawrence J. Lau, in late 2006. It was conceived as a university contribution to the long list of celebratory events officially recognized by the Hong Kong SAR government and organized by the Hong Kong community for this landmark occasion. Indeed, the conference was later incorporated into the roster of community events associated with the handover celebrations. The conference was held on campus on 18 June 2007. It involved a full day of presentation of papers and active participation in discussions, rounded off by a dinner.

Central to the organization of the conference and, thus of the production of this book, was the view that it is desirable for the first decade of the post-colonial Hong Kong to be fairly and systematically assessed by distinguished scholars from outside Hong Kong, from perspectives that relate closely to the subject of how the "one country, two systems" experiment came about or to the direction and weight of political and public opinion. Towards this end, scholars from Britain, North America, Beijing and Southeast Asia were invited to pass judgement on the outcome of the new political and administrative design prescribed by the Basic Law, a mini constitution for Hong Kong. In addition, it was felt that the birth of Hong Kong as an SAR within China had to be examined from the longer span of history, especially in the decades prior to the reversion of sovereignty surrounding Hong Kong. Hence, the first chapter of this book can essentially be viewed as an introductory essay that spells out the deep historical meanings in the return of Hong Kong to its motherland. To complete this first part of the book, which appraises Hong Kong from without, one chapter traces the often narrow confines within which Hong Kong's relations with Taiwan take place, under an overarching China-Taiwan cross-Strait policy. Another chapter was designed to tackle the subject of the international arena within which the Hong Kong SAR continues to operate as a separate entity within the one-China framework, but unfortunately this chapter failed to materialize.

The second part of the conference and the book is more straightforward. Sectors of the political, economic and social life of Hong Kong deemed to have undergone significant changes since 1997 are examined. Leading local scholars were invited to discourse on political changes, legal changes, economic development, the business environment, social transformation, education reform, cross-boundary integration, urban planning, environmental challenges and public health. Quite obviously, the list is partial and incomplete, but given the limited lead time for the conference and the measured scope of this book, many other important and worthwhile dimensions had to be forsaken. In any event, the chosen themes are sufficient to provide the reader with a sufficiently wide range of topics to appreciate the vicissitudes of life in Hong Kong and the wide swings in the SAR's economic cycles during a momentous and tempestuous decade. Individual authors provide reasoned accounts of how the past 10 years have affected Hong Kong and the Hong Kong people, and their views of what Hong Kong stands to expect at the threshold of the second decade.

I would like to thank many organizations and individuals, without whose cooperation and assistance this volume sizing up the success or otherwise of the first decade of the Hong Kong SAR would not have materialized. First and foremost, I wish to thank Vice-Chancellor Lau not only for his idea of holding a timely academic forum and compiling a book from the papers presented at that forum, but also for providing funding for the entire endeavour. I thank him also for the confidence he has shown in me. The staff of the Hong Kong Institute of Asia-Pacific Studies have demonstrated their usual efficiency and steadfastness of purpose in organizing the conference and preparing the related manuscript, often under stringent time constraints. Special thanks must go to Janet Wong, my long-time senior personal secretary, who was in charge of the overall handling of the conference and of my correspondence with the authors, in addition to preparing the manuscript in its many versions. Gorden Kee, my research assistant, deserves special mention, as he shouldered many responsibilities beyond the call of duty. The staff of The Chinese University Press were at their cooperative best, lending their support to the publication of this book within a relatively short period of time. This is especially appreciated as, during the summer, the press also underwent a change in director with the retirement of the previous director and the relocation of its office away from campus. Finally, I am indebted to all of the authors for their cooperation, understanding and forbearance through the greater part of the past year. Together, their exposition of their knowledge on Hong Kong has made this volume a valuable contribution to the documentation of an ever-changing world city within an emerging China in the era of globalization.

Yue-man Yeung
August 2007

Abbreviations and Acronyms

11th FYP	Eleventh Five-year Plan
AAT	Academic Attainment Test
ACE	Advisory Council on the Environment
AFC	Asian financial crisis
ANOF	anti-new order forces
API	Air Pollution Index
ASEAN	Association of Southeast Asian Nations
BL23	Article 23 of the Basic Law
CA	Conservancy Association
CASET	Computer Aided Evaluation Sustainability Tool
CBD	Central business district
CCG	Chinese Central Government
CCP	Chinese Communist Party
CDETO	Chengdu Economic and Trade Office
CE	Chief Executive
CEO	Chief Executive Officer
CEPA	Closer Economic Partnership Arrangement
CFA	Court of Final Appeal
CHP	Centre for Health Protection
CPG	Central People's Government
CPI	continuous public involvement
CPU	Central Policy Unit
DEP	Director of Environmental Protection
DPP	Democratic Progressive Party
EIAO	Environmental Impact Assessment Ordinance
EMB	Education and Manpower Bureau
EPD	Environmental Protection Department

EIU	Economist Intelligence Unit
EU	European Union
FCO	Foreign and Commonwealth Office
FDI	foreign direct investment
FTA	free trade area
G&M	The Globe and Mail
GDETO	Guangdong Economic and Trade Office
GDP	gross domestic product
GNP	gross national product
GPRD	Greater Pearl River Delta
ha	hectare
HA	Hospital Authority
HATS	Harbour Area Treatment Scheme
HKFDI	Hong Kong foreign direct investment
HKIA	Hong Kong International Airport
HKPC	Hong Kong Productivity Council
HKSAR	Hong Kong Special Administrative Region
HKTNC	Hong Kong transnational corporation
HMG	Her Majesty's Government
HN/AIDS	human immunodeficiency virus/acquired immuno-deficiency syndrome
ICCPR	International Covenant on Civil and Political Rights
IFC	international financial centre
IMD	International Institute for Management Development
IPO	initial public offering
IRP	International Review Panel
IVS	individual visitor scheme
JD	Joint Declaration
LegCo	Legislative Council
LPG	liquefied petroleum gas
MA	Management Agreement
MAC	Mainland Affairs Council
MNC	multinational corporation
MPH	Master's of Public Health
MSW	managerial solid waste
NCP	New Conservation Policy
NGO	non-governmental organization
NOx	nitrogen oxides
NPC	National People's Congress

NPCSC	NPC Standing Committee
NPO	new political order
NT	New Territories
NYT	*The New York Times*
OCTS	one country, two systems
ODM	original design manufacturer
OECD	Organization for Economic Cooperation and Development
OEM	original equipment manufacturers
OBM	original brand manufacturers
OZP	Outline Zoning Plan
Pan-PRD	Pan-Pearl River Delta
PCSSA	Portable Comprehensive Social Security Assistance
PISA	Programme for International Student Assessment
PLA	People's Liberation Army
PLC	Provisional Legislative Council
PNOF	pro-new order forces
PPP	Public Private Partnership
PRC	People's Republic of China
PRD	Pearl River Delta
PRS	producer responsibility scheme
QDII	qualified domestic institutional investors
ROC	Republic of China
RSP	respirable suspended particulate
SAR	Special Administrative Region
SARS	severe acute respiratory syndrome
SCNPC	Standing Committee of China's National People's Congress
SEZ	Special Economic Zone
SHETO	Shanghai Economic and Trade Office
SIJORI	Singapore Johore-Riau
SME	small and medium enterprise
SOE	state-owned enterprise
SSDS	Strategic Sewage Disposal Scheme
SUSDEV 21	*Study on Sustainable Development for the 21st Century in Hong Kong*
TCM	traditional Chinese medicine
TDS	Territorial Development Strategy
TEU	twenty-foot equivalent unit

TNC	Transnational corporation
TNI	transnationality index
tpd	tonnes per day
TSP	total suspended particulate
UNCTAD	United Nations Conference on Trade and Development
VOC	volatile organic compound
VR	village representative
WHO	World Health Organization
WTO	World Trade Organization

PART I

Hong Kong as Seen from Without

1

The First Decade: Historical Perspectives

Wang Gungwu *

Background to the 1997 Handover

Hong Kong's return to China was inextricably tied to conditions in China. Had the Cultural Revolution continued to 1997 or had there been any prospect of Hong Kong becoming independent as a nation-state after decolonization, Hong Kong would be a very different place today. Fortunately, when Mao Zedong died, he was not succeeded by his wife and her "Gang of Four" but by more pragmatic leaders who brought the visionary Deng Xiaoping back from his second stint in exile. Equally fortunate for the peace of the region was that in 1971 the People's Republic of China (PRC) had replaced the Republic of China as the only government of China in the United Nations (UN). When that was done, the PRC refused to allow Hong Kong to remain on the list of colonies under the supervision of the UN Special Decolonization Committee. That ensured that it was only a matter of time before Hong Kong would be returned to China.

Exactly how that was to happen was uncertain because China was in the grip of the Cultural Revolution and no one was sure how that would end. Finally, the internal struggles for power in Beijing that went on for another five years were resolved abruptly in 1976 following the arrest of the "Gang of Four." By 1978, Deng Xiaoping was in charge and he started

---

* The author and the editor, after due consideration, have decided not to include notes and references in this chapter. By providing historical perspectives predating the handover, this chapter can serve as a commanding introduction to the book, based on the perceptive reading of many. With the author's kind permission, the references for this chapter form part of the select bibliography at the end of this volume.

afresh by introducing deep and extensive economic reforms that turned the Chinese revolution on its head. It was in this extraordinary and unexpected context that the question of Hong Kong's eventual return to the motherland was brought to the negotiating table in 1982. This was doubly fortunate for Hong Kong. On the one hand, China's dependence on a flourishing Hong Kong economy was never greater. On the other, Britain had a stronger hand to play in trying to produce conditions of autonomy for Hong Kong people, who were used to a governance structure based on the rule of law and a free market economy. The timing was excellent when both sides agreed that the continued prosperity of Hong Kong was essential for the return to be widely welcomed. In addition, and this was possibly more decisive, was the fact that, even before the formal negotiations had begun, Deng Xiaoping had thought through the problem of reunification with Taiwan and had devised the formula of "one country, two systems" (OCTS) to deal with a more difficult issue of sovereignty left open by a long and bitter civil war. That formula, when applied to Hong Kong, helped to determine the extent to which Hong Kong people would have the chance to govern Hong Kong.

From China's point of view, the crucial problem was that only those Hong Kong people whom the Beijing authorities could trust should be allowed to govern the Special Administrative Region (SAR) after the handover. But they also had to be people who would know how to keep Hong Kong prosperous. The British, in turn, were concerned about protecting their economic interests for as long as possible and also about remaining influential in the SAR. But they were equally determined to achieve these things without being accused of "selling out the people of Hong Kong" or of abandoning them to the mercy of a Communist Party that had produced the horrors of the Cultural Revolution. Hence their belated attempts to introduce democracy to their colony at the last moment. As for the people of Hong Kong, their expectations varied considerably. Many chose to vote with their feet and made preparations to leave, following those who had already left in the late 1960s and early 1970s during the years of the excesses of the Cultural Revolution. Those who remained either had nowhere to go or accepted that they were, after all, Chinese. Hong Kong was Chinese territory and they should welcome the end of its colonial status. Indeed, many were grateful that there would be a period of 50 years for them and their compatriots on the Mainland to adjust fully to the differences that had grown between the cultures of each group. Yet others in Hong Kong, awakened to the possibility of exercising their political rights, decided to stay and fight for those rights, to the extent of encouraging those on the Mainland to recognize those rights together with them. Thus, for Hong Kong people, the decade-and-a-half before the actual handover was filled with a mixture of hope and disappointment. Some welcomed the pressure placed on the Chinese by the British and Americans over issues of human and political rights. Others were cheered by the efforts of various groups of Mainland Chinese officials to reassure Hongkongers, especially those who had always supported the return to China, that their lives could go on unchanged.

With this brief background, this chapter will examine the 10 years following the formal handover in 1997. It assesses what happened in response to what was promised, based on documents in the public domain, news reports and ongoing analyses that are widely distributed, the published views of the main protagonists, regular surveys of popular opinion, and innumerable anecdotes shared among aficionado in Hong Kong and elsewhere. The perspectives focus largely on what is most directly comparable with the decade immediately preceding, in particular 1997–2007, the first decade of the existence of the SAR (Decade C, or related to China after the return), with the long decade of 1984–1996, when Hong Kong was still a British colony (Decade B or that related to Britain). The latter was the decade during which the parameters for the first years after the handover were framed. In this chapter, the questions of how those parameters have or have not met the challenges they were crafted to deal with will be discussed, and perspectives that are largely holistic and impressionistic will be offered.

Roots in the Decade Before

The 10 years since Hong Kong's return to China have certainly been turbulent for the people of Hong Kong. But it is important to remember that the decade before the return was equally turbulent, if not even more so. That had begun with the colony recovering from the protracted uncertainty of the 1982–1984 negotiations. Following the Joint Declaration in 1984, community leaders struggled hard to spell out the details of Hong Kong's new constitution, the Basic Law. Although most people had accepted that the principle of OCTS was their destiny, no one really knew what that would do to their lives. Responses ranged from hope that the motherland would do its utmost to protect their well-being to great alarm among those who had earlier come to Hong Kong to seek refuge from communism. That they would before long again live under communist rule was unpalatable. While the extremes were far apart, the majority of people were ready to think their best thoughts about what might happen and to look for effective ways of facing the new challenges that lay ahead. These people would recall how Hong Kong people had always been flexible and adaptable in the past whenever they had to face the unknown. The optimistic felt that there would only be minimal differences between the pre- and post-1997 periods. The more realistic expected some of the adjustments they would have to make to be painful. They knew that hundreds of thousands of people had voted with their feet during Decade B, as they prepared to turn their backs on an uncertain future in Hong Kong. But the millions who had decided to stay and the millions on the Mainland who were hoping to go to Hong Kong obviously made different kinds of life choices.

During Decade C, the SAR had its share of turbulence, some of a very different nature from those of the previous decade. Some events might have been predicted, but many others were unexpected and most unwelcome. The most dramatic was the devaluation of the Thai baht on 2 July 1997, the day after the handover, and the resulting financial damage in many areas of the region, which inevitably and deeply hurt Hong Kong. Nothing like that happened in Decade B. On the contrary, the years after the signing of the Joint Declaration were marked by resilience and growth in most sectors of the economy. Although we can point to the effects of the Black Monday stock market crash on 19 October 1987 and to the problems of corruption and inflation in China prior to the Tiananmen Incident of 1989, each severe downturn was followed by a swift recovery. Even the impact of the June 4th tragedy and the negative reactions in Britain, Europe and the United States did not dampen Hong Kong's markets for long. Within two years, Hong Kong saw a spectacular boom in the property and stock markets. This brought great optimism to the colony, so much so that the consequent threat of inflation to the economy as a whole did not seem to have aroused much alarm.

The major anxieties among the middle classes during that earlier decade stemmed from other concerns. The beginnings of democratic politics, introduced by the British, had been coolly received by most, but many young educated people welcomed the possibility of having a more participatory form of politics. For those who hoped for a post-colonial Hong Kong that would give them more say in the city's future, this was a promising start. The British belatedly directed their senior administrative officers, normally regarded as staid and conservative, to be more responsive to popular sentiments and to be prepared to play semi-political roles. When the urban and regional councils began to have directly elected members, the lessons in democracy that Hong Kong people received were accompanied by their first taste of influence in some of the municipal decisions that concerned them. In addition, there was the intriguing idea of "No change for 50 years" that Deng Xiaoping had promised. Some read that as a reassuring promise for those who feared a rapid convergence with Mainland ways. Others saw it as a promise to keep in place the colonial executive-led system and to slow the development of democratic politics, or at least to not allow the process of democratization to move more quickly than would be acceptable within Mainland China itself.

The last-ditch efforts by Governor Chris Patten to support greater political participation were futile — something the Chinese authorities made clear at every step. Britain had no cards to play with and too little time to play. The firm responses from Beijing officials were in fact directed at Hongkongers who might have been encouraged to harbour unrealistic hopes. But the trenchant and exasperating exchanges during the last five years of colonial rule did reflect ideological positions on which neither side could afford to compromise and genuine differences about the nature of governance. In particular, China did not want Hong Kong to set the pace for China's own political reforms, and repeatedly stressed this point to the restless Hong Kong people. Nevertheless, there were Hongkongers who were not content to wait until China was ready to democratize. Both sides realized that, in the interstices of the Basic Law or through re-reading the small print of the 1984 Declaration, different interpretations were possible about what the Basic Law was really meant to do. One side emphasized that Hongkongers were ready to exercise their political rights and that the Basic Law promised to recognize this. The other, however, pointed to the prior need for national identity to take root among people who had lived their lives as the colonial subjects of a foreign power. The Basic Law must protect China's interests and the exercise of political rights should conform to a timetable that is acceptable to China. These differences have been elevated to almost irreconcilable positions. But it has been heartening to see how, despite these obvious differences, a strong sense of security can be seen among most people in Hong Kong. This sense of security comes from the fact that the common law system of justice has remained and that it can be monitored by other common law jurisdictions. In addition, there is also the fact that, although the Chinese found the system so unfamiliar, they knew that it was vital for sustaining and strengthening Hong Kong's financial services sector and, ultimately, the city's economic prosperity. It was, therefore, in their interest to retain this system.

The SAR's First Tests

Decade C began with the acknowledgement that the PRC is the sovereign state with the final say in all matters pertaining to Hong Kong. Since then, the authorities in Beijing have been willing to respect the system of governance in Hong Kong as long as they feel sure that the right person is the Chief Executive (CE). Having controlled that appointment through a limited electoral process and selected C. H. Tung and then Donald Tsang as the persons to whom they could entrust the SAR, they have apparently been content to leave developments largely in the hands of Hong Kong's leaders. They recognized the manifold benefits that the Hong Kong economy has brought and will continue to bring to China as a whole. But they expected that over the next few decades the people of Hong Kong would reorient themselves to the motherland and come to identify with China. In this context, the only major miscalculation in the PRC's dealings with the SAR during the decade was the pressure it put upon Hong Kong to speed up changes to the security laws as set out in Article 23 of the Basic Law. The intervention was untimely, and SAR officials were hard put to explain why it was necessary. All it succeeded in doing was to arouse some half a million Hong Kong people to do something they had rarely done, and that was to act together on an issue that was clearly political. This opposition to an unpopular move gave fresh encouragement to the democratic forces in Hong Kong. However complex the reasons for why people took to the streets on 1 July 2003, the fact that they did so was an awakening for all concerned.

From the time of Governor Patten's moves on behalf of the departing colonial power, setting a timetable for the introduction of universal suffrage to Hong Kong has been a contentious issue. During Decade C of the SAR, the issue turned on how to interpret what the Basic Law intended on this matter. Setting a date for the implementation of universal suffrage will continue to be a source of much dispute. No one doubts that the people of Hong Kong are ready to participate more fully in politics. The debates are really about the pace of political change that the PRC will permit, the dangers to China's stability with or without political reforms, and the degree to which Hong Kong people are willing to accept without criticism Beijing's version of what constitutes the national interest.

Decade C has seen the deepening of the debates that began in Decade

B, although it is clear that these debates cannot lead to decisive action until Beijing feels that it is prepared to introduce reforms to the national system. At that point, the question of whether or not the system in Hong Kong could provide useful lessons for the nation could come to the fore. Decade C has shown that the disciplined and responsible ways by which the Hong Kong people have made their views known could provide encouragement to their compatriots across the border. PRC leaders may have noted that, when a government is law-based and as relatively incorrupt as it is in the SAR, participation in the political arena by the people need not be destabilizing. Mainland Chinese who are disaffected could expect that, with further access to higher education and a continued rise in educational standards, they, too, could master the skills needed to get their demands accepted by the authorities. The outcry over Article 23, and the consequences of the actions taken on both sides, confirm that Hong Kong continues to stand for a law-based culture, economic efficacy and quality education. How have these three key elements in Hong Kong's distinctive system fared in Decade C?

The resignation of C. H. Tung on 12 March 2005 and the election of his successor, Donald Tsang, two years later caused the decade to end on a positive note. The post-handover arrangements have survived more or less intact, despite the efforts of detractors wedded to the doomsday scenario to find every possible reason to pronounce them a failure. Of the three elements, the most vulnerable to change after 1997 was the legal system because it is the most dissimilar from the system of governance that prevails in the PRC. Chief Justice Andrew Li has led the judiciary its efforts to adapt to the "two systems" environment with sensitivity, and has done so while retaining the trust of Hongkongers. With Elsie Leung as Secretary of Justice, the relationship between politics and law has been challenged on several occasions, but the people's faith in the SAR's legal culture has not been damaged. The mature professionalism of the SAR's legal practitioners is what has made the difference. The close-knit system of values that had developed during Decade B was impressive, and obviously provided a strong foundation to deal with the doubts and challenges that arose in Decade C. This survival of the legal culture is the most encouraging feature of Decade C. It is particularly important because, when the SAR faced the turbulent first years of an economic downturn for which economic solutions were not readily available, the stability of the legal system saw Hong Kong through this difficult period, by providing assurance of continuity to all investors, creditors and debtors both within and outside Hong Kong.

The best-known test of Hong Kong's economic efficacy was its success in fighting off several attacks on its currency. The institutions that protected the Hong Kong–U.S. dollar peg were well managed and withstood the financial chaos in the region. That success earned the confidence of the international community during the uncertain first six years of the existence of the SAR, which saw Hong Kong battered by several unfortunate events. For example, the collapse of the housing market and an outbreak of a deadly influenza epidemic arising from a virus in chickens, the so-called "chicken flu," threatened the economy within months of the handover. However, with a powerful financial structure in the background, the tough measures that were taken to overcome these threats to the economy were ultimately successful.

By the end of 1997, it was clear that the SAR government faced difficult new problems that were far more serious than anything that had been experienced during Decade B. Both of the abovementioned problems could largely be blamed on developments outside Hong Kong that were beyond the government's control. The question was whether the SAR had responded quickly and effectively enough and limited the damage, or had actually contributed to making the problems worse. Where the sharp downturn in the housing market was concerned, it is debatable what measures could have provided greater relief and protection. The effort to place the blame mainly on the Chief Executive's decision in 1997 to review the government's policy on public housing is unfair.

It is particularly helpful here to compare Decade C with Decade B. The exercise will show that the wild speculation seen during the housing boom in the years preceding the handover was fundamentally destabilizing. The steep price rises were unsustainable and the market was bound for a correction. With the long years of financial crisis after 1997, and the confusion and panic in the banking systems around the region, it was inevitable that the property bubble would burst and that housing prices would stay down for some time. C. H. Tung's willingness to apply aspects of Singapore's public housing policy to Hong Kong in order to alleviate the living conditions of Hongkongers who did not own their own home arose from a desire to pursue policies that would bring about greater social stability by nurturing new generations of stakeholders for the SAR. His was the long-term view and his new policies needed time to unfold. He was unfortunate in that the financial crisis also took a long time to resolve and that his new policies had the effect of further depressing the market. Hong Kong's politically powerful property developers could not wait. It is unfortunate that the changes he proposed were aborted and that this policy initiative has been chalked up as one of C. H. Tung's failures.

The chicken flu epidemic in 1997 was a problem of a different order. Although it emerged from the Pearl River Delta region, local conditions contributed to the widening of the threat. In the end, the drastic measures taken to slaughter one-and-a-half million chickens seem to have been effective in curbing the threat, and the same methods were used again when the threats returned in 2002–2003. The impact on the economy was noteworthy, but much of the damage was psychological. Again, the SAR government was tested. There was controversy as to whether other measures might have been more effective in ridding Hong Kong of that strain of flu altogether. Certainly the return in 2002–2003 of the chicken flu rocked the confidence of the people of the SAR as well as its neighbours. However, in March 2003 the first cases of something far deadlier were reported. Severe acute respiratory syndrome (SARS) had struck Hong Kong, rendering the earlier fears over flu insignificant by comparison.

With SARS, Hong Kong's civil and professional services faced their greatest challenge of the decade. The origins of SARS, its arrival in Hong Kong from Guangdong in Mainland China, and its spread around the world through Hong Kong, as well as the policies adopted both within and outside Hong Kong to contain its spread, have now been well documented. Many reports and influential books on the subject have been published around the world. There is no doubt that lessons have been learnt, not least from the work of the doctors and researchers in Hong Kong itself, where the virus was identified. Despite the fact that carriers of SARS fanned out from Hong Kong, leading to many deaths in Singapore, Taiwan and North America, and that more might have been done earlier to prevent the disease's spread, it is clear that the SAR government did act decisively when the nature of this previously unknown disease was identified. Together with the international agencies involved, SARS was suppressed. The number of people who died in Hong Kong, a total of 299, was the largest per head of population. In the face of the near suspension of all movements of people to and from Hong Kong, the government did well to limit the impact of SARS on Hong Kong's economy. Whatever doubts people may have had about the government's performance in the field of public health, the health of the economy was protected.

The quality of education in Hong Kong was not as seriously challenged as that of public health, but the subject has never ceased to be a focus of keen local attention because human resource questions have always been important in Hong Kong — now more so than ever as expectations for expertise keep rising in a globalized knowledge economy. C. H. Tung has long had a personal interest in education and, as Chief Executive, was quick to encourage changes to further raise the overall standard of education in Hong Kong. He gave strong support to those who sought more balanced development in the area of education, following the great leap forward in higher education during Decade B, especially after 1989. Under both Governors Wilson and Patten, there were major infusions of funds to increase student places and to encourage basic research in the universities. In addition to the establishment of a new university, the Hong Kong University of Science and Technology, two polytechnics and two liberal arts colleges were turned into universities to meet the great demand of university places. One key factor that led to this change in policy was the rising number of people emigrating from Hong Kong during the 1980s. There were fears that this would lead to a reduction in the size of the educated middle class in Hong Kong at a time when the city needed many more professionals and skilled young people to sustain its economy.

By 1997, additional funds were sought to strengthen education at other levels to ensure that the key high schools were equipped to prepare students to fill the university places that were available. Questions were again asked about whether a good balance had been achieved between the number of schools that were teaching in the mother tongue (still largely Cantonese) and those teaching in English. Certainly, Hong Kong students should acquire fluency in speaking Putonghua and improve their skills in writing standard Chinese. But there had long been concern about whether there were enough graduates with a mastery of the English language. In the end, the frequent complaints about the fall in English standards could not be ignored. It was widely noted that the students on the Mainland had begun to learn English in earnest because they could see that better career prospects as well as the chance to study abroad depended on additional language skills. In response to that challenge, the government renewed efforts to ensure that all parents who wanted their children to learn good English would be given opportunities to do so.

Thus, the whole school system was reviewed at the very beginning of Decade C. Primary education quickly received additional funding, with increased funds made available to upgrade secondary schools. It is significant that despite the economic downturn, there was an increase in educational funding of over 40% during the decade. There were also debates about the need for new curricula given the SAR's post-colonial situation, and also systematic reviews of teaching methods and technical facilities. Of special concern was the quality of teacher training. The decision-makers did not always appreciate that educational reforms are slow to show results because it normally takes a decade before reforms can be judged to be really successful. Thus, they continued to be troubled throughout the decade by criticisms from teachers, parents and students about how often education policies were being reviewed and how new polices were being implemented. Nevertheless, the actions taken by the government did reassure people that full attention was being given to the quality of Hong Kong's human resources.

At the same time, Hong Kong was facing a challenge from educational developments that were taking place on the Mainland. Since 2000, Beijing's Ministry of Education has raised the annual growth rate in college and university enrolment to 15% in over 700 institutions that now also provide post-graduate education. By 2006, over four million students were graduating and looking for jobs. Although the standards on the Mainland were and remain uneven, and few of the institutions were any match for those in the SAR, there were demands from Mainland China for university places in Hong Kong, something these universities had been preparing for and welcomed. At the same time, Hong Kong students could also apply to the many more Mainland universities, including several of the best ones there. Thus, despite the educational and employment differences between the SAR and the Mainland, this has been an area where the "two systems" have worked well without serious difficulties. There was appreciation in Beijing that Hong Kong's system was making a major contribution to the human resources environment of the whole country. Many students were also increasingly aware of the shortage of well-qualified personnel on the Mainland and ready to take advantage of the educational opportunities open to them there. They realized that Beijing would be increasingly concerned that future generations of SAR citizens should become loyal and patriotic Chinese citizens, and have come around to the view that in the long run this is in Hong Kong's and their own personal interest.

Respective Roles in OCTS: Hong Kong and Mainland China

Chinese views about what Hong Kong should do for Mainland China were always complicated because there were wide-ranging expectations in this regard. Since the early 1980s, the main reason why China's political leaders were willing to leave the governing of Hong Kong largely in the hands of local elites — the rationale for the "one country, two systems" formula of full autonomy — was to woo Taiwan back into the fold. Although events in Taiwan since the mid-1990s suggest that this approach may no longer be sufficient to win the hearts of most Taiwan people, that ultimate purpose cannot be ignored. Once it was clear that there was no alternative to resuming sovereignty over Hong Kong, other considerations had to be addressed. One was to keep faith with those Hong Kong leaders who had always supported China against Britain and who had the potential to give the necessary support for the ideal of two systems to become credible. Another vision, of a reformed China as a country that will play by the rules of the international system, has been exceptionally successful. China has shown, in Decade C, that it is standing by its promise to retain the status quo in Hong Kong. It has shown that it is not afraid to have the implementation of this policy open to outside scrutiny. Ordinary Chinese emphasized numerous other factors: the many roles that Hong Kong could perform for China, the fact that Hong Kong stood for the most accessible form of modernity for Mainlanders, and was the ideal place for people who want to be both inside and outside China at the same time. Not least, Hong Kong was where many could find a decent livelihood, the freedom to write and speak their minds, and even take refuge from the Mainland's one-child policy.

The net of relationships between Hong Kong and the Mainland has become much more complex during the last 10 years. One may argue about whether this was to be expected, but it is hardly surprising. At the same time, nothing has been left to chance, as can be seen in the long years of preparation, since the early 1980s, for the handover. During those years, China sent a very large number of officials, party leaders, soldiers and scholars to study the workings of Hong Kong. An impressive number of the Hong Kong elite also rendered valuable help to Beijing to ensure that both sides understood each other. In their way, the British, too, were willing to help, if only to assist in achieving a smooth transfer and to ensure that they and the world outside would continue to enjoy the benefits of China's growth with Hong Kong's active help. The Sino-British negotiations of 1982–1984 were tough, but the timing was good. China had just come out of 30 years of isolation with an uncertain vision of its new place in the world. It was eager to learn, not least from Hong Kong, how to make full use of the global market. And Britain, at the time, still had a few cards with which to play and enough time to ease the colony back to China without damaging its interests.

In 1997, China had the key people in place to enable Hong Kong to continue to assist China in its economic reforms and to remain prosperous and stable. No one could have predicted the outbreak of the Asian financial crisis, the chicken flu, the sudden collapse of the property market and the several concerted efforts in 1997 and 1998 from outside to force the devaluation of the Hong Kong dollar. During the critical first two years of the existence of the SAR, there was anxiety in Beijing as China had to consider how best to step in to help Hong Kong deal with its immediate troubles, and even moments of doubt about Hong Kong's capacity to turn things around. Certainly, the angry voices raised within Hong Kong at the time would have given cause for concern. When policies and actions were not in good accord, relations between the Chief Executive and the Hong Kong civil service became shaky. Beijing would have noted that Hongkongers were quick to show their dissatisfaction, and that Beijing's experts and friends on the ground seemed helpless to repair the diminishing faith among Hong Kong people in the success of this experiment with OCTS.

Most people acknowledged that making two such different systems work together was a new challenge and that, despite all efforts to keep the executive-led government strong, the teams in place had still to be tested. Increasingly clear was the cultural gap between tightly knit professionals in the Hong Kong civil service and the China-oriented businessmen that looked to C. H. Tung to cater to their wants. In comparison, democratic critics were not able to stay united in their efforts to challenge the administration. If anything, in the midst of trying times, their voices were muted and their organizations ineffectual. It was not they who were the most troublesome to the new Hong Kong regime. Instead, what turned out to be unsuccessful were the several attempts to mix businessmen and administrators in key executive positions that required the executive team to understand and trust each other. Some of the experiments had been introduced before the handover, but the changes that were made afterwards were not effective. Given the stresses that Hong Kong went through because of executive failures, the Beijing authorities showed a surprising amount of forbearance and patience.

In short, despite the many critics who were on the look-out for every possible infringement by China's agents and friends, the "two systems" worked surprisingly well. Beijing officials were careful to stay clear of anything that would suggest that they were out to subvert the authority of the Chief Executive or the work of any of his senior colleagues. This reminds us that Beijing has always looked at the larger picture of China's rapid economic growth, one that requires China to win the trust of the big players in the global market economy, notably North America, Western Europe and Japan. Having had to do that since 1978 meant that keeping Hong Kong stable and prosperous was a key pillar of national interest. Deng Xiaoping's team realized how suspicious most people were of China's communist political structure. A Hong Kong that has returned to Chinese sovereignty and that is doing well as part of China would do much to win trust and dispel fear. At first, China's leaders were seen as rational and purposeful, and people were hopeful that they would stand by the agreement that they had signed. That confidence had been seriously dented by the events leading up to the tragedy of June 4th 1989 in Tiananmen Square. Without doubt, most Hongkongers became fearful that divisions within the Chinese Communist Party (CCP) could make things unpredictable. That event left many questions unanswered and remains a taboo subject until today. As long as this is the case, there will be Hongkongers who feel that they cannot afford to trust the China's authoritarian leadership. It is in part because of this that well-briefed Beijing officials have tried their best not to be seen as interfering in the internal affairs of Hong Kong.

There remained the matter of C. H. Tung's skills in managing a civil service that he had never been a part of. Beijing had counted on him to work closely with a powerful Chief Secretary. Beijing hoped that their blessing would help the CE to lead and that the added support of Hong Kong's major businessmen would be enough to quell any residual doubts about this within the civil service. After all, the process did not seem very different from that of sending a governor out from Britain to head a Hong Kong government consisting of a mixture of businessmen and civil servants. But somehow, the formula that had worked so well for the British did not work this time. That the appointment did not produce a strong executive team was a disappointment, and further errors of judgement about the power spectrum in Hong Kong followed. Anson Chan's resignation did not ease the problem. C. H. Tung was supported for a second term in the belief that, with a new and less powerful Chief Secretary, the leadership issue would be solved. In that context, the decision to test that leadership by turning Article 23 of the Basic Law into new legislation was a mistake. Was the civil service in disarray by 2002? Did its senior officers not anticipate the depth of the people's unease and opposition?

It did matter who was in charge in Beijing. The changing of the guard in 2003 from Jiang Zemin to Hu Jintao led to belated reassessments of the role of the Hong Kong civil service in the SAR's governing structure. By that time, the distance from the earlier colonial authority had grown and the civil service in Hong Kong also better understood how to make the "two systems" work. The readiness to replace C. H. Tung with a British-trained civil servant, first as acting CE and then as the substantive CE in 2007, is a mark of administrative and psychological convergence. After 10 years of experimentation, Beijing officials and Hong Kong professionals seem to have found a more congenial basis for the kind of collaboration that Beijing had hoped for. Does this now mean that there is less room for miscalculation with a firmer platform for officials on both sides to build trust and work together? It is still too early to be sure but, unless Beijing radically changes its larger national objectives, the chances for a more transparent discourse about Hong Kong's future in China have improved. There had been signs of this happening, with conscious efforts to bring the Hong Kong economy closer to that of the Pearl River Delta and having Hong Kong assist South and Southwest China through the Mainland and Hong Kong Closer Economic Partnership Arrangement (CEPA). How this will evolve is still not clear. Hong Kong's precise role is still evolving, but the entity called the SAR is no longer seen across the Shenzhen divide as an awkward protuberance whose people are not truly patriotic and are also difficult to control. It has now gone beyond being China's window on the world and is ready to become an integral part of China's own development plans. That change has not come overnight. During the 10 years of adjustment, while remaining valuable as an international financial centre, Hong Kong is no longer just a model for wooing Taiwan. It is striving to be more than just a city in competition with the likes of Shanghai, Tianjin and Beijing, and it certainly does not want to be seen to be aloof from the dynamic transformations in the southern Chinese provinces in its backyard. If that continues, the first decade will have been more positive than anyone could have expected.

The Emergence of a New Hong Kong

The sleepy colony that turned into a heroic symbol of international capitalism on the borders of its communist enemy may seem to have changed again into something totally new: China's most cosmopolitan and international city. But what has really changed is not so much Hong Kong itself but the China that it was a gateway to for more than five decades. There is now a China that no one, not even Hong Kong's expert China watchers, could have anticipated 30 years ago. Hong Kong's own changes have hinged on the vitality of its financial sector that the Chinese have learned to use and trust. Hong Kong has responded with consistent efficacy to the opportunities that China's rise has offered to investors around the world. But even more significant has been the vital role it played in enabling Chinese firms to launch their initial public offerings (IPO) in Hong Kong, thus enabling them to enter the international economy with confidence. Only Hong Kong's reputation and experience could have ameliorated the serious doubts that most people have about the banking system in China.

There is also the spectacular impact of China's image as a future world power peacefully rising through its determined pursuit of economic reforms. How does Hong Kong look beside that image? At one end, there is the view that Hong Kong will inevitably converge with the Mainland to become just another of China's provincial cities. This would be a threat to Hong Kong's local freedoms and hold off its potential for democratic development. At the other end, Hong Kong is still the beacon of China's reform goals, and the place through which China mastered the basics of a modern market system that has brought prosperity to many Chinese cities. Except for the financial services that, within China, only Hong Kong can thus far reliably provide, Hong Kong's kind of dynamic and vibrant economy can now be found elsewhere in China. But the China cake has grown so large that Hong Kong's smaller share still leaves it as the most prosperous, progressive and cosmopolitan city in China.

In between, Hong Kong plays many more roles. It is still useful as a bridge to Taiwan, as there is now much more of a willingness in Hong Kong than there was in the 1990s to move towards a pan-Chinese identity that would assure China of the patriotism of Hongkongers. More conventionally, Hong Kong continues to command the respect and confidence of most ethnic Chinese overseas, especially those in Southeast Asia. Now that it is part of China and closer to local and provincial officials in southern China, Hong Kong has become more important than ever for those who seek to invest in South China, the region from where most ethnic Chinese overseas originated.

Nevertheless, proximity to China has its price. Hong Kong is defenseless against the pollution that now afflicts neighbouring parts of China. The world now has an increasingly negative image of Hong Kong's environment. Above all, there is now the question of how well Hong Kong will fare in the face of a rising middle class in China's major cities? Better educated Chinese surpass Hongkongers in their hunger for success. Their appetite for high-tech skills and foreign knowledge already challenges that of Hongkongers once renowned for their competitiveness. However, Hong

Kong still has many advantages and, except at the highest levels of science and engineering, the educational playing field is still tilted in its favour. Employers everywhere will watch Hong Kong's capacity to stay ahead through better research funding and academic standards, not least, through its ability to attract the best scholars from both China and abroad to the SAR.

Conclusion

The years after the handover have not, as many feared, weakened Hong Kong. Some may claim that this is the result of international supervision, monitored by Anglo-American idealists for whom democracy is the key test of progress. This has been indirectly supported by China's anxiety to improve its image as a modernizer. While that background should not be discounted, the overwhelming evidence suggests that the credit for Hong Kong's success in battling the uncertainties of returning to a vastly different motherland really lies with the people of Hong Kong, with important contributions coming from visionary but pragmatic Beijing leaders who kept their eyes firmly on the larger national agenda. For all its faults, the Basic Law has turned out to be a workable constitution in the hands of realistic administrators and professionals. Despite their lack of success in obtaining their key demands, in their pursuit of democratic guarantees, the articulate people of Hong Kong have ensured that the legal system is intact and that channels for dissent and criticism have remained open. The constraints on Hong Kong's very free media have been muted in spite of the "patriotic" voices that have complained from time to time about licence and bias. Business survived a severe downturn, with China offering a helping hand when the economy was in need. Most of all, the young have adapted to the new realities of a Hong Kong under Chinese sovereignty and an increasingly modern and economically powerful China, and are better prepared to venture forth across the border both to study and to work. The enormous gap between the Hongkongers of an earlier generation and their compatriots on the Mainland has narrowed significantly. The new norm of younger Mainland and Hong Kong professionals competing and cooperating in an increasing number of fields bodes well for the future.

The first decade thus suggests that the expected convergence will not be towards China becoming more like Hong Kong or Hong Kong conforming to Mainland ways, but will more likely be towards a distinct Chinese modernity to which both have contributed. There are reasons to believe that this will happen. It has been fascinating to witness the speed at which references to Hong Kong's British heritage have diminished. With the exception of mention of the legal system and of certain bureaucratic procedures, there has been less recalling of British ways among Hongkongers than many people expected. Even where key ideals and values may have their roots in the British-based education system, there is less consciousness of that background. Instead, and this may satisfy the British officials who have cared deeply for Hong Kong for generations, the values they helped to propagate in their colony are now taken to be part of the broader international criteria of what is essential for good governance, and which are also valued elsewhere in East and Southeast Asia.

There has been a rich flowering of East Asian cultural forms and styles over that past half century that have come from a merging of Euro-American and Asian tastes and sentiments. Hong Kong people have been more open to this phenomenon than their compatriots on the Mainland during the first 30 years of CCP rule, but until 1997 greater weight was placed in Hong Kong on the European side of the equation. The result was the rise of an Anglo-Cantonese perspective among the most educated of the first generation of Hongkongers. Hong Kong people also intermittently and selectively absorbed ideas from the emerging "Eurasian" mix drawn from the artistic and literary heritage of the most talented peoples of Japan, South Korea and Taiwan.

What has occurred to bring about a dramatic change in the perspective of Hong Kong people has been the economic and political opening of China in the 20 years before the handover. Everyone knows how quickly the Chinese have learnt from Hong Kong and elsewhere not only the skills of commercial organization, management, investment and finance, but also the importance of making massive investments in research and higher education to stimulate inventiveness. In many ways, China's economic, scientific and technological performance, especially in the major cities on the Mainland, has surpassed that of Hong Kong. But the broader and deeper realms of cultural values go beyond such skills. To the surprise of most observers, many Chinese who returned to the cities from a decade spent in the countryside joined a younger generation of students in seeking new ideas and inspiration from the outside world in such areas as literature, art and film, in the willingness to reassess the Chinese heritage, and in polemical debates about larger issues of social and cultural values. That they did so with such energy and determination was unexpected, and Hong Kong people did not appreciate the full impact of these changes until the 1990s on the eve of the handover. Together with the departure of the British, the explosive response to outside influences among a younger generation of Chinese on the Mainland began to change the perspectives of people in Hong Kong. More Hong Kong people are aware of how creative the new forces unleashed across the border are, and of how quickly these are beginning to contribute to the "Eurasian" mix of values that the region has spawned.

During the first 10 years of the existence of the SAR, Hong Kong people have become much more aware that young people on the Mainland are searching in a way that Hongkongers themselves had done decades earlier. Their bold restlessness and inventiveness, which are a match for anything found elsewhere in Asia, are qualities that generations of Hongkongers can identify with, and that the young Hong Kong people of today can respect. These developments seem to be merging into the wider river of social, psychological and cultural values that are still awaiting definition. In the meantime, those values are being modified and internalized as part of Hong Kong's own modern future. The more this happens, the easier it will be for Hong Kong's form of modernity to enter the mainstream of a new Chinese culture when the peoples of the "two systems" eventually converge on all fronts. If the past 10 years were any guide, when that convergence takes shape, who provided what, or who provided less and who more, will not really matter.

2

A British Perspective on Hong Kong: A Decade Later

Michael B. Yahuda

At the outset, it must be recognized that Hong Kong has not generally figured large in the political concerns of the British public. Despite the many and close educational, commercial and people-to-people ties between Britain and Hong Kong and, indeed, the presence of several tens of thousands of residents from the territory in the United Kingdom (U.K.), media attention is rarely drawn to Hong Kong. Before the handover, there were some exceptions, but these were of a parochial nature such as when there was a "scare" arising from the belief that millions of British passport holders in Hong Kong might be entitled to seek residence in the U.K., or in relation to the personal situation of Chris Patten, the high-profile British politician, and the colourful denunciations of him by the Chinese side. In the 10 years since 1997, public interest in China has exceeded any residual interest in Hong Kong. The latter has attracted media attention either because of an outstanding event such as the huge demonstration of 1 July 2003, or because of Prime Ministerial visits. The attention given to Hong Kong by the British public may at best be seen as episodic.

The principal focus of this chapter will be on how the British government followed developments in Hong Kong, and its attempts to fulfil its commitments on the implementation of the agreement that it reached with the Chinese government over the territory after its reversion to full Chinese sovereignty. But attention will also be paid to the extent to which Britain has retained or extended its commercial, educational, legal, social and other ties with Hong Kong. After all, Hong Kong is still very much an international city and the extent to which ties have been maintained with Britain, its former colonial master and still an important player on the international stage, ought to be a matter of interest.

In conclusion, I shall suggest that Beijing's aversion to the prospect of elections for the Chief Executive (CE) and the Legislative Council (LegCo) in Hong Kong based on universal suffrage arises in part from the distrust that Chinese leaders felt of the British during the Sino-British negotiations.

The Colonial Legacy

It is appropriate first to consider the question of the colonial legacy left by the British in Hong Kong. In the foreword to the first six-monthly report on Hong Kong to Parliament dated July 1997, the British Foreign Secretary claimed that the British had fulfilled their pledge in the Joint Declaration of 1984 to administer Hong Kong until 30 June 1997 "with the object of maintaining and preserving its economic prosperity and social stability." As evidence, he pointed to the fact that Hong Kong had become the world's seventh largest trading entity and the fifth largest banking centre, possessed the world's largest container port and had a GDP per person that was higher than that of the U.K. itself. He argued that "Britain's most important contribution to this remarkable success has been to endow Hong Kong with the rule of law, a level playing field in commercial matters and autonomy to take its own economic and commercial decisions." He later added that the Hong Kong government had sought to improve housing, education and social welfare, and that Hong Kong people enjoyed "a high degree of personal freedom as guaranteed by the International Covenant of Civil and Political Rights." Finally, he extolled Hong Kong's Civil Service as "apolitical, impartial, effective and accountable."[1]

More significant perhaps, was that beginning in the 1970s, much of the Hong Kong administration had been localized even to the highest levels in the civil service, the professions, and so forth, and that what the Foreign Secretary regarded as Britain's "contribution" had come to be regarded by most people in Hong Kong as their own achievement.[2] Hong Kong's economic success was largely the product of Chinese Hong Kong entrepreneurs, who were able to take advantage of the legal order and trading conditions provided by the British. Chinese manufacturers and traders ran virtually all of the small- and medium-sized enterprises and, by the 1970s and 1980s, their larger firms had outpaced and outgrown most of the British companies in Hong Kong (Welsh, 1994, pp. 495–99).

However, what is missing in official British statements about Hong Kong and the British legacy is the question of the failure to have introduced greater democratization at a much earlier stage in their administration.[3] Much of the tense negotiations and, indeed, arguments with the Chinese side for the previous 20 years and especially since the Tiananmen massacre of 1989, had centred on the pace and extent of democratization. Not only was there pressure from within the territory for representation based on universal suffrage, but the British, especially in the guise of the last Governor, Chris Patten, had come to realize that, ultimately, the key guarantor of the Hong Kong system was the people of Hong Kong and that this could only be assured by a genuinely representative government elected by and accountable to the people.

Nevertheless, there has not been a backlash against the British colonial period as has been the case in some of the other British former colonies. Indeed, most British expatriates found it congenial to stay on in Hong Kong. In its first report after the handover, the Foreign and Commonwealth Office (FCO) noted that although many expatriate civil servants and police officers left, about 760 remained in the civil service and a further 450 in the police force. Expatriate judges remained and the legal system was assessed as reassuring. The educational system was little changed and the FCO found little to complain about in the changes made to history textbooks. The decision to replace English with Cantonese as the normal medium of instruction from September 1998 was seen as reflecting a long-running debate and it was noted that some 100 suitably qualified schools could continue to use English. To be sure, there were changes in national symbols, including the flying of the Chinese flag and the singing of the Chinese national anthem in schools (FCO Report, July–December 1997, p. 12 and p. 22). But all of this did not add up to a critique of the colonial legacy, let alone its rejection.

Arguably, there were elements in the colonial legacy that could have been rejected to the betterment of Hong Kong. These included cosy relations between the government and big business, the excessive reliance on sales of land as a principal source of government revenue and the practice of often not offering government contracts to open tender. Interestingly, criticism of these practices tended to come from foreign observers and residents rather than from Hong Kong or the People's Republic of China (PRC) sources, who seemed quite happy to continue these practices (Vines, 1998; Goodstadt, 2005).

From a British perspective, the British legacy has been broadly retained, but not without struggles and lapses. In the 10 years since the return of Hong Kong to full Chinese sovereignty, the main problems that have arisen in the political field have been with regard to the autonomy of the legal system and the maintenance of the various freedoms of expression, assembly, and so on. Britain has also supported those within Hong Kong who have pressed for the extension of the franchise and for increasing governmental accountability to the people in whose name the Hong Kong Special Administrative Region (HKSAR) is ruled.

The Dual Approaches of the British Government

Long before the handover in 1997, British policies towards Hong Kong had been carried out within the context of British relations with China and in the knowledge that Britain could do little to stop a Chinese takeover of Hong Kong if the Chinese government were so determined. Given that the British government (HMG) had long expected that it would have to turn over responsibilities for Hong Kong to the Chinese central government, the British had to consider how best to ensure that Hong Kong's special system could be preserved after the handover and how British interests in relations with China should be balanced with British obligations to the people of Hong Kong. Ten years after Hong Kong's return to China, those dual concerns are still evident, even though Tony Blair and his governments had tried to draw a line between themselves and their predecessors. HMG still had to balance the pursuit of close relations with China, whose international weight was rapidly increasing, with continuing its obligations to Hong Kong even if at times that entailed openly disagreeing with policies of the Chinese government with the risk that the U.K.'s relations with China might be adversely affected.

This contradictory dualism of the British approach was evident as long ago as the 1960s when as Charge d'Affaires in Beijing, the then Mr. Percy Cradock, clashed with the Governor of Hong Kong, Sir David Trench. Cradock argued that Trench should release those serving prison sentences because of their convictions for violent behaviour during the riots in Hong Kong in order to meet the political demands set by the Beijing authorities for the release of British subjects who had been detained by the Chinese authorities. Trench held fast to the view that he would not bend the law and due process in Hong Kong to suit Beijing (Cradock, 1999, p. 83). Similar differences emerged during the early negotiations between the Chinese and British governments, when London did not contest Chinese objections to attempts by Governor Sir Edward Youde to include representatives from Hong Kong in the negotiations (Cottrell, 1993, p. 108). Perhaps the best known example of the clash of views on this question was the very public disagreements between Sir Percy Cradock and the last Governor, Chris Patten. Cradock argued against the electoral reforms introduced by Patten on the grounds that they were unacceptable to the Chinese side and that they would be undone by the Chinese, thereby disrupting a smooth transition in 1997. Patten, however, argued in favour of empowering the people of Hong Kong with greater democracy (albeit of only the limited kind that he could introduce) as this was their right and that it would stand them in good stead in the future.[4]

The tenth anniversary of the establishment of the HKSAR roughly coincides with the British Prime Minister Tony Blair's tenth year in office. In that context, it is worth remembering that prior to Blair's victory on 2 May 1997, the Labour Party had been out of office for 18 years. This meant that none of the members of the three governments headed by Tony Blair had been at all involved in the difficult and, at times, contentious negotiations with the Chinese authorities over the future of Hong Kong. Blair and his ministers began their dealings with Hong Kong without any of the baggage that attended the contentious past of Sino-British relations. In fact, on taking office in May, Tony Blair made it clear that he sought to establish a new and closer working relationship with the Chinese government than the one that existed under his conservative predecessor. Since the handover of Hong Kong was imminent, he decided not to change Britain's existing policy towards Hong Kong and also chose to leave Chris Patten in place to serve out the remainder of his term as governor despite condemnations of Patten by the Chinese side. Blair would start afresh after 1 July 1997.

As a co-signer of the 1984 Joint Declaration (JD), HMG claims responsibility for monitoring its implementation. Arising from that, the British FCO provides the British Parliament with six-monthly reports on significant developments within Hong Kong. These are not simply dispassionate accounts. They focus on the question of the PRC's implementation of the JD and on demonstrating Britain's continuing commitment to and interest in Hong Kong. The Declaration was lodged with the United Nations, indicating that both the U.K. and the PRC regarded it as an international agreement. Thus, despite occasional protests by the Chinese side that matters relating to the HKSAR fall within the domestic affairs of the PRC, HMG has from time to time expressed "concern" at what it has seen as adverse intervention by Beijing in what should properly lie within the jurisdiction of the HKSAR.

Notwithstanding the concerned scrutiny of the FCO and the professed commitments of the British Prime Minister, Tony Blair has indicated that in some respects, British interests in cultivating relations with China may claim a higher priority. To be fair to him, this view was put forward within a context in which the expressed and considered judgements of the FCO, the European Union (EU), the U.S. State Department and other interested governments have always been that "generally the 'One Country, Two Systems' principle has worked well in practice and that rights and freedoms promised to Hong Kong in the Joint Declaration and the Basic Law continue to be upheld" (FCO Report, July–December 2006, p. 17). It is not as if China had behaved towards Hong Kong in accordance with some of the dire expectations that were expressed in the Western media on the eve of the handover. Blair's approach may well have been different if that had happened. Indeed, the approach of the Western world as a whole towards China would undoubtedly have been different.

Be that as it may, during his visit to Hong Kong on 23 July 2003, Tony Blair did not appear as the zealous promoter of the cause of democracy for which he is well known in other contexts. He seemed more concerned with "stability" than with extending the franchise. Bearing in mind that he said this barely three weeks after the July 1st demonstration in which more than 530,000 people protested against the proposed security law, and with Tung Chee-hwa commanding an approval rating of only 12% in the opinion polls, Blair's emphasis on the need for "stability as the bedrock" of Hong Kong's success was welcomed by China's controlled press more than by the press elsewhere in the world.[5] Indeed, his own FCO's Six-monthly Report showed that "stability" was not the issue. The Foreign Office Minister Bill Rammell had issued a statement on 16 July paying "tribute" to the people of Hong Kong "that so large a demonstration could take place in such a peaceful manner." The FCO report noted that not a single person had been arrested. Yet on the same day, Gao Siren, Director of the Central Government Liaison Office in Hong Kong, had said earlier, "Hong Kong is an economic city rather than a political city. It will affect social stability if Hong Kong becomes too politicized" (FCO Report, February 2004, pp. 4, 6). It would seem that Blair paid more attention to the Chinese official than to his own minister.

Arguably, the British Prime Minister was concerned more about his larger agenda with China's leaders, including issues such as Iraq and overcoming the possible influence in Beijing of European leaders, Chirac and Schroeder. Tony Blair clearly saw himself as playing an important role on the world stage. Given the Chinese government's acute sensitivity about the mishandling of the situation in Hong Kong, the British Prime Minister was keen not to rub salt in their wounds precisely at that point. He also hoped to signal that he, at least, understood the concerns of China's leaders even as he also repeated the long-standing formal position of the FCO of favouring progress towards the "ultimate" aim of the election of the CE and the LegCo by universal suffrage.

A few years later, on a visit to Beijing in April 2007, Prime Minister Tony Blair said to reporters after talks with China's leaders that "there's an unstoppable momentum [in China] towards greater political freedom, progress on human rights and those other issues, and I think there's an understanding that this should happen."[6] Whatever the merits of his observation, the implications for Hong Kong were that, given the trends in China, there was no need to worry unduly about Beijing's implementation of the Joint Declaration as Hong Kong would in due course inevitably benefit from China's own progress towards democracy. Yet only three years earlier in April 2004, the British Foreign Minister, Jack Straw, made the point in his foreword to the FCO Six-monthly Report that a "decision" (his quotation marks) by the Standing Committee of China's National People's Congress (SCNPC) to rule out the possibility of universal suffrage in elections in 2007 and 2008 gave rise to "significant concerns in Hong Kong, many of which we have shared." He added that "our main concern has been that these moves seemed to erode the high degree of autonomy promised to Hong Kong in the Joint Declaration." These statements in the foreword by the Foreign Minister could not have been made lightly in a document that would have been subject to careful thought as to their impact. The contrast in the outlook between Blair and his Foreign Minister could hardly have been greater. Although the Foreign Minister's statement was made three years earlier, it is not unreasonable to suggest that before his visit, the Prime Minister would have been properly briefed about what his government considered to be an unfortunate intervention by Beijing in the affairs of the HKSAR that boded ill for its autonomy. If he believed that in the intervening three years, there had been a significant change in the views of China's leaders with regard to Hong Kong's autonomy or to the prospects for universal suffrage there, Blair failed to identify it. Yet, again, it must be assumed that as far as he was concerned, Blair's priority lay with cultivating China's leaders and not antagonizing them unnecessarily over Hong Kong.

The View of the FCO

The British Foreign Office has so far produced 20 reports to the British Parliament on the implementation of the 1984 Sino-British Joint Declaration on the Question of Hong Kong. Collectively, they add up to 308 single-spaced A-4 pages and they constitute close observations of the main developments in Hong Kong that have a bearing on the implementation of the JD. They also seek to demonstrate that Britain has maintained close ties with Hong Kong in many areas. The intent is to show that, in addition to its moral and legal obligations to the people of Hong Kong, Britain has continued to maintain close working relations with different sectors and peoples in Hong Kong.

The continuing judgement of the FCO and of the three Secretaries of State that have led it over the 10-year period is, to quote the opinion repeated at the end of each of the 20 Reports, that "we conclude that the 'one country, two systems' principle has *generally* (my emphasis) worked well in practice and that the rights and freedoms promised to Hong Kong in the Joint Declaration and the Basic Law continue to be upheld." It must be pointed out that this conclusion is in accord with the views of the governments of the United States, Canada, and Australia and of the EU Commission, even when they had occasion to express concern about certain developments within the HKSAR or in China's relations with the region.

Nevertheless, the Reports, which followed constitutional developments closely, have expressed criticism and concern on the three major occasions when the SCNPC has used its power to interpret the Basic Law. The FCO has regarded these interventions as "seeming" to weaken judicial independence and the high degree of autonomy promised to Hong Kong. For example, in April 2004 when the SCNPC ruled out the possibility of election by universal suffrage of the CE in 2007 and the LegCo in 2008, the British Foreign Secretary commented: "This unexpected *intervention* (my emphasis) of the NPC Standing Committee has given rise to significant concerns in Hong Kong, many of which we have shared." He added that British views were expressed "both privately and publicly. Our main concern has been that these moves *seemed* (my emphasis) to erode the high degree of autonomy promised to Hong Kong in the JD" (FCO Report, January–June 2004, p. iii). The FCO also rejected claims by Chinese officials that foreigners had no right to criticize or intervene in what they regarded as China's domestic affairs. For example, the FCO gave a robust response to China's expression of "strong dissatisfaction" to the British government's comments on the April 2004 decision: "The British Government stands by its judgement and will continue to comment on these matters as it judges appropriate, in particular where it believes that the principles of the Joint Declaration might be eroded. This is in line with the U.K.'s continuing obligations under the Joint Declaration" (FCO Report July–December 2004, p. 1).

In a similar vein, these Reports noted developments that seemed to limit freedom of expression in the press and the problems of self-criticism. These gave rise to repeated statements about the need for a more rapid advance to universal suffrage for the election of the CE and of LegCo. For example, "If Hong Kong's free society is to endure and fundamental freedoms are to be protected, Hong Kong needs a truly democratic system of government" (FCO Report January–June 2006, p. 4). This view was apparent from the outset when the FCO welcomed the preparations for elections to a LegCo to replace the provisional one, but expressed "regret" at the return to corporate voting in the functional constituencies (FCO Report July–December 1997, p. 3). But it was not formally expressed until the end of 2001. Successive Reports also urged the Chinese government to rescind the ban on those legislators who were not allowed to travel to the Chinese Mainland.

One theme that runs through the 20 Reports is that the future of Hong Kong ultimately depends on the Hong Kong people. Many of the criticisms levelled from time to time against the HKSAR or the Chinese central government pick up on views first expressed within Hong Kong. The Reports devote much space to constitutional issues and to the relevant performance of the HKSAR government to monitor not only the observance of the JD and the Basic Law, but also to encourage the authorities to pay more attention to the views of the people of Hong Kong.

The question arises as to what impact these Reports may have. British criticisms and objections are confined at most to "expressions of concern." Interventions by the Chinese central government are noted in some detail and careful explanations are provided on the ways in which these may be harmful, but at most, the FCO tends to admonish the Chinese authorities that these actions "*seem*" (my emphasis) to weaken the autonomy promised Hong Kong. In my view, these reports serve at least three purposes, as summarized below.

First, the public and detailed reports provide assurance for the people of Hong Kong that they have not been forgotten by Britain, despite the fact that the British media devote little space to the territory. The reports also provide a degree of support for those in Hong Kong who value their freedoms under the law and who wish to advance towards proper democratic and representative government. At least it shows that their voice is heeded and that their concerns are part of the agenda of Sino-British relations. However large China may loom in the calculations of the British government, relations with China would inevitably suffer if the Chinese government were to undermine Hong Kong's system of an independent judiciary, an impartial civil service and the basic freedoms that have underpinned its success as an international city.

Second, these Reports pave the way for the international community to take a legitimate interest in the development of the HKSAR. The FCO's public concern in the fate of Hong Kong provides the space and opportunity for other governments and international institutions to take up the cause of Hong Kong's autonomy and the preservation of its way of life. To be sure, the U.S. State Department would have continued to produce its own separate annual reports on Hong Kong, as it is mandated to do so by the Congress. But the fact that the British do so as an obligation arising out of the JD facilitates the American action, especially as the JD has the status of an international agreement.

Finally, these Reports have an impact on the Chinese government. Otherwise, its officials would not be so keen to register their disapproval. The British may lack the power to stop the Chinese from doing harm to Hong Kong, but a Chinese government that is eager to improve its standing in the world and to enhance its reputation as a responsible major power would seek to avoid outright British disapproval of its actions in Hong Kong unless it felt that something truly major was at stake. In fact, the Chinese government has taken steps from time to time to brief the FCO about Hong Kong matters.[7] So far the FCO has confined its expressions of disapproval to the relatively mild words of "expressing concern." Perhaps sterner words would be counterproductive as they might antagonize the Chinese side to no good purpose and extinguish such communication as does exist between London and Beijing on Hong Kong.

It is worth bearing in mind that the distrust of Britain by at least some Chinese officials has not entirely dissipated. To be sure, the Chinese side no longer gives credence to the warning of Zhou Nan (then head of the local Xinhua office, the Chinese government's representative in Hong Kong), made on his departure in 1997, that the British would leave behind "little or big trouble."[8] But according to a "well placed source," Beijing was concerned in the summer of 2003 that the unrest in Hong Kong (over the proposed security law) could spread to the Mainland and that "foreign elements" had been involved in recent mass protests in the territory. The source was then quoted directly as saying, "The U.S. and British government statements opposing the national security legislation seemed to have been timed to coincide with the demonstration" (Ching, 2003). While it's difficult to know how representative this "source" was, this account by a respected journalist suggests that the old suspicions of the British (and the Americans) have not gone away. Nevertheless, the indications are that the FCO Reports are noted in Beijing, even though the degree of attention paid to them cannot be determined.

British Bilateral Relations with Hong Kong

Arguably, British influence in Hong Kong derives not only from the residue of the colonial past, but is also the product of the depth and breadth of the current relationship. It is important to look at the state of current relations, as the influence from the past will inevitably erode with time, especially as Hong Kong deepens its relations with the Mainland, which it must for both economic and political reasons. The erosion of long-standing British influence perhaps can be slowed down through the maintenance of an active bilateral relationship.

The British government has worked hard to maintain and even improve relations with Hong Kong. There has been a continual exchange of visits by ministers and senior officials, and Britain has supported numerous programmes to boost trade. There have also been continual attempts to maintain educational exchanges and cultural and social contacts. There are some 30,000 British expatriates living and working in Hong Kong (about the same as before the handover), there is an active British Chamber of Commerce, and the British Consulate General Office is the largest of its kind in the world. The character of these relationships will be considered before the significance of the relationship is assessed.

Official Relations

According to the FCO Reports, there has been a continual stream of high-level visits in both directions every year. These include some three to four visits every year by British ministers and their equivalents from Hong Kong. The British Prime Minister has visited Hong Kong at least three times since the handover and Hong Kong's CE has visited the U.K. about five times.

There have been exchanges of visits between the higher levels of the legal professions and two leading British Law Lords sit in Hong Kong's Court of Final Appeal. The British government, through a subsidiary, has sent numerous trade missions to Hong Kong. Britain's largest Consulate General is based in Hong Kong, where inter-alia it deals with the 3.5 million holders of British National (Overseas) passports. The British Council regularly provides courses in English for 40,000–50,000 Hong Kong students a year and the FCO provides scholarships for roughly 50 Hong Kong students to pursue postgraduate studies in the U.K.

Educational Exchanges

Inevitably, the tertiary sector in Hong Kong is more open to staff and students from the Mainland than before. Australian and American universities have been more active in recruiting students from Hong Kong. Nevertheless, important links with the U.K. have been maintained, especially in the university sector where British academics still serve as external examiners and are consulted about the promotion of local academics. The U.K. is still seen as an attractive place to study. In the year 2000 for example, 9,000 Hong Kong students attended tertiary education institutions and a further 5,000 studied at British schools. By the academic year 2004–2005 (the latest for which there are statistics), the number of Hong Kong students studying in the U.K. had grown to nearly 20,000, with some 3,000 in postgraduate courses and a further 8,500 in tertiary education.

Trade and Commerce

According to The House of Commons Foreign Affairs Committee for the session 2005–2006, "there is a feeling that the relationship has not strengthened as much as it could have done since the 1997 handover." Total trade between the two grew from under US$11 billion in 1997 to US$12.8 billion in 2005 with most, if not all, of the growth being in Hong Kong's exports to the U.K. The performance was judged to be "relatively disappointing" when set against the 50% expansion in Hong Kong's total trade between 1997 and 2005. As a result, the U.K.'s share of Hong Kong's total trade fell from 2.8% in 1997 to 2.1% in 2005. It is possible to make the U.K.–H.K. economic relationship sound impressive in percentage terms. For example, Hong Kong is the second largest export market for the U.K.

in Asia, or the fourteenth largest in the world, while the U.K. is the fifth largest export market for Hong Kong and the second largest in the EU. Likewise, in terms of investment, Hong Kong is the seventh largest recipient in the world of U.K. direct investment and the U.K. is the second most favoured destination (excluding offshore financial centres) for HKSAR investors. But the actual figures tell a different story: As of the end of 2004, Hong Kong had invested a total of US$7 billion in the U.K., while the U.K. had invested US$9 billion in Hong Kong, each accounting for 2% of the total.[9]

Yet the U.K. Trade and Industry Office described Hong Kong as "a crucial centre for U.K. business interests in the Asia-Pacific region." Approximately 1,000 British companies have offices in Hong Kong and, of the 1,167 international companies that have made Hong Kong their regional headquarters, 115 are from the U.K. Hong Kong with its rule of law, clean civil service and efficient infrastructure, is seen as the gateway to China, just as the U.K. is Hong Kong's gateway to the EU. Nevertheless, according to the British Chamber of Commerce in Hong Kong, "the perception in the British, Hong Kong and Mainland business communities alike, has been that the U.K. has refocused its attention on the Mainland, at the cost of its involvement and profile in Hong Kong."[10]

Cultural Exchanges

The office of the British Consul General has made a difference to the cultural exchanges between the U.K. and Hong Kong. There was no equivalent during the colonial period that was specifically charged with promoting British culture in the territory. To be sure, the British Council has provided institutional continuity and, through the Consulate General in whose premises it is located, has promoted with greater vigour the teaching of English and the exchange of what might be called cultural events. Thus every year since 1997, the Council has provided English language courses for up to 40,000 Hong Kong people.[11] Perhaps such courses are needed more than before as most schools since 1998 have used Cantonese as the main language for general teaching. The enhanced interest in Mandarin (which is understandable, given Hong Kong's return to the Mainland and the growing economic integration with the Mainland) should not be at the expense of acquiring a workable knowledge of English. If Hong Kong is to retain its comparative advantage as Asia's key international city, it must retain competence in the universal language of international business and finance, namely English. The British Council, under the aegis of the Consulate General, has also taken the lead in arranging a whole variety of events, conferences, displays, and other activities, which bring together educationalists, designers, writers, lawyers, scientists, artists and performers of all kinds to Hong Kong. According to its website, the British Council arranges more than 20 such events every year.[12]

Hong Kong Residents in the U.K.

According to the British census of 2001, there were 243,000 "Chinese" people living in the U.K. (i.e., 0.4% of the total population). The census does not discriminate between those of Hong Kong origin and the rest. Thus, it states that the proportions of the "Chinese" born in the U.K. and Hong Kong are the same at 29%, with 19% born in China and 8% in Malaysia. Given the major wave of migration from Hong Kong in the 1950s, it would be fair to assume that the overwhelming majority of those born in the U.K. would be of Hong Kong origin. Thus, the residents in the U.K. of Hong Kong origin number around 125,000.[13]

The first wave of Chinese migrants was largely made up of sailors who came in the 1920s and settled near the port of major cities such as London (around the famous Limehouse Street) and Liverpool. The majority of Hong Kong people came in the 1950s and most initially found work by providing laundry services before moving on to establish restaurants throughout the country. They, like their predecessors, liked to live in close proximity to each other. On the whole, they kept themselves to themselves and their own communities were relatively self sufficient as, unlike many other groups of immigrants, they rarely called upon the services of the British social-security system. In the last two or three decades, as their second and third generations availed themselves of Britain's educational opportunities, they have entered the professions and have made contributions to British life and culture that go beyond the culinary. Chinese students are highly visible, particularly in the more prestigious universities, now that they attract some 50,000 a year from China and up to 10,000 a year from Hong Kong.

As a community, however, the Hong Kong Chinese have kept a low political profile in Britain. They have not sought to act as a political lobby, nor have they chosen to make their collective voice in Britain heard on issues affecting Hong Kong.

British Expatriates in Hong Kong

The British expatriate presence in Hong Kong has continued much as it had before the end of the colonial period. There was no mass exodus in 1997, although several thousands did leave. There are estimated to be up to 30,000 British people working and living in Hong Kong. The figure includes some 16,000 long-term residents and those who are there on a more temporary basis. They work mainly in the professions and in the financial sector. They constitute but a small percentage of the over one million foreign workers in the HKSAR. However, the overwhelming majority of these are guest workers from the Chinese Mainland, the Philippines and other countries in Southeast Asia who undertake manual and domestic work. The British expatriates, together with their equivalents from mainly Australia, Canada and the U.S., play a major role in enhancing Hong Kong's reputation as an international city. They have also been politically more active than Hong Kong residents in the U.K. When they perceived that their interests were threatened, as was the case when the security law was being drafted in 2003/2004, they were able to make their voices heard through their respective chambers of commerce and to bring about relevant changes in the next draft of the proposed bill. Otherwise, they do not play an active role in Hong Kong politics.

An Assessment

The significance of Britain's relations with Hong Kong would seem to be more than the sum of its parts. The British traditions continue to shape many aspects of the Hong Kong system. The political system of a CE (the equivalent to a Governor) with Executive and LegCo mirror the previous colonial system, despite the various changes since 1997. The legal system based on the common law and the judiciary with its judges and lawyers still echoes the British system. The same can be said for the civil service and its impartiality. It is within that context that the current levels of relations between Britain and Hong Kong must be assessed. The educational exchanges must be judged a success, especially in light of the enhanced competition for students from Australia and the U.S. in particular. Commercial relations are more disappointing. But here the Chinese imprint is more evident and it is growing fast. British officialdom continues to put much effort into the relationship and it plays a not unimportant role in helping Hong Kong to continue to develop its standing as an international city even as it is drawn closer to the embrace of the Mainland.

Conclusion: Britain and Beijing's Distrust of Greater Democratization in Hong Kong

Earlier, it was argued that, on the whole, the British legacy was beneficial to Hong Kong and that its people had been able to take over the better aspects of that legacy and, together with their own contributions, transform that into the success that the city is today. But one aspect of that legacy has proven to be a source of deep problems about the political character of governance in Hong Kong. As Chinese officials never tire of pointing out, the British did not introduce democracy into Hong Kong and Hong Kong was not ruled in a democratic way before 1997 even as it flourished under the rule of law and its people enjoyed the basic freedoms.

From the outset of the Sino-British negotiations, the British sought to ensure that what was called "the Hong Kong way of life" would be safeguarded and they endeavoured successfully to insert as many details as possible about that "way of life" into the JD of 1984. But, in addition to preserving the Hong Kong system, the British also sought to persuade the Chinese of the need to democratize the Hong Kong government even though they had not done so themselves. The British view was that the Hong Kong system would only endure and survive under Beijing's authority and enjoy genuine autonomy if the future HKSAR government was a representative government based on universal suffrage.[14] The Chinese, however, argued that the reason the British sought to introduce democracy at the very end of their rule was to preserve their influence.

The Chinese side distrusted the British position on several counts. First, British motives were suspect. After all, in the Chinese view, the only reason for the British acquisition of Hong Kong and for their continued rule there was to make money. Indeed, Deng Xiaoping was convinced that the British had a scheme to siphon off profits from the territory. Some of the provisions in the agreement affecting government land sales prior to the handover were framed precisely to prevent such a possibility. Similarly, the Chinese were concerned that some of the big projects that the then Hong Kong government sought to construct in the 1990s were being rushed through so as to enable British companies to make undue profits.

Second, the insinuation that the British knew how to run Hong Kong better than the Chinese was insulting and a challenge to Chinese sovereignty.

Third, especially after the Tiananmen disaster and the collapse of the Soviet Union in 1991, Chinese leaders became even more suspicious of the proposed democratization of Hong Kong. In their view, the West was seeking to undermine communist rule through a long-term scheme of "peaceful evolution," by which communist regimes would be destroyed from within. The question of Tiananmen became linked with some of the prominent democrats in Hong Kong. Once patriotism (*aiguo*) became synonymous with support for the government and hence communist party rule, as it did in the campaign of "patriotic education" in China of the early 1990s (Zhao, 2004, p. 219), it became possible to stigmatize democrats in Hong Kong as "unpatriotic." The fact that they tended to benefit most from the elections introduced by the British in the 1990s did little to endear them to the rulers in Beijing.

Finally, in the view of Deng Xiaoping and most of his successors, the Hong Kong system was above all a capitalist one. The point of "one country, two systems" was that a capitalist and a socialist system could co-exist within one China. It was not seen as a device for the co-existence of democracy and authoritarianism.

These Chinese perspectives provide the context within which China's leaders chose Tung Chee-hwa to be the first CE. If Hong Kong was a capitalist city, who better to run it than a capitalist — especially one who was beholden to Beijing for having saved his firm from possible bankruptcy some 15 years earlier? In other words, he was not only a capitalist, but a "loyal" one (Vines, 1998, p. 97).

It took several years and major demonstrations in Hong Kong before Beijing realized that it needed above all a competent CE, who knew about the governance of Hong Kong, and that such a person could be better found among the senior ranks of the civil service (even if they had served under British rule) than among Hong Kong's capitalists. Yet, even so, as Donald Tsang has observed, the abiding difficulty in promoting further democratization is the absence of trust in Beijing.

Obviously, the China of today is no longer the China of the 1990s, and the question of democracy may evoke different connotations. But many of the doubts and suspicions that underlie the current distrust between Beijing and those who seek to promote greater democracy in Hong Kong were sown in the Sino-British negotiations and exchanges before the handover in 1997.

As noted earlier, occasional echoes of Beijing's distrust of a possible Western disposition to create "trouble" in Hong Kong may still be heard. But clearly, as the FCO has argued, the British have a moral obligation to continue to press Beijing to live up to the commitments it made in the

JD and the Basic Law to allow Hong Kong to go forward to establish a government based on universal suffrage. At the same time, the FCO has noted repeatedly, such a development depends ultimately on the people of Hong Kong. In the longer term, British influence is bound to become less evident and less significant as an element affecting specific policies, but as Stephen Bradley, the British Consul General, observed, "Hong Kong ... is a real amalgam from which the non-Chinese elements simply cannot be extracted but are integral, and have become part of the Chinese clay from which the pot is made" (Bradsher, 2007).

Notes

1. Robin Cook, Secretary of State for Foreign and Commonwealth Affairs, *Foreword* to the "Six-monthly Report to Parliament, January–June 1997." July 1997 (hereafter "FCO Report").
2. For a broadly positive view by a veteran Hong Kong journalist, see Lau (1997).
3. A recently declassified British document of March 1969 stated that no "constitutional changes towards representative and more representative and more responsible government would be made" in Hong Kong lest it makes the eventual transfer of Hong Kong to the PRC more difficult. See Cheung (2006).
4. For Patten's side of the argument, see Dimbleby (1997), where it is claimed that throughout his governorship, Patten was weakened by resistance in the FCO by Cradock and his acolytes. For Sir Percy's account, see Cradock (1999, pp. 271–85). Interestingly, despite the vituperation hurled by the Chinese side at Patten as Governor, he was subsequently hailed by Jiang Zemin personally as an "old friend of the Chinese people" and as a "great expert on China." Indeed, Patten and his wife were invited to visit China as the personal guests of the then Chinese leader. But that was only after Patten's appointment as the Foreign Affairs Commissioner of the European Union.
5. See for example, the former editor of the *South China Morning Post*, Jonathan Fenby, "Why Blair Betrayed Hong Kong," *Wall Street Journal*, 29 July 2003.
6. BBC News, 26 April 2007. See http://news.bbc.co.U.K./go/pr/fr/-/2/hi/U.K._news/politics/4218080.stm.
7. To take but one example, the Chinese Ministry of Foreign Affairs briefed the British ambassador in Beijing and the Consul General in Hong Kong, and the Chinese ambassador in London briefed the Minister of State, about the SCNPC's decision on 26 April that ruled out universal suffrage for the 2007 and 2008 elections in Hong Kong. See FCO Report, January–June 2004, p. 11.

8. Confidential interview with an informally retired local communist official in 1999.
9. All figures were drawn from the House of Commons Foreign Affairs Select Committee Minutes of Evidence in http://www.publications.parliament.U.K./pa/cm200506/cmselect/cmfaff/860/6030812.htm. Accessed on 27 April 2007.
10. This paragraph has drawn greatly on the House of Commons Foreign Affairs Committee, *East Asia, Seventh Report of Session 2005–2006, Volume 1* (London: Stationary Office Ltd., 13 August 2006), pp. 121–23.
11. See http://origin-www.britishcouncil.org.
12. Ibid.
13. "Chinese: Guide to Ethnic Groups in Britain," http://www.cre.gov.U.K./diversity/ethnicit/chinese.html. Accessed on 31 April 2007.
14. This paragraph and the subsequent observations about Chinese attitudes and the Sino-British negotiations are drawn from my book. See Yahuda (1996).

References

Bradsher, Keith (2007), "In Hong Kong, No Looking Back at Britain," *The International Herald Tribune*, 2 April 2007.

Cheung, Gary (2006), "Why U.K. Held Back on Hong Kong Democracy," *South China Morning Post,* 20 November 2006.

Ching, Cheong (2003), "Beijing 'Concerned' that Hong Kong Unrest May Spread," *The Straits Times*, 15 July.

Cottrell, Robert (1993), *The End of Hong Kong.* London: John Murray.

Cradock, Percy (1999), *Experiences of China.* London: John Murray, new edition.

Dimbleby, Jonathan (1997), *The Last Governor.* London: Little Brown & Co.

Foreign & Commonwealth Office (FCO) Report (various years), Six-monthly Report in Hong Kong, http://www.fco.gov.hk.

Goodstadt, Leo (2005), *Uneasy Partners: The Conflict between Public Interest and Private Profit in Hong Kong.* Hong Kong: Hong Kong University Press.

Lau, C. K. (1997), *Hong Kong's Colonial Legacy.* Hong Kong: The Chinese University Press.

Vines, Stephen (1998), *Hong Kong China's New Colony.* London: Aurum Press.

Welsh, Frank (1994), *A History of Hong Kong.* London: HarperCollins.

Yahuda, Michael (1996), *Hong Kong, China's Challenge.* London: Routledge.

Zhao, Suisheng (2004), *A Nation-State by Construction: Dynamics of Modern Chinese Nationalism.* Stanford, CA: Stanford University Press.

3

A Decade of Responses in North America to the Handover

Janet W. Salaff and Arent Greve

Introduction

In this chapter, we explore the news reports that North Americans have been able to access in the major presses of Canada and the United States (U.S.) about the Hong Kong Special Administrative Region (SAR) through reviewing articles from *The Globe and Mail* (*G&M*) (Toronto) and *The New York Times* (*NYT*). We first comment on our institutional framework, which emphasizes how the press builds a consensus in meaning. We then discuss the particular frame that the press assumed in their discussions of the SAR. Over the 10-year period, most of the press were operating within the terms of predictions from influential presses, in particular, the 1995 *Fortune Magazine* article by Louis Kraar (1995). We turn to the review of the press materials. We conclude that, by the end of the decade, there has been a shift in meaning and in the frame employed by the press. Although slow to concede the case, near the end of the SAR's first decade, the press has come to the conclusion that Hong Kong is not "dead." What Kraar anticipated and feared has not come about. From heralding the end of Hong Kong, there has come to be a recognition that there is the beginning of a real government, a turn to a viable economy, and a real society in Hong Kong. In so doing, the commentators have provided a great deal of information about Hong Kong to readers, albeit with a slant.

The Press: A Framework for Unifying Meanings

We chose these two organs of the press as useful windows on what educated North Americans can learn about the SAR. Situated in a major global city, the *NYT* is an influential opinion maker. Its op-eds are widely read and discussed. Its articles are syndicated throughout the U.S. It was here that the colonial Hong Kong government took out ads to influence public opinion on its viability. The *NYT* is the most influential newspaper in North America. The *G&M*, while not from a central metropolitan node, is also a national paper. It holds a similar philosophical viewpoint. Its particularity is its representation of the leaders of the Canadian political economy and the nation's foreign policy. As well, it reflects Canada's vantage point as the recipient of a large number of Chinese immigrants from Hong Kong and China. Taken together, they are key sites for us to learn about the reporting of news from the press about the Special Administrative Region (SAR).

The press has a powerful role in forming public opinion and policy. However, what is presented is selective because material and institutional conditions shape the choice of topics and their presentation. Institutional analysis describes large-scale factors, as well as local structures of meanings that shape what the press presents as news. The market plays an important role in the presentation of what is deemed to be news, as do the larger context of social relations and the producers. Newspapers have become increasingly concentrated, and the cost of launching a press is high (McChesney, 2001). Publishers set their tone and content, with an eye to their audience, interest groups, the political economy of the region and ideological stance. The medium itself permits limited feedback, apart from highly selected letters to the editor, and advertisers that monitor sales. Further, there is no pretense at representative coverage. The media has its own social networks on which it draws for news. Certain figures are considered legitimate media sources, while others are not. For instance, most press coverage relies heavily on government officials (McChesney, 1996). In particular, the *NYT* tends to present press coverage that is closely aligned to the viewpoints of the political elite (Benson and Hallin, 2007).

In addition to such material and institutional conditions, there is the professional position of reporters, whose norms of appropriateness and professional norms influence the content of the press (Benson, 2004). The reporters of these presses are professionally trained, which gives them a common approach to news presentation. Journalism is their career, although they also write books. They move from press to press, and may also advance within their main press, to become bureau chiefs. They become personally associated with what they write. Their by-lines are on the articles, and they may receive awards for particular pieces. Their movement from region to region and their esprit de corps makes it likely that they will inherit from their predecessors a frame of writing about a location, and pass it on. Their informants are inherited as well.

The production of meaning is at the core of the role of the press. People develop beliefs and make sense of events (Boland and Tenkasi, 1995; Weick, 1995). Sensemaking is a social process; people discuss events in order to understand them. The beliefs that are the foundation for sensemaking become shared through interaction and become accepted facts; they may not even be questioned (Sperber et al., 1990). In most cases, we make sense of events retrospectively — even our own experiences (Garfinkel, 1967; Lindstead, 2006). When applied to future events, prior developed scripts heavily influence predictions and beliefs about causation. When people arrive at certain conclusions, they search their memory for beliefs that will support their reasoning. This includes applying biased beliefs about others as well as about events (Kunda, 1987). It is this consensus that is based on many foundations that accounts for news articles providing information within a constructed frame. For Hong Kong, there was ready agreement on the frame: the threats to decentralized, neo-liberal capitalism when Hong Kong reverted to a centralized government that had little understanding about what capitalism was based upon.

The Press: What Is Presented about Hong Kong

Together, the two papers produced a substantial amount of materials on the Hong Kong SAR, of which we reviewed a good segment. Although the two presses differ, their articles fell under the same ideological influence. Through the first decade of the existence of the SAR, these papers engaged with issues that Louis Kraar dramatically voiced in *Fortune Magazine* (1995), when he predicted that reversion to China meant "the death of Hong Kong" (Kraar, 1995). Many of the 131 articles that we reviewed, 119 for the 10-year period of the SAR alone, engaged, both directly and obliquely, with issues raised in Kraar's influential journalistic piece. When we present our analysis of the press coverage of Hong Kong during the handover years and afterwards, we will analyze how these beliefs influenced the press coverage. We also examine the great difficulty it took to change these beliefs.

The press reflects what reporters *see*. What they see is framed by what they expect. The interest of the two press organs we covered mainly centred on the foreign investor's mood. Or as one writer put it, the "economic mood of the city." Given this, it is unfortunate that the reports mainly framed

Hong Kong's political and economic life through an inheritance of a series of pre-1997 predictions of what would happen after retrocession. The retrocession shook the institutional framework that Western reporters took for granted about how capitalism works. Colonial Hong Kong held a unique place. Hong Kong embodied the North American investors' dream: British common law used in support of the free market. Its uniqueness was seen as being shored up by several pillars. The articles written after the handover placed their news against the background of the viability of these pillars after reversion to China.

What the public learns from the press is what the press presents as newsworthy. This is true for all reportage. However, in addition to their set framework on the eve of the handover, there was another unique feature about this reportage on Hong Kong. Western reporters faced major constraints of language, background, difficulty in gaining access to informants, culture, social networks closed to outsiders, and other factors that limited coverage of a range of viewpoints. Hence, they tended to gather their reportage from a small number of players, a handful of key respondents, such as, for example, academics or one or two dissidents.

Our chapter traces how the press handled the pillars that it sees as crucial in buoying up a strong capitalist economy. We conclude that, given these limits, the press has covered a lot of the political and economic activities that have taken place in Hong Kong in the past decade.

Data

Hong Kong is popular in North America. It is true that in the 1960s Hong Kong was considered *Britain's white elephant* (Catron, 1971). However, by the years leading up to the reversion, Hong Kong had become a talking spot in the North American media. Whereas many have the impression that Hong Kong has lost precedence and has fallen from the public eye since its reversion to Chinese rule, this is not what our review shows. Materials on Hong Kong in the *NYT* increased incrementally as reversion approached. The handover date itself was greeted with a large flurry of reports: We read four features and editorials in the *NYT* on that date alone. And after reversion to China, Hong Kong remained an *item*. For the *NYT* in particular, there was an explosion of coverage (see Appendix). We did not review pre-handover *G&M* coverage. Clearly what happens in Hong Kong is considered important in the media of the two countries, for the *NYT* in particular.

The Themes

We grouped the major themes of the articles into the twin terms of politics and the economy, which dominated the pre-retrocession rhetoric on the "death of Hong Kong." Of the two themes, politics dominated by far (see Appendix). Further, the discussions over economics and politics were closely intertwined, as the two were seen to inextricably affect each other. First, we discuss the assumptions and beliefs that shaped the content and judgements of the articles. Then, we review the content of the materials that were mainly published after reversion, turning first to the theme of politics and then to the theme of the economy.

Beliefs and Assumptions

First among the pillars are the political factors that were seen to promote and protect capitalism. The freedom to invest and make deals was freedom from state interference. This was crucial in a region that had been dominated by state investment in or heavy influence over the market. Next were democratic freedoms. In Europe, historically, the freedom of the marketplace and the ascendancy of the middle classes over the king, the church and royal courts were associated with democratic representation, the opportunity to assemble for unpopular causes and to voice ideas that were not liked, and to oppose the state. In colonial Hong Kong, while fighting for freedom of representation had not been a main feature of political life, it was emerging to become a force that was not easy to ignore. The issues were seen to be freedom of expression, important in its own right, and important for stability, essential to maintaining the confidence of investors. Finally, there was Hong Kong's split personality of Western and Chinese culture, which featured an English-based education and a key role for expatriate capitalists and managers.

The survival of these political economic and features became the major focus of press reports leading up to and after retrocession. The press was concerned about the possible changes after reversion, due mainly to Mainland Chinese misunderstanding of the complexities of this mixture of the ingredients of neo-liberal capitalism. Or, as was opined in the 1 July 1997 *NYT* op-ed on the reversion, the Mainland Chinese might try to open free markets, but fail to appreciate the *software* of the free market.

> The strength of Hong Kong was that it combined Chinese capitalist hardware — that is, Chinese entrepreneurial talent, energy and money — with British

software — the rule of law, an independent judiciary and the enforcement of contracts and property rights — and together they made Hong Kong rich and powerful.... ("Auld Lang Syne," Thomas L. Friedman, *NYT*, 1 July 1997).

An obvious feature of the construction of meaning in both presses is the unmistakable proprietary tone ("we know best") that intrudes into the reports. This is perhaps based on *nation first* perspectives in the North American press. Throughout, the views are presented through the national interests of the countries where the press originates. What goes reported needs to defend that country's own industry, its own products, and its ideology. This tone gives us, as readers, the uncanny feeling of a new form of colonialism, that of ideas. It is more than a tone, however. It is a taken-for-granted element of the framework within which what is done locally in Hong Kong is evaluated.

It needs to be pointed out that what the press takes for granted, the foundation of meaning, are assumptions about the good old days, before retrocession, which did not exist. Colonial Hong Kong did not have an unequivocally excellent showing on the political and economic fronts. For most of the colonial period, few democratic processes had been put into place, which had undoubtedly delayed interest among the public in democratic representation. The right to profess some ideas (anti-colonial, pro-PRC views) was suppressed. The property market was never free and was to hamper the economy during the Asian financial crisis (1997–1998). The state did not stay in the background, but had built the infrastructure to promote certain kinds of production as opposed to others. Mainland China had subsidized Hong Kong consumption and living costs and, in turn, its production. English education was not universally at a high level. Nevertheless, Hong Kong was an acclaimed success, as juxtaposed against what was seen to be the way the economy and political system worked in the People's Republic of China (PRC). Opinion leaders feared that these pillars of Hong Kong's success were liable to fall.

During the early years of the SAR, the press constantly challenged Hong Kong and China's leadership to demonstrate that they were maintaining these pillars. The press expressed fearful views as to what Hong Kong would become. Initially, doubts overrode assurances, and the calamitous economic and public health events of 1998–2003 reinforced their interpretations. It took some time for the news-makers to revise their perspectives, to establish a new frame. The change in stance occurred gradually, but one can see mainly around 2005 the emergence of a clearly articulated, albeit begrudging, assessment: Hong Kong has not *died*.

The change over time was captured in the *G&M* article "24/7 Boomtown." Geoffrey York recalled the fearful predictions:

> Just a decade ago, the Western media were announcing the demise of this former British colony. In the spring of 1995, a cover story in *Fortune* magazine proclaimed "The Death of Hong Kong." The events of the following years seemed to confirm the gloomy prediction.
>
> First there was the handover to Chinese control in 1997. It terrified so many Hong Kongers that 300,000 fled overseas in the 1990s — almost 70 per cent of them emigrating to Canada. Then there was the devastating Asian financial crisis of 1997–98, followed by years of deflation and a prolonged collapse in Hong Kong's property market. The culmination of it all was the SARS epidemic of 2003, which turned Hong Kong into a ghost city where mask-wearing residents were afraid to touch even a doorknob. The economy ground to a halt.

Geoffrey York continued:

> In 2001, when the Toronto-based Four Seasons group won the management contract for the first new luxury hotel to be built in Hong Kong in a decade, it must have seemed like a risky gamble. But when the 45-storey waterfront hotel opened this month [in 2005], its timing was exquisite. The hotel has caught the upsurge of a new boom that has brought confidence and optimism to this territory of seven million people ("24/7 Boomtown," Geoffrey York, G&M, 29 September 2005, p. H.1).

In the following sections, we describe in more detail the content of our press survey, the tone of which is reflected in this article. Economic and political issues dominate their concerns, and are intertwined. Politics are seen to control economics, and in turn to shape the identities of the Hong Kong people. There are major shifts over time, however, and as the years passed, the perspectives and their underlying beliefs have changed direction.

Theme 1: Politics

The majority, but not all of, the themes covered in our press articles under the political rubric revolve around the major issues that were prominent in the *Fortune* assessment of 1995. These are the adherence to the Basic Law and the stability of civil society. Included were issues that Americans take as their civic religion: political self rule and self determination, and the ability to vote and to protest.

As we reviewed the content of the articles of the decade with political themes, we find that at the outset of SAR, the articles treated political topics relatively rigidly. It was as if preconceived ideas overtook a fresh assessment of what was happening in Hong Kong. Over time, however, there were major shifts to a more flexible view of Hong Kong's polity.

We begin with crucial issues that appeared on the eve of or early in the SAR. Opinions on the *legitimacy of the reversion* of Hong Kong to China were conspicuous by their absence. The press coverage and views of the reversion appear to have been formed without attention to historical evidence. Few articles reflected on the historical legacy and commented on the importance of maintaining territorial integrity. Perhaps this omission was because this topic was not actually raised in the 1995 *Fortune* assessment of Hong Kong's future. Without reference to history, the Opium Wars, gunboat diplomacy, and the fact that Hong Kong had been part of Chinese territory were rarely mentioned. The 99-year lease was accepted flatly without evaluation; discussions started at the present, from the perspective of the here and now. An exception appeared in the 20 February 1997 obituary of Deng Xiaoping (Tyler, 1997).

Another theme early on was dropped fairly quickly. This was the discussion in the *NYT* that it was important for this nation state *to take on the British burden*. The day of the reversion was accompanied by soul-searching editorials in the *NYT* anguishing over the possible problems that Hong Kong's neo-liberal capitalism would meet up with after joining what was seen as a centralized giant, China. The American role was seen to be that of taking over the British political leadership's job of safeguarding human rights ("Auld Lang Syne," Thomas L. Friedman, *NYT*, 1 July 1997). The proprietorial tone (we know best) intruded into the reports. The Americans, or the Clinton administration, were committed to taking on the issue of Hong Kong's freedom as its burden (from the British) after reversion. These issues set the tone for the subsequent materials which followed and which we review.

NYT reporter, Steven Erlanger, contended that Hong Kong will look to the U.S. as an arbiter and protector in its relations with China; he maintained that while Britain is no longer an Asian power,

> ... the United States, with its self-confidence, global reach, economic might, military power and vocal push for democracy and human rights, is a different

matter. It remains the most important Pacific power, a source of enormous investment, trade and needed technology. And it is one of the few countries that commands Beijing's respect. In the case of Hong Kong, China needs decent relations with the United States, and Hong Kong is vital to that larger relationship. The people who hold power in Washington and Beijing understand this.... Ms. Albright said, "Hong Kong is very high on [the] long list of issues [with China]" ("Uncle Sam's New Role: Hong Kong's Advocate," *NYT*, 2 July 1997).

But interestingly, this theme was dropped, as it became clear that Hong Kong could handle its own political issues and no defence was needed.

Assurances of the *continuity of the Basic Law* were a major theme throughout the 10-year period. The main issue was whether or not the PRC and the Hong Kong SAR leadership were following the Basic Law. Since this theme was introduced early on and carried forward, we see considerable change in views over the 10-year period. At the outset, doubts were raised as to whether the PRC leadership would follow the Basic Law. Looking at the headline of one piece at the cusp of the reversion:

"The Mao Things Change, The song remains the same, Officials say Hong Kong won't change — can we believe them?" (Michael Grunwald, *G&M*, 28 June 1997, p. F-7).

In another example from the same early time period,

... [the] transfer of power ushers in time of uncertainty over whether China will honour [its] pledge to maintain Hong Kong's way of life largely unaltered for next 50 years. ("China resumes control of Hong Kong, concluding 156 years of British rule," Edward A. Gargan, *NYT*, 1 July 1997).

Subsequently, over the decade, as articles scrutinized the major happenings for evidence of whether the Basic Law was being followed. Most recognized that the PRC and SAR were adhering to the Basic Law.

... Mr. Tung has so far managed to preserve more autonomy for Hong Kong than many outsiders imagined possible. For the most part, Hong Kong's independent judiciary and free press have survived the transition (Editorial, "Hong Kong Votes for Democracy," *NYT*, 27 May 1998, Section A, p. 20).

It should be pointed out, in contrast, that the British role in establishing and changing Hong Kong's political institutions on the eve of the reversion was not equally scrutinized, and was taken as a given. We introduce these comments although they precede the handover date because they provide an early consensus among the press on what the institutions were that should be monitored.

It is true that some writers recognized that there had been scant *democratic development* under the British.

> The agreement governing the terms of the hand over was signed in 1984, at a time when China seemed to be liberalising both its economic and political systems. Hong Kong's political structure then was not strictly democratic, and the prospects for finding a workable accommodation between the two systems seemed difficult but not impossible (Editorial, "Hong Kong Votes for Democracy," *NYT*, 19 September 1995, Section A, p. 20).

Hence, there was little discussion that the British, late in the game, had itself unilaterally changed the political institutions, thereby departing from the Basic Law. Instead, the press took the political institutions on the eve of the retrocession as the real institutions. For example, the electoral system was a topic that was tracked throughout the period. The discussion of the evolution of electoral politics became muddled due to the assumption that the political institutions as created by Patten were the real institutions.

> Christopher Patten, Britain's last Hong Kong Governor, has sought to encourage and strengthen democratic institutions.... (Editorial, "Hong Kong Votes for Democracy," *NYT*, 19 September 1995, Section A, p. 20).

After the elections of May 1998, there was again reference to the inherited institutions as the genuine institutions.

> ... the democratic electoral system that was developing during the last years of British rule but was dismantled after the transfer to China last July ... (Editorial, "Hong Kong Votes for Democracy," *NYT*, 27 May 1998, Section A, p. 20).

Another issue in the handling of the Hong Kong electoral system was the view that the timetable should be sped up because of popular pressure. The establishment of democratic institutions was bound to happen anyway,

> But as Hong Kong's experience demonstrates, all people eventually want a role in their own governance. As Hong Kong people grew wealthier and better educated, they began to thirst for representative government (Editorial, "Message in Hong Kong," *G&M*, 26 November 2003, p. A-20).

> Since Hong Kong's people "clearly want" democratic institutions, the press fears that if the SAR government holds back, the people who demand

democracy may become unruly. That is bad for business, and may undermine the business confidence that makes the territory such a valuable asset. Political turmoil is the enemy of a flourishing economy (Editorial, "Hong Kong Votes for Democracy," 19 September 1995, *NYT*, Section A, p. 20).

Over the decade-long period after retrocession, there was increased recognition that there had been an evolution in political systems. Many wrote that the evolution was understandably slow, because what was forming was new to all parties. That there was political change was recognized. This was partly due to political interaction between Hong Kong and China.

Hong Kong and China political interaction: A theme in the press throughout this period was the dynamic exchange between the SAR and the motherland. The press recognized that there is interplay between the two locales. By pursuing this theme, the press became open to a vision that was wider than its focus on the pillars of democracy that China might undermine. That China may not understand parliamentary forms of political expression did not mean that China could not learn.

On the day of the reversion, the stress of the press articles was on how Hong Kong might change Mainland Chinese institutions:

> [The] most important question is not how China will change Hong Kong but how Hong Kong will change China — and the world beyond; Hong Kong could end up being a colossal Trojan horse that could threaten the lifestyle and leadership of Chinese Communist Party leaders ("Year of the Trojan Horse," Nicholas D. Kristof, *NYT*, 1 July 1997 Section A, p. 1).

Over time, commentators reported that China was learning to tolerate political expression in Hong Kong itself. China was learning about party politics from Hong Kong, and how to handle the public. The showdown over the effort to pass the Security Bill 23 revealed that,

> Hong Kong can be a test bed for new ideas.... Beijing has learned new tactics to placate the voters and boost its allies. With a combination of political concessions and economic gifts, the authorities are figuring out how to play the democratic game. "They are beginning to behave like the Republican Party in the U.S. or the Conservative Party in Britain," said Margaret Ng, a member of the Hong Kong legislature. "They're more responsive to people's views. They realize you have to give people what they want if you want them to support you. You can't just tell people to support you. From the Hong Kong experience, they're learning about election tactics. It's fascinating to see how they're getting better at it" ("China Learns to Play the Democracy Game," Geoffrey York, *G&M*, 3 October 2003, p. A-23).

The press has also emphasized that *conservation of the rule of law*, as interpreted by courts based on British constitutional principles, is a tenet that is central to protection of the Basic Law. Over this 10-year period, the press has concluded that this tenet, a condition of retrocession, has been respected. Observers find that Hong Kong has been allowed to preserve its own institutions, which do not have the same rights on the Mainland. As an example, the area of religion is one that the press closely tracks. Although before the handover the Catholic Church made preemptory moves to put into place a mechanism for selecting the successor to Hong Kong leader, Joseph Cardinal Wu, the press quoted Foreign Ministry spokesman Shen Guofang, who insisted that,

> "The religious policy on the Mainland will not be implemented in Hong Kong." (Church and State/Despite Vatican-China tensions, the faithful try their best to reconcile opposing loyalties, *G&M*, 18 January 1997).

In another example, the Falun Gong was outlawed in China in 1999, but the press noted that Hong Kong has not been included in this ban,

> Hong Kong has no plans to pass a law against the sect.... The protected status of Falun Gong in Hong Kong says a great deal about the limits of Beijing's power in this capitalist outpost.... As if to underscore the difference between Hong Kong and China, about 160 Falun Gong members gathered outside Mr. Tung's office on Friday to mark the anniversary of the crackdown [in China]. Sitting in the lotus position, with their eyes closed and hands raised in prayer, the crowd aroused little notice — let alone anger or alarm — from the police, or office workers who strolled past ("The World: Tolerating Falun Gong; Hong Kong Bows to Beijing. Except When It Doesn't," Mark Landler, *NYT*, 22 July 2001, Week in Review, Desk Section 4, p. 4).

That expressions of political opposition have been allowed in many realms has also been recognized by the press. In the realm of political protest, and the press is quick to note that annual demonstrations on 1 July, and others, are permitted. Further, the demonstrations have had an effect. The press cheered over the shelving of the discussion paper on Bill 23. The right to protest is acknowledged in Hong Kong, and furthermore, officials are heeding public opinion.

> Yielding to public pressure to an extent seldom seen in China, Hong Kong's chief executive announced yesterday he was withdrawing the internal-security legislation that provoked huge protests in July. Tung Chee-hwa said that while he still believed that legislation was needed here to protect China's national

security, he would not introduce a new bill until a clear public consensus supported the legislation ("Hong Kong withdraws security bill," Keith Bradsher, *G&M*, 6 September 2003, p. A-22).

Whether Hong Kong's legal institutions, in particular its courts, had been subjected to interference from Beijing was much discussed and made news throughout the spring of 1999. The Hong Kong Court of Final Appeal (CFA) had ruled in January 1999 that several children of Hong Kong and Mainland Chinese parents, who had been living in China at the time of the retrocession, but had entered Hong Kong on temporary visas and stayed on, were permitted to remain. The Standing Committee of China's National People's Congress reinterpreted the ruling on 31 March 1999. The key issue in the press was whether this was a constitutional crisis. Did Hong Kong challenge China? Was there a power play from China, compelling Hong Kong to comply? Or was there a procedural misunderstanding on the part of the CFA? The press discussed these issues in a fairly complex manner. The press presented many viewpoints without drawing conclusions. On the one hand, there were hints of PRC interference, as in the article titled, "China Tells Hong Kong It Wants Immigration Ruling *'Rectified'*" [emphasis added]

> Speaking on her return from a meeting in Beijing, Secretary of Justice Elsie Leung said officials had told her the ruling by the Court of Final Appeal was "contradictory to the principles in the constitution." ... [and that the] landmark ruling on immigration by the high court here violated the territory's constitution and "should be rectified" ("China Tells Hong Kong It Wants Immigration Ruling 'Rectified'," Mark Landler, *NYT*, 14 February 1999).

Alternative views of the Hong Kong government were only briefly aired. The *G&M* published a letter from the acting director of the Hong Kong Economic & Trade Office in Toronto, insisting that it was Hong Kong people themselves who had asked China for a clarification of the Basic Law, in order to keep out what they claimed would be an inundation of children from Mainland China.

> Since the CFA's judgement was founded on the Basic Law, which was enacted by the National People's Congress, we had no alternative but to seek interpretation of the true legislative intent of the provisions. We are not pretending when we said that this was a special case. We have exercised great care to ensure that the approach was entirely legal and constitutional and complies with legal procedures (Reader's letter: "Hong Kong's special case," Eddie Cheung, *G&M*, 12 July 1999, in reference to editorial 2 July 1999).

Other articles depicted a more human, but sad, side of the story of the desperate poverty of the new Mainland arrivals ("Promised land paved with broken dreams Mainlanders sour on pricey Hong Kong," *G&M*, 26 May 1999). The press sought a way out of the impasse, quoting Michael DeGolyer, a Hong Kong academic and frequent informant, who hinted at a humane way to solve this issue ("Hong Kong Seeks Its Own Chinese Wall," Mark Lander, *NYT*, 23 May 1999). From the treatment of this topic, we see that the press employed a multifaceted approach, characterized by locating viewpoints from diverse parties. A well-rounded approach was emerging.

The press noted that *a new sense of belonging* was being manifested in Hong Kong. In particular, they singled out the popular protests that have been taking place in Hong Kong. Many of the news articles on political issues contained the subtext that politics has become newly important to the people. Hong Kong can no longer be depicted as a "borrowed place, in a borrowed time." For example, the press observed that the demonstrations against the demolition of the Star Ferry in 2006 reflected the new Hong Kong identity. Furthermore, these demonstrations are seen as having an effect. The press quoted Chief Executive Donald Tsang as recognizing that people care about Hong Kong's heritage and that legislation on heritage needs to be strengthened. It further commented that this demonstration revealed the stability of Hong Kong.

> "Collective memory" — has emerged as a rallying cry for a young generation of activists who have rediscovered the city's history. Hong Kong ... once saw itself as merely a temporary place of business for capitalist refugees who fled Communist China.... After a long economic slump following the 1997 handover to China, the city survived and stabilized. The passport holders who escaped before the handover were returning. People began to think of Hong Kong as their home, a place with a "collective memory." In the aftermath of the Star Ferry battle, there is a growing movement to defend dozens of threatened sites — historic markets, piers, old apartment blocks and cluttered streets of shops that for decades were the heart of Hong Kong life ("Hong Kong suddenly seeks its soul," Geoffrey York, *G&M*, 31 March 2007, p. F-4).

By the end of our period, the press had conceded that the political pillars, the major political issues, appear to have stabilized. China has been keeping to its commitment to uphold the Basic Law. There is flexibility in the political system, which is slowly evolving. Seeing that their dire predictions have not come true, it has taken the press nearly a decade to change their beliefs about Hong Kong and PRC. Although the changes are more of degree than fundamental, the newspaper articles seem to reflect that more diverse beliefs are being held and expressed about the years after the handover.

Theme 2: Economy

The second major pillar of the Hong Kong liberal capitalist system was the nature of its economy. Soon after the retrocession, the Hong Kong economy faced major crises, which dominated press articles through 2003. It was only when the Hong Kong economy rebounded in recognized ways that these outside observers gave Hong Kong a clean bill of health, and refused to sign the death warrant. The turnaround was sealed in 2005.

Unlike the political discussions, in the discussions of the economy there was recognition that the economic downturn was not largely a direct result of the reversion to China. Nevertheless, the SAR government's handling of these several crises came under criticism. The press rapped the knuckles of Hong Kong Chief Executive Tung for handling the economy in an inept manner. Joseph Cheng, an oft-interviewed local academic, was cited as saying that "People respect Tung but HK people want results" ("Hong Kong Leader Tries to Cope with the Crisis," Mark Landler, *NYT*, 12 October 1998, p. A-6).

The press pointed out political aspects of the crises. The press was on the lookout for xenophobia. They noted that in key projects that went off the rails blame was placed on expatriates, events that they traced to political pressure from China. The press thought that Hong Kong's inherited script was: do not criticize Chinese; blame outsiders ("Hong Kong Blames Foreign Managers for Airport's Faulty Start," Mark Landler, *NYT*, 23 January 1999).

This spate of economic problems may not have been the government's doing. But it seemed that the government could not handle the tough issues involved.

Almost from the day he took over as chief executive of post-colonial Hong Kong in 1997, Tung Chee-hwa has been in trouble. First came the Asian financial crisis. Then, the mishandled opening of a big new airport. Next was the property-price bust. Then SARS. Now, Mr. Tung faces his biggest crisis: a popular revolt over his government's tough new anti-subversion bill.... Sixty-seven per cent of Hong Kongers tell pollsters Mr. Tung should quit. Even if he doesn't, his reputation and his authority are in ruins ("Tung Chee-hwa and the death of 'Asian values'," Marcus Gee, *G&M*, 10 July 2003, p. A-17).

The outbreak of severe acute respiratory syndrome (SARS) was another area that drew fire on the new government. The efforts that the government took to get people back out shopping and spending, and going to theatres and concerts, which included handing out salary tax rebates, were seen as akin to bread and circuses ("Trying to save Hong Kong," Frank Ching, *G&M*, 12 May 2003, p. A-13).

In other press themes of economic issues in the crisis-ridden early post-handover period, we find the theme that people are aware that this is their own place now. The ethos has changed. There was an observation that, in the economic crisis, the wealthy kept on earning. Yet the wealthy were more likely to hide ostentatious displays of wealth.

The regional economic crisis has compounded Hong Kong's identity crisis by slowing its capitalist heartbeat. Money is still being made here.... But the gaudy celebration of wealth that characterized Hong Kong during the go-go years has been replaced by a more sober recognition of hard times. Still, if you ignore the prevailing mood and walk the streets, Hong Kong feels very much like its old self ("What's Doing in; Hong Kong," Mark Landler, *NYT*, 18 April 1999).

Even the wealthy had to slow down their conspicuous consumption. For the first time, many went over the border to buy knock-offs of designer brands. In their new society, they were wary of displaying their wealth. The ability of people to respond to the poor economy was heralded as showing that even after reversion, Hongkongers maintained their spirit of innovation. For example, they evaded border controls and other sanctions in order to consume ("It's Not Hong Kong, but Then It's Not Gucci Either," Mark Landler, *NYT*, 2 February 1999).

The press was clear that the drop in property values, which lasted for years, greatly increased the suffering of the poor and middle class. The press discussion of the economic problems of ordinary people during this crisis focused especially on the housing issue, which those investors who read the paper could relate to ("Property Slump Ruins Many in Hong Kong," Keith Bradsher, *NYT*, 15 August 2003). There were critiques of the government's policy as well as the former British land policy, which made prices inflexible. Even after the economy began to recover by 2005, the housing market had yet to climb back to levels reached in late 1997. ("[Housing] Prices are on the way back to sky-high," Mark Graham, *G&M*, 29 September 2005, p. H-7).

By 2005, a turnaround was in the air. Appealing to its business readership, in 2005, Geoffrey York from *G&M* summed up the new press consensus: renewed optimism. The wheel had spun around since 1997.

> According to conventional wisdom in the 1990s, Hong Kong would soon be overshadowed by Shanghai, the Chinese glamour queen. But the rumours of Hong Kong's death were somewhat exaggerated. "The mood has turned around and it's much more positive," said Michael DeGolyer, director of the Hong Kong Transition Project at Hong Kong Baptist University. "I don't hear anyone in Hong Kong saying that Shanghai will take over. They're not worried about that any more."

The major barometers of an up-turn sparked investor confidence. York continued,

> More than 90 per cent of Canadian businesses in Hong Kong consider the territory to be an excellent place to do business, according to a survey this year by the Asia Pacific Foundation of Canada....
>
> The engine of China is behind Hong Kong, and there's a huge amount of pressure and demand building up. So many of our corporate clients are coming back to town and expanding their offices here. They're doing business in China, but they're setting up their offices here" ("24/7 Boomtown," Geoffrey York, *G&M*, 29 September 2005, p. H-1).

Far from being a liability, China is seen to have revived Hong Kong's economy.

In sum, throughout this first 10-year period of the existence of the SAR, we find a shift in frames. Initially, the articles on the economy predicted doomsday. The early years of the SAR did not dispel that belief. However, the attributions shifted. Instead of faulting the entire leadership system of governance of Hong Kong under China, the commentators turned to people. They emphasized how ordinary people could innovate, or how the Chief Executive was not able to handle the crises (Menon et al., 1999). This was a major shift and reveals that the paradigm, the "death of Hong Kong," has been reframed.

Conclusion

We have reviewed articles that appeared in two major North American newspapers, the *NYT* and Toronto's the *G&M* mainly during the 10 years after the establishment of Hong Kong as a special administrative region of China. We selected them in order to understand the main themes and main issues that they conveyed. We found a relatively narrow focus on politics and economics and, of the two, political issues overwhelmingly represented the depiction of Hong Kong in the press.

The press in those articles that we read largely focused on what they believed their public wanted to hear. The press, especially the *G&M*, appeared to define their public as investors first. The *NYT* went past investors to take into account the policy-makers, notably during the Clinton era.

Most of the articles that we reviewed for the first 10 years of the existence of the SAR jousted with the shadow of the Kraar (1995) *Fortune Magazine* article. The theme of the Kraar piece was that the reversion to China is a death sentence levelled on Hong Kong. This perspective was not foreign to the views of those journalists. Following this journalist heritage, the frame of what the key issues would be for Hong Kong in this period was fairly circumscribed. Hong Kong issues were crafted around the themes of its political struggles and the economic implications of these struggles. In another sense, however, they were not narrow. These articles touched on many issues and much information was presented in these articles, although they had a common take on the SAR, one that was heavily influenced by the ideology of the commentators and how they made sense of events.

Their beliefs changed slowly. In this heritage, the main emphasis was political. Through 2003, the political system of Hong Kong as an SAR was judged fairly severely. The political themes sought to find China plots behind many issues in Hong Kong. Gradually, by late 2003, after Hong Kong had weathered the Security Bill 23, and following the change of government after 2005, the press reported that the PRC appeared to maintain its political assurances in relation to Hong Kong.

The economy, on the other hand, took a bit longer to come around. But even here, by 2005, the press deemed Hong Kong to be free of the threat foretold by Kraar. Although slow to concede the case, near the end of the SAR's first decade, the press has come to conclude that Hong Kong has not suffered irrevocably. What Kraar (1995) had anticipated and feared has not come to pass.

APPENDIX: How We Assessed the Press

For our survey of the press, we used two search engines, Proquest and the internal search function of the *NYT,* to find instances of articles that mentioned *Hong Kong* and *handover.* We added articles from special searches, such as those pertaining to the 1999 court case of immigrant children from the PRC or SARS. We searched in the *NYT* from 1 January 1992 through 12 May 2007, representing 8 years of pre-handover and 10 years of post-handover articles, and Toronto's the *G&M* from January 1996 through 12 May 2007. We chose the *NYT* as the leading national American opinion-making piece. The *G&M* (Toronto) is Canada's national paper, the major receiving country for Hong Kong and Chinese immigrants.

The number of news articles that we tracked in the *NYT* increased after 1997. For the *NYT,* we found 93 relevant pieces[1] from 1 January 1992 through 12 May 2007. Eighty-one of these, or the vast majority, were from the SAR period. For the *G&M,* we read thirty-eight relevant articles from the SAR period.

In the two presses, we saw that between the economy and political issues the distribution of materials was heavily weighted in favour of the political scene. This was mainly because most economic issues were assessed in political terms. This tendency became more extreme after the handover. The ratio of economic to political articles in the *NYT* before 1997 was nearly even. But of the 76 articles we read in the *NYT* after 1997, nearly four-fifths dealt with politics (Table 3.1).

Slightly fewer *G&M* pieces dealt with political themes. What they did talk about was immigration and the effects of immigration on Canadian institutional and societal structures, as well as other topics, such as the price of housing, that Hong Kong immigrants might find relevant.

These figures are suggestive of the uneven coverage between the two papers and time spans (in the case of the *NYT*). However, since web search

Table 3.1 Number of Articles by Source and Topic

	NYT	G&M	Total > 1997
Economy before 1997	5	–	5
Politics before 1997	6	–	6
Economy after 1997	17	18	35
Politics after 1997	59	9	68
Other topics 1992–2007	6	11	17
Total	93	38	131

engines omitted reports, we cannot assess the complete count and coverage of articles. Our contribution lies rather in the overall assessment of the topics in the two national papers.

Apart from locating the main themes on Hong Kong's post reversion economy and society, we did not study the mass media *per se*. We did not focus on the presentation, the page of the paper, the tone or degree of sensationalism (Benson, 2002). We focused solely on the content.

Note

1. We excluded from our analysis and count pieces on Art and Travel, and on Macao and Taiwan, although many contained political sub-themes. For example, discussions on the reversion of Macao were presented in political terms, with comparisons to Hong Kong (Chan, 2003).

References

Benson, Rodney (2002), "Immigration News Coverage," *Journal of European Area Studies* 10 (1): 49–70.

—— (2004), "Bringing the Sociology of Media Back In," *Political Communication* 21 (3): 275–92.

Benson, Rodney and Daniel C. Hallin (2007), "How States, Markets and Globalization Shape the News," *European Journal of Communication* 22 (1): 27–48.

Boland, Richard J., Jr. and Ramkrishnan V. Tenkasi (1995), "Perspective Making and Perspective Taking in Communities of Knowing," *Organization Science* 6 (4): 350–72.

Catron, Gary W. (1971), "China and Hong Kong, 1945–1967." Ph.D. thesis, Harvard University, Cambridge, MA.

Chan, Ming K. (2003), "Different Roads to Home: The Retrocession of Hong Kong and Macau to Chinese Sovereignty," *Journal of Contemporary China* 12 (36): 493–518.

Garfinkel, Harold (1967), *Studies in Ethnomethodology*. London: Polity Press.

Kraar, Louis (1995), "The Death of Hong Kong," *Fortune* 131 (12): 118–27.

Kunda, Ziva (1987), "Motivated Inference: Self-serving Generation and Evaluation of Causal Theories," *Journal of Personality and Social Psychology* 53 (4): 636–47.

Lindstead, Stephen (2006), "Ethnomethodology and Sociology: An Introduction," *The Sociological Review* 54 (3): 399–404.

McChesney, Robert W. (1996), "Communication for the Hell of It: The Triviality of U.S. Broadcasting History," *Journal of Broadcasting and Electronic Media* 40 (4): 540–52.

——— (2001), "Global Media, Neoliberalism, and Imperialism," *Monthly Review* 52 (10): 1–19.

Menon, Tanya, Michael W. Morris, Chi-yue Chiu and Ying-yi Hong (1999), "Culture and the Construal of Agency: Attribution to Individual versus Group Dispositions," *Journal of Personality and Social Psychology* 76 (5): 701–17.

Sperber, Dan, Colin Fraser, George Gaskell, et al. (1990), "The Epidemiology of Beliefs." In Colin Fraser and George Gaskell (eds.), *The Social Psychological Study of Widespread Beliefs*. New York: Clarendon Press/Oxford University Press, p. xxx.

Tyler, Patrick E. (1997), "Deng Xiaoping: A Political Wizard Who Put China on the Capitalist Road," *New York Times*.

Weick, Karl E. (1995), *Sensemaking in Organizations*. Thousands Oaks, CA: Sage.

4

From Vision to Reality: Ten Years after Hong Kong's Return to China

Jia Qingguo

Time flies! Ten years has already passed since Hong Kong's return to China in 1997. Ten years ago, when the Chinese government started to put the "one country, two systems" (OCTS) principle into practice with the return of Hong Kong, the world was full of sceptics. It is not going to work, they said. Many predicted disaster. Now, 10 years later, not only is OCTS a reality, but also a success beyond expectations. Despite moments of uncertainty, Hong Kong has emerged to become a politically stable and economically vibrant city with greater prospects than it had before 1997. While Hong Kong is still confronted with various problems and challenges, its people have many good reasons to celebrate the 10-year anniversary of the handover and to be optimistic about their future.

This chapter represents a modest attempt to assess the application to date of the OCTS principle to Hong Kong from Beijing's perspective. A set of criteria with which to evaluate the application of the principle will first be developed. These criteria will then be used to assess the Hong Kong experiment. This is followed by an analysis of the findings. Finally, some speculations on the future of Hong Kong are put forward.

Criteria for Assessment

In anything, people can differ widely in their efforts at evaluation. This is primarily because they often proceed from different perspectives and use different criteria in conducting their evaluations. The same applies to efforts to evaluate the application of the OCTS principle in Hong Kong. In order to avoid such confusion, it is necessary to clarify from the outset from what perspective the evaluation is being conducted and with what criteria. This chapter approaches the evaluation of the perspective of Beijing and, therefore, uses the Chinese government's objectives in applying the OCTS as criteria in assessing the application of the principle to Hong Kong.

What were the objectives of the Chinese government when it took over Hong Kong 10 years ago? To begin with, the Chinese government anticipated that the OCTS principle would facilitate the recovery of sovereignty over Hong Kong from the British. In his talk with Li Ka-shing in 1992, Deng Xiaoping said that the Chinese government had to take back Hong Kong in 1997. The Chinese government would fail its historic mission to the Chinese people if it did not take back Hong Kong at that time. Li said that Deng told Mrs Thatcher, the then British Prime Minister, that there was no room for flexibility on the question of sovereignty.[1]

Second, the Chinese government anticipated that the OCTS principle would facilitate the transfer of administration over Hong Kong to the Hong Kong people. They rejected the British proposal to let the British continue to administer Hong Kong after the transfer of sovereignty. In a policy statement in 1984, Deng Xiaoping said that one should have confidence in the ability of the people of Hong Kong to administer the place on their own.[2] A few years later, he proposed to make it possible for the people of Hong Kong to participate in the management of Hong Kong's affairs beginning from 1990, including those relating to public administration, the judiciary, and economic and financial matters, so that they would be prepared for the return of Hong Kong.[3]

Similarly, former President Jiang Zemin stated in 1997 that increasing the participation of Hong Kong people in preparing for the return of Hong Kong had been a consistent policy of the Chinese government. The Chinese government had two objectives for doing so: One was to encourage Hong Kong people to advise the Chinese government as to how to manage the transition; the other was to enable Hong Kong people to become familiar with the administration of Hong Kong after its return to China.[4]

Third, the Chinese government hoped that the OCTS principle would help to ensure a smooth transfer of sovereignty over Hong Kong from Britain to China. It is always difficult for a colonial power to relinquish its rule over a place. It is also probably more difficult for a Western country to transfer a territory under its administration to a country with a different ideology and a different political system from its own than it would be to one with a similar ideology and political system. This was the case with Britain over Hong Kong. In the 1990s, as the day of Hong Kong's return to China drew nearer, the situation of Hong Kong became more complicated as the British became less cooperative than before and created various obstacles for the handing over of Hong Kong. At one point, even Deng Xiaoping became worried about the prospect of a smooth transfer. He said that he was concerned that a great deal of turmoil would erupt there (Deng, 1994, p. 14).

In his meeting with the representatives of the National People's Congress (NPC) from Hong Kong and Macao on 31 March 1993, Qiao Shi, the Chairman of the NPC at the time, said that the Chinese government was prepared to overcome difficulties so as to ensure the smooth transfer of Hong Kong and the latter's long-term economic prosperity.[5] In order to ensure Hong Kong's peaceful transfer, the NPC formed a special preparatory committee led by Vice-Premier Qian Qichen to study various issues related to the transfer. According to Vice-Premier Qian, by the end of 1995, the preparatory committee had held three plenary sessions and set up five study groups on political, economic, legal, cultural, social and security affairs. The study groups met 89 times and came up with 46 proposals and suggestions during their tenure.[6]

Fourth, the Chinese government ensured that the OCTS design would strengthen Hong Kong's position, so that it would not be used as a base for anti-China activities. Thus, Deng Xiaoping said during the drafting of the Basic Law that OCTS principle did not mean that the central government would not intervene at all. If Hong Kong were used as an anti-socialist, anti-Chinese government base, the central government would have to intervene. Otherwise, things would only get worse. The solution to the problem of Hong Kong should be one that the Chinese Mainland, Hong Kong and Britain would all be able to accept.[7]

Fifth, the Chinese government fully expected that the OCTS system would help to keep Hong Kong economically viable and politically stable. According to Deng Xiaoping, if the Chinese government had not guaranteed the right of Hong Kong and Taiwan to continue practising capitalism after their return to China, it would not be able to ensure their prosperity and stability.[8]

Finally, in the OCTS principle the Chinese government had a wider and bigger target. They anticipated that the new system would encourage people in Taiwan to be more amenable to peaceful reunification under the same arrangement.[9] Former Chinese President Jiang Zemin also stressed the point many times. He said that the successful application of the OCTS principle in Hong Kong would serve as an example for the resolution of the Taiwan problem. To him, the prosperity and stability of Hong Kong and Macao would provide the most effective way to remove doubts and suspicions concerning the feasibility and credibility of the principle on the part of the people in Taiwan.[10]

A Success beyond Expectations

Assessing the application of the OCTS principle in Hong Kong with the criteria discussed in the previous passages, one finds that the Chinese government has been quite successful in reaching its objectives. First, the Chinese government successfully recovered sovereignty over Hong Kong from the British according to its announced schedule. Moreover, it has firmly held on to this regained sovereignty since then.

Second, the transfer of sovereignty from Britain to China went smoothly. The People's Liberation Army (PLA) marched into positions in Hong Kong without any serious incidents. The handover ceremony was held punctually and solemnly. The ensuing celebrations took place in a genuinely festive mood. And the British left quietly. The transfer did not meet with any major political resistance. It did not have any significant negative impact on Hong Kong's economy.[11] No major social and political turmoil followed the transfer. No massive emigration took place. Those in Hong Kong who obtained British overseas passports did so primarily for insurance rather than out of panic or defiance. In fact, following Hong Kong's return to China in 1997 many Hong Kong residents who had migrated to Canada returned to Hong Kong after securing permanent residency there.[12]

Third, the administration of Hong Kong by Hong Kong people has been realized and, on the whole, has proceeded quite smoothly. Beginning from 1 July 1997, Hong Kong people took over the administration of the place. They also took over all of the important positions in the Legislative Council and the courts. Colonial rule over the city became history. Over time, with support from the central government, Hong Kong people proved that they could do as good a job as the British in running the place and, in fact, have made Hong Kong a better place.

Fourth, largely as Beijing hoped, Hong Kong has not been used as a base by hostile forces to launch activities to sabotage the Chinese government. It is true that some political forces like the Taiwan separatists, Tibetan independent advocates, Falun Gong protesters and human-rights critics wanted to make Hong Kong a base from which to stage activities against the Chinese government. It is also true that they have managed to organize some political activities in Hong Kong. However, they have never managed to make major infiltrations into China or to organize large-scale and persistent political protests against China in Hong Kong.

Fifth, since Hong Kong's return to China, it has remained economically viable and politically stable. Despite the shock of the Asian financial crisis of 1997, Hong Kong has remained an economically viable place with the strong support of the central government. According to the government of the Hong Kong Special Administrative Region (SAR), "Overall, the Hong Kong economy is expected to attain solid and broad-based growth of 4.5–5.5% in real terms in 2007. This, if realized, would signify another year of above-trend growth when compared with the trend growth at 4.1% over the past 10 years. The prevailing forecasts by the private sector are likewise upbeat about further expansion of the Hong Kong economy at a solid pace, which are mostly in the range of 5–5.5%" (Government of HKSAR, 2007, p. 33). Figure 10.1 (p. 219) shows the widely fluctuating trend of GDP performance over the past decade.

According to the Hong Kong SAR government, "The underlying trend of labour productivity, as measured by GDP per person engaged, is better revealed by examining its movement over a longer period, as the year-to-year movement may be susceptible to the influence of business cycles. Between 2000 and 2006, labour productivity in Hong Kong as crudely measured by GDP per person engaged rose by about 3.7% per year. This was notably higher than the 2.8% average increase in the 1990s, reflecting the on-going shift of the economy towards high value-added and knowledge-based activities, which has been matched by the continuous quality upgrading of Hong Kong's labour force" (Ibid., p. 5).

In addition, 10 years after Hong Kong's return to China, it has managed to maintain its position as the freest economy in the world, according to the *Index of Economic Freedom* of the U.S. Heritage Foundation. Among the 10 factors under evaluation, Hong Kong achieved the top score in 6. "Hong Kong scores exceptionally well in almost all areas of economic freedom. Income and corporate tax rates are extremely low, and overall taxation is relatively small as a percentage of GDP. Business regulation is simple, and the labour market is highly flexible. Inflation is low, although the Government distorts the prices of several staples. Investment in Hong Kong is wide open, with virtually no restrictions on foreign capital. The island is also one of the world's leading financial centres, with an extensive banking and services industry that is regulated non-intrusively and transparent. The judiciary, independent of politics and virtually free of corruption, has an exemplary ability to protect property rights" (Kane et al., 2007, pp. 60, 205).

Politically, despite continuous pressure from some political activists for speedier democratization and despite some protests, such as the massive demonstration in 2003 against the Hong Kong SAR government's efforts to implement Article 23 of the Basic Law, Hong Kong has generally remained politically stable. People may complain about the pace of democratization and the extent of press freedom. However, few would deny that a relatively high level of political stability has been maintained over the years. In 2001, about four years after Hong Kong's handover and the outbreak of the Asian financial crisis, Hong Kong was ranked the second politically most stable of 12 countries and regions in a study on the political risk for business investment.[13] If a similar study on political stability were to be carried out now, Hong Kong would likely also achieve quite a high ranking.

On the question of press freedom in Hong Kong, it appears that the trust that Hong Kong residents have in the news media has remained high and quite stable over the years. Opinion surveys about Hong Kong residents' views of Hong Kong's news media, conducted by The Chinese University of Hong Kong since Hong Kong's return to China, show that in 2006 the Hong Kong people's level of trust in Hong Kong's news media (6.41) was roughly similar to what it had been in 1997 (6.44).[14]

Despite what has been mentioned above, the Chinese government has encountered a number of problems in implementing the OCTS principle. To begin with, it has not convinced a large segment of Hong Kong's population that it is necessary to enact Article 23 of the Basic Law. On 24 September 2002, the Hong Kong SAR government initiated a three-month process of public consultation on the issue of legislating Article 23. The result of the consultation showed that a substantial number of Hong Kong residents did not support the legislation.[15] When the Hong Kong SAR government decided to press on with legislating Article 23, hundreds of thousands of Hong Kong residents took to the streets on 1 July 2003 to voice their opposition to the legislation. Faced with such unprecedented popular pressure, the Hong Kong SAR government decided to withdraw the bill on 5 September 2003. While the Basic Law requires that legislation be passed on Article 23, it is unclear when the Hong Kong SAR government will again propose it to the Legislative Council.

Moreover, Beijing has not convinced many in Hong Kong, especially the educated elite, that it is also in the best interests of Hong Kong to follow the schedule of democratization agreed upon prior to the return of Hong

Kong to China. Instead, some people have decided that Hong Kong needs a faster pace of democratization. This has led to persistent efforts to put pressure on the Hong Kong SAR government, including a mass demonstration on 5 December 2005, when an estimated 65,000 people participated in demanding direct elections for the Legislative Council and for the position of Chief Executive.[16]

Finally, Beijing has not been successful in persuading the people of Taiwan to become more receptive to the idea of unification under the OCTS arrangement. In fact, for various reasons, the people of Taiwan have not paid much attention to the positive developments in Hong Kong since its return to China, or for their positive relevance to Taiwan's future. Instead, they have been told to focus on the problems that have arisen during the implementation of the principle. The following polls conducted between 1995 and 2003 by Taiwan's organizations on Taiwan residents' view of the applicability of the OCTS principle to solving the Taiwan problem, suggest that Taiwan residents' view of the applicability of the OCTS formula has not changed much over the years despite its successful implementation in Hong Kong (Figure 4.1).

Another popular survey conducted in Taiwan on its residents' views of the question of unification and independence between 1994 and 2004 also suggests that on this question the view of Taiwan residents has not changed much over the years (Figure 4.2)

A more recent opinion survey conducted at the end of 2006 by Taiwan's Strait Exchange Foundation, a leading organization of the Taiwan authorities, suggests that support for unification has not been on the rise despite the successful application of the OCTS formula in Hong Kong.[17]

Despite these and other problems, one has to admit that from Beijing's perspective the application of the principle of OCTS in Hong Kong has been a great success 10 years after its return to China. Critics may fault Beijing for failing to bring greater freedom and faster democratization to Hong Kong. However, these were never among the central government's paramount stated objectives. In fact, the agreement between China and Britain on the return of Hong Kong called for a gradual and phased process of democratization, and Beijing has so far been faithful in observing this agreement.

Explaining the Successful Application of OCTS in Hong Kong

In retrospect, the following factors may explain Beijing's success in applying

Figure 4.1 Is the "One Country, Two Systems" Formula Applicable to Solving the Problems across the Taiwan Strait?

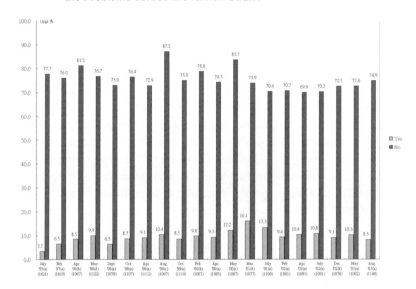

Organization conducting survey:

(a) Election Study Center, National Chengchi University, Taipei

(b) Burke Marketing Research, Ltd., Taipei

(c) China Credit Information Service, Ltd., Taipei

(d) Center for Public Opinion and Election Studies, National Sun Yat-sen University, Kaohsiung

(e) Survey and Opinion Research Group, Department of Political Science, National Chung Cheng University, Chiayi

(f) E-Society Research Group, Taipei

Respondents: Taiwanese adults aged 20–69 accessible to telephone interviewers

The numbers in parentheses denote the total number of respondents

Source: *Taiwan Yearbook 2004*, http://ecommerce.taipeitimes.com/yearbook2004/P087. htm

the OCTS principle to Hong Kong: (1) Beijing's adherence to the OCTS policy; (2) Beijing's commitment to a gradual process of democratization; (3) Beijing's proactive approach to supporting Hong Kong's economy; and (4) the Hong Kong SAR government's handling issues as they emerged.

To begin with, Beijing's adherence to the OCTS principle has effectively alleviated concerns on the part of Hong Kong residents and addressed concerns about the viability of OCTS on the part of some in the Mainland. Two responses were required from Beijing: to respect Hong Kong's

Figure 4.2 Changes in the Unification — Independence Stances of Taiwanese as Tracked in Surveys, 1994–2004

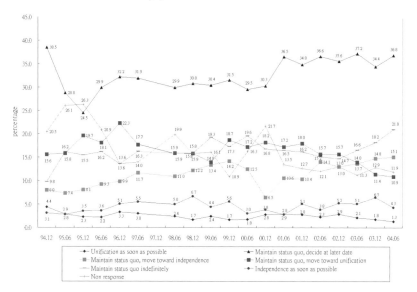

Source: Election Study Centre, NCCU.

autonomy and to defend the central government's authority and responsibilities.

Despite the numerous problems that it has had to confront since Hong Kong's return to China, Beijing has never relinquished its commitment to maintaining Hong Kong's high degree of autonomy. When Hong Kong was returned to China, many in Hong Kong doubted Beijing's commitment to the OCTS arrangement. Many shared the view that Beijing would not be able to resist the temptation of intervening in Hong Kong's internal affairs. Over time, however, Beijing's behaviour has effectively alleviated such concerns. Since Hong Kong's handover, the Chinese government has repeatedly stated its commitment to the OCTS arrangement and shown respect for the Hong Kong SAR government's way of managing Hong Kong's internal affairs. It has resisted internal demands to intervene, despite perceived provocations on the part of certain Hong Kong critics, even when confronted with a massive demonstration in July 2003 opposing the legislation of Article 23 of the Basic Law. Although it is perfectly legitimate for Beijing to demand such legislation, in deference to popular sentiment the central government decided to go along with its postponement. As a result of Beijing's adherence to its own end of the agreement regarding the handover, Hong Kong people have become increasingly confident in and supportive of the OCTS arrangement.

A recent opinion survey conducted by The University of Hong Kong has shown that 78% of Hong Kong residents have confidence in the OCTS arrangement, the highest level since the first such survey was conducted in 1993.[18] Another opinion survey conducted by the same university on the question of Taiwan and released in March 2007 has shown that 59% of the respondents said that OCTS arrangement suits Taiwan, the highest percentage since this survey was first conducted in 1996.[19] This is also a reflection of Hong Kong people's confidence in the OCTS arrangement.

Another opinion survey conducted by The University of Hong Kong on the question of identity earlier this year has shown that more than 80% of respondents identify with China and close to 40% of respondents said that they are fully identify with China. Only about 30% of the respondents expressed a wish to return to British rule.[20] Still another survey has shown that 89% of Hong Kong residents are confident about China's future and 81% are confident about Hong Kong's future, the highest levels since Hong Kong's return to China in 1997.[21]

In the meantime, Beijing has never given up its authority and responsibilities under the OCTS arrangement. Since Hong Kong's return to China, Hong Kong society has found itself mired in three controversies: in 1999 the right of abode issue, in 2004 the issue over the method of electing the Chief Executive of the Hong Kong SAR and members of the Legislative Council, and in 2005 the issue over the term of office of the new Chief Executive. In response to a request from the SAR government, the Standing Committee of the NPC stepped in and gave its interpretation of the Basic Law to resolve the controversies. Beijing has also insisted that the SAR legislate on Article 23 of the Basic Law, although it has allowed the matter to be postponed to a more opportune time. In doing this, Beijing has asserted its authority and fulfilled its perceived responsibilities to maintain stability and prosperity in Hong Kong. At the same time, it has assured its domestic audience that it has the means to defend China's legitimate interests through ensuring the proper implementation of the OCTS principle.

Second, Beijing's commitment to a gradual process of democratization has contributed to the maintenance of stability and a favourable business environment in Hong Kong. The rising demand for a faster pace of democratization in Hong Kong around the time of its return to China created a dilemma for Beijing. On the one hand, it placed Beijing in the difficult position of having to address a theoretically legitimate demand and maintaining political stability and economic prosperity in Hong Kong. On the other hand, the central government found itself caught between the need to address concerns on the part of some critics in China about a Western conspiracy to use democratization of Hong Kong to instigate a "colour revolution" in China and adhering to the OCTS principle.

There may be nothing wrong about people in Hong Kong demanding a faster pace of democratization. However, hasty democratization may also unleash forces that could lead to dire consequences. This had been the case in many countries, such as the former Soviet Union and eastern European countries, which underwent rapid democratization in the 1990s only to find themselves caught in subsequent political chaos and economic paralysis. Beijing certainly has no intention of being accused of opposing democratization in Hong Kong or of contributing to the repetition in Hong Kong of the traumatic experiences of failed democratization in other countries. Therefore, it felt that it had to achieve a delicate balance between supporting democratization in Hong Kong and maintaining political stability.

The demand for faster democratization in Hong Kong has also aroused much concern in Beijing. This was especially true when the so-called "colour revolution" led to regime change in some former Soviet republics. Western countries' public endorsement of anti-government forces in those countries appeared to suggest that they were behind these forces. Taking heed of this recent experience, some in Beijing concluded that the demand for faster democratization in Hong Kong is part and parcel of a conspiracy by Western countries to undermine governments with a political system different from their own. With government after government in the former Soviet states overwhelmed by popular uprisings, some in Beijing became increasingly worried about the implications of the demand for democratization in Hong Kong and in the Mainland. Therefore, they urged the central government to take effective measures to intervene and deflect such a demand. However, such intervention as they demanded would pose a threat to the implementation of the OCTS arrangement. The consequences would be equally grave, such as damage to Beijing's credibility, Hong Kong's political stability, Hong Kong's economic viability and the negative impact on residents of Taiwan.

After carefully balancing the alternatives, Beijing took what it believed to be the least harmful approach: adhere to a gradualist approach to Hong Kong's democratization process. From Beijing's perspective this approach has several virtues. First, it shows the outside world that it is not opposed to democratization, contrary to impression given by some of Beijing's critics. Second, it allows the central government to maintain some degree of control over the democratization process in Hong Kong. Beijing believes that this is crucial for Hong Kong's political stability and prosperity. It is also critical for the central government to control the perceived negative implications of democratization in Hong Kong on political stability in the Mainland. Third, it is useful for maintaining the OCTS arrangement, which Beijing believes to be crucial for Hong Kong's political stability and economic viability and for Hong Kong to serve as an example for Taiwan. Although such an approach has not satisfied China's critics, upon reflection, it has worked quite well except for the desired influence on Taiwan.

Third, Beijing's proactive approach to supporting Hong Kong's economy has also contributed to the successful application of the OCTS arrangement. Soon after Hong Kong's return to China, the Asian financial crisis broke out. Country after country fell in a vicious cycle of currency devaluation and ended up in economic crisis and political turmoil and, in the case of Indonesia, even in political collapse. Hong Kong's economy was in a state of crisis. Facing this situation, Beijing quickly announced that it would give full support to Hong Kong in its efforts to maintain the stability of the Hong Kong currency. Beijing's support is believed to have been crucial in helping to stabilize the Hong Kong dollar during what was a very difficult time.

Following the Asian financial crisis, Hong Kong's economy bounced back, but then became sluggish. Real estate prices plummeted. Many of the middle class in Hong Kong found themselves with negative assets. Furthermore, the outbreak of the SARS crisis threatened to send Hong Kong's economy into a recession. Under the circumstances, Beijing decided to take action to boost Hong Kong's economy. Among other things, it lifted control over the visits of individual Chinese tourists to Hong Kong[22] and concluded a Closer Economic Partnership Arrangement (CEPA) with the Hong Kong SAR government.[23] These measures provided a much-needed stimulus to Hong Kong's economy and contributed to the strong recovery and robust development that has since been experienced in Hong Kong.

According to one investigative report, in a little over three years after the lifting of travel restrictions, over 17 million tourists from Mainland China visited Hong Kong. Each such tourist is estimated to have spent an average of RMB5,000 in Hong Kong, for a total of more than RMB80 billion from this new source of visitors. This has effectively helped boost consumption and reduce unemployment in Hong Kong.[24]

Through CEPA, the Chinese government will make a greater effort to facilitate trade, services and investment between the Mainland and Hong Kong. Beginning from 1 January 2004, the Chinese Customs has collected zero tariffs on 273 kinds of goods made in Hong Kong and imported to the Mainland.[25] On 1 January 2005, another 713 kinds of imported goods made in Hong Kong became eligible for zero tariff treatment.[26] In part as a result of these and other measures, Hong Kong's economy has resumed its healthy growth. In 2004, Hong Kong's GDP grew by 8.6% compared to 3.2% in 2003, and average GDP growth between 2004 and 2006 was 7.5%. Hong Kong's unemployment rate dropped from 8.7% in 2003 to 4.4% in 2006.[27]

Beijing's continuous support for Hong Kong has not only bolstered Hong Kong's economic recovery and political stability, but has also cultivated good will among ordinary people in Hong Kong. This is seen in opinion surveys conducted by The University of Hong Kong since Hong Kong's return to China. According to these surveys, Hong Kong people's confidence in the Chinese government has remained high, about twice that of those who have no confidence. Moreover, their satisfaction with the central government and confidence in China's future has also remained highly positive.[28]

Finally, the Hong Kong SAR government's adherence to the Basic Law has also contributed significantly to the application of the OCTS principle. Since coming to power in 1997, it has confronted with a two-fold challenge in managing its relations with the central government. The first is how to exercise its "high degree of autonomy" while maintaining the trust and confidence of Beijing. The second is how to maintain the trust and confidence of Beijing while catering to the ever changing interests and demands of various sectors in Hong Kong.

Although the Basic Law has clearly prescribed that the Hong Kong SAR government has a mandate to exercise a "high degree of autonomy" in governing Hong Kong, it still needs to maintain the confidence and trust of Beijing. After all, the central government holds the power to appoint the Chief Executive and has extensive influence over Hong Kong through various networks cultivated over previous decades. In a way, only with the full confidence and trust of Beijing can the Hong Kong SAR government make full use of its "high degree of autonomy" in governing Hong Kong.

Meanwhile, although because of the OCTS principle Beijing and Hong

Kong are not supposed to have fundamental differences over the issue of how Hong Kong is governed, this is not always true in reality. After all, Beijing is supposed to represent China and the Hong Kong SAR government is supposed to represent Hong Kong. Because of the nature of central-local relations, in certain issues the interests of the central government and those of the local government will inevitably differ. This is especially true in the case of "two systems." The Hong Kong SAR government has to find a balance between these two sets of interests.

These are very difficult challenges for the Hong Kong SAR government. In retrospect, one finds that it has met these challenges quite successfully. It has maintained its high degree of autonomy. While the central government may have hoped that the Hong Kong SAR government would have done a better job in addressing local demands in a way consistent with China's national interests, it has sufficient trust and confidence in the latter that it is willing to provide whatever assistance it can to support the Hong Kong SAR government.

Looking Ahead

Looking to the future, there is good reason to be optimistic that OCTS will continue to be implemented in a manner that is mutually beneficial to the Mainland and Hong Kong. Among other things, as a result of rapid and sustained development and reforms, Beijing commands greater respect from the people of Hong Kong. In addition, during the past 10 years, the two sides have accumulated much experience in managing their relationship. New problems will continue to emerge. However, both Beijing and the Hong Kong SAR government are in a better position to handle them. The future of Hong Kong is brighter than it has ever been.

Notes

1. http://www.singtaonet.com/reveal/200702/t20070213_469604.html.
2. http://www.china.com.cn/chinese/2004/Feb/501260.htm.
3. http://www.singtaonet.com/reveal/200702/t20070213_469604.html.
4. *Renmin Ribao* (People's Daily), 26 June 1997.
5. *Renmin Ribao* (People's Daily), 1 April 1993, http://www.people.com.cn/GB/ 14576/28320/35439/35441/2661784.html.
6. http://www.law-lib.com/fzdt/newshtml/22/20050810233136.htm.
7. http://www.singtaonet.com/reveal/200702/t20070213_469604.html.

8. http://cache.baidu.com/c?word=%B5%CB%3B%D0%A1%C6%BD
   %2C%D2%BB%B9%FA%C1%BD%D6%C6%2C%BE%AD%BC%C3%3B%B7%
   B1%C8%D9&url=http%3A//www%2Eckzl%2Enet/obicn/paper/show%2
   Easp%3Fid%3D35518&p=9e759a4193904eaf5ba5e62a464c&user=baidu.
9. http://cache.baidu.com/c?word=%B5%CB%3B%D0%A1%C6%BD%2
   C%D2%BB%B9%FA%C1%BD%D6%C6%2C%BE%AD%BC%C3%3B%
   B7%B1%C8%D9&url=http%3A//www%2Eckzl%2Enet/obicn/paper/show
   %2Easp%3Fid%3D35518&p=9e759a4193904eaf5ba5e62a464c&user=baidu.
10. http://wm.61yz.com/lwsx/HTML/lwsx_52469.shtml.
11. Although Hong Kong's economy suffered a severe blow in 1997, the cause is generally believed to have been the Asian financial crisis rather than the transfer of sovereignty.
12. http://www.qdzhaosheng.com/LiuXue/2005/05-31/141053312/01.shtml.
13. http://news.sina.com.cn/c/224630.html.
14. http://hk.news.yahoo.com/061026/12/1vbiv.html/.
15. "Forward," http://www.basiclaw23.gov.hk/english/.
16. http://www.zaobao.com/special/china/hk/pages1/hk051205.html.
17. http://cn.bbs.yahoo.com/message/read_interfoc_12028.html.
18. http://news.xinhuanet.com/tai_gang_ao/2007-04/27/content_6035609.htm.
19. http://forum.xinhuanet.com/detail.jsp?id=40772066.
20. http://gb.chinareviewnews.com/doc/1003/4/7/7/100347794.html?coluid= 2&kindid=0&docid=100347794.
21. http://news.xinhuanet.com/tai_gang_ao/2007-04/27/content_6035609.htm.
22. http://news.xinhuanet.com/newscenter/2003-09/03/content_1059598.htm.
23. http://finance.sina.com.cn/g/20040101/0949586004.shtml.
24. http://news.xinhuanet.com/tai_gang_ao/2007-02/20/content_5758786.htm.
25. http://finance.sina.com.cn/g/20040101/0949586004.shtml.
26. http://finance.sina.com.cn/g/20041029/07101117531.shtml
27. http://news.xinhuanet.com/tai_gang_ao/2007-02/20/content_5758786.htm.
28. For example, http://news.enorth.com.cn/system/2002/04/16/000314152.shtml; http://china.qianlong.com/4352/2003/10/24/1160@1664656.htm; http://news.sohu.com/20060505/n243117183.shtml; http://news.sohu.com/20070222/ n248315291.shtml.

References

Deng Xiaoping wenxuan (Selected Works of Deng Xiaoping) (1994), Beijing: Forcign Languages Press.

Government of HKSAR (2007), *2006 Economic Background and 2007 Prospects*, February.

Kane, Tim et al. (2007), *2007 Index of Economic Freedom*. Washington, D.C.: Heritage Foundation.

5

The Triumph of Pragmatism: Hong Kong–Taiwan Relations

Timothy Ka-ying Wong

Introduction

Historically, Hong Kong–Taiwan relations have been closely linked with and very much affected by the state of relations between Mainland China and Taiwan, which have been in a continuous state of separation and confrontation since 1949. Hence, the reunification of Hong Kong with China in 1997 should have a significant impact on existing Hong Kong–Taiwan relations. In retrospect, the first milestone in the development of cross-Straits relations came in 1979, when China started to implement the policy of reform and opening up to the outside world. The second milestone occurred in 1987, when Taiwan relaxed controls on visits to and investments in the Mainland. These historic changes led to increased interactions between the Mainland and Taiwan after nearly 40 years of complete separation. However, as the political conflict between the two sides over the issue of reunification has not yet been resolved, the much-discussed "three direct links" of transport, postal services and commercial exchanges across the Straits have yet to be realized.

Under such circumstances, Hong Kong, insulated as a British colony from the political disputes between Mainland China and Taiwan, played a significant mediatory role in the rapid growth of economic and trade activities and non-governmental exchanges across the Straits. Consequently, Hong Kong has developed very strong ties with both the Mainland and Taiwan. According to Taiwan's statistics, the total value of trade between Hong Kong and Taiwan rose from US$5.83 billion in 1987 to US$20.04 billion in 1996,[1] of which more than 70% is estimated to consist of indirect trade between the Mainland and Taiwan (Sung, 1995). In 1996, Hong Kong was Taiwan's third largest trading partner and the region with which it had the largest trade surplus, while Taiwan was Hong Kong's fourth largest trading partner. In that same year, there were more than 3,000 Taiwanese firms registered in Hong Kong, with a total investment of over US$4 billion (Mainland Affairs Council, 1996, p. 47). With such sustained growth in economic ties between Hong Kong and Taiwan and the increased importance of Hong Kong as a transit centre between the Mainland and Taiwan, the number of passengers travelling between Hong Kong and Taiwan also increased rapidly, from 296,302 people (60,092 of whom were Taiwanese visiting Hong Kong) in 1987, to over 2,005,172 people (1,822,062 of them Taiwanese visiting Hong Kong) in 1996.[2] As Taiwanese tourists constituted 15.56% of the total of 11,702,735 visitors to Hong Kong in 1996 and were the third largest group of visitors to Hong Kong (*Hong Kong Annual Digest*, 1996), they certainly played an important role in Hong Kong's tourist boom.

Nevertheless, the return of Hong Kong to Chinese sovereignty has inevitably brought changes to the previous political status of Hong Kong. As mentioned above, the political reality across the Straits is still that of separation and confrontation. It follows that the relations between Hong Kong and Taiwan that were established under British colonial rule must now be undergoing re-examination and re-definition. Consequently, this chapter discusses developments in Hong Kong–Taiwan relations under a situation of cross-Straits conflict in the decade following the handover. Since Hong Kong–Taiwan relations have become a special part of the larger sphere of Mainland-Taiwan relations after Hong Kong's return to China, the first aspect to be analyzed will be the policies of Beijing and Taipei towards Hong Kong–Taiwan relations, and then how Hong Kong has managed to maintain and develop its relations with Taiwan within the confines of these policies.

Beijing's Policy

Hong Kong is not an independent "political entity" in terms of sovereign power. Before its reunification with China, the territory was a British colony; its government a local one. What took place in 1997, therefore, was a transfer of sovereignty over Hong Kong from Britain to China. In other words, when British rule came to an end and Hong Kong was reunited with China, Hong Kong then came to be ruled by the central authorities in China. In accordance with the principles laid down by the Sino-British Joint Declaration, in April 1990, the National People's Congress of the People's Republic of China (PRC) passed the Basic Law of the Hong Kong Special

Administrative Region (HKSAR) of the PRC (henceforth referred to as the Basic Law), which contains provisions on the post-handover relations between the Chinese central government and the HKSAR.

The guiding principle of the Basic Law is "one country, two systems" and "Hong Kong people ruling Hong Kong." This principle is also the fundamental principle in the Sino-British Joint Declaration.[3] Specifically, there are two aspects to the provisions of this principle in the Basic Law: one is on the division of powers between the HKSAR and the central government; and the other on the delineation of the socio-political system of Hong Kong. It is the former that may significantly affect post-1997 Hong Kong–Taiwan relations.

On the issue of the division of powers, the Basic Law stipulates that the central government shall handle Hong Kong's diplomatic affairs and national defence, while the HKSAR government shall handle its own internal affairs.[4] The HKSAR government can also make decisions on issues relating to its "external relations," which are considered lower in status to the diplomatic relations of a sovereign state.[5] However, Beijing has always insisted that Taiwan is an inalienable part of China and that the government of the PRC is the country's sole legitimate government, and has denounced Taipei's legal status as an independent "political entity."[6] Therefore, the HKSAR's limited authority over its own external affairs cannot be extended to its relations with Taiwan (Chen, 1996, p. 156). To state this more clearly and, from Beijing's perspective, Hong Kong's relations with Taiwan are an internal matter for China, and in such matters the HKSAR government must follow the decisions of the central government.

On 22 June 1995, Vice Premier and Foreign Minister Qian Qichen, representing the State Council, declared a Seven-point statement to regulate Hong Kong–Taiwan relations after Hong Kong's reunification with China in 1997 (henceforth referred to as Qian's Seven-point Statement) (*Hong Kong Standard*, 23 June 1995, p. 1). Qian's Seven-point Statement makes it clear that "in issues concerning Hong Kong's relations with Taiwan, those related to national sovereignty and relations across the Taiwan Straits shall be handled by the Central People's Government or the HKSAR government with authorization from the Central People's Government." The release of Qian's Seven-point Statement has at least two implications. First, by formally declaring its policy, Beijing makes it known to both Hong Kong and Taiwan that the central government is in effective control over Hong Kong's relations with Taiwan. Second, the Beijing government's basic principles and policies in handling Hong Kong's relations with Taiwan shall comply with these seven points. In other words, the conduct of Hong Kong's relations with Taiwan after 1997 is not a matter relating to the autonomous rule of the HKSAR; rather, it must comply with the decisions and arrangements made by the Beijing government. As it stands, Qian's Seven-point Statement has so far been the most important guiding principle on the formulation of policies on Hong Kong–Taiwan relations.

Qian's Seven-point Statement laid out rather extensive and specific provisions on the relationship between the HKSAR and Taiwan. The unstated aim was to maintain and promote Hong Kong's economic and non-governmental ties with Taiwan under the guidance of Beijing as the central government and, at the same time, to strictly limit Taiwan's political influence in Hong Kong. Points I, II, III and V clearly indicate that economic and non-governmental activities between Hong Kong and Taiwan shall remain intact after 1997 and that such activities shall be governed and protected by existing laws in Hong Kong. Point VI particularly stresses the point that in accordance with the "one China" principle, direct air and sea links between Hong Kong and Taiwan shall be managed in the form of "special local transportation routes," giving further assurance of the smooth carrying over of such links beyond 1997. Clearly, the intention behind these points was to ease any tensions arising from the 1997 reunification over existing economic and non-governmental relations between Hong Kong and Taiwan.

From a political point of view, Points VI and VII are the most important ones for the HKSAR government and the Taipei government. Point VI stipulates that "official contacts, exchanges, consultations, agreements signed and establishment of institutions by the HKSAR and Taiwan shall be submitted to the Central People's Government for ratification or be ratified by the Chief Executive of the HKSAR with the authorization of the Central People's Government on a case-by-case basis." It reiterates that the power to make decisions in matters concerning Hong Kong's relations with Taiwan rests with the central government, and that Hong Kong must seek approval or authorization from Beijing when dealing with such issues.

Point VII explicitly stipulates the sphere of activities that Taiwan's agencies in Hong Kong may engage in after 1997: "Taiwan's agencies currently stationed in Hong Kong as well as their staff members may be permitted to stay. However, they are required to strictly obey the Basic Law of the HKSAR of the PRC, to adhere to the 'one China' principle, and to refrain from engaging in activities that may damage the peace and prosperity of Hong Kong or in any other activities that are deemed inappropriate to their stated purposes for staying." The focus of this point is that it prescribes that Taiwan's agencies in Hong Kong must obey the Basic Law. The text that makes possible restriction to the activities of these agencies is Article 23, which states that "the HKSAR shall enact laws on its own to prohibit any act of treason, secession, sedition, subversion against the Central People's Government or theft of state secrets, to prohibit foreign political organizations or bodies from conducting political activities in the Region, and to prohibit political organizations or bodies in the Region from establishing ties with foreign political organizations or bodies." While under British colonial rule, Taiwan's agencies in Hong Kong had often acted in defiance of Beijing's "one China" policy (for instance, by using the name Republic of China [ROC], displaying the ROC flag, and national day of the ROC on October 10th), since 1997, such activities have been restricted in various degrees by the HKSAR government. However, the restrictions have been implemented by political instead of legal means. The fact is that, although 10 years have passed since Hong Kong's return to China, Article 23 has not been enacted into law. In 2003, the HKSAR government attempted to translate the article into law, but the attempt was aborted after a massive anti-government protest on 1 July 2003.[7] The aim of the proposed legislation was to create the specific offence of secession, which is currently absent from the existing legal system of Hong Kong. Should a similar attempt succeed in the future, the activities of Taiwan's agencies in Hong Kong as well as Hong Kong–Taiwan exchanges in general will certainly be affected.

At any rate, according to the foregoing analysis, the development of relations between Hong Kong and Taiwan after 1997 is clearly restricted by Beijing's policies in the following respects. First, the HKSAR government is not empowered to make decisions on matters related to Taiwan. Consequently, any arrangements in dealing with such matters shall be in conformity with the stipulations of Qian's Seven-point Statement and those of the Basic Law. In the case of a contravention or possible contravention against either of the two documents, the central authorities in Beijing must be consulted and their prior consent, endorsement, or authorization obtained on any action taken. Second, when handling affairs involving Hong Kong–Taiwan relations, the central authorities clearly separate political from non-political issues. That is, politically the principle of "one China" based on the PRC shall not be compromised, while flexibility is accorded to economic and non-governmental activities. Third, the activities of Taiwan's agencies stationed in Hong Kong are essentially subject to the restrictions laid down in Article 23 of the Basic Law. Consequently, in order to obtain a clear understanding of the sphere of activities permitted to these organizations, any related legislation should be noted. Fourth, now that the power to make decisions on Hong Kong's relations with Taiwan rests with the central government, the HKSAR government must maintain close contact and consultations with Beijing if it intends to play an active role in Hong Kong–Taiwan relations and, at the same time, to be in line with Beijing's policies and principles towards Taiwan. Fifth, as Hong Kong does not have the autonomy to handle its Taiwan-related affairs, Taipei must hold direct consultations with Beijing or put up with provisions unilaterally laid down by Beijing, if it wants to maintain and promote its ties with Hong Kong. Sixth, Hong Kong–Taiwan relations after 1997 are part of the larger sphere of cross-Straits relations. While they are admittedly of a special nature and hence must be given special treatment by all of the parties involved, the development of cross-Straits relations will inevitably have a large impact on Hong Kong–Taiwan relations. Thus, an improved relationship between the Mainland and Taiwan should be an important condition under which Hong Kong–Taiwan relations may be maintained and further developed.

A review of the development of Hong Kong–Taiwan relations since the declaration of Qian's Seven-point Statement seems to show that Beijing has adhered to the above principles in dealing with issues of Hong Kong–Taiwan relations during the transitional period and afterwards. This is reflected in the following aspects. First, at the time that Qian's Seven-point Statement was made public, the relationship between the Mainland and Taiwan was deteriorating alarmingly because of Taiwanese President Lee Teng-hui's sudden visit to the United States. As one way of expressing its displeasure of the visit, during the transitional period, Beijing gave the cold treatment to issues relating to Hong Kong–Taiwan relations by rejecting the holding of any direct talks with Taipei, particularly on the question of the continued presence of Taiwan's agencies in the territory. This shows the direct consequences that Mainland-Taiwan relations can have on Hong Kong–Taiwan relations. Second, in separating economic issues from political ones, Beijing took a rather pragmatic attitude towards Hong Kong–Taiwan economic and trade relations, especially on such problems as air and sea links, by authorizing different non-governmental organizations to carry out negotiations with their Taiwanese counterparts. As a result, the problems pertaining to aviation between Taiwan and Hong Kong were satisfactorily resolved in July 1996 (Wong, 1996, pp. 147–49). An agreement on shipping arrangements was also reached with Taipei in May 1997, so that direct shipping would not pose a problem after the 1997 handover. Third, while Beijing refused to hold talks with Taipei on the post-1997 arrangements for Taiwan's agencies in Hong Kong, Beijing did not see the need to expel them from the territory after 1997 since these agencies have played quite an important role in Hong Kong–Taiwan relations.

There is an obvious need for such agencies as the Chung Hwa Travel Service, whose function is to help visitors from the Mainland, Hong Kong and foreign countries obtain visas to Taiwan. Yet, before 1 July 1997, the Chung Hwa Travel Service was not registered in Hong Kong and only operated under special diplomatic-like arrangements unilaterally extended by the British colonial government. To deal with the problem of the status of the Chung Hwa Travel Service in the post-handover period, the Chinese Central Broadcasting Station revealed in April 1997 that the HKSAR government would ask the agency to re-register and that Beijing would find a practical solution to the issue as long as Taipei was willing to cooperate (*China Times*, 9 April 1997, p. 7). For unknown reasons, while the HKSAR government never made such a request after the handover, the Chung Hwa Travel Service has continued to operate in the decade following 1997. Thus, we may conclude from this that the continued existence of Taiwan's agencies in Hong Kong is no longer a problem, although their status remains ambiguous. In fact, on 3 July 1997 — only two days after Hong Kong's return to China — the Chief Executive of the HKSAR government, Mr Tung Chee-hwa, held a meeting with Mr Koo Chen-fu, the Director of the Straits Exchange Foundation, a semi-official organization set up in 1990 by Taipei as a way of dealing with cross-Straits affairs without resorting to direct official exchanges, and Mr Cheng An-kuo, the Managing Director of the Chung Hwa Travel Service. After the meeting, Mr Tung reiterated that the *status quo* in Hong Kong–Taiwan relations would remain unchanged. He also announced the appointment of Mr Yip Kwok-wah, his Special Advisor, who would hold exclusive responsibility for exchanges and consultations with Mr Cheng on matters concerning Hong Kong–Taiwan relations (*Ming Pao*, 4 July 1997, p. A2). As these were extremely politically sensitive decisions, it is inconceivable that Mr Tung could have made them without the prior approval of Beijing.

It is thus apparent that while Mainland-Taiwan relations have continued to deteriorate in the past decade, particularly since the rise to power in 2000 of the pro-independence Democratic Progressive Party (DPP), Beijing has continued to demonstrate a rather pragmatic attitude towards handling issues concerning Hong Kong–Taiwan relations during and after the handover, in an attempt to minimize any negative impact on trade and non-governmental activities as far as possible. Beijing knows very well that during the sensitive period of Hong Kong's transition to Chinese rule, any significant interruption in Hong Kong's *status quo* may destabilize Hong Kong, with damaging consequences not only to Hong Kong's international status, but also to China's national pride and to the country's modernization programme (Yahuda, 1996, pp. 135–42). Any radical changes to the existing close Hong Kong–Taiwan ties could be harmful. Hence, it is worth noting that, Beijing has consistently implemented its policy of separating trade and non-governmental activities from political issues as stated in Qian's Seven-point Statement, simply to avoid putting Hong Kong–Taiwan relations at risk. Strategically, Beijing's bottom line for Hong Kong–Taiwan relations is quite clear — that is, that Hong Kong–Taiwan relations must develop in a de-politicized direction at the least and, at best, in a direction that is politically favourable to Beijing. However, as pushing Taipei too hard to accept Beijing's political position could cause Taipei to withdraw or reduce its presence in Hong Kong, the second-best — and certainly more realistic — approach is that of the de-politicization rather than politicization of Hong Kong–Taiwan relations.

While pragmatic in its economic approach, the political position adopted by Beijing is more or less based on the consideration that before any breakthrough can be made on the cross-Straits political conflict, Taiwan's political influence in Hong Kong after 1997 must be kept to a minimum. Taiwan must be given no chance to interfere in the affairs of the HKSAR or to use Hong Kong–Taiwan relations to promote separatist political goals (*Ming Pao*, 8 May 1997, p. 7).[8] Beijing also wants to maintain its dominant position in handling Hong Kong–Taiwan relations and, if possible, to force Taipei to accept the "one China" principle as defined by the Mainland side.

Taipei's Policy

Taiwan has huge economic interests in and involving Hong Kong, as a result of the unexpected surge in cross-Straits economic exchanges beginning in the mid-1980s and mediated through Hong Kong. Thus, Taipei decided that Taiwan's government agencies and other Taiwanese interests would not pull out of Hong Kong, at least in principle. What the Taiwan authorities did was to begin drafting the Statute Governing the Relations between People of the Taiwan area and the Hong Kong and Macao area.

The Statute attempted to treat people in Hong Kong and Macao as a separate category from those on the Mainland, in conformity with the National Unification Guidelines enacted by Taipei in 1991. According to the Guidelines, Taipei will not establish any direct links of mail, transport and trade with the Mainland prior to Beijing's recognition of Taiwan as an equal political entity. Singling out Hong Kong and Macao from the rest of the Mainland area means that the existing Taiwan–Hong Kong and Taiwan–Macao direct links fall outside the restraints of the National Unification Guidelines. In other words, under the definition of the Statute Governing the Relations between People of the Taiwan Area and the Hong Kong and Macao Area, Hong Kong retains its status as a "third party"; henceforth, its existing direct links and non-governmental ties with Taiwan shall not be affected by Hong Kong's reunification with China, as they are independent of Mainland-Taiwan relations (Zhu, 1996, p. 134).

In addition, at the end of 1996, Taipei openly endorsed its "no-pullout" policy for its agencies in Hong Kong, and made detailed proposals in response to Qian's Seven-point Statement. These included the following: First, Taiwan's agencies in Hong Kong shall seek to perform their stated functions legally and openly after 1997, as they have done in the past. Second, the establishment of any institutions in Hong Kong shall be based on realistic grounds and mutual benefits. Third, the mode of operation of any agencies in Hong Kong shall be determined according to developments in the situation. Fourth, the functions of Taiwan's agencies in Hong Kong include visa services, notarization, civil services and other activities. Consular and civil services call for the setting up of official establishments. Fifth, if it is not possible to set up official agencies in Hong Kong, their services can be provided by non-governmental bodies, commissioned and regulated by law. Sixth, these non-governmental bodies shall not be allowed to enter into any agreement with the HKSAR government or any other non-governmental bodies on behalf of the HKSAR government without prior authorization by their managing departments (Mainland Affairs Council, 1996, pp. 49–50).

Taipei also adopted a pragmatic attitude towards the handling of the existing direct air and sea services between Taiwan and Hong Kong to guarantee their continued operation after 1997. The problem of air services was settled in July 1996. The two parties agreed that their national flags and emblems would not be displayed on their planes. Taipei also agreed to permit Hong Kong Dragon Airlines Limited, 64% of the shares of which are held by Mainland companies, to fly between Hong Kong and Taiwan

(Mainland Affairs Council, 1996, p. 51). As for shipping, in April 1997, Taipei also compromised on the issue of the hoisting of national flags by ships entering Hong Kong waters; it dropped its requirement that all such ships hoist the flag of the ROC and agreed with the arrangement that no flags were to be required of ships of the two territories when entering the other's waters (*China Times,* 25 May 1997, p. 1).[9]

On the eve of Hong Kong's return to China on 16 June 1997, the cabinet-level Mainland Affairs Council (MAC) of the Executive Yuan released a formal statement entitled "The Stand and Policy of the ROC regarding the Situation of Hong Kong's 1997 Handover," which explained the basic policies of the Taipei government on Hong Kong's return to the Mainland. The statement contains four major points: 1) The ROC government in Taiwan expresses its delight at the return of Hong Kong from Britain to the Chinese nation; 2) The arrangement of "one country, two systems" for Hong Kong after its return to the Mainland is a compromise made by the Chinese Communist Party (CCP), which sees that communism would not work in Hong Kong but which still has an interest in maintaining Hong Kong's prosperity. Hence, the arrangement should not be seen as evidence of the CCP's kindness to the Hong Kong people. In view of Beijing's ever-tightening grip on Hong Kong even before the handover, it is clear that the communist government on the Mainland cares more about the "one country" component of the formula, and less about the "two systems"; 3) Whether or not the "one country, two systems" promise pays off for Hong Kong, it is not an acceptable scheme for the reunification of Taiwan with the Mainland as it establishes a central-to-local power structure. Taiwan, unlike the British colony of Hong Kong, is an independent sovereign state. The Taipei government will not accept any deal that will reduce Taiwan to a local government under a communist state; and 4) A peaceful and stable Hong Kong–Taiwan relationship is, of course, conducive to the development of cross-Straits relations, but faith and goodwill from Beijing will be required if there are to be positive interactions among the Mainland, Hong Kong and Taiwan. The future of Hong Kong–Taiwan relations will depend not only on Beijing's adherence to the pledge of "one country, two systems," but also on Beijing and Taipei taking a practical attitude towards relations across the Taiwan Straits (*China Times,* 17 June 1997, p. 7).

As Taiwan had always been sceptical and critical of the "one country, two systems" scheme, what was new in this statement was that, for the first time, Taipei was recognizing that the return of Hong Kong was a historic event of justice for the Chinese people. Even though the Taiwan authorities did so by using the vague term "the Chinese nation" instead of the "PRC," in order to shun the political reality that it can no longer refer to the ROC as the legitimate government of China, it showed that Taipei is taking a very pragmatic attitude towards the return of Hong Kong to Mainland China.

To cope with the changing situation in Hong Kong, the MAC officially set up a Hong Kong Affairs Office on 30 June 1997 to openly and legally coordinate the different agencies of the Taiwan government stationed in Hong Kong. Mr Cheng An-kuo, the Managing Director of the Chung Hwa Travel Service, was appointed as the first director of the office (*China Times*, 1 July 1997, p. 1). The move was significant for several reasons. First, the Chung Hwa Travel Service, as Taiwan's top representative in Hong Kong, was formerly under the Ministry of Foreign Affairs. Thus, its reshuffling to come under the MAC, which is exclusively in charge of Mainland-Taiwan relations, has been seen as a sign that Taipei officially recognizes Hong Kong–Taiwan relations as part of Mainland-Taiwan relations and that Taiwan accepts the fact that Hong Kong is part of the PRC. Second, upgrading the handling of Hong Kong–Taiwan relations from the departmental level to the office (sub-ministerial) level indicates that Taipei is attaching more weight to its relations with Hong Kong than it did before the handover. Third, establishing the Hong Kong Affairs Office to coordinate the Taiwan's agencies in Hong Kong is conducive to improving the internal communication and management of resources of such agencies, and therefore to improving the services they render in Hong Kong.

Taipei has largely stuck to a pragmatic approach in dealing with Hong Kong after 1997, and this position has not changed much even with the rise to power of the pro-independence DPP in 2000. Taipei's agencies in Hong Kong, particularly, the Chung Hwa Travel Service, have largely confined themselves to non-political activities. Even when they have had to engage in some political activities, they have largely kept a low profile. In addition, to improve Taiwan's interactions with Hong Kong, in July 2001, Taipei unilaterally simplified the procedures for Hong Kong residents visiting Taiwan by giving ground visas to those who had previously been to Taiwan. In June 2002, this ground visa policy was further extended to all Hong Kong permanent residents born in Hong Kong (*Hong Kong and Macao*, July 2002, p. 31).

In short, Taipei's policy on Hong Kong–Taiwan relations after 1997 has been quite pragmatic, positive and flexible. Like Beijing, Taipei officially regarded the return of Hong Kong to Chinese rule as an act of historical justice and wanted its existing ties with Hong Kong to continue after 1997.

However, Taipei is also aware of the fact that Hong Kong is now part of the PRC and that the political indifference it enjoyed in its dealings with Hong Kong under British colonial authorities is a thing of the past. Therefore, Taipei is ready to make appropriate readjustments to cope with the terms set up by Beijing and the HKSAR government. Yet, there is always a limit to such readjustments, and the bottom line is that in the maintenance of Hong Kong–Taiwan relations, pressure should not be exerted on Taipei to abandon its political autonomy vis-à-vis Beijing (Wong, 1997a, p. 192). While working hard to maintain Hong Kong–Taiwan ties, Taipei will not be forced into accepting the "one country, two systems" scheme under the PRC for its own future or to give the international community the impression that it is willing to do so (Mainland Affairs Council, 1996, pp. 51–52).

HKSAR's Policy and the Development of Hong Kong–Taiwan Relations after the Handover

Hong Kong–Taiwan relations raise difficult policy problems for the HKSAR government for which there are no precedents. The difficulty lies in the fact that in any kind of Taiwan policy that the HKSAR were to pursue, there would be various implications for the intricate political game involving Mainland China, Hong Kong and Taiwan. Under PRC rule, Hong Kong is only a local government. Although the PRC central government has granted it a high degree of autonomy, this autonomy does not cover the sensitive area of Hong Kong–Taiwan relations, especially on matters relating to national sovereignty and cross-Straits political relations. As the Mainland and Taiwan are still in a state of intense political conflict and competition, the HKSAR could easily become entangled in the political conflict between the two sides. Hence, the HKSAR government must achieve a delicate balance between the central government's policy towards Taiwan and Hong Kong's own interests. The lack of any precedents in the matter is due to the fact that the policy decisions of the former British colonial government on Hong Kong–Taiwan relations were made by the Britain's Foreign Affairs Ministry. The Hong Kong government even had to receive the prior approval of the British Political Advisor from Britain's Foreign Affairs Ministry on a matter as routine as the granting of entry visas to Taiwanese officials. When the British left Hong Kong, the institutions, skilled personnel and established cases for handling matters in this domain went with them and are largely lacking in the HKSAR government.

However, this did not prevent the HKSAR government from making its own Taiwan policy. From the beginning, the HKSAR government learned that it should not delegate responsibility for the issue entirely to the central government in Beijing, as the colonial government had done with London. The reason for this is that the nature of the relationship between the Mainland and Taiwan is different from that between Britain and Taiwan. The Mainland is one of the parties involved in the cross-Straits conflict. If Hong Kong–Taiwan relations are to be totally subsumed under Mainland-Taiwan relations, the former will be damaged by the political conflict between the two rival parties. The colonial government of Hong Kong was basically free from, or at least not directly involved in, the Mainland-Taiwan conflict. As a result, it could make its own policies in Hong Kong's own interests (and in the interests of Britain, of course). The HKSAR government knows that it, too, must have its own Taiwan policy if it wants to maintain a stable relationship with Taiwan, as long as this policy does not directly and openly run counter to the Taiwan policy of the central government.

As discussed earlier, Qian's "Seven-point Statement" has, in principle, set the framework for Hong Kong–Taiwan relations after 1997. The guiding principle is to leave intact current economic trade and non-governmental relations, while preventing Taipei from using Hong Kong–Taiwan relations to promote a separatist programme. Similarly, Taipei has taken a pragmatic stance in dealing with issues relating to the return of Hong Kong to the Mainland, while remaining wary of Beijing's attempts to force Taiwan into accepting an unequal and dependent political status following the return of Hong Kong. In other words, neither Beijing nor Taipei would want Hong Kong–Taiwan relations to deteriorate and, therefore, they are both trying to be pragmatic and flexible towards each other. With so many overlapping interests between the Mainland and Taiwan, the HKSAR government has a great deal of room in which to manoeuvre.

A quick analysis of developments in the post-handover period reveals that the HKSAR government has done a relatively satisfactory job in maintaining and developing post-1997 Hong Kong–Taiwan ties grounded upon the huge overlapping interests between the Mainland and Taiwan. In essence, the Taiwan policy pursued by the HKSAR government is also built upon a pragmatic strategy that was not only largely followed by its colonial predecessor, but which also wisely falls within the baselines of Beijing's and Taipei's equally pragmatic policies on Hong Kong–Taiwan relations. The HKSAR government recognizes the reality of its political subordination to the central government in Beijing, and is therefore ready to identify, at least rhetorically, with Beijing's insistence on the "one

China" principle in dealing with Hong Kong–Taiwan ties in exchange for Beijing's political trust and support (Wong, 1997b, pp. 45–46). Yet, in practical terms, it has tried its best to steer clear of the cross-Straits political conflict and to create conditions for strengthening exchanges between the two sides.

On the matter of siding with Beijing's political position towards Taiwan, we observe the following: 1) Soon after Mr Tung Chee-hwa was chosen to become the first Chief Executive of the HKSAR, he repeatedly stated that the unification of China must be affirmed and that Hong Kong would not tolerate any acts in the HKSAR that promote the splitting up of the motherland (Wong, 1997b, p. 39). In addition, on various occasions, both local and international, Mr Tung openly praised the applicability of Hong Kong's "one country, two systems" model to Taiwan. He also warned in several public remarks that it would be a "dead end" for Taiwan to seek independence (*Wen Wei Po,* 4 April 2000, p. 1); 2) As mentioned earlier, to minimize political influence from Taiwan in Hong Kong, in 1997, the Provisional Legislature of the HKSAR approved a controversial ban on Taiwan funds and ties to local political parties; 3) In order not to provoke Beijing, Taiwan's high-ranking officials are still, as was the case during colonial times, banned from entering Hong Kong without prior approval from the ruling authorities — in this case, Beijing; 4) After 1997, ROC Nationalist flags flown in public areas by pro-Taiwan groups to celebrate the Double Tenth Festival were torn down in accordance with the Public Property Ordinance (*SCMP,* 11 October 1997, p. A1); and 5) Despite practical needs and repeated request from Taiwan, the HKSAR government has until now refused to set up a representative office in Taiwan to manage Taiwan-related affairs. It is widely believed that the HKSAR government's inflexible attitude arises from an unwillingness to upset Beijing, which has taken a hard-line position in dealing with the pro-independence DPP government on political matters.

With regard to the HKSAR government's efforts to prevent Hong Kong–Taiwan ties from being damaged by cross-Straits political disputes and to create conditions for strengthening exchanges between the two areas, the following developments are noted: 1) Mr Tung's appointment of Mr Yip Kwok-wah as his Special Advisor to handle Hong Kong's relations with Taiwan was regarded as an important breakthrough in Hong Kong–Taiwan relations, as there had been no such appointments under British colonial rule; 2) In March 1998, the HKSAR government announced that residents of Taiwan with valid visas to the Mainland were now eligible to enter and stay in Hong Kong for up to seven days without applying in advance for a visa to Hong Kong; 3) On 9 April 2000, after the pro-independence, DPP candidate Chen Shui-bian won the presidential election in Taiwan in March of the same year, Hong Kong Cable Television Limited broadcast an interview with Vice-president Annette Lu. For this, the station was roundly criticized by local pro-Beijing groups, including Deputy Director Wang Feng-chao of the PRC Central People's Government Liaison Office in Hong Kong, who stated that the media should not broadcast speeches and views advocating the "two-state theory" or "Taiwan independence" (*Wen Wei Po*, 18 April 2000, p. 2). Mr Wang's opinion was consistent with that of the State Council's Hong Kong and Macau Affairs Office and its Information Office. However, the HKSAR government did not follow suit. Instead, it released a statement saying that freedom of press was protected under the Basic Law and that the media were free to comment and report on all events of current interest (*Hong Kong Economic Journal*, 18 April 2000, p. 5); 4) On 31 May 2000, in a luncheon hosted by the Chinese General Chamber of Commerce, Mr He Zhi-ming, the deputy head for Taiwan Affairs in the PRC Central People's Government Liaison Office, "reminded" Hong Kong businessmen to refrain from trading with Taiwanese businessmen who supported Taiwan independence, or to bear the consequences. Mr He's remarks immediately triggered an uproar in both the local and international communities. In response, Chief Executive Tung Chee-hwa contacted Mr Jiang En-zhu, the Director of the Central People's Government Liaison Office, about the remarks. Mr Jiang indicated to Mr Tung that the Liaison Office would not interfere with Hong Kong's commercial activities. The HKSAR government also issued a statement saying that it would continue to firmly protect principles of economic freedom and free trade, and that investors and businessmen operating in Hong Kong remained free to choose their business partners (*Ming Pao*, 1 June 2000, p. A1); 5) In early 2001, the HKSAR government went one step further to simplify visa application procedures for residents of Taiwan. At the end of the same year, it further allowed Taiwanese to apply for visas to Hong Kong via the internet; 6) While in principle banning Taiwan's high-level officials from entering Hong Kong, the HKSAR government permitted many of these people to visit Hong Kong in various capacities, including the Chairman of the ministerial-level Economic Planning and Construction Committee Chen Po-chi, the Minister of Finance Yan Sing-cheong, Taipei City Mayor Ma Ying-jeou, Kuomintang Chairman Lien Chan, and People's First Party Chairman James Soong; 7) With the permission of the HKSAR government, in May 2002, the Chung Hwa Travel Service set up its first branch office at the Hong Kong International Airport to provide more convenient services for both Hong Kong and Mainland residents going to Taiwan; 8) As has been pointed out before, in the absence of direct cross-Straits links, Hong Kong and Taiwan have managed to maintain direct air and shipping services after 1997. On 29 June 2002, both the HKSAR and Taiwanese governments successfully reached a new deal to continue their air links by avoiding the sensitive political issues of "one China" principle and state sovereignty; 9) On 29 June 2002, the HKSAR government announced that starting from 1 July 2002, Mr Yip Kwok-wah would not be reappointed to the post of Special Advisor, and that the Constitutional Affairs Bureau would henceforth deal with all unofficial links with Taipei. The move was widely interpreted as an attempt by the HKSAR government to institutionalize Hong Kong–Taiwan relations (*SCMP,* 1 July 2002, p. 2); and 10) Since assuming the role in mid-2002 of dealing with all unofficial links with Taipei, the Constitutional Affairs Bureau has increased contacts and exchanges with Taiwan's visitors and civil organizations to strengthen communication and interactions between Hong Kong and Taiwan (*Taipei Times*, 17 January 2003, p. 4).

It is under the above delicately calculated pragmatic approach that Hong Kong–Taiwan relations have been conducted since 1997, largely free from the continuing cross-Straits conflict. In fact, despite the turbulence in the cross-Straits relationship stirred up by Taiwanese president Lee Teng-hui's sudden announcement of the "two-state theory" in 1999 and the unexpected rise of the pro-independence DPP to power in 2000, Hong Kong–Taiwan exchanges have so far remained largely unaffected, especially on the economic front. For example, the total value of trade between Hong Kong and Taiwan, which fluctuated between 1997 and 2002, has since started to rise steadily, at US$20.66 billion in 1997, US$17.68 billion in 1998, US$17.10 billion in 1999, US$21.06 billion in 2000, US$18.62 billion in 2001, US$19.35 billion in 2002, US$21.52 billion in 2003, US$26.07 billion in 2004, US$28.07 billion in 2005 and US$31.57 billion in 2006.[10] The fluctuations in the early years were mainly caused by the economic cycles in the region, not by the cross-Straits conflict. In addition, largely because of expanded interactions in the region and because of the HKSAR and Taiwan governments' efforts to simplify visa application procedures, the number of visitors between Hong Kong and Taiwan has continued to grow, from 2,074,789 (of whom 1,896,866 were Taiwanese visitors) in 1997 to over 3,288,880 (of whom 2,955,602 were Taiwanese visitors) in 2006.[11]

Obviously, in terms of trade and passenger flows, Hong Kong–Taiwan exchanges after 1997 have increased, especially in recent years.

Nevertheless, it must be pointed out that when we say that Hong Kong–Taiwan ties after 1997 have been largely free from the impact of the continuing cross-Straits conflict, this is true not in absolute terms but only in terms of degree. The truth is that no matter how pragmatic the HKSAR government is, it must work within the policy confines set out by the central government in Beijing; and that the baseline is that the HKSAR cannot develop any official ties with Taiwan without the permission of Beijing. When Hong Kong is prohibited from having official relationships with Taiwan, it is very difficult, if not impossible, for Hong Kong–Taiwan relations to develop to their full potential.

What is more, because Hong Kong is now under PRC sovereignty, the HKSAR government sometimes has to take Beijing's side in the cross-Straits conflict, even at the expense of Hong Kong–Taiwan relations, to demonstrate its political loyalty. Examples of this include Tung Chee-hwa's open support for the applicability of Hong Kong's "one country, two systems" model to Taiwan and his unequivocal condemnation of Taiwan independence; the inability of Chung Hwa Travel Service's Managing Director Cheng An-kuo to extend his work visa after defending Lee Teng-hui's "two state" theory in a radio programme in Hong Kong; and over one-year delay his successor, Chang Liang-jen, encountered in obtaining his work visa to go to Hong Kong. Three years later, in 2004, Chang's successor Pao Cheng-kang also experienced similar difficulties. Such remarks and acts have led to negative feelings and criticisms in Taiwan, and are, therefore, not conducive to the normal development of Hong Kong–Taiwan relations.

Conclusion and Discussion

The maintenance and development of Hong Kong–Taiwan relations are basically in the interests of all parties involved: the Mainland, Hong Kong and Taiwan. Because of this, both Beijing and Taiwan have made efforts to ensure that such relations continue to operate smoothly after 1997, to seek a balance between economic and political considerations, and to avoid any adverse effects on the relationship from political considerations alone. At the same time, the HKSAR government, positioned in between the two conflicting parties, also has realized that Hong Kong–Taiwan relations are not only a legacy of a historical complication but are also important to

Hong Kong's economic well-being. Therefore, grounded on the pragmatism shown by Beijing and Taipei, the HKSAR government has also developed a similarly pragmatic policy to deal with Hong Kong–Taiwan relations, trying its best to achieve a balance between Beijing's political position of not compromising on the "one China" principle and Hong Kong's practical interests. In this way, in the decade following Hong Kong's return to China, the HKSAR government has been able to maintain and develop Hong Kong–Taiwan relations, especially in economic and non-governmental areas, with a minimum of political disturbance.

However, as a Chinese SAR, Hong Kong's calculatedly pragmatic policy inevitably has its structural limits. First and foremost, in its relations with Taiwan, Hong Kong cannot run counter to Beijing's political position, otherwise it will lose Beijing's political trust and support, which would be disastrous for Hong Kong. Yet, siding with Beijing's political position, even passively, may have an adverse effect on Hong Kong–Taiwan relations, since Taipei may see this as an attempt by Beijing to use Hong Kong to exert pressure on Taiwan. If the efforts to support Beijing are active, like some of the examples mentioned earlier, the result will be to make Taiwan uncomfortable and even angry (*The Standard*, 9 May 2005, p. 4).[12] Since the cross-Straits political conflict shows no signs of being resolved but actually seems to be intensifying over time, in the near future, it will be almost impossible for the HKSAR government to completely stay away from it, given Hong Kong's political subordination to Beijing. This, of course, will create many uncertainties in the future for Hong Kong–Taiwan relations.

For Beijing, official ties between Hong Kong and Taiwan are the last thing it wants to see before achieving a breakthrough with Taiwan over the issue of cross-Straits reunification. Under this constraint, Hong Kong–Taiwan relations can only develop to a severely limited degree. Hence, even though the HKSAR government has advanced relations by letting the Constitutional Affairs Bureau deal with all unofficial links with Taipei starting on 1 July 2002, the HKSAR government has remained extremely cautious in its communication and interactions with its Taiwan counterpart, even in an unofficial capacity. In fact, any contact between the Constitutional Affairs Bureau and the Taiwan authorities, including the Chung Hwa Travel Service, the island's *de facto* representative office in Hong Kong, is likely to be regarded as official and may spark criticism from local pro-Beijing groups or even directly from Beijing.

All in all, while Hong Kong–Taiwan relations have been able to make it through the 1997 transition rather peacefully, there have been constraints and disruptions, which have limited the development of these relations and created uncertainties. Yet, since these constraints and interruptions largely arise from the cross-Straits political conflict and the HKSAR government is unable to steer clear of them, the genuine solution lies in achieving a real compromise between Beijing and Taipei over the issue of reunification. Before this happens, Hong Kong must continue to adhere to its approach of calculated pragmatism in handling its relations with Taiwan, and especially try its utmost not to get involved in the cross-Straits political conflict.

Notes

1. Mainland Affairs Council website, 15 May 2007: http://www.mac.gov.tw/big5/statistic/ass_hm/table1.pdf.
2. Mainland Affairs Council website, 15 May 2007: http://www.mac.gov.tw/big5/statistic/ass_hm/table8.pdf.
3. See Annex I of the Sino-British Joint Declaration and Chapter I: General Principles of the Basic Law. The edition of the Basic Law quoted in this article is that of *The Basic Law of the Hong Kong Special Administrative Region of the People's Republic of China* (Hong Kong: One Country Two Systems Economic Research Institute Ltd., 1992).
4. See Chapter II of the Basic Law: Relationship between the Central Authorities and the HKSAR.
5. See Chapter VII of the Basic Law: On External Affairs. Limited authority on external affairs mainly refers to exchanges that are below the level of diplomatic affairs that are conducted only by sovereign states. It may also refer to participation in multilateral organizations or to the signing of multilateral agreements other than those in which only sovereign states are represented.
6. Beijing's consistent stand can be seen from its diplomatic exchanges with countries all over the world.
7. For the causes of the protest, see Cheng (ed.) (2005).
8. Beijing's efforts to curb Taiwan's political infiltration into Hong Kong's politics can be seen from a law passed by the HKSAR Provisional Legislature to prohibit Hong Kong's "political organizations or bodies" from accepting foreign financial support or from affiliating with any foreign organizations or bodies. It is explicitly stated that the legislation is applicable to Taiwan.
9. In the course of negotiations, the Hong Kong delegates initially rejected the proposal that neither side would display their flags, arguing that the act was against the established international practice and suggested that Taiwan displays

the flag with the plum flower design (Taiwan's national flower) and Hong Kong displays the HKSAR flag with the bauhinia flower design. The Taiwanese delegates expressed reservations about the proposal, suspecting that Beijing might use this to degrade Taiwan's status to that of a "special local region" similar to Hong Kong. However, a compromise was eventually reached by both parties: commercial ships registered in Taiwan that enter HKSAR waters with advance notice shall not be requested to hoist flags on the mizzenmast or on the mainmast; commercial ships registered in Hong Kong entering Taiwan waters with advance notice need only display the HKSAR flag on the mizzenmast and no flags on the mainmast.

10. Mainland Affairs Council website, 15 May 2007: http://www.mac.gov.tw/big5/statistic/ass_hm/table1.pdf.

11. Mainland Affairs Council website, 15 May 2007: http://www.mac.gov.tw/big5/statistic/ass_hm/table8.pdf.

12. For example, in late April to early May 2005, two top Taiwanese opposition leaders, Kuomintang Chairman Lien Chan and People's First Party Chairman James Soong, passed through Hong Kong en route to the Mainland, but Chung Hwa Travel Service's Managing Director Pao Cheng-kang was barred by the HKSAR government from meeting them. Later, Pao openly criticized the HKSAR government for not being sufficiently open-minded about Hong Kong's relations with Taiwan.

References

Chen, Albert H. Y. (1996), "The Impact of the 1997 Handover on Hong Kong–Taiwan Relations: A Legal Perspective." In Hung-mao Tien (ed.), *The 1997 Transition and Taiwan–Hong Kong Relations*. Taipei: Ye Qiang Publication House, pp. 153–77.

Cheng, Joseph Y. S. (ed.) (2005), T*he July 1 Protest Rally: Interpreting a Historic Event*. Hong Kong: City University of Hong Kong Press, Chapter 1.

China Times, 9 April 1997; 25 May 1997; 17 June 1997; 1 July 1997.

Hong Kong and Macao, No. 96, July 2002.

Hong Kong Annual Digest (1996), Hong Kong: The Census and Statistics Department of the Hong Kong Government, pp. 148–49.

Hong Kong Economic Journal, 18 April 2000.

Hong Kong Standard, 23 June 1995.

Mainland Affairs Council of the Executive Yuan (1996), *National Development Conference: Information and Analyses of Mainland-Taiwan Relations*. Taipei: The Mainland Affairs Council of the Executive Yuan.

Ming Pao, 8 May 1997; 4 July 1997; 1 June 2000.

One Country Two Systems Economic Research Institute Ltd. (1992), *The Basic Law of the Hong Kong Special Administrative Region of the People's Republic of China*. Hong Kong: One Country Two Systems Economic Research Institute Ltd.

South China Morning Post (SCMP), 11 October 1997; 1 July 2002.

Sung, Yun-wing (1995), "Direct 'Trade' between the Mainland and Taiwan." In Kuang-sheng Liao (ed.), *Economic and Trade Exchanges between the Mainland and Taiwan: Problems and Potentials.* Hong Kong: Hong Kong Institute of Asia-Pacific Studies, The Chinese University of Hong Kong, pp. 35–47.

Taipei Times, 17 January 2003.

The Standard, 9 May 2005.

Wen Wei Po, 18 April 2000; 4 April 2000.

Wong, Timothy K. Y. (1996), "Hong Kong–Taiwan Relations." In Mee-kau Nyaw and Si-ming Lee (eds.), *The Other Hong Kong Report 1996.* Hong Kong: The Chinese University Press, pp. 129–52.

—— (1997a), "Constraints on Tung Chee-hwa's Power and His Governance of Hong Kong," *Issues & Studies,* 33 (8): 26–48.

—— (1997b). "The Impact of State Development in Taiwan on Cross-Straits Relations," *Asian Perspective,* 21 (1): 171–212.

Yahuda, Michael (1996), *Hong Kong: China's Challenge.* London: Routledge.

Zhu, Y. H. (1996), "Exploring the Taiwan–Hong Kong Consultation Mechanism and the Status and Function of Taiwanese Agencies in Hong Kong." In Hung-mao Tien (ed.), *The 1997 Transition and Taiwan–Hong Kong Relations.* Taipei: Ye Qiang Publication House, pp. 121–51.

6

Hong Kong–ASEAN Economic Relations

Henry Yeung

Introduction

Hong Kong has always had deep social and economic relations with Southeast Asia. From the much earlier waves of Chinese sojourners in the nineteenth century and early twentieth century to the post–World War II period of massive social and economic transformations, Hong Kong has consistently maintained intimate economic relations with Southeast Asian countries. In the economic realm, this relationship has historically been manifested in the form of two-way trade and investment flows (Yeung, 1994; 1995; 1996). Not only are there many traders and investors from Hong Kong who transact with counterparts, mostly the so-called "overseas Chinese," in Southeast Asia; more interestingly, some of Hong Kong's established families have businesses with a vast presence in Southeast Asia (e.g., the Shaw brothers and Sing Tao's Aw family). Since its reversion to Chinese rule in July 1997, Hong Kong's economic outlook has been increasingly oriented northwards, towards intensified economic integration with the Mainland. While economic relations with Southeast Asia remain reasonably visible, the relationship is becoming increasingly one-way in nature, with Hong Kong serving as Southeast Asia's gateway to Mainland China. Meanwhile, Hong Kong is playing a much less significant role in the economic development of Southeast Asia.

Few recent studies have been conducted on these changing two-way economic relations between Hong Kong and Southeast Asia. Some studies have examined the possibility of monetary cooperation between Hong Kong and Southeast Asia (e.g., Ahn et al., 2006) and the work organization of East Asian firms, including those from Hong Kong, in Southeast Asia (e.g., Gamble et al., 2004). This dearth of academic studies can be largely explained by the weakening economic relations between Hong Kong and Southeast Asia since the mid-1990s. In this chapter, I aim to trace these changing economic relations between Hong Kong and five member countries in the Association of South East Asian Nations (ASEAN) — Indonesia, Malaysia, the Philippines, Singapore and Thailand.[1] In particular, I examine trade and investment data from numerous official sources in Hong Kong and ASEAN countries. Collectively, these time-series data on trade and investment shed intriguing light on the economic relations between the city-state and ASEAN countries. This examination is divided into two sections: a look at Hong Kong–ASEAN economic relations prior to 1997, followed by an analysis of trade and investment relations between Hong Kong and ASEAN from 1998 to 2006.

Three possible explanations are offered for the shift from active two-way economic relations between Hong Kong and ASEAN prior to 1997 to mostly one-way economic interactions (ASEAN to Hong Kong) in the past decade. Here, the 1997/1998 Asian economic crisis, the rise of China's economic might, and changing global production networks are critical factors in accounting for this shift in economic relations. The chapter concludes with a discussion of some of the implications of the above developments for the policy and business communities.

Leading up to 1997: Hong Kong–ASEAN Investment and Trade in the 1990s

Prior to the mid-1990s, entrepreneurs and companies based in Hong Kong were among the most active in spearheading cross-border trade and investment in Southeast Asia. Some large non-Chinese transnational corporations from Hong Kong (HKTNCs) had emerged as early as the late nineteenth century, in particular those controlled by British capital in Hong Kong (Yeung, 1998, Chapter 4). Some of these British establishments had their origins as colonial trading houses, known as *hongs* locally in Hong Kong and Southern China (e.g., Jardine Matheson, Swire Group and Wharf Group). Some of these *hongs* and commercial firms had also made substantial overseas investments, mostly in the then Imperial China and Southeast Asia (e.g., the Hongkong and Shanghai Banking Corporation in Malaysia, Singapore, Thailand, and so on). This was thus a historical period in which foreign direct investment from Hong Kong (HKFDI) in Southeast Asia resulted primarily from the colonial and expansionist tendencies of the British Government and British-controlled HKTNCs. HKFDI in the

ASEAN region was also controlled, to a large extent, by British colonial trading houses.

From 1945 to the late 1960s, moderate changes were observed in the composition of HKFDI in the ASEAN region. Particularly prominent among these changes was the fact that such investment was increasingly coming from businesses owned and controlled by ethnic Chinese in Hong Kong. For example, some large textile companies from Hong Kong, owned and operated by emigrant industrialists who had fled Shanghai before the communist takeover of China in 1949, began to venture into Southeast Asia and selected countries worldwide (e.g., South Africa). Some of these textile mills later became the pioneers of integrated textile mills in the host countries (e.g., Malaya; see Wong, 1988). This was also the period during which Hong Kong experienced dramatic changes in its industrial structure and economic development processes. Manufacturing industries came to the forefront of the domestic developmental agenda. These internal developments resulted in certain spin-offs of FDI from Hong Kong into the ASEAN region. Meanwhile, the imposition of voluntary quota restrictions on Hong Kong textile firms via the Multi-Fibre Agreement in the late 1950s and the early 1960s by developed countries in Europe and America effectively induced many textile HKTNCs to venture into overseas locations where export quotas were available (Lui and Chiu, 1994). Southeast Asia was deemed a favourable location due to its geographical and cultural proximity to Hong Kong (e.g., Wing Tai in Singapore).

By the late 1960s, the Hong Kong government was following an export-oriented industrialization strategy. Under a general *laissez-faire* approach to the economy, various liberal fiscal and monetary measures, such as tax incentives and free capital mobility, were implemented to stimulate industrial and economic development (Ho, 1992; Eng, 1997; Yu, 1997). These historically specific policies contributed to a spectacular process of industrialization in Hong Kong that triggered off a strong centrifugal force. By the late 1960s and the early 1970s, a number of HKTNCs had emerged and were investing in other parts of the world. This was the first phase of major growth in outward FDI by HKTNCs in Southeast Asia. Manufacturing HKTNCs had a head start when those engaged in electronics and textiles and garments expanded into lower-cost production sites in Southeast Asia and other developing countries (Ho, 1992; Yeung, 2000; Chiu and Wong, 2004). In contrast to pressures from quota restrictions in the earlier phase, this outward movement of manufacturing HKTNCs was primarily a spatial manifestation of ongoing restructuring efforts taking place within Hong

Kong, together with an increasingly open attitude in ASEAN countries towards foreign investment. Meanwhile, the "open-door" policy adopted by Mainland China since the late 1978 has fundamentally changed the ways in which most Hong Kong firms plan for the future. Mainland China, particularly Guangdong, has since attracted a huge influx of Hong Kong firms in all types of industries and sectors, ranging from large listed corporations to small family operators (see Thoburn et al., 1990; Leung, 1993; Ho and So, 1997; G. Yeung, 2001; Huang, 2002).

Another major wave of overseas investment from Hong Kong occurred during the early 1980s, when the future of Hong Kong became increasingly uncertain. The Sino-British Joint Declaration in December 1984 represented the single most clear-cut watershed in the historical development of HKTNCs and outward FDI flows from Hong Kong. Major companies in Hong Kong began to rethink their strategies for the next 10 years and beyond 1997, acted in diverse ways. One of the first signals of a strategic re-orientation in corporate investment was evident in Jardine Matheson's relocation of its holding company to Bermuda in 1984. Mr Simon Keswick, Chairman of the Jardine Matheson Group, announced on 28 March 1984 that "[w]hen we are competing in the market place for major long-term contracts, it is undoubtedly a disadvantage to have to deal with questions regarding the long-term future of Hong Kong. We want to put these questions behind us once and for all" (quoted in *The Economist*, 31 March 1984).

This second phase of rapid growth and consolidation of HKFDI coincided with rapid growth and a further opening-up of the ASEAN region to foreign investors. HKFDI in the ASEAN region was also much more diversified than before in industrial structure, in response to different factor endowments in different ASEAN countries. Between 1984 and 1988, the average outflow of HKFDI was US$2.5 billion, while the average inflow of FDI US$1.8 billion (UNCTC, 1992, p. 103). In other words, Hong Kong experienced a period of negative FDI flows. HKFDI was largely biased towards intra-regional flows. More than two-thirds of HKFDI went to East, South and Southeast Asia, with another one-third to North America and Western Europe. Within the Asia-Pacific region, a large proportion of HKFDI was invested in China, in particular Guangdong and Fujian.[2] Southeast Asia, in particular ASEAN countries, also captured a large share of these FDI outflows from Hong Kong. By the late 1980s, HKTNCs had established a strong foothold in many countries within the region. Hong Kong had become a net exporter of FDI. UNCTAD (1996, Annex Table 4) estimates that outward FDI stock from Hong Kong was US$9.4 billion in

1985 and reached US$85 billion in 1995. By 1995, HKTNCs controlled more than 4,317 foreign affiliates in host countries worldwide (UNCTAD, 1996, Table I.4).

Significant Hong Kong Investments in ASEAN

Generally speaking, the spatial and temporal distributions of HKFDI and HKTNCs in different ASEAN countries are highly uneven. There was a sharp break in continuity due to the sharp decline in HKFDI in 1985–1986. This phenomenon can be attributed to the sudden and unexpected collapse of the Hong Kong dollar in the foreign exchange market and its subsequent recovery (pegged in October 1983 against the U.S. dollar at HK$7.8 for US$1) after the conclusion of the Sino-British Joint Declaration in December 1984. In the post-1985 period, however, the flow of HKFDI to ASEAN increased dramatically, especially to Indonesia, Singapore and Thailand. Geographically, HKFDI in the ASEAN region tended to be biased towards three ASEAN countries: Indonesia, Singapore and Thailand. Most HKFDI projects in Indonesia and Thailand involved large capital commitments. In the first six months of 1990, the average value of approved projects in Indonesia was US$44 million, whereas the corresponding figure for Thailand was US$19 million (Federation of Hong Kong Industries, 1990, p. 16). In the first three quarters of 1994 alone, Hong Kong investors had committed some US$5.7 billion in Indonesia, with most of this sum going into two mega-projects, one in power generation wholly owned by Gordon Wu's Hopewell (US$1.8 billion) and the other in oil refining, wholly owned by Li Ka-shing (US$3.5 billion) (*The Straits Times*, 1 August 1994; *Far Eastern Economic Review*, 1 September 1994).

Between 1980 and 1996, in terms of *cumulative* FDI stock (see Figure 6.1), Hong Kong was consistently among the top three largest investors in Indonesia, the Philippines and Thailand. But during the same period its position in Singapore fell to fifth. Between 1967 and January 1997, Hong Kong investors poured some US$14.6 billion (8.3% of total FDI) in approved projects in Indonesia, making Hong Kong the third largest investor in that country after Japan (US$30 billion) and the U.K. (US$21.9 billion). In Malaysia, Hong Kong's paid-up capital in approved FDI projects in the manufacturing sector as at 31 December 1994 was RM$637 million or US$256 million (4.2% of the total), ranking Hong Kong only sixth after Japan, Singapore, the U.K., Taiwan and the U.S. In the Philippines, Hong Kong firms invested up to US$233 million (6.3% of the total) in cumulative

Figure 6.1 Geographical Origins of Cumulative Foreign Direct Investment in Five ASEAN Countries, 1965–1997

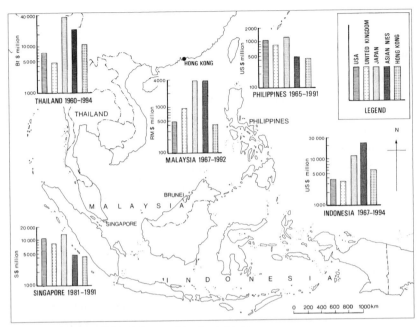

Sources: Same as Table 6.1 except for the following:
¹ Malaysia: The data refer to total paid-up capital in manufacturing FDI projects in production as at 31 December 1994, except for hotel and tourist projects.
Source: Malaysian Industrial Development Authority.
² The Philippines: The data refer to data from the Central Bank of the Philippines on cumulative foreign equity investment stock from 1965–1991; supplied by Eric Ramstetter, December 1993.

foreign equity investment stock from 1965 to 1991, third after the U.S. and Japan. In Singapore, Hong Kong's cumulative foreign equity investment between 1981 and 1994 was S$5 billion or US$3.3 billion (2.8% of the total). During the same period, Hong Kong stood was the fifth largest investor after Japan (S$16.9 billion), the U.S. (S$14.1 billion), the U.K. (S$9.1 billion) and Switzerland (S$5.8 billion). In Thailand, it was the third largest investor after Japan (Bt$140 billion) and the U.S. (Bt$86.7 billion), with cumulative net flows of HKFDI from 1965 to September 1996 amounting to Bt$73.4 billion or US$2.9 billion (15.1% of the total).

Table 6.1 presents some statistics on annual HKFDI *inflows* to the ASEAN-5 countries since 1980. In Indonesia (see also Figure 6.2), HKFDI in approved projects in all sectors except oil, banking, non-banking financial institutions, insurance and leasing, increased more than 300 times from US$19.5 million in 1980 to a record of US$6 billion in 1994. During this period, HKFDI inflows to Indonesia enjoyed accelerated growth, with the exception of the years 1984–1986 when Hong Kong faced significant domestic economic challenges. These HKFDI inflows were generally significant. In 1981 and 1994, HKFDI inflows accounted for almost a quarter of total FDI inflows into Indonesia. In some other years (1982, 1987, 1990 and 1992), they remained significant at about 10% of total FDI inflows. In Malaysia, a similar pattern was seen in HKFDI in approved manufacturing projects. In 1981, it was RM$35 million, but decreased to RM$9.5 million in 1984. In subsequent years, approved HKFDI inflows rose significantly to a record high of RM$3.6 billion in 1994. The subsequent three years leading up to 1997 witnessed a slowdown in HKFDI

Figure 6.2 Geographical Origins of Inflows of Foreign Direct Investment into Five ASEAN Countries, 1965–1997

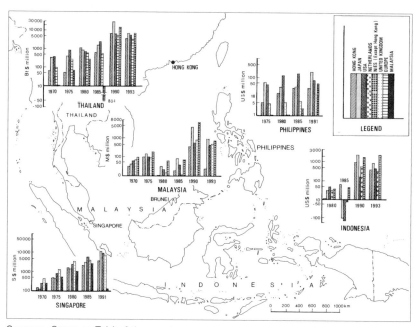

Sources: Same as Table 6.1 except
[1] The Philippines: Data refer to inflows of foreign equity investment (see Figure 1), except data for 1996 that refer to approved FDI.
[2] Singapore: Data are cumulative total foreign equity investment.

Table 6.1 Foreign Direct Investment Flows from Hong Kong to Five ASEAN Countries, 1980–1997

Country	1980	1982	1984	1986	1988	1990	1992	1994	1996	1997
Indonesia[1]										
(US$mil)	19.5	207.2	48.6	9.6	231.4	993.3	1,020.6	6,041.7	1,105.6	251.0
% of Total	2.50	13.35	4.36	1.16	5.22	11.35	9.87	24.47	3.69	0.74
Malaysia[2]										
(RM$mil)	319.6	4.9	9.5	27.5	298.4	375.0	1,089.0	3,589.0	912.0	628.0
% of Total	10.81	0.93	3.45	5.24	6.12	2.13	7.67	12.43	2.93	1.74
Philippines[3]										
(US$mil)	15.4	12.0	10.6	-15.2	7.0	15.2	37.8	48.7	76.2	59.8
% of Total	6.71	3.49	7.23	-14.05	10.94	7.76	11.52	5.52	5.95	5.68
Singapore[4]										
(S$mil)	1,707.0	459.7	48.3	-231.0	249.9	690.5	335.5	-3.4	650.4	39.8
% of Total	13.13	12.51	1.80	-7.50	3.71	6.33	13.75	-0.03	3.96	0.17
Thailand[5] (Bt$mil)	1,114	593.5	351.7	955.7	2,795	6,944	14,549	8,004	5,444	14,817
% of Total	N.A.	N.A.	9.5	10.2	10.1	10.8	15.4	N.A.	9.47	12.59

[1] For Indonesia, the data refer to FDI approvals in all sectors by the BKPM, excluding oil, banking, non-banking financial institutions, insurance and leasing. Investment value is the total investment value of new projects and their expansion and change of status.

Sources: Unpublished database generated by the Capital Investment Coordinating Board (BKPM), 15 June 1994; Bank Indonesia (various years).

[2] For Malaysia, the data refer to foreign capital investment in approved projects. From 1983 to 1986, the data refer to proposed foreign paid up capital.

Sources: Malaysian Industrial Development Authority (various years). Bank Negara Malaysia (various years).

[3] For the Philippines, the data refer to registered direct foreign equity investment in all sectors.

Sources: Central Bank of the Philippines (various years). Department of Economic Research (various years).

[4] For Singapore, the data refer to the total equity investment of all companies from Hong Kong in all sectors. Total equity investment refers to (1) their direct equity investment plus (2) their portfolio equity investment plus (3) their indirect equity investment.

Source: Department of Statistics (various years).

[5] For Thailand, the data refer to net flows of foreign direct investment in all sectors. For 1984–1993, percent of total refers to Hong Kong's share of total FDI stock.

Sources: Unpublished memos from the Bank of Thailand, supplied by Eric Ramstetter, 20 October 1993. Bank of Thailand (various years).

inflows to Malaysia's manufacturing sector. While the significance of HKFDI inflows in Malaysia might not be as high as in Indonesia, these inflows remained fairly substantial, hovering between 7% and 12% of total FDI inflows.

In the Philippines, following a sharp rise of inflows from US$39 million in 1981 to US$28 million in 1985, HKFDI inflows experienced a decline in the subsequent two years. The first half of the 1990s was a golden era of HKFDI in the Philippines, with the figure surging to US$235 million in 1995. HKFDI inflows were quite significant for the Philippines. Throughout the 1980s, they exceeded 10% of total FDI in the Philippines in 1981, 1985 and 1987–1988. By 1995, this ratio had climbed to 28.9%, clearly a very substantial figure compared to HKFDI in Indonesia and Thailand. In Singapore, foreign equity investment from Hong Kong in all sectors in Singapore started modestly at S$148 million in 1970 and S$515 million in 1975 (Chia, 1993, Table 8.5). It grew steadily in the 1980s, from S$1.7 billion in 1980 to S$5 billion in 1994, representing almost a 30-fold jump over a period of two-and-a-half decades. When we examine the flow data, however, it is apparent that there was a great deal of instability in HKFDI in Singapore. Negative inflows were registered for 1984–1985, 1991 and 1994. Still, HKFDI inflows were quite important for the Singaporean economy. In some years (1981–1982, 1989, and 1992), HKFDI inflows accounted for up to 13% of net total FDI inflows. An equally striking growth rate was seen in net HKFDI inflows to Thailand from 1980 to 1997. Although there was a minor disruption in 1984 and 1985, HKFDI inflows to Thailand increased 45-fold from Bt$323 million in 1981 to a record high of Bt$14.5 billion in 1992. The figures for the period 1993–1996 show a relative decline in HKFDI inflows to Thailand (Table 6.1). In 1997, however, they hit a new record high of Bt$14.8 billion. Between 1986 and 1997, the contribution of HKFDI to total FDI inflows to Thailand rose from 10% to 15.4% in 1992 and subsequently declined slightly to 12.6% in 1997.

Although Hong Kong was clearly an important investor in ASEAN prior to 1997, it is unclear if ASEAN countries were significant investors in Hong Kong. While data on inward FDI in all sectors in Hong Kong are only available from 1995 onwards, we can glean from Tables 6.2 and 6.3 that none of the ASEAN countries except Singapore had a substantial amount of investment in Hong Kong prior to 1997. Table 6.2 shows that inward direct investment flows to Hong Kong were mostly concentrated in non-manufacturing sectors such as financial services, property development, and other business and consumer services industries. In the case of

Table 6.2 Inward Direct Investment Flows in All Sectors in Hong Kong by Country of Origin, 1996–2005 (in HK$ million)

	1996	1997	1998	1999	2000	2001	2002	2003	2004	2005
Mainland China	39,200	51,900	20,200	38,600	110,700	38,500	31,700	38,000	62,000	72,900
Japan	81,500	65,900	600	6,800	25,800	8,500	15,300	14,200	10,900	14,100
Singapore	21,400	23,800	500	5,900	60,000	11,400	6,400	-9,900	3,200	11,000
Thailand	–	–	–	–	–	200	3,100	-1,800	1,300	28,100
Netherlands	–	–	13,200	24,300	7,400	-2,300	10,300	24,700	8,800	17,000
United Kingdom	26,600	34,200	8,300	1,900	-41,300	7,200	8,600	4,500	18,200	13,700
U.S.A.	25,100	32,600	6,600	19,000	18,800	11,800	-11,000	22,000	48,400	-29,700
British Virgin Islands	58,100	99,200	30,300	48,800	238,400	74,700	59,400	19,800	62,700	47,000
Bermuda	20,900	19,100	20,700	24,600	36,900	9,900	2,100	-13,600	8,900	36,000
Cayman Islands	–	–	–	1,300	11,100	10,900	-68,700	2,900	6,500	12,000
Others	120,000	142,400	14,000	17,900	16,800	12,600	20,700	5,600	34,100	39,400
Total	392,700	469,000	114,400	190,700	482,600	185,400	75,500	106,300	265,100	261,500
% of manufacturing	0.7	0.6	7.0	8.1	1.0	1.1	13.2	5.1	5.1	2.8

Note: The first survey was conducted in 1969 and others in 1970, 1975 and 1981. The first regular survey was published in 1985.
Source: Census and Statistics Department (various years).

Table 6.3 Inward Direct Investment Stock in All Sectors in Hong Kong by Country of Origin, 1996–2005 (in HK$ million)

	1996	1997	1998	1999	2000	2001	2002	2003	2004	2005
Mainland China	114,200	142,400	213,700	814,800	1,112,200	958,100	594,600	770,100	1,020,100	1,271,900
Japan	94,400	97,900	108,800	111,500	113,200	116,600	141,400	142,200	148,200	131,700
Singapore	10,700	15,500	43,300	143,100	98,200	88,800	73,500	58,000	87,100	84,300
Thailand¹	22,600	34,600	–	–	–	3,700	6,200	5,100	6,500	33,200
France	7,100	14,500	–	–	–	–	–	–	–	–
Germany	9,100	11,400	–	–	–	–	–	–	–	–
Netherlands	19,700	27,400	124,500	207,000	224,800	199,900	204,900	256,100	307,200	327,100
Switzerland	8,900	9,700	–							
United Kingdom	168,700	184,300	153,400	195,800	55,300	45,400	55,800	48,100	70,000	88,500
U.S.A.	110,800	128,600	115,500	170,400	161,400	193,700	186,600	187,600	243,500	205,800
British Virgin Islands	4,800	9,400	542,600	924,700	1,131,400	943,600	779,400	935,200	1,029,300	1,270,700
Bermuda	–	–	202,000	–	317,200	315,700	273,200	254,800	272,200	271,500
Cayman Islands	–	–	–	993,000	90,200	119,500	44,900	53,100	61,800	66,700
Others	75,400	91,400	240,200	192,700	214,700	256,400	223,700	249,900	275,900	304,900
Total	623,900	732,400	1,744,000	3,149,300	3,550,800	3,269,700	2,622,300	2,960,400	3,521,900	4,056,300
% of manufacturing	7.7	6.9	4.9	3.2	2.1	2.2	2.8	2.2	2.0	1.7

¹ Thailand: Stock data between 1994 and 1997 refer to total net assets in non-manufacturing sectors at net book value.
Note: The first survey was conducted in 1969 and others in 1970, 1975 and 1981. The first regular survey was published in 1985.
Source: Census and Statistics Department (various years).

Singapore, with similar historical and geographical circumstances, that country did play a substantial role in inward investment into Hong Kong. Between 1995 and 1997, Singapore was the fifth largest identifiable investor in Hong Kong, if we exclude tax havens such as the British Virgin Islands, Bermuda and the Cayman Islands where it is almost impossible to identify the country of origin of FDI. Still, Singapore's FDI inflows during this period were not too far from those from the U.S. and the U.K. Major Singaporean operations in Hong Kong then were in financial services (e.g., UOB, DBS and OCBC), property development (Sino Land and CDL International) and other services (e.g., SingTel, PSA and Singapore Press Holdings).

Table 6.3 offers some statistics on inward FDI stock in Hong Kong from 1994 onwards. Between 1994 and 1997, FDI stocks from Singapore and Thailand were quite substantial. Measured by total net assets in non-manufacturing sectors at net book value, Thailand's FDI stock in Hong Kong in 1997 was higher than such European developed countries as France, Germany, the Netherlands and Switzerland. It grew very rapidly at a rate of 835% from HK$3.7 billion in 1994 to HK$34.6 billion in 1997. This rate was far greater than that from any other country of origin. Major Thai operations in Hong Kong were in financial services (e.g., Bangkok Bank) and trading (e.g., CP Pokphand).

More specifically, Hong Kong emerged during this period as the transit point through which Southeast Asian firms ventured into China (Zhang and Ow, 1996; Nyaw et al., 2001). Many Southeast Asian investors channelled their investments in China through their listed and non-listed corporate vehicles in Hong Kong and these investments were counted in official statistics as Hong Kong investments (see Low et al., 1998; Yeung, 2004). A substantial amount of annual FDI from these ASEAN countries to China was registered as investments from their Hong Kong offices and/or subsidiaries. For example, it is well known that Indonesia's Liem Sioe Liong made investments in China through its Hong Kong listed vehicle First Pacific Group. So did Malaysia's Robert Kuok (Kerry Group and Shangri-la Hotels in Hong Kong) and Quek Leng Chan (Guoco Group in Hong Kong), Singapore's Ng Teng Fong (Sino Land in Hong Kong), Thailand's Dhanin Chearavanont (CP Pokphand in Hong Kong) and the Philippines' Lucio Tan (Eton Properties in Hong Kong). This phenomenon of indirect investment implies that FDI inflows from Hong Kong into China might be inflated because some of these inflows were actually from Southeast Asian (and Taiwanese) investors.

Table 6.4 Hong Kong's Total Trade with Ten Main Countries/Territories, 1972–2006 (in HK$ million)

Year	Total	China	U.S.A.	Japan	Taiwan	Singapore	South Korea	Germany	U.K.	Malaysia	Thailand
1972	41,164	3,950	9,084	6,359	1,893	1,453	588	2,326	3,731	218	645
1976	84,849	7,908	17,400	12,249	4,192	4,237	2,112	5,476	5,234	767	1,341
1980	209,893	28,195	38,886	30,174	11,026	11,685	4,999	11,003	13,066	1,590	2,641
1984	444,811	95,101	97,861	62,405	23,825	19,367	11,139	16,414	20,175	3,277	4,120
1988	991,867	288,572	163,714	121,861	61,947	32,389	39,292	38,581	34,866	8,723	10,381
1992	1,880,248	628,412	283,694	214,653	119,675	63,314	59,157	70,970	52,353	19,268	20,005
1996	2,933,499	1,049,815	417,260	299,727	156,545	119,892	96,002	92,487	79,851	47,092	37,737
1997	3,071,040	1,116,117	441,826	310,011	161,158	116,975	94,876	95,174	86,073	51,329	40,526
1998	2,776,741	1,044,045	421,236	250,576	137,948	92,185	82,640	84,605	81,988	43,035	33,640
1999	2,741,717	1,057,149	419,374	235,616	133,386	92,415	86,725	80,780	82,893	40,994	34,859
2000	3,230,652	1,257,968	478,286	286,110	163,972	111,742	109,232	92,107	93,834	51,971	42,306
2001	3,049,181	1,228,101	434,720	264,210	143,295	102,477	96,735	84,901	84,218	51,777	41,803
2002	3,179,936	1,330,317	424,429	266,281	150,487	107,325	106,351	81,836	80,313	55,182	46,336
2003	3,548,206	1,528,169	422,945	307,997	167,473	126,274	122,866	97,444	81,597	60,044	51,116
2004	4,130,237	1,806,818	453,594	363,686	202,924	154,563	144,536	102,899	94,690	69,800	58,376
2005	4,579,643	2,061,900	479,892	375,079	218,654	181,731	151,277	113,774	100,220	75,738	68,557
2006	5,060,831	2,349,162	494,699	388,562	247,024	213,449	171,519	120,091	105,058	82,295	77,944

Source: Internet download from the Trade Analysis Section, Census and Statistics Department, 27 February 2007.

Table 6.5 Hong Kong's Imports from Ten Main Countries/Territories, 1972–2006 (in HK$ million)

Year	Total	China	Japan	Taiwan	U.S.A.	Singapore	South Korea	Malaysia	Germany	Thailand	Philippines
1972	21,764	3,847	5,045	1,309	2,595	668	409	78	752	465	81
1976	43,293	7,761	9,348	3,057	5,309	2,517	1,636	368	1,314	795	199
1980	111,651	21,948	25,644	7,961	13,210	7,384	3,869	850	2,906	1,578	929
1984	223,370	55,753	52,620	17,347	24,377	12,229	7,289	1,367	5,725	2,199	1,886
1988	498,798	155,634	93,008	44,357	41,347	18,462	26,257	5,769	13,356	5,993	2,270
1992	955,295	354,348	166,191	87,019	70,594	39,087	44,155	12,825	21,911	11,811	3,458
1996	1,535,582	570,442	208,239	123,202	121,058	81,495	73,302	33,994	33,884	23,748	7,360
1997	1,615,090	608,372	221,646	124,547	125,381	79,186	73,226	38,008	38,518	26,070	9,815
1998	1,429,092	580,614	179,947	104,075	106,537	61,457	68,836	32,479	32,639	22,234	10,248
1999	1,392,718	607,546	162,652	100,426	98,572	60,017	65,432	30,010	28,114	22,798	12,307
2000	1,657,962	714,987	198,976	124,172	112,801	74,998	80,600	37,906	32,215	28,001	16,247
2001	1,568,194	681,980	176,599	107,929	104,941	72,898	70,791	39,200	33,309	27,370	15,408
2002	1,619,419	717,074	182,569	115,906	91,478	75,740	75,955	39,729	32,997	29,556	21,135
2003	1,805,770	785,625	213,995	125,203	98,730	90,570	87,340	44,637	41,222	33,194	29,227
2004	2,111,123	918,275	256,141	153,812	111,994	110,986	100,467	51,941	39,999	37,782	33,735
2005	2,329,469	1,049,335	256,501	168,227	119,252	135,190	103,035	57,153	41,054	46,455	38,278
2006	2,599,804	1,192,952	268,140	194,917	123,569	164,837	119,647	60,339	44,428	53,081	40,847

Source: Internet download from the Trade Analysis Section, Census and Statistics Department, 27 February 2007.

Table 6.6 Hong Kong's Re-exports from Ten Main Origin Countries/Territories, 1992–2006 (in HK$ million)

Year	Total	China	Japan	Taiwan	South Korea	U.S.A.	Malaysia	Germany	Singapore	Thailand	Philippines
1992	690,829	403,782	84,966	54,442	19,391	32,113	5,096	9,134	8,269	3,077	819
1993	823,224	474,007	109,949	64,649	21,685	37,424	6,660	14,256	11,836	3,986	1,203
1994	947,921	545,831	121,936	72,060	27,444	43,678	9,461	14,588	15,069	5,716	1,701
1995	1,112,470	636,392	130,511	83,307	37,615	55,636	13,334	14,886	21,678	8,049	2,234
1996	1,185,758	683,514	129,292	82,177	38,049	62,192	16,951	16,448	25,464	9,835	2,570
1997	1,244,539	723,416	133,825	83,341	39,672	62,633	19,806	16,616	27,869	10,037	2,742
1998	1,159,195	691,219	123,879	71,782	39,637	54,530	17,473	15,633	20,175	10,990	3,488
1999	1,178,400	720,126	121,265	71,957	38,822	56,737	19,031	15,558	13,805	10,582	4,695
2000	1,391,722	849,517	137,338	87,942	46,057	65,465	27,050	18,790	14,991	14,145	7,293
2001	1,327,467	808,370	125,649	80,321	39,775	65,193	27,170	20,322	14,650	13,297	8,273
2002	1,429,590	863,967	135,793	94,275	47,218	62,900	27,412	21,890	16,676	16,352	13,210
2003	1,620,749	967,104	161,231	107,144	57,000	63,158	33,933	26,583	23,479	21,368	19,873
2004	1,893,132	1,135,469	194,247	133,874	64,358	61,771	42,571	27,369	25,379	24,737	21,102
2005	2,114,143	1,313,211	186,065	152,496	74,030	64,304	49,008	28,554	27,313	27,587	22,893
2006	2,326,500	1,461,292	188,649	166,731	84,996	69,589	50,249	29,566	26,493	34,830	27,915

Source: Internet download from the Trade Analysis Section, Census and Statistics Department, 27 February 2007.

Rapidly Growing ASEAN Trade with Hong Kong

With the above significant HKFDI flows to Southeast Asia, we would expect Hong Kong–ASEAN trade relations to be commensurate with the deep economic links established by Hong Kong–based companies. In Tables 6.4 to 6.6, I present some important statistics on Hong Kong's trade relations with 10 major trading partners, including several ASEAN member states such as Malaysia, Singapore and Thailand. In Table 6.4, it is clear that Singapore, Malaysia and Thailand were not significant trading partners with Hong Kong back in 1972. By 1984, however, Singapore had emerged as Hong Kong's sixth largest trading partner, narrowly trailing Taiwan and the U.K; and by 1997, Singapore had become Hong Kong's fifth largest trading partner. Throughout the 1990s, Hong Kong's total trade with Singapore, Malaysia and Thailand grew phenomenally. While Singapore's total trade with Hong Kong more than doubled between 1990 and 1997, the growth rates for Malaysia and Thailand were 300% and 145%, respectively.

More specifically, Hong Kong's trade relations with Southeast Asian countries before 1997 can be expressed in two forms: imports and re-exports. First, with regard to imports, Hong Kong's trade relations with four ASEAN countries strengthened significantly over the period 1986 and 1997, as can be seen in Table 6.5. Hong Kong's imports from Malaysia, in particular, grew dramatically from HK$1.8 billion in 1986 to HK$38 billion in 1997, representing over a 19-fold increase in just one decade. During the same period, Hong Kong's imports from Thailand and Singapore also increased, by over 760% and 620%, respectively. To put these figures in perspective, Hong Kong's total imports during this one-decade period grew by 485%. In other words, the growth rates of Hong Kong's imports from Malaysia, Thailand and Singapore far exceeded the growth in total imports.

Second, Hong Kong served as an important entrepôt for these ASEAN countries during the first half of the 1990s. Table 6.6 shows that between 1992 and 1997, Hong Kong's re-exports to ASEAN from 10 main territories of origin grew by more than 80%. During the same period, the growth rates in Hong Kong's re-exports originating from Malaysia, Singapore, Thailand and the Philippines were, respectively, 280%, 230%, 220% and 230%. Again, these rates were significantly higher than the total re-exports by Hong Kong of products originating from 10 trading partners.

To sum up this section, throughout the 1980s and the 1990s, Hong Kong invested quite significantly in such ASEAN countries as Indonesia, the Philippines, Singapore and Thailand. In these countries, inflows of investment from Hong Kong could be very substantial. The role of investment in Hong Kong from ASEAN, however, remained relatively modest, with the exception of Singapore and, more recently, Thailand. Some of these ASEAN investments in Hong Kong were destined for Mainland China. Meanwhile, Hong Kong's trade relations with ASEAN countries took the form not so much of direct exports from Hong Kong to ASEAN, but mostly of imports and re-exports from ASEAN to Mainland China in particular. During this period, Hong Kong imported a large amount of materials and products from ASEAN countries and served as an important centre for re-exporting these ASEAN-origin products. Overall, Hong Kong–ASEAN economic relations prior to 1997 were very much predicated on inflows of investment to ASEAN by Hong Kong firms and on imports and re-exports from ASEAN to Hong Kong. It is fair to conclude that these investment and trade flows contributed significantly to two-way economic relations between Hong Kong and ASEAN.

Ten Years On: What Has Changed?

On 1 July 1997, Hong Kong was returned to China and became the Hong Kong Special Administrative Region (HKSAR) of China. A separate, but no less significant, event in the second half of 1997 was the onslaught of the Asian financial crisis that started with the collapse of the Thai baht in the international currency market. For the next several years, the HKSAR experienced significant economic difficulties. Similarly, most ASEAN economies — particularly Indonesia and Thailand — were badly damaged by the Asian financial crisis. Their recovery took a long time and remains an unfinished business as of today. Situated within this context of a changing political jurisdiction and a region-wide economic crisis, the HKSAR's economic relations with ASEAN have weakened substantially. In this section, I will document some of these weakened relations in the areas of investment flows and bilateral trade.

Table 6.7 presents the latest available data on *investment inflows* from the HKSAR to ASEAN countries since 1997. In Indonesia, HKFDI inflows between 1997 and 2006 were highly variable, peaking at US$1.7 billion in 2002. Still, during this period, they accounted for very insignificant proportion of total FDI inflows in Indonesia, except for the year 2002. Unlike the pre-1997 period, when HKFDI inflows often amounted to more than 10% of total FDI inflows, the post-1997 era saw a substantial decline

Table 6.7 Foreign Direct Investment Flows from Hong Kong to Five ASEAN Countries, 1997–2006

Country	1997	1998	1999	2000	2001	2002	2003	2004	2005	2006*
Indonesia[1]										
(US$mil)	251.0	549.0	76.9	105.4	39.7	1,712.0	169.5	20.1	101.9	353.4
% of Total	0.74	4.05	0.71	0.68	0.26	17.57	1.28	0.20	0.75	2.54
Malaysia[2]										
(RM$mil)	628.0	620.0	893.0	1,798.0	350.0	407.0	2,786.0	1,765.0	1,169.0	425.0
% of Total	1.74	1.91	2.72	4.87	0.75	1.14	8.74	6.36	1.80	1.40
Philippines[3]										
(US$mil)	59.8	21.3	20.0	16.5	4.4	N.A.	N.A.	N.A.	N.A.	N.A.
% of Total	5.68	2.41	0.95	1.18	0.51	N.A.	N.A.	N.A.	N.A.	N.A.
Singapore[4]										
(S$mil)	39.8	134.8	−921.6	1,100.8	−425.1	−479.4	−719.1	525.7	N.A.	N.A.
% of Total	0.17	0.75	−11.87	4.49	−1.88	−3.48	−6.03	2.22	N.A.	N.A.
Thailand[5]										
(Bt$mil)	14,817.0	16,571.0	8,862.0	13,356.0	6,709.0	3,698.0	24,873.0	5,555.0	14,679.0	10,686.0
% of Total	12.59	7.90	6.58	11.59	2.98	2.51	11.64	2.79	4.91	3.45

* The data for 2006 are up to October–November.
Source: Same as Table 6.1.

in the role of Hong Kong as a leading investor in Indonesia. In Malaysia, the post-1997 trend was equally unimpressive. With the exception of 2003, HKFDI inflows to Malaysia remained at less than 3% of total FDI inflows in the three periods of 1997–1999, 2001–2002 and 2005–2006. The same pattern of low HKFDI inflows occurred in the Philippines during the period 1997–2001. Prior to 1997 (Table 6.1), HKFDI inflows to the Philippines consistently made up between 5% and 29% of total FDI inflows. In Singapore, negative HKFDI inflows were registered for 1999 and 2001–2003. Only in Thailand did HKFDI maintain its lead in such years as 2000 and 2003. In both years, HKFDI made up over 10% of total FDI inflows. In short, there has been a significant decline in HKFDI in ASEAN since 1997, with the exception of Thailand. As a consequence, Hong Kong is no longer one of the largest foreign investors in most ASEAN countries, unlike during the 1980s and the first half of the 1990s when it ranked among the top three investors in the region.

Meanwhile, ASEAN investment in the HKSAR in the post-1997 period has not been substantial. As indicated in Table 6.2, inflows of FDI from Singapore to the HKSAR declined sharply in 1998 and 1999, before regaining ground in 2000. Since then, however, Singapore's FDI in Hong Kong continued to dwindle, and took a severe beating in 2003 when an outbreak of SARS hit both cities to reach a negative HK$9.9 billion. On the other hand, there was a modest amount of FDI in Hong Kong from Thailand during the 2001–2005 period. While the inflow of FDI from Thailand was negative in 2003, it peaked at HK$28 billion in 2005. As Table 6.3 shows, Thailand remains as a relatively modest investor in Hong Kong. The overall picture of ASEAN–Hong Kong investment relations between 1997 and 2005 is that of declining FDI inflows from Singapore and Thailand. The lack of data on FDI inflows from other ASEAN countries such as Indonesia, Malaysia and the Philippines precludes further analysis. But it is likely that the general trend of declining FDI inflows from ASEAN to the Hong Kong SAR holds true for those countries as well.

In terms of bilateral *trade relations* since 1997, the rapid rise of ASEAN's total trade with Hong Kong prior to 1997 began to ease during the past decade. Table 6.4 shows that, as expected, Hong Kong's total trade with Singapore, Malaysia and Thailand experienced different degrees of decline immediately after 1997. In the case of Singapore, the decline in its total trade with Hong Kong lasted for five years until 2003, whereas it took Malaysia and Thailand three years to recover in their total trade relations with Hong Kong. Still, the post-2000 growth in bilateral trade between

Hong Kong and these three ASEAN countries was relatively slow, indicating the changing global and regional context of international production activity.

Despite this declining trend in total trade with ASEAN, Hong Kong's imports from Singapore, Malaysia, Thailand and the Philippines increased quite dramatically between 2003 and 2006 (Table 6.5). If we measure the growth rates between 1997 and 2006, imports from Singapore, Thailand and the Philippines grew faster than the total imports from all of Hong Kong's trading partners. In the case of the Philippines, Hong Kong's imports from that country increased over 300% between 1997 and 2006 to reach HK$40.8 billion, a level not too far from its imports from Germany, at HK$44.4 billion. In particular, these ASEAN countries are significant suppliers of important raw materials and basic consumer goods to the Hong Kong SAR. In 2002, for example, ASEAN countries were leading suppliers of petroleum, rice, plywood, rubber latex, and frozen shrimps and prawns to Hong Kong (Trade and Industry Department, 2007):

- Singapore is the largest supplier of petroleum: 48% (HK$10 billion) of total imports.
- Thailand is the largest supplier of rice: 83% (HK$834 million) of total imports.
- Malaysia and Indonesia are the first and third largest suppliers of plywood, respectively: together they supply 40% (HK$674 million) of total imports of these products.
- Thailand and Malaysia are the two largest suppliers of rubber latex: together they supply 84% (HK$85 million) of total imports of this product.
- Indonesia and Vietnam are the second and third largest suppliers of frozen shrimps and prawns: together they supply 28% (HK$245 million) of total imports of these products.

During the same period, Hong Kong became an even more important entrepôt for such ASEAN countries as Malaysia, Thailand and the Philippines (Table 6.6). While the growth rate in re-exports from Singapore to Hong Kong stagnated between 1997 and 2006, the growth rates for the other three ASEAN countries were phenomenal, at 150% for Malaysia, 250% for Thailand and over 900% for the Philippines. These figures demonstrate that Hong Kong continues to play a critical role as a conduit for trade between these ASEAN countries and their final export destinations such as Mainland China, Taiwan and Japan. Four re-export categories that are particularly important are: electrical machinery and appliances, office machines, telecommunications equipment, textiles, and fabrics and made-up articles (Trade and Industry Department, 2007).

To sum up this section, the past decade has witnessed dramatic changes in the economic relations between the HKSAR and ASEAN. Hong Kong has clearly lost its role as one of the leading investors in ASEAN countries. Due to internal economic problems in ASEAN countries, ASEAN investment in Hong Kong has also been modest and has weakened. HKSAR–ASEAN trade relations have not performed much better either, with the exception of re-exports. Total trade between the HKSAR and ASEAN declined until 2000 and has not increased much since. During the past 10 years, therefore, there seems to be an increasing tendency towards a decoupling of economic relations between the HKSAR and ASEAN. This change is clearly not coincidental, but an outcome of the complex interplay of different factors that will be explained in the next section.

Accounting for Changes in Economic Relations

This section considers some of the key factors that might explain the changing economic relations between the HKSAR and ASEAN in the past decade. The three factors that are considered are no doubt interrelated, but for reasons of clarity, they are analyzed separately. In particular, the 1997/1998 Asian financial crisis has certainly had an impact in transforming the economic relations between Hong Kong and ASEAN. Meanwhile, the rise of Mainland China as the globally preferred investment location and market has diverted the investment and trade interests of many leading Hong Kong firms away from Southeast Asia. Finally, global production networks in several key sectors, such as electronics and apparel, have been reconfigured in such a way that there has been a great deal of relocation of manufacturing activity from Southeast Asia to China. This in turn is having a significant impact on Hong Kong–ASEAN trade relations.

Asian Financial Crisis

Apart from the reversion of rule over Hong Kong to Mainland China, the second half of 1997 was overshadowed by a region-wide financial crisis that swept virtually all Asian economies. Starting with the devaluation of the Thai baht in August 1997, the crisis seriously disrupted the expanding economies of Indonesia, Thailand and South Korea, decapitalized much of the Malaysian economy, and popped the property bubble in Hong Kong.

During the second half of 1997 and the first half of 1998, many Asian economies saw their currencies depreciate rapidly against the U.S. dollar,[3] their stock markets tumble, their banks and other non-bank financial institutions run into serious trouble, and their annual growth rates plummet downwards. In the words of Mahathir Mohamad, then Prime Minister of Malaysia, the economic turmoil caused by the devaluation of Asian currencies "reduced the [Asian] tigers to whimpering kittens and forced them to seek help from international agencies" (*The Straits Times*, 3 March 1998; see also Krugman, 1998).

Two of the hardest hit ASEAN economies, Indonesia and Thailand, had been very attractive to Hong Kong investors in the period preceding the 1997/1998 crisis. But at a time when Hong Kong itself was facing severe financial strains, many Hong Kong firms understandably took the defensive strategy of pulling back their investments in Southeast Asia, particularly in Indonesia and Thailand. The shrinking domestic markets and limited growth potential in the near future in these hard-hit ASEAN economies were also not encouraging to Hong Kong investors. As indicated in Table 6.7, HKFDI inflows in Indonesia did not recover to pre-1997 levels until at least 2002. In Malaysia, the recovery was slightly faster. In Thailand, HKFDI inflows were highly volatile during the post-crisis period.

The Rise of China

While the Asian financial crisis seriously dampened the interest of Hong Kong investors in ASEAN, it has arguably not been the key factor in driving HKFDI away from Southeast Asia. It is the rise of Mainland China as a major economic powerhouse in the global economy that represents an important challenge to HKSAR–ASEAN economic relations (see also Yeung, 2006, pp. 235–38). On the one hand, the emergence of Mainland China as the world's largest recipient of FDI among developing countries in 2002 has diverted some of the HKFDI inflows that might otherwise have gone to Southeast Asia (Wu and Puah, 2002). Although Table 6.8 shows that Mainland China's inward FDI performance index over the periods 1988–1990 and 1998–2000 remained fairly stable at 53rd and 59th in world rankings, respectively, it is clear that the inward FDI performance indexes and relative rankings of all five ASEAN countries (Singapore, Malaysia, Thailand, the Philippines and Indonesia) deteriorated during the same period. Moreover, the relative share of FDI in the GDP figures of all five Southeast Asian countries between 1988–1990 and 1998–2000

Table 6.8 The Inward FDI Performance Index, 1988–1990 and 1998–2000, for Selected Asian Countries and the U.S.

| | 1988–1990 | | | | | 1998–2000 | | | | |
| | | FDI inflow share over: | | | | | FDI inflow share over: | | | |
	GDP share	Employment share	Exports share	FDI index	Rank	GDP share	Employment share	Exports share	FDI index	Rank
Singapore	12.7	26.5	1.4	13.5	1	2.2	7.5	0.3	3.3	13
Hong Kong	5.0	11.8	0.7	5.9	4	6.3	24.5	1.1	10.6	2
United States	1.1	4.7	2.2	2.7	16	0.9	4.3	1.8	2.3	23
Malaysia	4.3	2.4	1.1	2.6	17	1.6	1.0	0.3	1.0	55
Thailand	2.4	0.6	1.4	1.5	37	0.9	0.3	0.4	0.5	86
Philippines	1.6	0.3	1.1	1.0	48	0.6	0.1	0.3	0.3	103
Taiwan	0.9	1.5	0.3	0.9	51	0.3	0.6	0.1	0.4	98
China	1.0	0.1	1.3	0.8	53	1.3	0.1	1.3	0.9	59
Indonesia	0.8	0.1	0.6	0.5	66	-0.7	-0.1	-0.4	-0.4	136
South Korea	0.4	0.5	0.3	0.4	75	0.6	0.9	0.3	0.6	81
Japan	0.0	0.0	0.0	0.0	101	0.1	0.3	0.1	0.2	120
Asia	1.1	0.2	0.6	0.6	–	0.9	0.2	0.6	0.6	–

Note: The index is based on an unweighted average of three ratios that reflect a country's propensity to attract FDI, taking into account the size and strengths of the economy. The three ratios were obtained by dividing the country's share of global FDI with its shares of global GDP, employment and exports.

Source: Wu and Puah (2002: Table 1; 47).

decreased quite significantly, a reflection of rapid GDP growth in some countries (e.g., from 12.7% to 2.2% for Singapore) and of a dramatic *net* decline in inward FDI in others (e.g., from 0.8% to –0.7% for Indonesia). Mainland China, on the contrary, has seen FDI make up an increasing share of GDP, from 1% during the 1988–1990 period to 1.3% during the 1998–2000 period. This increase in relative share has occurred in spite of dramatic economic growth in the country during the 1990s, underscoring the concurrent rapid influx of FDI during the same period.

This emerging diversion effect of Mainland China as a major destination for HKFDI poses two significant challenges for Southeast Asian economies. First, it has had implications for the post-crisis recovery of Southeast Asia. During the 1999–2003 period, the real GDP growth rates of most Southeast Asian countries remained fairly modest when compared to the pre-crisis 1991–1996 period. To a certain extent, the economic "miracle" in the region prior to the 1997 crisis was facilitated by the rapid influx of FDI into Southeast Asia during the 1980s and the 1990s (see Lim and Fong, 1991; Dobson and Chia, 1997; Giroud, 2003). FDI and limited technology transfers from Hong Kong firms were important in Southeast Asia, in view of the higher "appropriateness" of the technology and production processes of these Hong Kong firms (see Yeung, 1998). The collaborative business relationships between Hong Kong firms and ethnic Chinese manufacturers in Southeast Asia were highly conducive to the development of a Southeast Asian ethnic Chinese form of capitalism (Yeung, 2004). While the trend of diversion is not yet entirely clear, it is conceivable that new waves of FDI from Hong Kong will be more oriented towards penetrating the Mainland Chinese market and further strengthening Mainland China's already strong manufacturing base. This, in turn, presents a significant challenge to the continual survival of ethnic Chinese manufacturers in Southeast Asia who are tending, in turn, to initiate defensive efforts to expand into Mainland China to secure their existing customer base and to develop new market opportunities.

Second, the post-crisis diversion of HKFDI into Mainland China and that country's rapid export-oriented industrialization also imply that ethnic Chinese firms in Southeast Asia will increasingly face formidable competition from Mainland China's exports of manufactured goods.[4] This competition can present itself in two significant forms. Ethnic Chinese firms in Southeast Asia will experience a growing influx of manufactured goods from Mainland China into their home turfs in Southeast Asia. While foreign competition is not necessarily new to Southeast Asian economies, this influx of cheaper imports from China could erode the steady profits that these ethnic Chinese manufacturers have long enjoyed because of their monopolistic positions and cost advantages in their home countries. This problem of competition at home is less significant than that of competition from Mainland China in export markets because of the latter's success in competing on the basis of price. Apart from domestically oriented manufacturers, many ethnic Chinese-owned and controlled manufacturing firms in Southeast Asia are involved in regional production networks that export mainly to North America and, to a certain extent, to Western Europe (e.g., Borrus et al., 2000; Yeung, 2001). The growing competition from foreign- and domestically-owned manufacturers in Mainland China could squeeze out a significant number of these Southeast Asian firms that are involved in the relatively labour-intensive and low-tech production of manufactured goods. Even in the categories of high-tech and value-added manufactured products such as hard disk drives, Southeast Asian suppliers are facing strong competition from Mainland China (McKendrick et al., 2000).

While Southeast Asian investments in China may not yet appear to be very significant, it is clear that China may be a significant destination for outward investment from some Southeast Asian countries. In particular, China is quickly emerging as the most significant destination for the largest investor from Southeast Asia — Singapore. In 1985, China was a relatively insignificant target for outward FDI from Singapore, at S$57.6 million that year or only 2.6% of the city-state's total outward FDI. This trend of the relatively insignificant role of China as a host for Singapore's FDI was maintained throughout the 1990s. By 2000 and 2001, however, China had emerged as that country's single most important destination for outward FDI. China is now the largest host country for Singapore's outward investments and will likely remain very important for Singaporean investors. In cumulative terms, China received S$20.9 billion of FDI from Singapore by the end of 2004, representing 12% of the city-state's total cumulative FDI abroad (Department of Statistics, 2006, p. viii). In view of the Singapore government's emphasis on the regionalization of Singaporean firms into China, this trend of the growing importance of China for Singapore's outward investment is likely to continue into the twenty-first century. The same trend may also occur among other Southeast Asian countries such as Malaysia and Thailand. Manufacturing firms in these two Southeast Asian countries are facing increasing cost pressures to seek alternative production sites and China is likely to be a favourable location for their labour-intensive manufacturing activities. The exact location of these future Southeast Asian investments in China, however, remains unclear. It is quite likely that Southeast Asian investors may move away from the coastal locations of southern China and the Pearl River Delta to seek locations that offer even cheaper labour and land costs.

While no hard data are publicly available on the specific industries and sectors in which Southeast Asian investments in China are concentrated, we can broadly speculate that manufacturing industries and property and infrastructural investments are the two key sectors. The implication of this trend for Hong Kong–ASEAN relations is quite positive in the sense that there are likely to be complementarities in FDI from Hong Kong and Southeast Asia. In fact, many Southeast Asian investors have entered into joint ventures and partnerships with Hong Kong–based investors to invest in China. This trend of co-investment will tend to benefit the Hong Kong economy in the medium and long run for two reasons. First, such partnerships between Hong Kong and Southeast Asian investors in southern China are likely to be more successful than if each were to go it alone because of the complementary resources of the two parties in terms of personal connections, financial backing and international management experience. Second, many of these Southeast Asian investors operate through their offices and subsidiaries in Hong Kong, thereby contributing directly to the demand for Hong Kong's financial, information-related and other professional services.

The role of Hong Kong as a major "stepping stone" for Southeast Asian investors interested in establishing a presence in (southern) China is likely to remain very important in the near future. Most Southeast Asian investors are still hesitant about going into China directly due to both geographical and psychological distances and to China's relatively opaque business environment. Given the trend of growing Southeast Asian investments in southern China, Hong Kong's business services sector will likely benefit from the greater demand for their professional advice and management skills — both in Hong Kong and in China. More Southeast Asian firms are likely to establish regional offices and/or headquarters in Hong Kong to manage and control their China-bound investments.

The recently announced Closer Economic Partnership Arrangement (CEPA) between China and the HKSAR is likely to generate substantial interest among Southeast Asian investors who are keen on investing in China. In those sectors covered under the CEPA (e.g., financial services and professional services), the HKSAR is likely to receive more investments and joint partnership attention from Southeast Asian investors than ever before. These investors are likely to tap into their existing operations in Hong Kong or to establish new operations in Hong Kong if they have not already done so. For example, Singapore's DBS Bank has been aggressively building its presence in Hong Kong's financial sector, acquiring Dao Heng Bank and Kwong On Bank. In the manufacturing sector, however, Southeast Asian investors are unlikely to invest much in Hong Kong to take advantage of the CEPA arrangement (zero tariffs for some goods). This is primarily because Hong Kong's production costs are rather high for most Southeast Asian manufacturers. The lack of many high-tech and world-class manufacturing firms in Southeast Asian countries also explains why Hong Kong is unlikely to receive more manufacturing FDI from Southeast Asia. The net effect of the CEPA will be that Hong Kong's service industries will see growing investment from Southeast Asian firms that are interested in both the Hong Kong market and the China market (via CEPA).

Changing Global Production Networks

Finally, the rapid economic growth of Mainland China represents a much-welcomed opportunity to those ethnic Chinese firms from Southeast Asia that are well positioned and plugged into major global production networks (Fruin, 1998; Borrus et al., 2000; McKendrick et al., 2000; Henderson et al., 2002; Coe et al., 2004; Hess and Yeung, 2006). Their favourable articulation into global production networks can be explained by the early internationalization of these ethnic Chinese firms prior to the mid-1990s, which has already given them substantial operating experience and firm-specific knowledge in manufacturing for major brand-name producers in a variety of industries, e.g., consumer electronics and personal computers (see also Yeung, 2007). The rise of Mainland China thus presents a golden market opportunity for these ethnic Chinese capitalists from Southeast Asia to follow their lead-firm customers who have increasingly established and grounded their global production networks in Mainland China.

Some ethnic Chinese-owned and controlled transnational corporations (TNCs) from Malaysia and Singapore have been quite successful at internationalizing their operations to tap into business opportunities associated with selected global production networks (e.g., Hume Industries from Malaysia, and Wearnes Electronics and MMI Holdings from Singapore). In some cases (e.g., Creative Technology), ethnic Chinese manufacturers from Southeast Asia have grown and/or leapfrogged from original equipment manufacturers (OEMs) to original design manufacturers (ODMs) and original brand manufacturers (OBMs). The emergence of Mainland China as a major market relatively unexploited by leading global firms has exerted a very attractive centrifugal force to induce these ethnic Chinese firms to establish their operations in Mainland China. This centrifugal force has already operated very well on large manufacturing firms from Hong Kong, Taiwan and Singapore (Mathews, 2002; Yeung, 2002; 2007; Chen and Ku, 2004).

Partly due to this reconfiguration of global production networks towards Northeast Asia, Hong Kong–ASEAN investment and trade relations have deteriorated, as fewer Hong Kong firms are investing in Southeast Asia to serve their global lead-firm customers. Instead, these Hong Kong firms are serving these customers through their direct operations in Mainland China. Equally significant is the fact that bilateral trade in intermediary goods has not increased substantially because of this reconfiguration of global production networks.

Conclusion

This chapter has examined the changing economic relations between Hong Kong and Southeast Asia, with a focus on five ASEAN countries. Through a descriptive analysis of official statistics, I have shown how Hong Kong played a fairly significant role as a leading investor in the region prior to 1997. Equally important is the fact that Hong Kong–ASEAN trade was growing very rapidly during this period up to the mid-1990s. There was also a modest amount of Southeast Asian investment in Hong Kong, particularly from Singapore and Thailand. The period prior to 1997 can be described as one in which two-way economic relations were present and strong. Since Hong Kong's reversion to Chinese rule and the concomitant occurrence of the Asian financial crisis in July 1997, however, economic relations between Hong Kong and ASEAN have become changed. Instead of investing heavily in Southeast Asia, Hong Kong is mostly serving as the gateway through which Southeast Asian firms are investing in Mainland China. Hong Kong is no longer contributing significantly to the economic development of Southeast Asia. In accounting for this post-1997 change in the economic relations between Hong Kong and ASEAN countries, I have examined the specific effects of the Asian financial crisis, the rise of Mainland China as a "global factory," and the reconfiguration of global production networks in favour of China. These are powerful forces at play that are drawing the attention of Hong Kong's investors and traders away from Southeast Asia in favour of furthering their existing and/or future activities in Mainland China. The post-1997 weakening of the Hong Kong economy has also substantially affected the financial position of many potential investors who might otherwise have invested in Southeast Asia. Similarly, countries in ASEAN that were hit particularly hard by the Asian financial crisis, such as Indonesia and Thailand, have also become less attractive destinations for investment and trade from Hong Kong.

Several implications for the policy and business communities can be drawn from the above analysis. First, while Mainland China will continue to hold the key to the future of Hong Kong's economy, for strategic reasons, it is perhaps imperative for Hong Kong firms to continue to play the Southeast Asian card. The issue of investment diversification comes to mind. Since Hong Kong has a long history of engaging with Southeast Asia, it would be a strategic failure to write off the region from future plans. The importance for Hong Kong of refocusing on ASEAN has a lot to do with the fact that both Hong Kong and Singapore are "twin cities" for ethnic Chinese capital that will continue to remain strong in the near future (see Wu and Duk, 1995; Wu, 1997). The point here is that Southeast Asia's temporary displacement from the development track, with the exception of Singapore and, perhaps, Thailand, does not necessarily mean that it is impossible for rapid development to take place there in the future. The region has great potential because of its enormous size, resources and diversity. I, therefore, venture to argue that the future of Hong Kong rests as much on Southeast Asia as it does on China.

Second, Southeast Asian investments in Hong Kong remain relatively modest today. There is much more that the policy and business communities in Hong Kong can do to attract greater Hong Kong and/or China-bound investment. Today, Singapore remains the dominant investor from ASEAN in Hong Kong, accounting for perhaps up to 80% of total ASEAN investments in Hong Kong. Still, it is entirely reasonable to expect a greater influx of FDI from other ASEAN countries, particularly by ethnic Chinese capitalists. In Indonesia, Malaysia and Thailand, ethnic Chinese capitalists have continued to dominate the domestic corporate sectors in the post-crisis era (see Yeung, 2004). More importantly, some of the old patriarchs have lost much of their family fortunes during the crisis and have been replaced by a new wave of ethnic Chinese capitalists (see Brown, 2006). Some of these newly rich businessmen do not yet have a significant presence in Hong Kong and/or China. They will be the critical conduits through which Hong Kong–ASEAN economic relations can be strengthened in the future.

Finally, as the global economy continues to undergo drastic restructuring (see Dicken, 2007), the economic relations between Hong Kong and ASEAN will be (re)shaped by these global forces. I have alluded earlier to the role of global production networks in changing Hong Kong–ASEAN relations. Looking ahead, it is foreseeable that global lead firms will manage their supply chains much more efficiently, reducing the need to establish multiple locations throughout East and Southeast Asia. In the computer and electronics industries, for example, the Silicon Valley–Taiwan–China nexus has emerged as the most dominant segment of the global supply chains in these industries. On the other hand, some Japanese electronics manufacturers have made a strategic decision to expand their regional production networks in Southeast Asia to counterbalance their excessive exposure in Mainland China. The manufacturing of some specialized modules such as hard disk drives remains firmly in Southeast Asia (see McKendrick et al., 2000). We are beginning to observe the emergence of a regional production mosaic in East and Southeast Asia that comprises different but increasingly specialized networks. Hong Kong can clearly play a leading role in coordinating these diverse regional production networks that extend from Northeast to Southeast Asia. This would require the policy and business communities in Hong Kong to assume an outlook that is not exclusively oriented towards Mainland China, but towards the world economy as a whole. After all, Hong Kong aims to become Asia's world city, a vision clearly shared by its Southeast Asian counterpart — Singapore.

Notes

1. The choice of these five ASEAN countries is intentional, as these countries and their economic relations with Hong Kong were the focus of a study of mine conducted prior to 1997 (see Yeung, 1998). The same five ASEAN countries have been chosen for this chapter to facilitate a comparative analysis of dynamic changes in Hong Kong–ASEAN relations in the 10 years following Hong Kong's return to Chinese sovereignty in 1997.
2. A note of caution should be mentioned here. Hong Kong investments in China are a post-1979 phenomenon, whereas Hong Kong investments elsewhere within the Asia-Pacific region have taken place since the turn of the twentieth century. Official statistics published by the Chinese authorities, particularly those prior to 2000, must also be read with scepticism. Although Hong Kong

accounts for more than half of the total FDI in China, it is unlikely that all of this investment originates from companies headquartered in Hong Kong (see Low et al., 1998). Rather, a significant proportion of it is from Mainland Chinese and foreign companies that invest in China through their offices in Hong Kong (Fung, 1996). This observation applies to Taiwanese investors in particular (Chiu and Chung, 1993).

3. The only exception was Hong Kong where a pegged rate of US$1 to HK$7.8 was defended at the expense of high domestic interest rates and a severe credit crunch. In Southeast Asia, the Indonesian rupiah depreciated by as much as 72% against the U.S. dollar by early 1998. Other Southeast Asian currencies also depreciated by about 30–40% (*The Straits Times*, 3 March 1998).

4. Interestingly, one may argue that much of Mainland China's exports is accounted for by foreign-owned manufacturing firms, some of which are managed and controlled by ethnic Chinese capitalists from East and Southeast Asia.

References

Ahn, Changmo, Hong-Bum Kim and Dongkoo Chang (2006), "Is East Asia Fit for an Optimum Currency Area? An Assessment of the Economic Feasibility of a Higher Degree of Monetary Cooperation in East Asia," *Developing Economies*, 44 (3): 288–305.

Bank Indonesia (various years), *Indonesian Financial Statistics*. Jakarta: Bank Indonesia.

Bank Negara Malaysia (various years), *Monthly Statistical Bulletin*. Kuala Lumpur: Bank Negara.

Bank of Thailand (various years), *Economic and Financial Statistics*. Bangkok: Bank of Thailand.

Borrus, Michael, Dieter Ernst and Stephen Haggard (eds.) (2000), *International Production Networks in Asia: Rivalry or Riches*. London: Routledge.

Brown, Raj (2006), *The Rise of the Corporate Economy in Southeast Asia*. London: Routledge.

Census and Statistics Department (various years), *External Direct Investment Statistics of Hong Kong*. Hong Kong: Government Printer.

Central Bank of the Philippines (various years), *Annual Report*. Manila: Central Bank.

Chen, Tain-Jy and Ying-Hua Ku (2004), "Networking Strategies of Taiwanese Firms in Southeast Asia and China," in Edmund Terence Gomez and Hsin-Huang Michael Hsiao (eds.), *Chinese Enterprise, Transnationalism, and Identity*. London: RoutledgeCurzon, pp. 151–71.

Chia, Siow Yue (1993), "Foreign Direct Investment in the Singapore Economy." In Ippei Yamazawa and Fu-Chen Lo (eds.), *Evolution of Asia-Pacific*

Economies: International Trade and Direct Investment. Kuala Lumpur: Asian and Pacific Development Centre, pp. 183–232.

Chiu, Lee-in Chen and Chin Chung (1993), "An Assessment of Taiwan's Indirect Investment Towards Mainland China," *Asian Economic Journal*, 7 (1): 41–70.

Chiu, Stephen W. K. and K. Wong (2004), "The Hollowing-out of Hong Kong Electronics: Organizational Inertia and Industrial Restructuring in the 1990s," *Comparative Sociology*, 3 (2): 199–234.

Coe, Neil, Martin Hess, Henry Wai-chung Yeung, Peter Dicken and Jeffrey Henderson (2004), "'Globalizing' Regional Development: A Global Production Networks Perspective," *Transactions of the Institute of British Geographers*, New Series, 29 (4): 468–84.

Department of Economic Research (various years), *Yearbook*. Manila: DER.

Department of Statistics (various years), *Foreign Equity Investment in Singapore*. Singapore: DOS.

—— (2006), *Singapore's Investment Abroad, 2004*. Singapore: DOS.

Dicken, Peter (2007), *Global Shift: Mapping the Changing Contours of the World Economy*, 5th edition. London: Sage.

Dobson, Wendy and Chia Siow Yue (eds.) (1997), *Multinationals and East Asian Integration*. Singapore: Institute of Southeast Asian Studies.

Eng, Irene (1997), "Flexible Production in Late Industrialization: The Case of Hong Kong," *Economic Geography*, 73 (1): 26–43.

Federation of Hong Kong Industries (1990), *Hong Kong's Offshore Investment: A Survey on Hong Kong's Industrial Investment in Overseas Countries*. Hong Kong: Federation of Hong Kong Industries.

Fruin, W. Mark (ed.) (1998), *Networks, Markets, and the Pacific Rim: Studies in Strategy*. New York: Oxford University Press.

Fung, K. C. (1996), "Mainland Chinese Investment in Hong Kong: How Much, Why, and So What?" *Journal of Asian Business*, 12 (2): 21–39.

Gamble, J., J. Morris and B. Wilkinson (2004), "Mass Production is Alive and Well: The Future of Work and Organization in East Asia," *International Journal of Human Resource Management*, 15 (2): 397–409.

Giroud, Axele (2003), *Transnational Corporations, Technology and Economic Development: Backward Linkages and Knowledge Transfer in Southeast Asia*. Cheltenham: Edward Elgar.

Henderson, Jeffrey, Peter Dicken, Martin Hess, Neil Coe and Henry Wai-chung Yeung (2002), "Global Production Networks and the Analysis of Economic Development," *Review of International Political Economy*, 9 (3): 436–64.

Hess, Martin and Henry Wai-chung Yeung (2006), "Whither Global Production Networks in Economic Geography? Past, Present and Future," *Environment and Planning A*, 38 (7): 1193–204.

Ho, Kong Chong and Alvin So (1997), "Semi-periphery and Borderland Integration:

Singapore and Hong Kong Experiences," *Political Geography*, 16 (3): 241–59.

Ho, Yin-Ping (1992), *Trade, Industrial Restructuring and Development in Hong Kong*. London: Macmillan.

Huang, Yasheng (2002), *Selling China: Foreign Direct Investment during the Reform Era*. Cambridge: Cambridge University Press.

Krugman, Paul (1998), "Asia: What Went Wrong?" *Fortune*, 137 (4): 32.

Leung, Chi-kin (1993), "Personal Contacts, Subcontracting Linkages, and Development in the Hong Kong–Zhujiang Delta Region," *Annals of the Association of American Geographers*, 83 (2): 272–302.

Lim, Linda Y. C. and Pang-Eng Fong (1991), *Foreign Direct Investment and Industrialization in Malaysia, Singapore, Taiwan and Thailand*. Paris: OECD.

Low, Linda, Eric D. Ramstetter and Henry Wai-chung Yeung (1998), "Accounting for Outward Direct Investment from Hong Kong and Singapore: Who Controls What?" In Robert E. Baldwin, Robert E. Lipsey and J. David Richardson (eds.), *Geography and Ownership as Bases for Economic Accounting*. Chicago: University of Chicago Press, pp. 139–68.

Lui, Tai Lok and W. K. Stephen Chiu (1994), "A Tale of Two Industries: The Restructuring of Hong Kong's Garment Making and Electronics Industries," *Environment and Planning A*, 26 (1): 53–70.

McKendrick, David G., Richard F. Doner and Stephan Haggard (2000), *From Silicon Valley to Singapore: Location and Competitive Advantage in the Hard Disk Drive Industry*. Stanford: Stanford University Press.

Malaysian Industrial Development Authority (various years), *Annual Report*. Kuala Lumpur: MIDA

Mathews, John A. (2002), *Dragon Multinational: A New Model for Global Growth*. Oxford: Oxford University Press.

Nyaw, Mee-kau, Gordon C. K. Cheung and C. Y. Chang (2001), "Money Migration: An Assessment of ASEAN's Investment in China with Special Reference to Chinese Diaspora Investment After 1979," *Journal of World Investment*, 2 (3): 339–455.

Thoburn, John T., H. M. Leung, Esther Chau and S. H. Tang (1990), *Foreign Investment in China under the Open Policy: The Experience of Hong Kong Companies*. Aldershot: Avebury.

Trade and Industry Department, Hong Kong SAR government (2007), *Fact Sheet on ASEAN Countries*, http://www.tid.gov.hk, accessed on 5 March 2007.

United Nations Conference on Trade and Development (UNCTAD) (1996), *World Investment Report 1996: Investment, Trade and International Policy Arrangements*. New York: United Nations.

UNCTC (1992), *World Investment Directory 1992: Foreign Direct Investment, Legal Framework and Corporate Data. Volume 1: Asia and the Pacific*. New York: United Nations.

Wong, Siu-lun (1988), *Emigrant Entrepreneurs: Shanghai Industrialists in Hong Kong*. Hong Kong: Oxford University Press.

Wu, Friedrich (1997), "Hong Kong and Singapore: A Tale of Two Asian Business Hubs," *Journal of Asian Business*, 13 (2): 1–17.

Wu, Friedrich and Sin Yue Duk (1995), "Hong Kong and Singapore: 'Twin Capitals' for Overseas Chinese Capital," *Business and the Contemporary World*, 7 (3): 21–33.

Wu, Friedrich and Kok Keong Puah (2002), "Foreign Direct Investment to China and Southeast Asia: Has ASEAN Been Losing Out?" *Journal of Asian Business*, 18 (3): 45–58.

Yeung, Godfrey (2001), *Foreign Investment and Socio-Economic Development in China: The Case of Dongguan*. Basingstoke: Palgrave.

Yeung, Henry Wai-chung (1994), "Hong Kong Firms in the ASEAN Region: Transnational Corporations and Foreign Direct Investment," *Environment and Planning A*, 26 (12): 1931–56.

—— (1995), "The Geography of Hong Kong Transnational Corporations in the ASEAN Region," *Area*, 27 (4): 318–34.

—— (1996), "The Historical Geography of Hong Kong Investments in the ASEAN Region," *Singapore Journal of Tropical Geography*, Singapore, 17 (1): 66–82.

—— (1998), *Transnational Corporations and Business Networks: Hong Kong Firms in the ASEAN Region*. London: Routledge.

—— (2000), "Neoliberalism, *Laissez-faire* Capitalism and Economic Crisis: The Political Economy of Deindustrialisation in Hong Kong," *Competition and Change*, 4 (2): 121–69.

—— (2001), "Organising Regional Production Networks in Southeast Asia: Implications for Production Fragmentation, Trade and Rules of Origin," *Journal of Economic Geography*, 1 (3): 299–321.

—— (2002), *Entrepreneurship and the Internationalisation of Asian Firms: An Institutional Perspective*. Cheltenham: Edward Elgar.

—— (2004), *Chinese Capitalism in a Global Era: Towards Hybrid Capitalism*. London: Routledge.

—— (2006), "Change and Continuity in Southeast Asian Business," *Asia Pacific Journal of Management*, 23 (3): 229–54.

—— (2007), "From Followers to Market Leaders: Asian Electronics Firms in the Global Economy," *Asia Pacific Viewpoint*, 48 (1): 1–25.

Yu, Fu-Lai Tony (1997), *Entrepreneurship and Economic Development in Hong Kong*. London: Routledge.

Zhang, Zhaoyong and Chin Hock Ow (1996), "Trade Interdependence and Direct Foreign Investment between ASEAN and China," *World Development*, 24 (1): 155–70.

PART II

❖ ❖ ❖

Hong Kong as Seen from Within

In Search of a New Political Order

Lau Siu-kai

The restoration of sovereignty over Hong Kong by China on 1 July 1997 signified a fundamental transformation in the political status of the former British crown colony. Despite assurances by both Beijing and London that there would be no change to Hong Kong's institutional structure and lifestyle for 50 years following the handover and the enshrinement of these promises in the Sino-British Joint Declaration and the Basic Law, there is no denying that the formation of a new political order under the "one country, two systems" (OCTS) framework is proving to be a difficult and uncertain process. The decade after Hong Kong's handover to China has witnessed a tortuous and occasionally tumultuous process of building a new political order consistent with Beijing's design for Hong Kong (Lau, 2000a). Substantial progress has definitely already been made. However, the process of building a new political order under OCTS is still an ongoing process fraught with uncertainties, contestation and difficulties. By now, it is clear that an embryonic political order that complies with the original intentions of Beijing's policy towards Hong Kong has emerged. We can anticipate with some degree of optimism that, barring unforeseen circumstances, this new political order will be further consolidated in the years ahead, allowing Hong Kong to continue to progress as a Special Administrative Region (SAR) of China while enjoying a more cooperative relationship than before with both the Mainland and the Central People's Government (CPG).

The New Political Order under "One Country, Two Systems"

In contrast with the experience of decolonization in most of the former

British colonies, Hong Kong's exit from colonial rule did not take the form of independence. Instead, Hong Kong underwent a unique process of "decolonization without independence" (Lau, 1990, 1997a). In addition, the end of colonial rule in Hong Kong was not the result of a powerful independence movement led by strong and charismatic political leaders. Instead, it was achieved by peaceful negotiations between China and Britain. Consequently, Hong Kong's post-colonial fate was arranged from "above" without the involvement of local leaders. In fact, not only was the process of "decolonization" in Hong Kong not conducive to the rise of popular political leaders, it actually further weakened and divided Hong Kong's political leaders, due to the ferocious tug-of-war that took place between Beijing and London. The continued mistrust of Beijing, nostalgia for colonial governance, and anxieties about the future among Hongkongers, together with the debilitated and polarized local leadership on the eve of the departure of Britain, have created a situation uncongenial to the formation of a new political order that is compatible with the requirements of the OCTS design conceived by Beijing.

In accordance with China's policy towards Hong Kong, any new political order (NPO)[1] under the framework of OCTS should have the following features:

(1) Acceptance of the new political status of Hong Kong as an SAR of China, with its corresponding privileges and duties. There should be no return to colonial rule or quasi-colonial rule (i.e., "rule by Britain without the British").

(2) Acceptance of China's sovereignty over Hong Kong, recognition of the legitimacy of the CPG, and respect for the constitutional powers and prerogatives of the central authorities.

(3) Acceptance of the OCTS arrangements for Hong Kong and faithful compliance with and full-scale implementation of the Basic Law.

(4) Trust in the CPG and its sincerity in abiding by the OCTS policy.

(5) Belief in the primacy of mutual interests between Hong Kong and the Mainland and in the centrality of a cooperative relationship between Hong Kong and the CGP.

(6) Willingness to take account of the interests, views and concerns of the central authorities when handling Hong Kong's affairs, particularly in areas relating to national security, sovereignty and territorial integrity. More specifically, Hong Kong should abstain from interfering in the Mainland's affairs and should not allow

the territory to become a base for anti-communist activities or of subversive activities against the CPG.

(7) Recognition of the constitutional superiority of the central authorities in constituting Hong Kong's political system. This recognition is based on the constitutional principle that Hong Kong's high degree of autonomy is delegated by Beijing and not derived from the people of Hong Kong.

(8) Acceptance of the "executive-led" political system, particularly the electoral system, the division of powers between the executive and the legislature, and the division of powers between Hong Kong and the central authorities, stipulated by the Basic Law as well as the principles and rules governing its modification.

(9) The Hong Kong SAR to be governed by "patriots" who are defined as Hong Kong people who are sincerely willing to accept and uphold China's policy towards Hong Kong and the Basic Law.

(10) Hegemony of the beliefs and ideology behind the NPO in Hong Kong.

Before the handover in 1997, as a result of numerous statements from state leaders and Beijing officials, the basic features of the NPO were to a certain degree known to Hongkongers, even though they did not accept all of them, especially the gradualist pace of democratic development, the supremacy of the executive over the legislature and the primacy of the "central authorities" over the SAR. The political opposition, by nature the anti-new order forces (ANOF), contested the NPO all along. The departing colonial rulers also played a prominent role in disseminating ideas that impeded the acceptance of the NPO by Hong Kong people. At the same time, the colonial regime in its twilight days actively unleashed and organized the ANOF and partnered with them to counteract the political offensive of Beijing before the handover, with the expectation also that they would play a salient political role after 1997. After the handover, for about six years, the central authorities decided to adopt an inactive approach towards Hong Kong to demonstrate to Hongkongers and the international community their sincerity in observing Hong Kong's high degree of autonomy. One aspect of this approach was the absolute silence maintained by state leaders, Mainland officials and scholars with regard to Hong Kong affairs, even though the place was embroiled in political turmoil and the ANOF were in the ascendance. Consequently, the ANOF were able to present their ideas of what the post-colonial order should be and have gained much approval from the populace. The pro-new order forces (PNOF) in Hong Kong, being fragmented and unpopular, were unable to contain the ANOF's offensive. In the better part of the first decade of the Hong Kong Special Administrative Region (HKSAR), therefore, the idea of the NPO is understood by Beijing and the PNOF failed to achieve ideological hegemony.

The NPO propagated by the ANOF differs from the NPO as conceived by Beijing in a number of fundamental aspects. The ANOF basically want to define a high degree of autonomy as "complete" autonomy, where the powers and prerogatives of the central authorities are greatly reduced and their exercise of them circumscribed. They place primacy on Hong Kong's system as against that of the country, betraying a strong streak of "intransigent localism." They defy the authority of the executive and seek to arrogate more constitutional powers to the legislature and the judiciary. They advocate a programme of fast-pace democratization. And they take an adversarial approach towards the central authorities. The ascendancy of the ideas of the ANOF is inevitably making it difficult in post-1997 Hong Kong to establish an NPO that is compatible with China's OCTS policy, unavoidably complicating the problem of governance in the territory.

Some Basic Contradictions in the Post-1997 Situation

On the surface, China's OCTS policy is a wise strategy to deal with the problem of Hong Kong's post-1997 future. Formulated back in the early 1980s, OCTS in fact was the outcome of a rare coincidence of the interests of China, the Chinese Communist Party (CCP) and Hong Kong people at an important juncture in China's historical development. At that juncture, the replacement of class struggle by economic development as the primary task of the CCP after the end of the Great Proletariat Cultural Revolution means that Hong Kong's prosperous capitalist system could play a critically important role in China's economic modernization. Although Hong Kong's economic contribution to China had been of much value even before that juncture, the value was much more appreciated by the state leaders in view of China's needs and challenges in the years ahead. As a result, the preservation of Hong Kong's capitalist system was to the mutual interest of China and Hong Kong. Not surprisingly, OCTS was very much welcomed by Hongkongers and instrumental in maintaining a decent level of public confidence in the future of the territory.

Nevertheless, the attractiveness of OCTS to Hongkongers does not mean that the NPO as conceived by China will easily take root in the HKSAR. There are several basic contradictions in the post-handover situation that inhibit the formation of the NPO. These contradictions are inherent in Hong Kong's historical background and in the way it has "decolonized."

For one-and-a-half centuries, Hong Kong people, many of whom had fled the Mainland to avoid political oppression, treasured the protection against the various Chinese regimes that the colonial rulers provided. Colonial rule was also associated with Hong Kong's post–World War II economic miracle and social progress. Many Hongkongers were resistant to and fearful of Hong Kong's return to China, even though they had won the best possible deal from Beijing. In this politico-psychological context, it was natural that the majority of Hong Kong people would succumb to the political persuasions of the ANOF. The ANOF represent a conglomeration of elements that cut across social classes and previous political allegiances. The main components of the ANOF are the political parties (notably the Democratic Party and the Civic Party), a number of politicians and retired senior civil servants groomed by the colonial regime, democratic activists who once were viewed by the colonial regime with suspicion and apprehension, intellectuals steeped in Western political ideals, anti-communists and public personalities with liberal proclivities. What unite them are mistrust and hostility towards Chinese communists and their desire to see China democratizing in the Western fashion. Their common goal is to bring about "full democracy" in Hong Kong as soon as possible so that Hongkongers can have more power at their disposal to withstand any possible political interference from Beijing after the handover. They portray themselves as the guardians of Hong Kong's interests and the spokesmen of Hong Kong citizens. Since the early 1980s and before the handover, they were deliberately and effectively cultivated and promoted by the departing British, who apparently wanted them to control the reins of power after the handover and, before that, serve as political allies of the colonial regime to withstand Beijing's political offensive. In fact, in spite of the departure of the British, in the better part of the first decade after 1997, the ANOF enjoyed both ideological hegemony and popular support, despite their inability to obtain the highest position in the HKSAR. Still, they have managed to exert varying degrees of influence in the government, the Legislative Council, the district advisory bodies, the political parties and the media. The middle classes are particularly susceptible to their political appeals.

On the contrary, the PNOF, the chief supporters and advocates of the

NPO conceived by Beijing, are fragmented and unpopular. The PNOF are composed of leading businessmen, the Leftists who owe their loyalty to the CCP, community leaders who jumped on the Beijing bandwagon after the future of Hong Kong was sealed, and Hongkongers with strong nationalistic sentiments. The two major political parties of the PNOF are the Democratic Alliance for Betterment of Hong Kong and the Liberal Party. The PNOF are also a cross-class grouping whose unifying tie is their cooperative and deferential attitude towards Beijing. Even though the PNOF potentially have a lot of economic resources at their disposal, the fragmented nature of the business community, its ability to engage in back-door political manoeuvring and its wariness about entering into popular politics have rendered them largely irrelevant as a potent political force in the mass political arena. In any case, the PNOF's pro-Beijing position has become a liability, hampering them in their efforts to win the hearts and minds of Hong Kong people, especially the more educated segment of the population. With only minority support in the territory, the PNOF are not accepted by Hongkongers as the post-colonial governors of Hong Kong.

Since both the ANOF and the PNOF are made up of people with heterogeneous socioeconomic interests, both political groupings are afflicted with the problems of serious conflicts of interest and of personality. In addition, unlike charismatic independence leaders in other former colonies, both political groupings lack strong mass support and have limited capacity to mobilize politically. Still, the ANOF are much more organized and influential than the PNOF in the arena of popular politics.

Beijing fully understood the resistance of Hong Kong people to the handover. In order to placate the population and to bolster their confidence in the future of Hong Kong, Beijing decided not to allow the PNOF to take over the post-1997 Hong Kong regime, instead only giving them a minority place in it. But Beijing did not dare to entrust governing power to the ANOF either, as they were viewed with apprehension and fear. Instead, by appointing Tung Chee-hwa as the first Chief Executive of the HKSAR and relying heavily on the civil servants who used to serve the colonial regime as the principal officials, Beijing hoped to attain a tolerable level of governability in post-1997 Hong Kong.

Nevertheless, the inability of the PNOF to assume power after 1997 means that the NPO as envisaged by Beijing will not be realized. *The need to build the NPO and the marginalization of the PNOF represents the first basic contradiction in the post-1997 political situation.* Even though Tung viewed the idea of the NPO with approval, he lacked sufficient charisma, public support and sympathy from his own government to single-handedly install the NPO in Hong Kong. Moreover, in both his first term and his truncated second term as the Chief Executive of the HKSAR, Tung did accord a great deal of symbolic recognition to the PNOF, but refrained from giving them substantive powers and influence within his administration. As a result, the PNOF were bitter, frustrated and demoralized, further eroding their ability to promote the NPO.

A second basic contradiction lies in the discrepancy between the democratic aspirations of Hongkongers and the institutional requirements of OCTS. The central objective of China's policy towards Hong Kong is to fully implement the policy of OCTS, which is an integral part of China's comprehensive developmental strategy. A core component of the OCTS policy is an executive-led political system that is very similar to the previous colonial political system. At the apex of the political system is the Chief Executive of the HKSAR who, being responsible to the CPG and the HKSAR, is the key person to ensure that the project of OCTS is fully realized in Hong Kong. The partial democratic political system of Hong Kong will then gradually evolve to become more democratic in character. Under no circumstances, however, should democratic development be allowed to undermine the OCTS project. On the contrary, democratic development should contribute to the success of OCTS and the attainment of its major goals. In short, the implementation of OCTS comes before democratization.

Undeniably, the political system stipulated by the Basic Law is much more "democratic" than the previous colonial system, where all political powers were in the hands of the colonial governor and there were no autonomous political powers outside the colonial regime. Nevertheless, the promise of "Hong Kong run by Hong Kong people" made by Beijing, the inactive approach of the central authorities in the first six years of the HKSAR, the gradual rise in public confidence in Hong Kong's political future and, most unexpectedly, the strengthening of the belief among Hongkongers that Beijing is vulnerable to popular pressure have led to a visible increase in democratic aspirations in Hong Kong. The ANOF have deliberately positioned themselves as the champions of those with rising democratic aspirations — aspirations that were further raised by the less-than-satisfactory performance of the government and the mounting economic difficulties in the first year of the HKSAR. Needless to say, the widening gap between the rising democratic demands of Hongkongers and their incompatibility with the institutional requirements of OCTS is making the installation of the NPO and the situation of the PNOF extremely difficult.

A third basic contradiction is the incompatibility between the inactive approach of Beijing towards Hong Kong and the requirements for building the NPO. Inasmuch as creating the NPO is essential to the successful implementation of the OCTS policy, and in view of the comparative weakness of the PNOF, it is necessary for Beijing to play a role in promoting the NPO in Hong Kong. It is not advisable for the central authorities to encroach upon the autonomous powers that have been granted to Hong Kong; however, as the success of OCTS is a matter of serious concern for both Hong Kong and China, Beijing does have the right to ensure that the practice of OCTS in Hong Kong follows the blueprint laid down by Deng Xiaoping. In fact, even when Hong Kong went through a prolonged period of economic and political turbulence immediately after the handover and state leaders and CPG officials were of the view that the SAR had gone off on a wrong track, Beijing managed to adhere to its policy of non-intervention. The central government's self-restraint went a long way towards reassuring Hongkongers and the world of its sincerity in adhering to the policy of OCTS. This inactive stance, however, further weakened the PNOF and the Tung administration and, at the same time, provided a boost to the ANOF. Under these adverse circumstances, not only was it impossible to create the NPO, it was well-nigh impossible to maintain strong governmental authority and effective governance.

In retrospect, Beijing's policy of inactivity after Hong Kong's return to China was made before 1997 and was intended to bolster the authority of Tung Chee-hwa by demonstrating to the world that Tung was his own man. It was also an approach based on a number of assumptions about post-handover Hong Kong that were refuted by subsequent developments. Beijing assumed that post-handover Hong Kong would continue to enjoy economic prosperity. It also assumed that Hong Kong people would understand and respect Beijing's interests and concerns, that all of the senior civil servants inherited from the colonial regime would change their allegiance and wholeheartedly serve the new administration, that the political forces antagonistic to the CCP would exercise self-restraint and pursue a peaceful though separate coexistence with it, that the news media would be friendly or at least not too hostile towards Beijing, and that the new HKSAR government and the PNOF would expand greatly because of the change in "political master." Even though the central authorities came increasingly to realize that these assumptions lacked validity, it took some time for them to acknowledge that their policy of inaction was inappropriate and that a new approach to handling post-1997 Hong Kong was needed. In fact, it was the large-scale popular demonstration against the Tung administration that took place on 1 July 2003, instigated by the HKSAR government's attempt to push through legislation on Article 23 of the Basic Law, which prompted Beijing to take active steps to prevent the derailment of the OCTS project in Hong Kong.

The fourth basic contradiction is the need to achieve ideological decolonization and the lack of will to do so. Despite Beijing's pledge to maintain Hong Kong's pre-1997 status quo after the end of colonial rule, the implementation of OCTS still requires an ideological reorientation towards China, the CCP, the central authorities and compatriots in the Mainland. It also necessitates a rethinking of Hong Kong's relationship with the country and the outside world. Making ideological changes in these respects, however, does not entail the denigration of colonial rule and rejection of colonial legacies. It certainly calls for the imaginative crafting of a new Hong Kong identity that creatively combines patriotic sentiments, a pragmatic understanding of Hong Kong's situation and the selective preservation of those aspects of the colonial legacy that represent "modernity." Nevertheless, very little has been done since the handover to respond to the imperative of ideological reorientation. Strong psychological resistance to anything that smacks of political "brainwashing" has been one reason for the lack of such efforts. The weakness of the PNOF and the Tung administration has been another reason. What is worse is that the ANOF is taking advantage of the situation to reorient Hongkongers towards a direction marked by nostalgia for colonial rule, Hong Kong localism, and mistrust of Beijing and indifference to its OCTS policy.

The fifth basic contradiction is the need for a political coalition that can sustain Beijing's OCTS framework and the lukewarm attempts that have been made so far to bring this about. The composition of the political coalition should be inclusive enough so that it can enjoy a broad base of social support. Theoretically, the coalition should include not only the PNOF, but also centrist forces in society. In order to succeed, the encouragement and endorsement of the central authorities for such a grouping are indispensable. Beijing's inactive approach after the handover was not conducive to the formation of the coalition. Beijing's wariness of the emergence of organized political forces in Hong Kong is easily understood. If the central government were to encourage any particular political grouping, its actions might be criticized as political interference in Hong Kong affairs. Moreover, Beijing was worried about the possibility of the coalition being "captured" by local forces and opinion (Lau and Kuan,

2000, 2002). In any case, the unpopularity of the PNOF remains an insurmountable obstacle in any effort at coalition-building. Moreover, the embattled Tung administration was in no position to initiate a coalition-building project even with Beijing's endorsement. Worse, not only was no attempt at coalition-building made, but the PNOF became even more disorganized, divided and weaker because of growing conflicts of interest and personal rivalries (Lau, 1999a). Without a powerful and dedicated political coalition that identifies with the NPO and that will spearhead its development, no serious and effective effort at achieving it can be started.

The sixth basic contradiction is the discrepancy between the intention behind the OCTS arrangement of maintaining the status quo and a fast-changing Hong Kong society. The elaborate specification of various public policies inside the Basic Law is supposed to convince Hong Kong people that the institutions and lifestyle of Hong Kong will remain unchanged for 50 years after the handover. By and large, the provisions in the Basic Law represent the "consensus" in Hong Kong in the 1980s. But fast and unpredictable social changes are the norm in the territory. In reality, the transition that occurred in Hong Kong around 1997 was more than just the political one of going from a British colony to an SAR of China. It also represented the dramatic transformation of Hong Kong into a knowledge- and service-based economy, with all of the attendant social dislocations. The widening income gap between the rich and the poor has given rise to many palpable social grievances and accusations of social injustice. Increasingly, the existing economic and social policies are being regarded with public scepticism and uneasiness. Consequently, in some aspects, the "consensus" that was reached on Hong Kong's social, economic and political needs and policies had eroded even before the handover. Gradually, to some people, the Basic Law appears to be constraining Hong Kong's long-term development. Awareness of the inadequacies of the Basic Law, however, will not immediately lead to a new "consensus" on Hong Kong's developmental and policy needs. In the transitional stage, which covers the whole first decade of the HKSAR, where the weakened "old" consensus jockeyed for ideological dominance with the yet-to-be-formed "new" consensus, society was riven by conflicting interests and viewpoints. It is almost impossible to create a new political order when there is no consensus on the kind of social and economic order that should prevail in the territory (Lau, 1997b).

The seventh basic contradiction is the inconsistency between the promise of maintaining Hong Kong's pre-1997 status quo and the need to create the NPO. Naturally, there exists in Hong Kong different understandings of what constitutes the status quo ante, but there is a tendency for different people to characterize it in accordance with their own interests and values. The ANOF are particularly prone to "romanticize" the past in order to thwart any changes to which they are opposed. As nostalgia about life under colonialism is widespread, particularly in view of the dramatic economic downturn that occurred after the handover and the enormous sense of uncertainty about the future that this downturn has generated, there is a tendency among many Hong Kong people to "rigidify" the status quo ante. This conservative mentality is impeding the making of major changes in institutions, policies and ways of doing things. Under these circumstances, the building of the NPO is bound to encounter psychological resistance.

The eighth basic contradiction has to do with the dual allegiance of the Chief Executive of the HKSAR. Article 43 of the Basic Law stipulates that the "Chief Executive of the HKSAR shall be accountable to the Central People's Government and the HKSAR in accordance with the provisions of this law." The use of the term "Hong Kong Special Administrative Region" instead of the term "Hong Kong residents" was deliberate and well thought out. It carries the implication that the responsibility of the Chief Executive is to ensure the faithful implementation in Hong Kong of the OCTS project in accordance with China's policy. In doing so, the Chief Executive would be executing a function whose success or failure involves the basic interests of all Chinese people. This means that the Chief Executive's responsibility is not to the people of Hong Kong alone, but also to the people of the whole of China. If this interpretation of Article 43 is shared by both the central authorities and Hongkongers, there should be no basic contradiction between them. However, many Hong Kong people, the ANOF in particular, understand Article 43 to mean that the Chief Executive should be *equally* accountable to the CPG and to Hong Kong residents. On the other hand, in the NPO formulated by Beijing, the Chief Executive is the only interface between the two "systems" under "one country." He has a responsibility to the CPG to faithfully implement the grand project of OCTS in Hong Kong *in spite of* the preferences of Hongkongers, as OCTS is in the latter's ultimate interest. Since many Hong Kong people have a different understanding of OCTS from that of Beijing in some fundamental aspects, and since they are demanding primary accountability from the Chief Executive, a collision between these Hongkongers and Beijing is inevitable. Such a collision would not auspicious to the building of the NPO.

The Gradual Emergence of the Embryonic New Political Order

Notwithstanding the basic contradictions existing in post-1997 Hong Kong, by the end of the HKSAR's first decade, an embryonic NPO has eventually emerged. Although there is still a long way to go before the full-blown NPO can be realized, decent progress has been made in making governance in post-handover Hong Kong less difficult. Needless to say, the process of building the embryonic NPO is a messy one. No deliberate plans have been made, nor has such planning been possible. Instead, the embryonic NPO is the result of a prolonged process of conflictive interactions among various political actors, changes in the political mentality of Hongkongers, improvements in the governing strategy of the HKSAR government, an economic recovery and the inexorable decline of the ANOF. Behind all of this is the rise of China as a great power in the world and the surge of nationalism and patriotism in Hong Kong that this has aroused. One may surmise that the eventual emergence of the NPO is preordained by history because, given the balance of powers between the central authorities and the ANOF on the one hand, and the changing balance of power between the PNOF and the ANOF on the other, Hong Kong has no choice but to embrace the NPO as conceived by Beijing. At the same time, the interplay between Beijing and Hong Kong would also result in some modifications of the NPO, which would make it more acceptable to Hong Kong people.

Beijing's strategic reorientation of its approach towards Hong Kong immediately after the huge mass demonstration in mid-2003 has had a crucial impact on Hong Kong's political landscape. While the central government's apprehension about the derailment of the OCTS project in Hong Kong grew continuously before the event, its worries over the governability of the territory and the rapid build-up of the ANOF reached a critical threshold that compelled them into action. From this point onwards, Beijing openly and vocally showed its unhappiness with and anxiety over Hong Kong's post-handover development. State leaders, Mainland officials and scholars issued numerous messages that in effect reiterated China's policy towards Hong Kong and the proper way to understand the arrangement of OCTS. Beijing also made known its displeasure and disagreement with the ANOF; at the same time, it has been engaging them in dialogue so as not to offend public sentiment. Most important, Beijing acceded to the request from the Tung administration for a closer economic partnership between Hong Kong and the Mainland. The central government unveiled several economic measures in rapid succession, with the purpose of boosting Hong Kong's lacklustre economy and the confidence of Hong Kong people in the territory's future. These measures included intensifying economic cooperation between Hong Kong and Guangdong, the Closer Economic Partnership Arrangement (CEPA), the Individual Visit Scheme, and authorizing Hong Kong to conduct some forms of *renminbi* business. All of these measures had an immediate and dramatic economic impact, earning Beijing a great deal of goodwill from Hongkongers. The steps taken by Beijing simultaneously improved Hongkongers' trust in the central authorities, boosted public confidence in OCTS, bolstered the prestige of the Tung administration, restored a degree of political tranquillity to Hong Kong, afforded breathing room for the PNOF to recover and regroup, and restrained the ANOF. At the same time, Beijing took active steps to protect its vital interests. The most important of these steps was the "unsolicited" interpretation of the Basic Law by the Standing Committee of the National People's Congress in April 2004, which rejected the selection of the Chief Executive of the HKSAR by popular election in 2007 and of the Legislative Council in 2008. As the ANOF was always exploiting the issue of popular elections against the Tung administration, the temporary removal of the issue from the public agenda gave considerable relief to the embattled Hong Kong government. Surprisingly, though the ANOF cried foul and accused Beijing of undermining Hong Kong's high degree of autonomy and making a travesty of the principle of "Hong Kong people running Hong Kong," Hongkongers took Beijing's actions in stride. Hong Kong people might not welcome Beijing's move to take an active and proactive approach towards Hong Kong; however, they responded in a calm and ambivalent manner. Apparently, Hongkongers are fed up with the political conflicts and turmoil that have beset the territory after 1997 and are unhappy with the performance of both the Tung administration and the political opposition. The political assertiveness of Beijing is a timely response to the craving of Hong Kong people for authority and order. All in all, Beijing's political and economic initiatives have drastically changed the political landscape of Hong Kong.

The transformation of the governing strategy of the HKSAR government has also gone a long way in changing the political situation in Hong Kong. The major effects of the new strategy are the enhancement of governmental authority, a steady rise in the popularity of the government, and the gradual political marginalization of the ANOF. These effects have been further magnified by the replacement of Tung Chee-hwa by Donald

Tsang Yam-kuen as the Chief Executive in mid-2005. The new strategy, initially formulated during Tung's second term and largely inherited by Donald Tsang, has the following main components:

(1) Intensified economic cooperation between Hong Kong and the Mainland as the mainstay of the strategy of economic development;

(2) Creation of a layer of politically appointed "ministers" to replace the former "politically neutral" civil-servant "ministers" for the purpose of strengthening the political capability of the government.

(3) "People-based" governance, where the well-being of the people is the major responsibility of government and where responsiveness to public opinion is given strong emphasis.

(4) Developing a new mode of policy-making by involving various sectors of the community in the early stages of policy formulation, particularly at the time when a broad strategic or policy direction is charted.

(5) Engagement with the political opposition to reduce political confrontation.

(6) Closer cooperation with political friends and allies to form a loose "governing coalition."

(7) Promoting social harmony through more concern for the needs of the man in the street.

(8) Fostering a new Hong Kong identity of pride in being both Hongkongese and Chinese.

The implementation of the new strategy over a few years has borne visible political fruit. The incremental accumulation of political experience by the governing elites is also enabling them to handle political issues more skilfully, at the very least to avoid unnecessary mistakes that can be blown out of proportion to become political crises. By the end of the first decade of the HKSAR, the popularity of the government has come to surpass that of the opposition, even though public support for the PNOF still lags behind that for the ANOF. Public aspirations for democratic development are still strong, but Hongkongers have become more ambivalent and pragmatic about the idea of holding popular elections of the powerholders (Lau, 2005). The issue of democratic reform has become less salient as people are now attributing less importance and urgency to it.

The strategy of economic development that leverages on the Mainland's robust economic growth has finally produced magnificent results. Since the last two to three years of the first decade of the HKSAR, economic growth has resumed and decent growth appears to be sustainable. Unemployment has dropped to a tolerable level, although it is still higher than that before 1997. Hong Kong's economic productivity has risen and is comparable to that of its major competitors in the region. The proportion of GDP comprised by high value-added economic activities with substantial knowledge content has increased. Real per capita GDP has also surpassed that in 1997. The eventual end of the prolonged economic downturn since the handover, however, has not benefited everyone in Hong Kong, for the unrelenting and accelerated process of economic restructuring has left many Hong Kong people behind. The uneven distribution of the benefits generated by the economic recovery is manifested in the continual widening of the income gap between the rich and the poor, with an even more staggering wealth gap. Still, by the end of the first decade of the HKSAR, the economic nightmare that had for so long tormented Hongkongers had become history.

Significant changes in the political attitudes of Hong Kong people are another factor conducive to the emergence of an embryonic NPO. Apart from a rise in the public's trust in the government and a decrease in their sense of urgency for democratic change, Hongkongers are more trusting of the CPG, more confident about OCTS, more optimistic about Hong Kong's future and highly optimistic about China's future.[2] They are basically happy with Hong Kong's development in the first decade after the handover.[3] Although their support for the PNOF remains at a low level, in the last few years Hongkongers' attitudes towards the ANOF, and their political parties in particular, have become significantly less favourable. These changes in the political attitudes of Hong Kong people go a long way towards bringing about a less tense political atmosphere, making it much more difficult for the ANOF to mount mass-based challenges against the government.

The increasing political marginalization of the ANOF is probably the most important factor facilitating the rise of the NPO. Once Hongkongers have accepted the effectiveness of the strategy of economic development adopted by the government, the eligibility of the ANOF to be the governing force of a post-handover Hong Kong will be called into doubt. As the approval and support of Beijing are needed if that economic strategy is to succeed, any government of the HKSAR has to be trusted by the central authorities first before it can successfully pursue such a strategy. The ANOF's antagonistic stance towards Beijing, which is fully reciprocated by the latter, naturally disqualifies them from being a practitioner of that economic strategy, and Hongkongers fully understand this. Increasingly, the ANOF are perceived by Hongkongers as unable to play the positive role of promoting the territory's development. Moreover, the ANOF have so far not been able to formulate a comprehensive political and policy agenda that is viable and useful to Hong Kong's development as a part of China. As such, they have not been able to convince the majority of Hong Kong people that they can play a constructive role in a post-handover Hong Kong. Even though their role as a force that plays a check-and-balance function against the "Beijing-appointed," "pro-big business" Chief Executive is still appreciated and valued, their status as a "permanent" political opposition group is not likely to win them enough support from Hong Kong people to enable them to expand greatly. In its political instrumentalism, the political culture of Hongkongers greatly resembles the political culture in traditional China and in Asia in general (Moody, Jr., 1988). As long as the ANOF are judged by Hong Kong people to be of limited political utility, their future prospects are bound to be poor. At the end of the day, the ability of a weakened ANOF to contest the NPO being promoted by Beijing and the PNOF, as well as to win public support for an alternative new political order based on assumptions different from those underlying China's policy towards Hong Kong, is likely to be limited. Furthermore, the marginalization of the ANOF has greatly reduced the incidence of political conflict in Hong Kong, as Hongkongers are increasingly turned off by confrontational behaviour. When the issue of democratic development loses appeal, when adversarial politics is no longer popular and when socioeconomic issues come to the fore, not only do these events indicate that the political influence of the ANOF on the decline, but also that the grouping is ridden by internal fissures springing from irreconcilable differences on socioeconomic issues.

Over the years, the PNOF have also grown more politically united and capable. In the last several years, they have visibly recovered from the severe setback they experienced, stemming from the mass demonstration in 2003 against the government and the subsequent political fallout. The PNOF are better able to come together than before partly because of the common threat posed by the ANOF, which benefited for a while from the demonstration. The central authorities have also played a crucial role in constructing a united front among them. Both the Tung and the Tsang administrations have enhanced their political influence by involving more of their people in the process of governance, and brokering between their diverse interests and beliefs. The belated increase in political activism on the part of business, a major partner in the PNOF, is helping to buttress their political capability. Most important, the PNOF's "pro-Beijing" orientation, for a long time a political liability, has increasingly taken on positive political value due to the improvement in the relationship between the central authorities and Hong Kong people. In view of the increasing awareness of the existence of mutual interests between Hong Kong and the Mainland, Hongkongers are now more appreciative of the PNOF's role as an intermediary between the two "systems" under one country. Capitalizing on their perceived influence on the CPG and the local authorities in the Mainland, the PNOF are increasingly able to convince Hongkongers that they can advance their long-term economic interests. With their improved political situation, they can more openly and effectively articulate the ideas behind the NPO.

The palpable appearance of nationalistic sentiments among Hong Kong people has fostered an atmosphere that is more favourable than before to the creation of the NPO. "Inchoate" nationalistic feelings have always been present in Hong Kong, since Hong Kong is a predominantly Chinese society (Lau, 2000b). In fact, even before the handover, the "Hong Kong identity" and the "Chinese identity" were not separate, but very much overlapping. While most Hongkongers identify themselves as Hong Kong people, they are also proud to be Chinese. All along, they have been regarding themselves as Chinese in the ethnic, historical and cultural sense. Few identify themselves with the People's Republic of China (PRC) or the CCP. In the last couple of years, a discernible change has taken place. Even though the majority of Hong Kong people still identify themselves as Hong Kong people, they are increasingly proud to be citizens of the PRC and proud of the achievements of the Chinese government.[4] Most noteworthy was the finding that Hongkongers are more and more certain that China will achieve great power status in the foreseeable future. The idea of a "China threat" propagated by Westerners and the glorification of China's economic achievements are further fuelling their sense of national pride. Concomitantly, there has appeared a barely perceptible sense of a threat to the nation coming from the West, as Hongkongers increasingly subscribe to the view that the West is determined to block China's rise. A sense that they share a common fate with their Mainland compatriots has slowly emerged. The strengthening of nationalistic feelings is making the NPO conceived by Beijing more acceptable to Hongkongers.

The social, economic and political changes in Hong Kong in the first decade of the HKSAR, particularly in the last few years, have in varying degrees lessened the adverse effects of the basic contradiction inherent in OCTS on the building of the NPO in post-1997 Hong Kong. The successful implementation of OCTS has been embraced by Hongkongers as being in line with their basic interests. The central authorities are perceived as being not only sincere in following the OCTS policy, but also in wishing Hong Kong well and in being willing to render assistance whenever the territory is in need. Hong Kong's economic future is seen as part and parcel of China's economic future. The constitutional powers and privileges of the central authorities are now more recognized and respected than before. The importance of having a cooperative and cordial relationship with Beijing has been recognized. The idea that China's interests are also at stake in the success of Hong Kong's OCTS project and that China has the right to safeguard its interests in Hong Kong are increasingly acknowledged. More and more people are accepting the political rules of the game as prescribed by the Basic Law. The fact that the ANOF were willing to field a candidate to contest the Chief Executive in March 2007 testifies to their changed stance towards the political system under the Basic Law. Instead of treating the political system as "illegitimate," the ANOF are prepared to grant it a certain degree of legitimacy and to work within the system. On the other hand, there is lingering mistrust of CCP and persistent nostalgia about the "good old (colonial) days." Democratic aspirations, although less urgent today than before, are still quite strong.

A Modified New Political Order?

Even if the factors favourable to the formation of the NPO continue to operate, it will be some time yet before the NPO comes into existence, inasmuch as the underpinning of the NPO is a changed or new political mentality among Hongkongers. Over the first decade of the existence of the HKSAR, the political attitudes of Hong Kong people have changed dramatically, but as far as building the NPO is concerned, these changes are far from sufficient. Judging from past experience, it can be predicted that the political mentality of Hong Kong people will in the future be favourable to the realization of the NPO in a manner consistent with the OCTS project.

Nevertheless, it can always be anticipated that the content of the NPO as conceptualized by Beijing will also be modified to a certain extent. The interplay between Beijing and various political actors, particularly the ANOF, over more than 20 years on the one hand, and the central authorities' changing understanding and reactions to "the Hong Kong problem" on the other, will inevitably affect China's conception of the appropriate NPO for post-1997 Hong Kong. In this connection, a major factor will be the unavoidable, eventual acceptance of the OCTS by the ANOF and by those Hongkongers whose acceptance of the post-handover order has been at best lukewarm and at worst reluctant. Once these "hostile" elements are ready to accept the fact that Hong Kong is an integral part of China and that there is no viable alternative to OCTS as the framework for Hong Kong's post-colonial future, they will be willing to take into account the interests and concerns of Beijing and China. A *modus vivendi* would then appear to shape their relationship with the central authorities, making certain forms of political cooperation possible. The overall "legitimacy" of the new order after 1997 in Hong Kong will grow enormously, creating conditions favourable to effective governance and political stability in the territory, and a better relationship between the HKSAR and Beijing, as well as a more cordial partnership between Hong Kong and the Mainland.

It is important to point out here that Beijing does not have an ossified conception of the NPO, nor is Beijing totally inflexible in dealing with different views. Over the last 20 years, the attitudes of the central authorities towards Hong Kong's political system, political parties, executive-legislative relationship and the role of the judiciary in the NPO have undergone palpable and incremental changes as they have developed a better understanding of Hong Kong's reality and of the political thinking of Hongkongers. In essence, Beijing is willing to accept more political participation by Hong Kong people and different understandings of OCTS as long as the overall OCTS project is not jeopardized, and a broader definition of the "patriots" eligible to govern Hong Kong. The central government is even willing to experiment with step-by-step democratization in Hong Kong if it can smooth the process of building the NPO.

Generally speaking, looking into the future, it is quite possible that the gap between Beijing and Hong Kong people in their understanding of what the post-1997 order should be like will narrow. The new political order would be more or less similar to that envisaged by Beijing. Nonetheless, it will be modified here and there by inputs from Hong Kong. Once the modified NPO is in place, the project of OCTS will be brought to fruition.

Notes

1. In this chapter, the term NPO represents the post-1997 political order envisaged by Beijing in accordance with China's policy towards Hong Kong.
2. The findings from a poll (N=1,014) commissioned by the Central Policy Unit (CPU) of the HKSAR government and conducted on 15–17 December 2006

are illuminating. About half (51%) of the respondents were satisfied with the achievements of OCTS so far, with 14.3% not satisfied. 64.1% agreed that OCTS was in Hong Kong's interests, while 10.9% disagreed. 61.5% agreed that the CPG was sincere in taking care of Hong Kong's interests, while 13.3% disagreed. A total of 66.1% thought that Hong Kong and the Mainland shared similar interests, while 22.7% regarded their interests as being in conflict. Similarly, 62.2% felt that Hongkongers and the CPG had mutual interests, whereas 22.5 felt that they had conflicting interests. Another 32.6% of the respondents expressed great confidence in Hong Kong's future, while 16.3% having little confidence and 48.3% had moderate confidence.

3. In a poll (N=1,003) commissioned by the CPU of the HKSAR government and conducted on 20–23 April 2007, a plurality (42.4%) of the respondents were of the view that the development of Hong Kong in the first decade of the HKSAR was good, with 35.2% seeing it as being about average and 20.6% as not good.

4. In a poll commissioned by the CPU of the HKSAR government and conducted on 13–15 April 2007 (N=1,013), 72% of the respondents said that they would be or probably would be proud of being Chinese and 61.9% said that they would be or probably would be proud to be a citizen of the People's Republic of China. In the past, Hongkongers were proud to be a member of the Chinese nation but not proud to be a citizen of the People's Republic of China, which was treated as the creation of the Chinese Communist Party. The fact that more than half of Hongkongers were willing to identify with the People's Republic of China showed that the latter had gained substantial endorsement in Hong Kong.

References

Lau, Siu-kai (1990), *Decolonization without Independence and the Poverty of Political Leaders in Hong Kong*. Occasional Paper No. 1. Hong Kong Institute of Asia-Pacific Studies, The Chinese University of Hong Kong.

——— (1997a), Occasional Paper No. 1, "Decolonization *à la* Hong Kong: Britain's Search for Governability and Exit with Glory," *The Journal of Commonwealth and Comparative Politics*, 35 (2): 28–54.

——— (1997b), "The Fraying of the Socioeconomic Fabric of Hong Kong," *The Pacific Review*, 10 (3): 426–41.

——— (1999a), "The Rise and Decline of Political Support for the Hong Kong Special Administrative Region Government," *Government and Opposition*, 34 (3) (Summer): 352–71.

——— (1999b), "From Elite Unity to Disunity: Political Elite in Post-1997 Hong Kong." In Wang Gungwu and John Wong (eds.), *Hong Kong in China: The Challenges of Transition*. Singapore: Times Academic Press, pp. 47–74.

—— (2000a), "The Hong Kong Policy of the People's Republic of China 1949–1997," *Journal of Contemporary China*, 9 (23) (March): 77–93.

—— (2000b), "Hongkongese or Chinese: The Problem of Identity on the Eve of Resumption of Chinese Sovereignty over Hong Kong." In Lau Siu-kai (ed.), *Social Development and Political Change in Hong Kong*. Hong Kong: The Chinese University Press, pp. 255–84.

—— (2002), "Tung Chee-hwa's Governing Strategy: The Shortfall in Politics." In Lau Siu-kai (ed.), *The First Tung Chee-hwa Administration: The First Five Years of the Hong Kong Special Administrative Region*. Hong Kong: The Chinese University Press, pp. 1–39.

—— (2005), "Democratic Ambivalence." In Lau Siu-kai et al. (eds.), *Indicators of Social Development: Hong Kong 2004*. Hong Kong: Hong Kong Institute of Asia-Pacific Studies, The Chinese University of Hong Kong, pp. 1–30.

Lau, Siu-kai and Kuan Hsin-chi (2000), "Partial Democratization, 'Foundation Moment' and Political Parties in Hong Kong," *The China Quarterly*, 163: 705–20.

—— (2002), "Hong Kong's Stunted Political Party System," *The China Quarterly*, 172 (December): 1010–28.

Moody, Peter R. Jr. (1988), *Political Opposition in Post-Confucian Society*. New York: Praeger.

8

"One Country, Two Systems" from a Legal Perspective

Albert H. Y. Chen

Introduction

The experiment of "one country, two systems" (OCTS) is, in the final analysis, an experiment in the practice of the Rule of Law and constitutionalism. OCTS involves the legal delineation and guarantee of a high degree of autonomy for Hong Kong as a Special Administrative Region (SAR) of the People's Republic of China (PRC). It depends on the effective constitutional regulation of the relationship between the SAR and the Central Government in Beijing. It presupposes respect for and adherence to the constitutional norms and legal rules underpinning the powers of the SAR government and the rights of its citizens on the part of the PRC regime and the Chinese Communist Party.

When China decided to embark upon and commit herself internationally to this experiment by signing the Sino-British Joint Declaration on the Question of Hong Kong in 1984, the level of the Rule of Law and constitutionalism in the PRC was quite low: "socialist legality" was only beginning to be rebuilt from scratch after the "Cultural Revolution" era, during which the legal system was one of the targets of attack and had basically been dismantled. Thus, in the mid-1980s, when work on the drafting of the Basic Law of the Hong Kong SAR Region began, to have faith in the successful legal and constitutional practice of OCTS after 1997 was to take a leap in the dark.

The Basic Law was formally enacted by the National People's Congress (NPC) of the PRC in April 1990, less than one year after the earth-shattering Tiananmen Incident of June 1989. Its great length, complexity and level of legal sophistication make it one of the most remarkable constitutional instruments ever promulgated in the legal history of modern China. Its promulgation is also an important milestone in the constitutional history of the PRC itself. The Basic Law defines the constitutional relationship between the Hong Kong SAR and the central government in Beijing. It guarantees the human rights and various other rights of the residents of Hong Kong. It establishes a political order for the Hong Kong SAR that includes as its basic elements free elections by universal suffrage (of some though not all legislators), the separation of powers, checks and balances, judicial independence, the Rule of Law and the logic of phased democratization. It also stipulates the social, economic and other systems and policies to be practised in the SAR. In short, it promises a bright future for the people of Hong Kong.

Yet, for several years after the handover in 1997, that bright future did not materialize. Instead, Hong Kong descended into the gloom of the Asian financial crisis. The property market collapsed; several years of "negative economic growth" were experienced; and the government suffered from huge budget deficits. At the same time, controversies surrounding the implementation of the Basic Law created the impression of constitutional confrontation and crisis in Hong Kong. The abyss was reached in 2003, with the severe acute respiratory syndrome (SARS) epidemic in the spring and the march of half a million people in the summer against the proposed law to implement Article 23 of the Basic Law.

Fortunately, the people of Hong Kong and all other parties concerned have stood up to the trials and challenges of the initial practice of OCTS. The 10-year history of the Hong Kong SAR demonstrates that "Hong Kong people ruling Hong Kong" has not been an easy task. Yet, it is not an impossible task. The late Deng Xiaoping, architect of OCTS, said in 1984:

> We should have faith in the Chinese of Hong Kong, who are quite capable of administering their own affairs. The notion that Chinese cannot manage Hong Kong affairs satisfactorily is a leftover from the old colonial mentality.... All Chinese have at the very least a sense of pride in the Chinese nation, ... The Chinese in Hong Kong share this sense of national pride. They have the ability to run the affairs of Hong Kong well and they should be confident of that (Deng, 2004, p. 16).

Ten years of the practice of OCTS suggest that Deng's confidence in the people of Hong Kong had not been misplaced. According to a poll conducted by researchers at The University of Hong Kong in April 2007, "Hong Kong people's confidence in the central government and in 'one country, two systems' both reached a record high since the relevant surveys were initiated in 1992 and 1993, respectively; people's confidence in Hong Kong's future and in China's future also reached record highs since 1997."[1]

This chapter reviews the legal and constitutional history of the Hong Kong SAR since its establishment in 1997. Due to space limitations, it will only focus on what the author considers the most important events, cases or developments, but will provide considerable details on these. It divides the legal history of the 10-year period into four periods. The following four sections will deal with these periods respectively, followed by a concluding section.

1997–1999: Trial and Error, Confrontation and Adaptation

After the establishment of the Hong Kong SAR in July 1997, it was immediately plagued by two legal or constitutional problems regarding the interpretation of the Basic Law. The problems concerned the legality of the establishment of the Provisional Legislative Council (PLC) in 1997, and the right of abode in Hong Kong of the Mainland-born children of Hong Kong residents. These issues were litigated all the way from the Court of First Instance to the Court of Appeal, and then finally to the Court of Final Appeal (CFA). On 29 January 1999, the CFA rendered its judgements in the cases of *Ng Ka Ling v. Director of Immigration*[2] and *Chan Kam Nga v. Director of Immigration*.[3] In retrospect, these were the most momentous decisions of the Hong Kong courts in the last 10 years.

Both *Ng Ka Ling* and *Chan Kam Nga* were cases litigated against the government with the support of legal aid by seekers of the "right of abode" in Hong Kong. The applicants were children of Hong Kong permanent residents, but they were born on the Mainland. The children (some of whom were already adults) — who did not have any right of abode in Hong Kong under pre-1997 Hong Kong law (Chan and Rwezaura, 2004) — claimed the right of abode in Hong Kong under the Basic Law,[4] which came into full force on 1 July 1997, and argued that the immigration legislation (passed by the PLC)[5] that defined who were entitled to such a right (thereby excluding some of them from such an entitlement) and regulated the procedures for migration to Hong Kong for settlement was invalid because it contravened the Basic Law. Two controversies stemmed from the CFA's decisions in these two cases.

The first arose in the context of the CFA's handling of the issue of the legality of the PLC. In *Ng Ka Ling*, the CFA, like the Court of Appeal below it in *HKSAR v. Ma Wai Kwan*,[6] had to deal with the question of the legality of the PLC. This was because it was argued that the immigration legislation passed by the PLC was invalid, as the PLC itself had not been lawfully established. The PLC had been established by the Preparatory Committee for the SAR appointed by the NPC Standing Committee (NPCSC). It was argued that the PLC had not been lawfully established, as provision for such a body had not been made in the Basic Law. Since the Basic Law had been enacted in 1990 on the assumption that there would be a political "through train" in the sense that the members of the pre-1997 legislature would become members of the first legislature of the SAR,[7] there was indeed no provision for the establishment of the PLC (whose members were chosen by the 400-member Selection Committee for the first Chief Executive). The PLC was basically a contingency measure to deal with the "derailing" of the through train as a result of political reforms introduced by Governor Chris Patten in the mid-1990s, which Beijing considered to be contrary to the Basic Law and to the understanding reached between the Chinese and British governments when the Basic Law was enacted in 1990.

While the CFA reached the same conclusion as the Court of Appeal in affirming the legality of the PLC, it attempted in its judgement to overrule the Court of Appeal's ruling that Hong Kong courts had no jurisdiction to overturn acts of the NPC or NPCSC. The CFA stated in *Ng Ka Ling* that Hong Kong courts have the jurisdiction "to examine whether any legislative acts of the National People's Congress or its Standing Committee are consistent with the Basic Law and to declare them to be invalid if found to be inconsistent."[8] This immediately provoked a strong reaction from the Mainland Chinese side,[9] which led to the SAR government's unexpected and unprecedented application to the CFA on 26 February 1999 requesting it to "clarify" the relevant part of its judgement. The CFA acceded to the request and stated that (1) the Hong Kong courts' power to interpret the Basic Law is derived from the NPCSC under Article 158 of the Basic Law; (2) any interpretation made by the NPCSC under Article 158 would be binding on the Hong Kong courts; and (3) the judgement of 29 January did not question the authority of the NPC and its Standing Committee "to do any act which is in accordance with the provisions of the Basic Law and the procedure therein."[10]

The practical significance of the "clarification" (Chen, 1999; Ling, 1999), which is also a consequence flowing directly from the Basic Law itself, is that the Hong Kong courts' power to interpret the Basic Law and to determine whether an act of any governmental authority is consistent with the Basic Law, albeit a real and important power, is nevertheless not an absolute one. It is not absolute because it is subject to the overriding power of the NPCSC. In the absence of an interpretation by the NPCSC, the Hong Kong courts have full authority to interpret the Basic Law on their own and to decide cases in accordance with their own interpretation. But once the NPCSC has spoken, the Hong Kong courts must comply. But when can or will the NPCSC speak? This question was answered in the course of the second controversy flowing from the CFA's decisions on 29 January 1999.

This controversy stemmed from the CFA's interpretation of Articles 24(2)(3) and 22(4) of the Basic Law, and its decision not to refer the latter to the NPCSC for interpretation even though Article 22(4) seems to fall within Article 158(3) of the Basic Law (Chen, 2002a).[11] The SAR Government estimated that the implementation of Articles 24(2)(3) and 22(4) as interpreted by the CFA would mean that Hong Kong would need to absorb a migrant population from Mainland China of 1.67 million in the coming decade.[12] In the government's opinion, Hong Kong need not bear this burden because the CFA's interpretation of the relevant Basic Law provisions was of dubious validity. On 21 May 1999, despite strong opposition from certain sectors of the community, particularly legal professionals and pro-democracy politicians, the Chief Executive, Mr Tung Chee-hwa, asked the State Council to refer the relevant Basic Law provisions to the NPCSC for interpretation.[13] The request was acceded to, and the NPCSC issued an interpretation on 26 June 1999.[14] The NPCSC adopted the same interpretations as those adopted by the Court of Appeal before its decision was overturned by the CFA. The CFA's interpretations on these points were effectively overruled. In the text of its decision, the NPCSC also pointed out that the litigation did involve Basic Law provisions concerning the central government's responsibility or the central-SAR relationship that ought to have been referred to the NPCSC for interpretation by the CFA in accordance with Article 158(3) of the Basic Law in the first place.

The reference to the NPCSC for interpretation was extremely controversial because there is nothing in the Basic Law suggesting that the executive branch of the SAR government can ask the NPCSC to interpret the Basic Law. Furthermore, the reference to the NPCSC was criticized as a self-inflicted blow to Hong Kong's autonomy, judicial authority, Rule of Law and system for protecting the rights of individuals.[15] With respect, most of the criticisms cannot be sustained. First, as was acknowledged by the CFA in December 1999 in *Lau Kong Yung v. Director of Immigration*,[16] the NPCSC's power to interpret the Basic Law under Article 158(1) of the Basic Law is a "free-standing" one, in the sense that it can be exercised at any time, even in the absence of a reference by the CFA in accordance with Article 158(3) of the Basic Law. Any interpretation issued by the NPCSC, whether on its own initiative or upon a reference by the CFA, is binding on the Hong Kong courts. Second, the CFA also acknowledged in *Lau Kong Yung* that since the preamble to the NPCSC interpretation of June 1999 suggests that a reference to the NPCSC for interpretation should have been made by the CFA in this case, it might be necessary for the CFA to re-visit in future the test (such as the "predominant provision" test) for determining when a reference should be made to the NPCSC. This means that the CFA implicitly conceded that it might have been a mistake for it to decide in *Ng Ka Ling* not to refer Article 22(4) of the Basic Law to the NPCSC for interpretation. Third, it should be stressed that the parties to the litigation in the *Ng* and *Chan* cases were not affected by the NPCSC's interpretation.[17] This means that the interpretation only operates as a guide to Hong Kong courts on how to interpret the relevant Basic Law provisions in cases that come before the courts after the interpretation was made.

Although the 1999 NPCSC interpretation should not in itself, given the circumstances in which it was made, be regarded as a blow to Hong Kong's Rule of Law or autonomy, the concern is valid that if the NPCSC were to frequently exercise its overriding power to interpret the Basic Law, the autonomy and authority of the Hong Kong courts in deciding cases on their own (at least cases that touch upon an interpretation of the Basic Law) would be severely hampered. Fortunately, this has not happened. The NPCSC has practised self-restraint in exercising its power of interpretation of the Basic Law. Since its interpretation of 1999, only two other interpretations have been issued — one in 2004 on the issue of political reform and democratization in Hong Kong and the Beijing authorities' role in the process (Chen, 2004; Chan and Harris, 2005); and one in 2005 on the issue of the term of office of the successor (to be elected in Hong Kong and appointed by Beijing) to Chief Executive Tung Chee-hwa, who resigned in March 2005 before completing his second term of office of 2002–2007 (Chen, 2005). The 2004 interpretation was issued on the NPCSC's own initiative in the absence of any litigation on the matter or any request for interpretation by the Hong Kong government. The 2005 interpretation was issued at the request of the Hong Kong government at a time when litigation (to challenge a bill introduced in the Hong Kong legislature on the Chief Executive's term of office) was pending but before a full trial in any court.

To conclude this section, it may be said that 1997–1999 was a period of the initial trial operation of the Basic Law. The CFA's decisions on 29 January 1999 did precipitate two constitutional crises or "confrontations" between the legal orders of Hong Kong and of the PRC, one leading to the "clarification" by the CFA and the other leading to the June 1999 interpretation by the NPCSC. How the legal order of Hong Kong should position itself with regard to the power of the NPCSC was a fundamental problem raised by the 1997 handover. By the time of the CFA's decision in *Lau Kong Yung*, the Hong Kong courts led by the CFA had adjusted themselves to this new constitutional order.

2000–2002: The Elaboration and Consolidation of the Regime of Rights

The CFA delivered its judgement in *Lau Kong Yung* on 3 December 1999. On 15 December 1999, the same court rendered its decision in *HKSAR v. Ng Kung Siu*,[18] which inaugurated what this author would classify as the second period of the legal history of the Hong Kong SAR. The developments in this period should be understood against the background of Hong Kong's pre-1997 regime of rights protection.

Hong Kong's pre-1997 constitution was contained in the Letters Patent issued by the British Crown (Miners, 1995, chap. 5; Wesley-Smith, 1995, chap. 2). Before its 1991 amendment, the Letters Patent provided only a crude and rudimentary written constitution for the colony. In particular, it did not contain any guarantee of civil liberties and human rights. In 1991, in an attempt to restore confidence in Hong Kong's future, which had been deeply shaken by the Tiananmen incident of 4 June 1989, the Hong Kong government introduced the Hong Kong Bill of Rights Ordinance ("the Bill of Rights"), which the local legislature passed.[19] The "Bill of Rights" incorporated into the domestic law of Hong Kong the provisions of the International Covenant on Civil and Political Rights (ICCPR) that had already been applied by the U.K. to Hong Kong on the level of international law since 1976. A corresponding amendment was made to the Letters Patent to give the ICCPR supremacy over laws enacted by Hong Kong's legislature. Since 1991, the courts of Hong Kong have on such a constitutional basis exercised the power of judicial review of legislation (striking down any existing law that they considered failed to meet the human rights norms embodied in the Bill of Rights and the ICCPR), and developed a solid body of case law on the protection of human rights (Ghai, 1997; Chan, 1998a; Byrnes, 2000). Thus the era of constitutional adjudication began in Hong Kong.

Upon the establishment of the SAR in July 1997, the colonial constitution embodied in the Letters Patent lost its force. Article 8 of the Basic Law provides for the continued validity of the laws previously in force in Hong Kong except for any law that contravenes the Basic Law and subject to any amendment by the SAR legislature. Under Article 160 of the Basic Law, the NPCSC may declare which of Hong Kong's pre-existing laws contravene the Basic Law and cannot, therefore, survive the 1997 transition. Such a declaration was made by the NPCSC on 23 February 1997 in its Decision on the Treatment of the Laws Previously in Force in Hong Kong.[20] The Decision declared the non-adoption, *inter alia*, of three interpretative provisions in the Hong Kong Bill of Rights Ordinance,[21] apparently on the ground that they purported to give the Ordinance a superior status overriding other Hong Kong laws, which is inconsistent with the principle that only the Basic Law is superior to other Hong Kong laws. Does this mean that the pre-existing regime of legal protection of rights in Hong Kong before 1997 will be dismantled or weakened? An examination of various major judicial decisions in the second period of the post-1997 legal history of the SAR suggests that it will not.

The CFA's decision in *Ng Kung Siu* is thus far probably the most theoretically significant constitutional case on civil liberties and human rights in the legal history of the Hong Kong SAR. In this case, the defendants had participated in a demonstration in Hong Kong for democracy in China during which they displayed a defaced national flag (of the PRC) and a defaced regional flag (of the SAR). They were subsequently charged with violations of Section 7 of the National Flag and National Emblem Ordinance[22] and Section 7 of the Regional Flag and Regional Emblem Ordinance. The sections provide for the offences of desecration of the national and regional flags and emblems.

The defendants were convicted by the magistrate; they were neither fined nor imprisoned, but bound over[23] to keep the peace on a recognizance of HK$2,000 for each of the two charges for 12 months. They successfully appealed against their conviction before the Court of Appeal.[24] The government appealed the case to the CFA, which rendered its judgement in December 1999. The appeal was allowed by the CFA unanimously, and the impugned ordinances were upheld as constitutional and valid. The CFA pointed out that the national and regional flags are important and unique symbols of the nation and of the Hong Kong SAR, respectively. There exist, therefore, societal and community interests in the protection of the flags. Such protection constitutes the objective behind the flag desecration laws. Such protection was held to fall within the concept of "public order (*ordre public*)" as used in the ICCPR. It was held that the lower court below adopted too narrow a conception of "public order (*ordre public*)."[25]

The next questions for the CFA to consider were whether the flag desecration laws impose restrictions on the freedom of expression, and, if so, whether such restrictions can be justified on the ground that they are necessary for the protection of "public order (*ordre public*)" and proportionate to the objective sought (and thus not excessive). This is the application of the principles of rationality and proportionality that are well established in human rights jurisprudence elsewhere and that had already been introduced into Hong Kong since 1991. The CFA held that flag desecration is indeed "a form of non-verbal speech or expression,"[26] and the impugned laws do constitute a restriction thereon. However, the court pointed out that the restriction is a limited one, because while one mode of expression is prohibited, the same message that the actor wants to express can still be freely expressed by other modes.[27] It was, therefore, concluded that the "necessity" and "proportionality" tests had been satisfied.[28]

Although the CFA's actual decision in *Ng Kung Siu* was to uphold the flag desecration law, the approach and mode of reasoning adopted by the CFA in this case have far-reaching positive implications for the regime of rights protection in post-1997 Hong Kong. The case demonstrates that the operative force of the Bill of Rights and the ICCPR, and the Hong Kong courts' power to review the constitutionality of Hong Kong legislation on human rights grounds, and, if necessary, to strike down such legislation, have survived the non-adoption (by the NPCSC) of the relevant provisions in the Hong Kong Bill of Rights Ordinance as mentioned above. More particularly, the SAR courts may review whether any legislative or executive action in Hong Kong violates the human rights guaranteed by Chapter III of the Basic Law or by the ICCPR (the applicable provisions of which have, as mentioned above, been reproduced in the Bill of Rights), to which Article 39 of the Basic Law gives effect. Article 39 has been interpreted to mean that the relevant provisions of the ICCRP have the same constitutional force as the Basic Law itself, thus overriding laws that are inconsistent with these provisions.

We now turn to two other cases decided in 2000–2002 that demonstrate the vitality of judicial protection of human rights in post-1997 Hong Kong. *Secretary for Justice v. Chan Wah and Tse Kwan Sang*[29] concerns the system of local village elections in the New Territories (NT). Some of the residents of the villages of the NT are known as "indigenous inhabitants" or "indigenous villagers," defined[30] as descendents through the male line of residents in 1898 of villages in the NT.[31] The rules governing the election of village representatives (VR) in most villages in the NT limited the right to vote and the right to stand as candidates to indigenous inhabitants. In the *Chan* case, Chan and Tse were non-indigenous inhabitants of the villages in which they lived. They challenged the electoral rules as discriminatory in denying them their right to take part in the conduct of public affairs under Article 21(a) of the Bill of Rights (Article 25 of the ICCPR).

In the final judgement delivered in December 2000 in this case, the CFA held that the impugned electoral rules in this case imposed unreasonable restrictions on Chan's and Tse's right to take part in the conduct of public affairs through freely chosen representatives. In response to this ruling, the government subsequently reformed the village election system by introducing legislation providing for a dual system in which each village would elect two VRs, one serving only the indigenous inhabitants and the other all of the villagers.[32]

The *Chan* case concerns discrimination on the basis of origin or status, while the next case concerns gender discrimination. In *Equal Opportunities Commission v. Director of Education*,[33] the Equal Opportunities Commission challenged the Education Department's policy regarding the system of allocating secondary school places to students who have completed their primary school education. The effect of the operation of this system was that where a boy and a girl were of equal academic merit (as measured by scores), the boy stood a better chance of being admitted to his preferred secondary school than did the girl. The policy was based on the finding that the academic achievements (as measured by scores) of girls at the time they completed their primary education were on average higher than those of boys. This was presumably because, at that age, girls develop more quickly intellectually than boys, although boys are able to catch up later. The policy was designed to ensure a more balanced ratio between male and female students in the elite schools (i.e., schools to which admission is most competitive).

The Court of First Instance of the High Court[34] held that the Education Department's policy discriminates against female students and that none of the reasons advanced by the Department can justify such discrimination. Referring to Article 25 of the Basic Law, Article 22 of the Hong Kong Bill of Rights, the Sex Discrimination Ordinance and the Convention on the Elimination of All Forms of Discrimination Against Women (which was extended to Hong Kong in 1996), the court stressed that the right to equal treatment free of sex discrimination in this case is the individual's fundamental right, and cannot be easily subordinated to considerations of "group fairness"[35] or to the interest in achieving a better balance in schools between boys and girls as two groups. Any restriction of the girls' right in this case must pass the stringent standards of scrutiny of the "proportionality test"[36] in order to be justified. After examining the government's arguments and the evidence submitted by it, the court held that the impugned scheme of allocation of school places fails to pass this test. As a result of this decision, the Education Department changed its original policy.

Both the *Chan* case and *Equal Opportunities Commission* case concern matters of public policy; their ramifications extend far beyond the individual litigants or complainants in the cases. They demonstrate the increasingly significant role played by the courts in Hong Kong in shaping social policy and in promoting social reform by employing jurisprudential concepts — in these two cases, the right to the equal protection of the law without discrimination.

The three cases above elucidate the structural components of the post-1997 regime of rights protection in Hong Kong: They include Article 39 of the Basic Law, the ICCPR and the Hong Kong Bill of Rights. But the significance of rights-conferring provisions in the Basic Law other than Article 39 should not be ignored. After the Basic Law came into effect in 1997, the grounds on which legislative and executive actions may be challenged by way of judicial review have actually been broadened. After 1991 but before 1997, it was possible to launch such a challenge on the basis of the provisions of the Hong Kong Bill of Rights, which are identical to those provisions of the ICCPR that are applicable to Hong Kong. After 1997, a challenge may still be launched on this basis, but in addition, a challenge may also be based on other provisions of the Basic Law, particularly those that confer rights that are not expressly or adequately provided for in the ICCPR, such as the right of abode or the freedom to travel.[37]

The years 2000–2002 may be described as a period during which the regime of rights in the Hong Kong SAR was elaborated and consolidated. The CFA's decision in *Director of Immigration v. Chong Fung Yuen,*[38] another landmark case decided in this period, also marks such a consolidation. In this case, the issue was whether, as a matter of interpretation of Article 24(2)(1) of the Basic Law, the right of abode in Hong Kong vests in children born in Hong Kong to Chinese parents who are not Hong Kong residents but who are Mainlanders visiting Hong Kong temporarily or illegally staying in Hong Kong. On a literal interpretation of Article 24(2)(1), such children are Hong Kong permanent residents and enjoy the right of abode. However, the Preparatory Committee for the SAR in 1996 had suggested otherwise when it issued an opinion on the implementation of Article 24. In the NPCSC's interpretation of June 1999, it stated, *inter alia*, that the Preparatory Committee's 1996 opinion "reflected" the "legislative intent" behind Article 24(2) of the Basic Law. The question for the CFA in *Chong Fung Yuen* was whether it should follow the views of the Preparatory Committee in this regard.

The CFA's judgement in this case was an emphatic statement that when Hong Kong courts interpret the Basic Law, they should adopt the common law approach to interpretation, and do not need to resort to or otherwise take into account any principle or norm of the Mainland legal system. Applying the common law approach to interpretation in this case, the CFA held that there was only one possible answer to the legal question raised: The child concerned was entitled to the right of abode in Hong Kong. The CFA did not attach any weight to the passage in the June 1999 interpretation by the NPCSC suggesting that the Preparatory Committee's opinion reflected the legislative intent behind Article 24 of the Basic Law. The CFA stressed that the June 1999 interpretation was an interpretation only of Articles 22(4) and 24(2)(3) of the Basic Law. It was not an interpretation of Article 24(2)(1) of the Basic Law, which was the provision being interpreted in the *Chong Fung Yuen* case. In the absence of any binding interpretation by the NPCSC of Article 24(2)(1), the CFA was free to interpret it on its own, applying the common law approach to interpretation.[39]

The case aroused public concerns about pregnant women from the Mainland coming to Hong Kong to give birth. The concerns proved to be justified; in the next few years following the CFA's decision in the *Chong* case, increasing numbers of pregnant women from the Mainland visited Hong Kong in order to give birth, placing a great strain on Hong Kong's hospitals. In 2007, administrative measures were adopted to reduce the influx.

2003–2004: The Article 23 Saga

The next period of the SAR's legal history was dominated by a 10-month drama that culminated in a march by about half a million people through the streets on Hong Kong Island. This was one of the greatest events in the political, legal and social history of Hong Kong, which also changed the course of PRC policy towards the Hong Kong SAR. The drama had a specifically legal theme, namely the implementation of Article 23 of the Basic Law (Fu, Petersen and Young, 2005).

Article 23 of the Basic Law ("BL 23") requires the Hong Kong SAR to "enact laws on its own to prohibit any act of treason, secession, sedition, [or] subversion against the Central People's Government." It also deals with the issues of state secrets and the activities of foreign political organizations in Hong Kong. Many of the issues raised by BL 23 are considered to be politically sensitive. Ever since the Basic Law was enacted in 1990 and brought into effect in July 1997, there had been anxieties over the implementation of BL 23.

It was, therefore, understandable that the publication by the SAR government on 24 September 2002 of the Consultation Document on *Proposals to Implement Article 23 of the Basic Law*[40] caused much public anxiety as to whether the Hong Kong or Beijing government had the sinister intention of curtailing human rights in Hong Kong and extending to Hong Kong Mainland standards regarding matters such as subversion or the theft of state secrets. During the three-month consultation period for the legislative proposal, public opinion in Hong Kong was sharply divided. The debate was at times impassioned, and demonstrations were organized by both supporters and opponents of the proposal.

The consultation period ended in December after a demonstration on 15 December 2002 of nearly 60,000 people against the legislative proposal. In response, the government amended the proposal by giving several major "concessions" on its substance,[41] but rejected the call for a White Bill — a bill published for public consultation but not yet introduced into the Legislative Council. The National Security (Legislative Provisions) Bill ("the Bill"), designed to implement BL 23, was introduced into the legislature in February 2003.

In this author's opinion (Chen, 2003a), the proposed reforms to the law on treason and sedition contained in the Bill demonstrated that the BL 23 exercise was not primarily intended to make Hong Kong's laws more draconian. Instead, it was an exercise to review and reform the existing law in the light of the principles enshrined in BL 23, and to remove repressive laws that Hong Kong had inherited from its colonial era, which are now out-of-date and inconsistent with progressive notions of human rights. As regards subversion and secession, the Bill did not import the relevant Mainland laws and standards to Hong Kong; rather, it creatively designed for these two crimes legislative models that would be unique to the Hong Kong SAR. As regards state secrets, the proposed amendments to the Official Secrets Ordinance were not unreasonable and were basically consistent with the spirit of "one country, two systems." The most controversial provisions in the Bill related to "proscribed organizations." The Bill proposed a set of amendments to the Societies Ordinance to the effect that where a local organization (a) has the objective of engaging in or (b) has committed or is attempting to commit treason, secession, subversion, sedition or spying, or (c) is "subordinate to" an organization in Mainland China that has been proscribed by open decree by the central authorities for reasons of national security, the Hong Kong SAR's Secretary for Security may proscribe the local organization "if he reasonably believes that the proscription is necessary in the interests of national security and is proportionate for such purpose." Part (c) of the proposal aroused much public opposition.

After the Bill was introduced into the Legislative Council (LegCo) in February 2003, a Bills Committee under LegCo was set up to examine the Bill. During the Bills Committee's deliberations on the Bill, the government agreed to some amendments. However, critics said that the amendments were insufficient, and in any event the government's timetable of passing the Bill in the LegCo's week-long meeting beginning on 9 July did not allow sufficient time for deliberation. Meanwhile, the onslaught of SARS, or atypical pneumonia, in March 2003 distracted public attention from the Bill. There was, therefore, little understanding of the Bill on the part of members of the public in Hong Kong. As Hong Kong began to recover from the SARS crisis in June, opponents of the Bill woke members of the public up to the fact that the Bill was to be pushed through LegCo in early July.

On 1 July 2003, a hot summer's day that was also a public holiday marking the sixth anniversary of Hong Kong's return to China, half a million Hong Kong residents took to the streets to demonstrate against the Article 23 legislative exercise and to express other grievances against the Tung Chee-hwa administration that had accumulated since the 1997 handover. Opponents of the Bill immediately demanded that the Bill be shelved, and announced plans to organize a rally of tens of thousands to surround the LegCo building on 9 July if proceedings on the Bill were to go ahead on that day. The government finally decided to postpone the Bill. The decision came three hours after the Liberal Party, on the evening of 6 July, withdrew from the "governing coalition" of political parties in protest against the Tung administration's original decision on 5 July to adhere to the 9 July deadline for the passage of the Bill.[42] On 17 July 2003, Chief Executive Tung Chee-hwa announced that the government would re-open public consultation on the Bill to ensure that its contents would receive broad public support before it was passed into law. However, in an about-face on 5 September 2003, Tung announced that the Bill was to be withdrawn from LegCo. Since then, the implementation of BL 23 has been shelved indefinitely.

In the circumstances, the government's decision to postpone the national security bill was to be welcomed (Chen, 2003b). It would have been a flagrant violation of the democratic principle of law-making for a government or legislature to enact a controversial law hastily in the face of extremely strong public opposition. On the other hand, it should also be recognized that BL 23 does impose a legal obligation on the SAR government to enact laws on the matters covered by the article. This constitutional duty cannot be abdicated indefinitely. BL 23 will, therefore, return one day to the agenda of the SAR government.

2005–2007: Continued Active Exercise of Judicial Power

The fourth and most recent period of the SAR's legal history saw the further consolidation of the regime of rights that had been elucidated in the second period as discussed above, as well as the further strengthening of the role of the courts as the guardian of constitutional rights in the Hong Kong SAR. The NPCSC's second and third interpretations of the Basic Law in 2004 and 2005, respectively (on the mechanics of further democratization and on the term of office of the Chief Executive as mentioned above), did not have any adverse impact on the position of the courts. Unlike the first interpretation, they were not targeted at any judicial decision in Hong Kong and did not detract from the authority of the Hong Kong courts. Indeed, the courts in this fourth period exercised their power as actively as, or even more so than before. Three leading cases are discussed below as examples.

The first case is *Yeung May-wan v. HKSAR*,[43] concerning the prosecution of Falun Gong protesters in 2002, in which the police resorted to the law of obstruction of public places[44] in dealing with demonstrators. The case arose from a small-scale demonstration staged by 16 Falun Gong activists[45] outside the entrance to the Liaison Office of the Central People's Government in Hong Kong on 14 March 2002. Since the number of demonstrators was small, there was no need under the Public Order Ordinance to notify the police in advance or to comply with procedural requirements, which are only applicable to assemblies involving more than 50 persons or processions involving more than 30 persons. After the protesters refused to leave despite repeated police warnings, the police arrested them. There was some physical violence during and after the arrest. The protesters were charged with obstruction of a public place, and obstructing or assaulting police officers in the execution of their duty. After a 27-day trial, the protesters were in August 2002 convicted by the magistrate, who imposed fines ranging between HK$1,300 and $3,800 on them. They appealed to the Court of Appeal, which gave its judgement in November 2004.[46] The appeal against the conviction for obstructing a public place was successful, although the appeal against the conviction on the other charges failed. In a unanimous decision, the Court of Appeal held that due regard to the protection of the right of assembly should be given in applying the law of obstruction of public places. It overturned the conviction for obstruction on the ground that the magistrate had failed to address sufficiently whether the manner in which the protesters exercised their right of assembly was so unreasonable as to constitute an unlawful obstruction. The defendants appealed further to the CFA against the conviction on the other charges.

The appeal was successful. On 5 May 2005, the CFA[47] unanimously held that the arrest of the defendants had been unlawful, since the police officers who carried out the arrest were not able to satisfy the court that they had reasonable grounds for suspecting that the defendants had committed the offence of obstruction of a public place. The court stressed that the offence is not constituted by mere obstruction; the use of the public place or highway must be unreasonable, otherwise there could be a lawful excuse for the obstruction, in which case no offence has been committed. The court held that in determining what is unreasonable use of the pavement or lawful excuse, the defendants' right to peaceful assembly and demonstration should be given due weight. The court further held that the defendants in the present case could not be convicted for obstructing or assaulting police officers in the execution of their duty, even though physical resistance was involved. Since the arrest was unlawful, the police officers were not actually acting in the due execution of their duty when they encountered resistance from the defendants. It was also pointed out that citizens have a right to use reasonable force to resist an unlawful arrest and detention.

In this case and in the related case of *Leung Kwok Hung v. HKSAR*,[48] the CFA stressed the importance of the constitutional right to freedom of peaceful assembly and demonstration, which is guaranteed by the Basic Law, the Hong Kong Bill of Rights and the ICCPR. The decision in the Falun Gong case testifies to the equality of all before the law, so that Falun Gong members, although persecuted in the Mainland, are accorded the right to demonstrate directly in front of the Liaison Office of the Central Government in Hong Kong. The landmark decision epitomizes the vibrancy of the life of the law and the spirit of human rights in Hong Kong, and reveals the deeper meaning of "one country, two systems."

The second case, *Leung Kwok Hung and Koo Sze Yiu v. Chief Executive of the HKSAR*,[49] is probably the most important constitutional law case in this fourth period of the SAR's 10-year legal history, because it led to a comprehensive legislative overhaul of the existing law on the relevant issues. The issues concern covert surveillance conducted by law enforcement officers on suspected criminals. Covert surveillance activities include the wire-tapping of phones, interception of postal communications, and covert sound or video recording of people's conversations or activities. The legal basis for covert surveillance first came under critical scrutiny in two criminal cases in the District Court in 2005. It was pointed out that the existing practice was probably a violation of Article 30 of the Basic Law, which protects the "freedom and privacy of communication" and permits interception of communication only if it is done "in accordance with legal procedures to meet the needs of public security or of investigation into criminal offences." Also relevant is Article 17 of the ICCPR, which prohibits "arbitrary or unlawful interference with … privacy, family, home or correspondence." To plug the legal loophole, the Chief Executive in August 2005 promulgated the Law Enforcement (Covert Surveillance Procedure) Order ("the 2005 Order").[50]

Leung and Koo, two political activists who claimed that they had probably been targets of covert surveillance, brought an action before the court to challenge the constitutionality of the practice of covert surveillance. They were successful before the Court of First Instance, which delivered its judgement on 9 February 2006.[51] The court held that both Section 33 of the Telecommunications Ordinance (which dealt with wire-tapping) and the 2005 Order were unconstitutional: The former created the power to intercept communications without adequate legal safeguards against its abuse; the latter failed to comply with the procedural requirements of Article 30 of the Basic Law.

What is most interesting and significant about the court's decision is that the court (contrary to the request of the litigants against the government) did not declare that the impugned legislative provision and order should be immediately regarded as invalid and void, which is what would normally be the case where a law is determined by the court to be unconstitutional. Instead, the court agreed to the request by the lawyers acting for the government[52] in this case to suspend the effectiveness of the declaration of invalidity for six months, and held that the impugned legislative provision and order may still be regarded as temporarily valid during this six-month period. The purpose of this arrangement was to give the government time to propose and enact new legislation to replace the defective laws that had been challenged and held to be unconstitutional in this case. The court recognized that this arrangement was an exceptional course of action for the court, but declared that the court in the exercise of its inherent jurisdiction had the power to make this arrangement. For if law enforcement agencies were to suddenly lose their powers of conducting covert surveillance, this would be tantamount to "an amnesty for conspirators"[53] and "would give rise to the probability of danger to Hong Kong residents, disorder by way of a threat to the rule of law and deprivation to Hong Kong residents generally."[54]

The decision of the Court of First Instance was affirmed on appeal to the Court of Appeal.[55] The further appeal to the CFA was also unsuccessful.[56] However, unlike the courts below it, the CFA drew a distinction between granting a declaration of temporary validity (for six months) with regard to the impugned laws and suspending (for six months) the declaration of invalidity of such laws. The CFA only agreed to grant the latter remedy in this case. In the event, the government did comply with the six-month deadline for introducing new legislation to regularize the practice of covert surveillance in Hong Kong. The Interception of Communications and Surveillance Ordinance was passed by LegCo at around 2 a.m. on 6 August 2005 after a 58-hour marathon debate, which started on 2 August. More than 200 amendments proposed by the "democrats" were voted down by pro-government legislators, although some other amendments proposed by them had been incorporated into amendments proposed by the government and were adopted.

In the *Leung Kwok-hung* case, the courts refrained from immediately outlawing the practice of covert surveillance even though the existing legal basis for it was found to be defective, and gave the government and legislature a "grace period" of six months to rectify the legal situation. This seems to reflect an attitude of judicial restraint. However, insofar as the remedy granted by the court in this case is innovative, unprecedented in the legal and constitutional history of Hong Kong, and represents a breakthrough in the creative fashioning of judicial mechanisms to deal with novel situations, it may also be considered an example of judicial activism. Judicial activism is further demonstrated by the next case to be discussed.

In *Leung T C William Roy v. Secretary for Justice*,[57] Leung, the applicant for judicial review, was a homosexual aged 20 at the time he brought this action before the court. He challenged the constitutionality of certain provisions in the existing criminal law on the grounds that they were discriminatory on the basis of sex or sexual orientation and violated the constitutional rights to equality and privacy. The main provision that was controversial in this case was Section 118C of the Crimes Ordinance, which provided that if two men committed buggery with each other and one or both of them were under the age of 21, then each of them was guilty of a criminal offence, the maximum punishment for which would be life imprisonment. Both the Court of First Instance and the Court of Appeal held that this provision was unconstitutional and invalid, because it discriminated against male homosexuals and the government was not able to give good reasons to persuade the court that the discrimination or differential treatment was justified. The impugned provision was discriminatory against male homosexuals because under Hong Kong's existing law, in the case of consensual sexual intercourse between heterosexuals, no criminal liability exists so long as both parties are above the age of 16. Thus, homosexual males between the age of 16 and 21 were discriminated against.

This case has been controversial as it involved the judiciary stepping into the domain of social or sexual morality and overturning a law (made by the legislature) reflecting what was supposed to be the moral standards of the community. It may be questioned whether judges in Hong Kong may legitimately set the behavioural norms for the community in this regard. However, the court's decision may be defended on the ground that one of the legitimate functions of the constitutional review of laws by the courts is to protect the fundamental rights of minorities against oppressive or unjust laws enacted by a legislature that represents only the views or interests of the majority in society. In any event, the *William Roy Leung* case underscores the increasingly important role played by the courts in Hong Kong society — the main theme of the fourth period of the SAR's legal history under review here.

Conclusion

Can one make any sense out of this 10-year constitutional and legal history of the Hong Kong SAR? The following general observations may be made from the perspective of the Rule of Law and constitutionalism — as pointed out at the beginning of this chapter, OCTS is ultimately an experiment in the practice of the Rule of Law and constitutionalism.

First, autonomy, the Rule of Law, human rights and civil liberties have successfully been practised in the Hong Kong SAR under the constitutional framework of OCTS and on the basis of the Basic Law. Both the people of Hong Kong and the international community would appreciate that the central government in Beijing has indeed respected the high degree of autonomy enjoyed by the Hong Kong SAR, and has not interfered with the SAR government's policy-making and policy-implementation activities.[58] The common law-based legal system, judicial independence and the tradition of the Rule of Law have continued to flourish in post-1997 Hong Kong. As promised by the Sino-British Joint Declaration, the "life-style" of the people of Hong Kong has remained unchanged. The level of protection of human rights and civil liberties has not dropped as some had feared before 1997.

Second, the three interpretations of the Basic Law by the NPCSC and the legislative exercise to implement Article 23 of the Basic Law were indeed among the most significant legal events in the history of the Hong Kong SAR. They were indeed highly controversial. The Article 23 incident indeed shook the whole of Hong Kong society. However, the power of the NPCSC to interpret the Basic Law is an integral part of the new legal order of post-1997 Hong Kong. It has been built into the structural design of the Basic Law itself. Each of the three interpretations has its own rationale and justification; none may be regarded as an arbitrary or irrational exercise of power by the NPCSC. The power of the Hong Kong courts to try and decide cases has been left intact. As regards the Article 23 episode, the government's intention was not to curtail human rights and civil liberties in Hong Kong. The trauma of this legislative exercise was the result of the convergence of various circumstances, including the hasty legislative process, the lack of a white bill for prior consultation, the failure of communication between the government and the people, the incidence of SARS, the economic downturn and the accumulated social dissatisfaction with the Tung administration over the years.

Third, in the post-1997 era, the courts of Kong Kong have flourished as the guardian of the Rule of Law, constitutionalism, human rights and civil liberties. Increasing numbers of major issues of social and public policy have been litigated in the courts, as members of the public become more aware of the possibilities of the judicial review of governmental and legislative measures and more conscious of their rights. The discourse of the law has become more powerful than ever before in Hong Kong society. At the same time, the courts have been careful not to over-extend their jurisdiction in a manner that would upset the delicate balance of judicial, executive and legislative powers in the SAR and the even more delicate power relationship between the SAR courts and the central authorities in Beijing. As I have written elsewhere:

> [C]onsidering the inevitable tensions that inhere in the constitutional experiment of "one country, two systems," the record of the Hong Kong courts in dealing with these challenges has thus far been positive. The judiciary, led by the Court of Final Appeal, has chosen the middle path[59] or the "golden mean"[60] between confrontation with and subservience to Beijing, and between judicial activism and judicial restraint. In tackling their relationship with Beijing, the courts have adopted an approach that may be described — in a phrase translated from the Chinese — as "neither too proud nor too humble" (*bukang bubei*). In the domain of human rights, the tenor of the courts' decisions may be described as moderately liberal — neither radically liberal nor conservative ... such a middle path is indeed appropriate in the context of Hong Kong under "one country, two systems" (Chen, 2006, pp. 629–30).

Fourth, 10 years after the handover, the linkage between the legal systems of Hong Kong and Mainland China has remained weak and loose. The level of judicial cooperation between the two jurisdictions is still lower than that between Hong Kong and many other jurisdictions overseas, particularly common law jurisdictions. This is because of the huge differences between the two legal systems and the political sensitivity of some issues of judicial assistance, such as extradition or rendition. In this regard, what I wrote on the fifth anniversary of the Hong Kong SAR remains true even today:

> The constitutional and legal design of "one country, two systems" is such that the points of contact and interface between the two systems are few, and in

the overwhelming majority of cases and circumstances, the two systems operate autonomously without any interaction with one another.... The looseness of the connection between the two systems (at least from the legal point of view) is exemplified by the fact that despite the long negotiations between the SAR Government and Beijing on a possible rendition agreement on fugitive offenders, no agreement has yet been reached, and neither side sees the matter as a pressing one (Chen, 2002d, pp. 85–86).

Nevertheless, there are some recent signs of increasing linkage between the two legal systems. July 2006 saw the conclusion between the two sides of a judicial cooperation agreement known as the Arrangement on Reciprocal Recognition and Enforcement of Judgements in Civil and Commercial Matters by the Courts of the Mainland and of the Hong Kong SAR Pursuant to the Choice of the Court Agreement between Parties Concerned. In October 2006, the NPCSC passed a decision authorizing the Hong Kong SAR authorities to exercise jurisdiction in a port control zone located in a spot in Shenzhen where immigration and customs officers of both the Mainland and Hong Kong sides would be "co-located" to facilitate travel between Hong Kong and Shenzhen on the new Shenzhen–Hong Kong Western Corridor. On the basis of the NPCSC decision, legislation to implement the co-location scheme was enacted by LegCo in Hong Kong in April 2007.

As mentioned in the introduction to this chapter, given the low level of the Rule of Law and constitutionalism in the PRC as of 1984, to have faith then in the successful implementation of OCTS after 1997 was to take a leap in the dark. Even 10 years ago, it was still a complete unknown as to whether OCTS would work from a legal and constitutional perspective. The past 10 years have been a real learning experience for all who have a stake in the success of OCTS. By trial and error, episode by episode, sometimes painful, sometimes joyful, we have gradually mastered the legal art of the practice of OCTS. Tuition fees have been paid; lessons have been learned; and history has been written. It is, I believe, a history that we have all participated in making; a history that we can justifiably feel proud of; and a history that inspires confidence about ourselves, faith in our partners, and hope for the future.

Notes

1. *Xinbao* (*Hong Kong Economic Journal*), 27 April 2007, p. 12 (in Chinese).
2. [1999] 1 H.K.L.R.D. 315.

3. [1999] 1 H.K.L.R.D. 304.
4. Basic Law, Article 24(2)(3).
5. The Immigration (Amendment) (No. 2) Ordinance 1997 and the Immigration (Amendment) (No. 3) Ordinance 1997.
6. [1997] H.K.L.R.D. 761, (1997) H.K.C. 315. The court judgements in the cases discussed in this article are all available at the website of the Hong Kong Judiciary, http://legalref.judiciary.gov.hk.
7. See the Decision of the National People's Congress on the Method for the Formation of the First Government and the First Legislative Council of the Hong Kong SAR, enacted at the same time as the enactment of the Basic Law on 4 April 1990 and published together with the Basic Law. The Decision is reproduced in Ghai (1999, pp. 568–69).
8. [1999] 1 H.K.L.R.D. 315, at 337.
9. In a highly publicized seminar reported in the Hong Kong and Mainland Chinese media on 7 February 1999, four leading Chinese law professors, who were also former members of the Drafting Committee for the Basic Law and the Preparatory Committee for the establishment of the Hong Kong SAR, attacked the statement. They suggested that it had the effect of placing Hong Kong courts above the NPC, which is the supreme organ of state power under the Chinese Constitution, and of turning Hong Kong into an "independent political entity." After the visit of the Hong Kong SAR's Secretary for Justice Elsie Leung to Beijing on 12–13 February 1999 to discuss the matter, it was reported that Chinese officials had criticized the statement as unconstitutional and called for its "rectification." See generally Chan, Fu and Ghai (2000, p. 73).
10. [1999] 1 H.K.L.R.D. 577.
11. Article 158(3) of the Basic Law requires the CFA to refer to the NPCSC for the interpretation of relevant Basic Law provisions "concerning affairs which are the responsibility of the Central People's Government, or concerning the relationship between the Central Authorities and the Region."
12. This figure is the sum total of 690,000 (being the "first generation," consisting of children of current Hong Kong permanent residents) and 980,000 [being the "second generation," consisting of children (already born) of the "first generation" who will be entitled to the right of abode after their parents — as members of the "first generation" — have migrated to Hong Kong and resided there for seven years]. See generally Fung (2004); Chen and Cheung (2004, pp. 253–60).
13. It should be noted that although article 158(3) provides for reference by the CFA of a Basic Law provision to the NPCSC for interpretation in certain circumstances, Article 158 does not expressly state that the HKSAR government may ask the NPCSC to interpret the Basic Law. Article 158(1) does stipulate, however, that "[t]he power of interpretation of this Law shall be vested in" the NPCSC. See Chen (2000).

14. Government of the Hong Kong SAR Gazette Extraordinary, Legal Supplement No. 2, 28 June 1999, p. 1577 (L.N. 167 of 1999).
15. See generally Chan, Fu and Ghai (2000); Wesley-Smith (1999); Lin (2000); Xiao (2000).
16. [1999] 3 H.K.L.R.D. 778.
17. This is provided for in Article 158(3) of the Basic Law and is also reiterated in the text of the NPCSC's interpretation.
18. [1999] 3 H.K.L.R.D. 907, [1999] 2 H.K.C.F.A.R. 442.
19. Cap. 383, L.H.K. See generally Wacks (1990); Chan and Ghai (1993); Wacks (1992); Chan (1999).
20. For an English translation of this Decision, see 27 H.K.L.J. 419 (1997).
21. The interpretative provisions concerned were Sections 2(3), 3 and 4 of the Ordinance. For the effect of the non-adoption of these provisions, see Wesley-Smith (1997); Chan (1998b).
22. This section was basically reproduced from Article 19 of the PRC Law on the National Flag and Article 13 of the PRC Law on the National Emblem. These two PRC laws had since 1 July 1997 been listed in Annex III to the Basic Law as being among those Mainland laws that are applicable to Hong Kong under Article 18 of the Basic Law.
23. For the practice of "binding over," see Wesley-Smith (1992, pp. 26–27).
24. [1999] 1 H.K.L.R.D. 783.
25. Both the English and French expressions appear in the text of Article 19 of the ICCPR. In its judgement, the court below (the Court of Appeal) referred to two decisions of the American Supreme Court that determined that the criminalization of flag desecration violates the "free speech" clause in the U.S. Constitution and is unconstitutional: *Texas v. Johnson* 491 U.S. 397 (1989); *United States v. Eichman* 496 U.S. 310 (1990). Each of these cases was decided by a majority of five to four in the Supreme Court and was extremely controversial in the U.S.A.
26. Ibid. at 455.
27. Ibid. at 456.
28. Ibid. at 460–61.
29. [2000] 3 H.K.L.R.D. 641, (2000) 3 H.K.C.F.A.R. 459.
30. See the Government Rent (Assessment and Collection) Ordinance, Cap. 515. L.H.K.
31. 1898 was the year in which the British colony of Hong Kong — then comprising Hong Kong Island and Kowloon Peninsula — was expanded in size to include the New Territories north of Kowloon.
32. See the Village Representative Election Ordinance, Cap. 576, L.H.K. (Ord. No. 2 of 2003).
33. [2001] 2 H.K.L.R.D. 690.
34. The case was not appealed to any higher court.

35. Para. 80 of the judgement.
36. Para. 121 of the judgement.
37. For example, in *Bahadur v. Director of Immigration* (2002) 5 H.K.C.F.A.R. 480, which reached the CFA in July 2002, Bahadur, a citizen of Nepal living in Hong Kong as a non-permanent resident, successfully asserted his freedom to travel, which was held by the CFA to include as its essential element the right to re-enter Hong Kong after travelling. The CFA reiterated the approach it stated in previous cases that the rights and freedoms guaranteed by the Basic Law should be given a generous interpretation ("whilst restrictions to them should be narrowly interpreted") and that "these rights and freedoms lie at the heart of Hong Kong's separate system" under "one country, two systems." For a commentary on this case and its significance, see Young (2004).
38. [2001] 2 H.K.L.R.D. 533.
39. In a very unusual manner not seen since the constitutional crisis of February 1999, Beijing reacted publicly to the decision as well. On 21 July 2001, the morning immediately following the day of the CFA's decision, a spokesman from the Legislative Affairs Commission of the NPCSC, in a widely reported press statement, pointed out that the CFA's decision in *Chong Fung-yuen* was "not consistent" with the NPCSC's interpretation, and "expressed concern" about the matter. However, apart from this terse statement, no further action on the matter was taken by the Beijing side. In particular, no interpretation on the issue was issued by the NPCSC. See generally Chen (2001).
40. For discussion of the issues by this author, see Chen (2002b; 2002c).
41. On 28 January 2003, the government published the multi volume *Compendium of Submissions* and announced nine sets of clarifications or modifications of the original proposal.
42. On 5 July, the government also announced three major "concessions" on the content of the Bill — deleting the provision on the power to proscribe a local organization that is subordinate to a Mainland organization proscribed on the Mainland; introducing a public interest defence in the state secrets law; and deleting the provision on the power of the police to conduct searches without a warrant.
43. The citations of the Court of Appeal's and the CFA's decisions in this case are provided below.
44. See the Summary Offences Ordinance, ss. 4(28) and 4A.
45. For Falun Gong in Hong Kong, see Chen and Cheung (2004, pp. 261–62).
46. *HKSAR v. Yeung May Wan* [2004] 3 H.K.L.R.D. 797.
47. *Yeung May Wan v. HKSAR* [2005] 2 H.K.L.R.D. 212.
48. (2005) 8 H.K.C.F.A.R. 229.
49. The citations of the courts' decisions in this case are provided below.
50. The order was promulgated under Article 48(4) of the Basic Law.

51. *Leung Kwok-hung and Another v. Chief Executive of the HKSAR* (HCAL 107/ 2005; 9 February 2006).
52. They relied strongly on the Canadian case of *Manitoba Language Rights* [1985] 1 S.C.R. 721.
53. Para. 159 of the judgement.
54. Para. 165.
55. *Leung Kwok-hung and Another v. Chief Executive of the HKSAR* (CACV 73/ 2006; 10 May 2006).
56. *Koo Sze-yiu and Another v. Chief Executive of the HKSAR* [2006] 3 H.K.L.R. D. 455.
57. [2006] 4 H.K.L.R.D. 211.
58. I do not consider the interventions by the NPCSC in 2004 on the question of political reform and democratization an interference with the autonomy of the Hong Kong SAR. The Basic Law establishes a particular political system in Hong Kong and authorizes the government under this political system to exercise autonomy. The autonomy of Hong Kong is the autonomy of the government under this political system to govern Hong Kong. Such autonomy does not include the autonomy to change the political system itself.
59. [Footnote from the original text of the quotation] In the language of Chinese philosophy, such a middle path may be called "*zhongyong zhidao.*" The *Zhong Yong* (Book of the Mean) is one of the "Four Books" in the Confucian classics. See generally Fung (1966, pp. 172–74).
60. [Footnote from the original text of the quotation] As discussed in Aristotle's philosophy.

References

Byrnes, Andrew (2000), "And Some Have Bills of Rights Thrust Upon Them: The Experience of Hong Kong's Bill of Rights." In Philip Alston (ed.), *Promoting Human Rights Through Bills of Rights: Comparative Perspectives*. Oxford: Oxford University Press, chapter 9.

Chan, Johannes M. M. (1998a), "Hong Kong's Bill of Rights: Its Reception of and Contribution to International and Comparative Jurisprudence," *International and Comparative Law Quarterly*, 47: 306.

—— (1998b), "The Status of the Bill of Rights in the Hong Kong Special Administrative Region," *Hong Kong Law Journal*, 28: 152.

—— (1999), *The Annotated Ordinances of Hong Kong: Hong Kong Bill of Rights Ordinance*. Hong Kong: Butterworths Asia.

Chan, Johannes M. M., H. L. Fu and Yash Ghai (eds.) (2000), *Hong Kong's Constitutional Debate: Conflict Over Interpretation*. Hong Kong: Hong Kong University Press.

Chan, Johannes and Yash Ghai (eds.) (1993), *The Hong Kong Bill of Rights: A Comparative Approach*. Hong Kong: Butterworths Asia.

Chan, Johannes and Lison Harris (eds.) (2005), *Hong Kong's Constitutional Debates*. Hong Kong: Hong Kong Law Journal Limited.

Chan, Johannes and Bart Rweraura (eds.) (2004), *Immigration Law in Hong Kong: An Interdisciplinary Study*. Hong Kong: Sweet & Maxwell Asia.

Chen, Albert H. Y. (1999), "Constitutional Crisis in Hong Kong: Congressional Supremacy and Judicial Review," *The International Lawyer*, 33: 1025.

—— (2000), "The Interpretation of the Basic Law — Common Law and Mainland Chinese Perspectives," *Hong Kong Law Journal*, 30: 380.

—— (2001), "Another Case of Conflict Between the CFA and the NPC Standing Committee?" *Hong Kong Law Journal*, 31: 179.

—— (2002a), "Ng Ka-ling and Article 158(3) of the Basic Law," *Journal of Chinese and Comparative Law*, 5: 222.

—— (2002b), "Proposals a Credit to '1 Country, 2 Systems,'" *China Daily* (Hong Kong edition), 7 October 2002, pp. 3–4.

—— (2002c), "Will Our Civil Liberties Survive the Implementation of Article 23?" *Hong Kong Lawyer*, November, pp. 80–88.

—— (2202d), "The Constitution and the Rule of Law." In Lau Siu-kai (ed.), *The First Tung Chee-hwa Administration: The First Five Years of the Hong Kong Special Administrative Region*. Hong Kong: The Chinese University Press, chapter 3.

—— (2003a), "How Hong Kong Law Will Change When Article 23 of the Basic Law is Implemented," *Hong Kong Law Journal*, 33: 1.

—— (2003b), "Hong Kong's Political Crisis of July 2003," *Hong Kong Law Journal*, 33: 265.

—— (2004), "The Constitutional Controversy of Spring 2004," *Hong Kong Law Journal*, 34: 215.

—— (2005), "The NPCSC's Interpretation in Spring 2005," *Hong Kong Law Journal*, 35: 255.

—— (2006), "Constitutional Adjudication in Post-1997 Hong Kong," *Pacific Rim Law and Policy Journal*, 15: 627.

Chen, Albert H. Y. and Anne S. Y. Cheung (2004), "Debating Rule of Law in the Hong Kong Special Administrative Region, 1997–2002." In Randall Peerenboom (ed.), *Asian Discourses of Rule of Law*. London: Routledge, chapter 8.

Cheung, Anne S. Y. and Albert H. Y. Chen (2004), "The Search for the Rule of Law in the Hong Kong Special Administrative Region, 1997–2003." In Wong Yiu-chung (ed.), *"One Country, Two Systems" in Crisis*. Lanham: Lexington Books, chapter 3.

Deng, Xiaoping (2004), *Deng Xiaoping on "One Country, Two Systems."* Hong Kong: Joint Publishing.

Fu, Hualing, Carole J. Petersen and Simon N. M. Young (eds.) (2005), *National Security and Fundamental Freedoms: Hong Kong's Article 23 Under Scrutiny.* Hong Kong: Hong Kong University Press.

Fung, Ho-lup (2004), "The 'Right of Abode' Issue: A Test Case of 'One Country, Two Systems.'" In Wong Yiu-chung (ed.), *"One Country, Two Systems" in Crisis.* Lanham: Lexington Books, chapter 4.

Fung, Yu-lan (1966), *A Short History of Chinese Philosophy*, first published 1948. New York: The Free Press.

Ghai, Yash (1997), "Sentinels of Liberty or Sheep in Woolf's Clothing? Judicial Politics and the Hong Kong Bill of Rights," *Modern Law Review*, 60: 459.

Lin, Feng (2000), "The Constitutional Crisis in Hong Kong — Is It Over?" *Pacific Rim Law and Policy Journal*, 9: 281.

Ling, Bing (1999), "Can Hong Kong Courts Review and Nullify Acts of the National People's Congress?" *Hong Kong Law Journal*, 29: 8.

Miners, Norman (1995), *The Government and Politics of Hong Kong*, 5th edition. Hong Kong: Oxford University Press.

Wacks, Raymond (ed.) (1990), *Hong Kong's Bill of Rights*. Hong Kong: Faculty of Law, The University of Hong Kong.

—— (ed.) (1992), *Human Rights in Hong Kong*. Hong Kong: Oxford University Press.

Wesley-Smith, Peter (1992), "Protecting Human Rights in Hong Kong." In Wacks (1992), chapter 1.

—— (1995), *Constitutional and Administrative Law in Hong Kong*. Hong Kong: Longman Asia.

—— (1997), "Maintenance of the Bill of Rights," *Hong Kong Law Journal*, 27: 15.

Xiao, Yongping (2000), "Comments on the Judgment on the Right of Abode by Hong Kong CFA," *American Journal of Comparative Law*, 48: 471.

9

A Decade of Change in the Business Environment

Qin Xiao

Introduction

Since the handover in 1997, Hong Kong has been undergoing many radical changes that have not only fascinated the world but also profoundly affected the people, the businesses and the political-social outlook of this Special Administrative Region (SAR) that is governed under the unique arrangement of "one country, two systems." These changes have drastically altered the local and even regional economic, social and business environments.

When academics discuss the business environments, their analytic units have traditionally been national-level home economies. However, as businesses have become more and more globalized in nature, the distinction between home economies and international markets has become blurred. As a city economy, Hong Kong has never been a close-ended system. This chapter is a discussion of the local business environment within the context of the global economy. In addition to globalization, another approach to understanding the Hong Kong business environment is the increasing economic and social integration that has been occurring between Hong Kong and the Mainland since the handover.

The aim of this chapter is to reflect upon the changes that have occurred in different dimensions of Hong Kong's business environment after 1997. While the study of national-level business environments has a long history, the analysis of city business environments is relatively new. In observing the changes that have taken place in Hong Kong in the last decade, three main driving forces that have shaped the business landscape of Hong Kong as "Asia's world city" should be kept in mind — reunification, globalization and integration.[1]

Therefore, the main theme of this chapter is the changes in Hong Kong's business environment under the process of national reunification, economic globalization and regional integration. In subsequent sections, I shall (1) briefly review the original design of Deng Xiaoping and the Basic Law for Hong Kong's post-handover economic system; (2) summarize the general contours of Hong Kong's economic performance after 1997; (3) explore Hong Kong's investment environment from the perspective of globalization and foreign direct investment; (4) describe the increasingly integrated Greater Pearl River Delta (GPRD) region, which provides an explanation for the changes that have been taking place in Hong Kong's competitiveness in the global economy; (5) review the rankings of Hong Kong's business environment from the perspectives of different international indices; and (6) discuss from different dimensions issues relating to Hong Kong's business environment that are being debated and disputed.

Deng Xiaoping's Design for Hong Kong: "One Country, Two Systems"

To understand the changes in Hong Kong over the last decade, it is of interest to recall Deng Xiaoping's original design for the concept of one country, two systems (OCTS), which was proposed primarily to achieve the dual objectives of preserving a prosperous Hong Kong, while securing China's wider national interests by providing a framework to resolve the Taiwan issue.

Some 20 years ago, Deng told Hong Kong's leading businessmen that "… after China resumes the exercise of its sovereignty over Hong Kong in 1997, Hong Kong's current social and economic systems will remain unchanged, its legal system will remain basically unchanged, its way of life and its status as a free port and an international trade and financial centre will remain unchanged and it can continue to maintain or establish economic relations with other countries and regions" (Deng, 2004, pp. 11–12).

In accordance with this design, Hong Kong's constitutional document, the Basic Law, guarantees that the existing economic, legal and social systems of Hong Kong will remain unchanged for 50 years. In addition, Hong Kong's capitalist system and way of life will continue. Hong Kong maintains a free and open market economy with a free flow of capital, goods, information and services, and a freely convertible currency. In terms of the reunification with Mainland China, the boundary between Hong Kong and the Mainland is clearly delineated and properly managed. In terms of foreign business and investment, Hong Kong welcomes and encourages the participation of foreign enterprises, and provides a level-playing field for all.

From the designer's perspective, the whole logic of Hong Kong's handover has been to maintain "stability and prosperity," and to effect minimum changes except for the transition to sovereignty. Since the handover, the Hong Kong Special Administrative Region (HKSAR) has indeed maintained its capitalist economic and legal systems, and retained its status as a free port with the free movement of goods and capital.

Hong Kong's fundamental institutions and systems have remained unchanged; but dramatic economic, social and cultural transformations are taking place in Hong Kong. Outlining the driving forces behind those changes will enhance our understanding of what has happened in this tiny geographical area during the last 10 years.

Hong Kong's Economic Development

Due to space constraints, a detailed analysis of Hong Kong's economic performance since 1997 is beyond the scope of this chapter. However, a brief review of what has happened in the last decade is of importance in helping us to understand the overall background of Hong Kong's business environment.

On the one hand, major events in the last decade have had a severe impact on Hong Kong's society and economy. These include the Asian financial crisis, the bursting of the dotcom bubble, the global economic recession related to the September 11th terrorist attacks, and the outbreak of severe acute respiratory syndrome (SARS). In the face of these happenings, it was no longer viable to maintain the status quo in Hong Kong. On the other hand, Hong Kong's integration with Mainland China has provided strong support for economic growth in Hong Kong. It is likely that, without this support, Hong Kong would have fared poorly economically, socially and politically during the last decade. The Closer Economic Partnership Arrangement (CEPA), the Individual Visit Scheme, and many other preferential measures and policies were introduced, and these contributed to a quick rebound in Hong Kong in the period 2003–2006 (Figure 9.1).

Figure 9.1 Hong Kong Real GDP Growth (%)

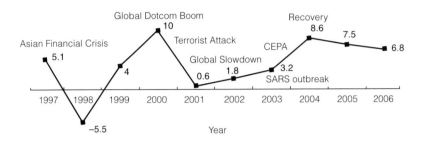

Source: Census and Statistics Department, HKSAR government, *2006 Gross Domestic Product*. From www.censtatd.gov.hk.

Asian Financial Crisis, 1997–1998

On 2 July 1997, the day after Hong Kong's return to Chinese sovereignty, the Asian financial crisis broke out in Thailand. The turmoil soon spread to Hong Kong. As interest rates rose to defend the Hong Kong dollar's peg to the U.S. dollar, the stock market plunged and the property bubble burst. Hong Kong abruptly entered a period of economic stagnation of a magnitude that Hong Kong people had not experienced since Hong Kong's industrialization in the 1970s. The GDP growth rate declined from 5.1% in 1997 to minus 5.5% in 1998, the first negative growth in 13 years. During 1998, the property market was highly depressed, with prices down 45% from their peak in the previous year. Similarly, the stock market was 55% below its peak in August 1997. Unemployment rate rose to 4.2%, the highest level recorded in Hong Kong in 14 years.

The first Chief Executive, Mr Tung Chee-hwa, unaware of the severity of the coming recession, set out a series of ambitious development targets in his first policy address in October 1997. One controversial policy was his target of building 85,000 flats each year to cool down the heated property market. Unfortunately, that policy was announced in the same month as the fall of Hang Seng Index, and the beginning of the macro-economic recession in Hong Kong brought about by the Asian financial crisis. Critics later frequently linked Mr Tung's housing policy with the subsequent decline in the property market.

Another debatable issue with regard to Hong Kong's business environment was the government's role in making economic policy at a time when Hong Kong was going through the worst recession in its recent history. On the one hand, the government faced growing pressure from the public to act as quickly as possible to stimulate the economy and create jobs through increased government spending — leading to more interventionist economic polices. As a result, the HKSAR government announced a series of policy measures to stimulate the economy, stabilize the property market, secure the banking system and, of course, create jobs. In June 1998, Tung Chee-hwa unveiled a four-point package to stimulate the economy, in particular the property sector. Another symbolic action was taken by the government on 14 August 1998 when, under the threat of continued attacks on the Hong Kong dollar and the capital market by international speculators, it began to make direct purchases on the stock market. In the end, the government spent HK$120 billion intervening in the stock market. These measures were generally well received by the business and financial sectors. However, the government's interventions were also criticized by individual interest groups, political parties and academics.

The High-tech Boom and the Dotcom Bubble, 1999–2000

After being hit heavily by regional crises, Hong Kong's economy bounced back in the second half of 1999. That year, Hong Kong recorded a real GDP growth rate of 4%, due mainly to an economic recovery in Asia and elsewhere, as well as to the high-tech and dotcom boom in stock markets worldwide. In 2000, Hong Kong's GDP growth was even stronger, at 10%. Economic integration with the Pearl River Delta (PRD) region continued to gain momentum. The optimism was sustained until 2001, the year when China was scheduled to enter the World Trade Organization (WTO). An increase in export activity in China helped Hong Kong to recover, but domestic demand and investment growth remained weak.

In order to stimulate the economy, the government announced the Cyberport development plan. The development rights were granted to a group led by Richard Li Tzar-kai, an act that created a storm of controversy among local developers. Another symbolic move was the government's participation in the building of a Disneyland theme park, aimed at promoting Hong Kong's tourism sector.

Global Slowdown, Terrorist Attacks and SARS, 2001–2003

However, the global economy experienced a slowdown beginning in the second half of 2001 due to the bursting of the dotcom bubble, and was further adversely affected by the September 11th terrorist attacks in the U.S. Once again, Hong Kong fell into a two-year economic recession. Hong Kong recorded only 0.6% and 1.8% growth in GDP in 2001 and 2002, respectively. Hong Kong also entered a period of prolonged deflation.

During this period, Hong Kong was undergoing painful economic restructuring. In his 2001 Policy Address, Tung Chee-hwa announced a number of policies and measures on education and training, in order to transform Hong Kong into a knowledge-based economy. That same year saw a major in Tung's administration with the resignation of Chief Secretary Anson Chan and her replacement by Donald Tsang Yam-kuen.

Hong Kong's economy improved in the second half of 2002. People began to expect an end to two lean years and to look forward to a full recovery in the coming year. However, in February 2003, Hong Kong was badly hit by a previously unknown disease, which subsequently was named SARS. A total of 299 lives were lost and 1,755 people were infected over the course of a 100-day nightmare. The tourism, retail, entertainment and catering sectors were particularly hard hit. The SARS outbreak had serious economic consequences for Hong Kong in 2003.

When Hong Kong experienced serious difficulties, Mainland China offered a helping hand. The outbreak of SARS in Hong Kong resulted in a sharp drop in the number of both Mainland and overseas visitors. In order to boost Hong Kong's tourism industry and economy, the Individual Visit Scheme was launched in July 2003, allowing Mainland visitors to enter Hong Kong on an individual basis. At the same time, the central government introduced other initiatives to help revitalize Hong Kong's economy, and placed a strong emphasis on regional economic integration. Both the Mainland and HKSAR governments accelerated negotiations over a free-trade arrangement between Hong Kong and Mainland China. This led to the signing of CEPA on 29 June 2003, an arrangement to eliminate import tariffs on most Hong Kong–made goods (accounting for 60% of Hong Kong's exports to the Mainland) from 1 January 2004, and to open up the Chinese services sector, giving Hong Kong firms greater and earlier access to the Mainland market, ahead of China's WTO timetable.

The year 2003 proved to be the most challenging year for Hong Kong in the first decade after the handover, whether politically, economically or socially. While economic integration with Mainland China gained momentum and concrete progress was made there that year, Hong Kong's political landscape deteriorated. On 1 July 2003, half a million people took to the streets to protest against the Article 23 legislation[2] and to demand "democracy."

CEPA and Recovery, 2004–2006

Beginning in the second half of 2003, Hong Kong's economy started to recover strongly. An unexpected real GDP growth rate of 3.2% was achieved in for the year 2003 as a whole. Hong Kong's recovery was widely attributed to its external sectors, and to the fact that the SAR was benefiting continually from its integration with Mainland China.

CEPA came into effect in January 2004. In June 2004, the first Pan–Pearl River Delta (Pan-PRD) Regional Cooperation and Development Forum was held, bringing together the governors of nine Chinese provinces and the chief executives of the Hong Kong and Macao SARs. The aim of this forum was to expand the economic ties between Hong Kong (and Macao) and southern China, known as the "9 plus 2" region, and to achieve an agreement to cooperate on broad agendas for economic and social development.

The momentum for growth was maintained in 2004 and 2005, when strong GDP growth rates of 8.6% and 7.5%, respectively, were realized. In 2005, Tung Chee-hwa chose to step down early on health grounds. He announced his resignation on 10 March. According to the Basic Law, the Chief Secretary for Administration, Donald Tsang Yam-kuen, assumed duties as the acting Chief Executive. Six months later, he received nominations from most members of the Election Committee and was appointed by the State Council as the Chief Executive of the HKSAR.

Hong Kong continued its strong recovery in 2006. An increasing number of Mainland tourists visiting Hong Kong, and more and more Mainland companies listing in Hong Kong helped Hong Kong to record a GDP growth rate of 6.8% that year. In addition, in terms of funds raised, Hong Kong's stock market ranked second in the world that year.

Is Hong Kong back on track for continued economic growth? After several years of stagnation, optimism in society has been in short supply. Looking back at 1997, when Hong Kong was celebrating its return to China, optimism was high among Hong Kong's 6.5 million residents probably in large part because of, not despite, the bubble in the stock and property markets. Over the last decade, Hong Kong has gone through the painful process of economic transformation and developed into a service-based economy in line with increased integration with Mainland China. Today, Hong Kong's role is clearly defined, that is, to serve its hinterland. Thus, further integration with the PRD is undoubtedly the only path to Hong Kong's economic future. In this sense, we should all be optimists.

Globalization and Hong Kong

The term "globalization" itself seems to have many meanings, but it mainly refers to a more connected world in which barriers and borders of many kinds are coming down, felled both by technological change, and by ideas and policies (Yergin and Stanislaw, 2000). Globalization brings down the barriers to the movement of people, goods, capital and information. Along with economic globalization, foreign direct investment (FDI) — productive investment across borders — has been growing at a dramatic pace in the last several decades. The flow of FDI has constantly changed the world's economic landscape, and in turn defined the level of competitiveness of specific cities. It also has become a much more important engine of economic growth both in the home and host economies.

FDI Inflows: Hong Kong Remains a Favoured Location

As the first free port in Asia, Hong Kong has attracted significant inflows of FDI in its history. During the last decade, Hong Kong has maintained its position as one of the most favoured destinations for global FDI inflows (Table 9.1). As the figure shows, Hong Kong's FDI inflows rose from US$11.4 billion in 1997 to an all-time high of US$61.9 billion in 2000,[3] owing to the global economic recovery, high-tech fever and mergers & acquisitions (M&A) boom worldwide. FDI inflows then declined to US$9.7 billion in 2002 and US$13.6 billion in 2003, when Hong Kong was suffering economic difficulties and undergoing painful economic restructuring. Since 2004, Hong Kong has regained its growth momentum in FDI inflows. Such inflows reached US$35.9 billion in 2005, followed by a further increase to US$41.4 billion[4] in 2006.

In rankings of FDI inflows in Asia, Hong Kong is second only after Mainland China, and has outperformed Singapore since 1998. This shows Hong Kong's competitive edge over other Asian economies as a preferred

Table 9.1 FDI Inflow into Hong Kong (Unit: US$ million)

	1997	1998	1999	2000	2001	2002	2003	2004	2005	2006
HKSAR	11,368	14,766	24,580	61,939	23,775	9,682	13,624	34,032	35,897	41,400
Singapore	13,533	7,690	16,067	17,217	15,038	5,822	10,376	14,820	20,083	31,900
China	44,237	45,463	40,319	40,715	46,878	52,743	53,505	60,630	72,406	70,000

Source: UNCTAD, 2006.

destination for FDI. In its annual "World Investment Report," UNCTAD publishes an "Inward FDI Performance Index," which shows the ratio of an economy's share of global FDI inflows to its share of global GDP, reflecting the extent to which a host economy receives FDI inflows relative to its economic size. This index thus captures the factors of attractiveness to inflows of FDI other than market size such as a location's business climate, economic and political stability, natural resources, infrastructure, skills, technologies and the effectiveness of its promotion of FDI.

In the Inward FDI Performance Index, Hong Kong ranked third globally in 1990, rose to second place in 2000, dropped to sixth in 2004, and bounced back to third place in 2005. Again, Hong Kong has outperformed Singapore since 2000 and has proven to be one of the most attractive destinations for foreign investment after 1997. However, in 2004 Hong Kong was only positioned at fifteenth in UNCTAD's rankings of places in the "Inward FDI Potential Index," a measure based upon 12 economic and structural variables,[5] which captures several factors (apart from market size) that are expected to affect an economy's attractiveness to foreign investors (UNCTAD, 2006, p. 277). This was well below Singapore's fifth-place ranking that year. This index attempts to assess an economy's potential in attracting FDI inflows (Table 9.2).

UNCTAD has also ranked the degree of transnationality of a host economy by using the "transnationality index" (TNI), composed by the average of four ratios.[6] In its 2006 report, UNCTAD gave Hong Kong's TNI an assessment of 85.5%, ranking it first in the world and well above second-placed Iceland with 63.7, and sixth-placed Singapore with 59.3% (Figure 9.2).

FDI Outflows: Hong Kong Leads in Asia

In outflows of FDI, Hong Kong has maintained a leading position in Asia. The pattern of its FDI outflows is roughly the same as that of its inflows. Its FDI outflows plunged from US$24.4 billion in 1997 to US$17 billion in

Figure 9.2 Transnationality Index of Host Economies, 2003

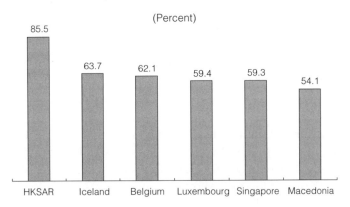

Source: UNCTAD, 2006, p. 11.

Table 9.2 Ranking in the Indices of Inward FDI Performance and Potential, 1990–2005

Economy	Inward FDI performance index					Inward FDI potential index			
	1990	2000	2004	2005		1990	2000	2003	2004
Azerbaijan	–	10	1	1	Netherlands	8	8	11	11
Brunei Darussalam	93	7	2	2	Iceland	14	15	13	12
Hong Kong, China	3	2	6	3	Finland	9	9	12	13
Estonia	–	19	15	4	Belgium	–	–	–	14
Singapore	1	5	7	5	Hong Kong, China	20	13	14	15
Luxembourg	–	–	4	6	France	7	12	15	16
Lebanon	99	31	8	7	Korea	21	18	16	17
Malta	21	6	30	8	Australia	12	20	20	18
Bulgaria	106	30	9	9	Taiwan	22	21	17	19
Congo	85	14	10	10	Switzerland	11	14	18	20

Source: UNCTAD, 2006, pp. 277–78.

1998 and US$19.3 billion in 1999. It reached a peak of US$59.4 billion in 2000, then again declined significantly and reached a low in 2003 of only US$5.5 billion. As its economy recovered in 2004 and 2005, Hong Kong's FDI outflows rebounded strongly, at US$45.7 billion and US$32.6 billion, respectively.

After the launching of economic reforms in China, Hong Kong

manufacturers were among the first and the largest investors in Mainland China, particularly in the PRD region. During the last decade, Hong Kong's FDI outflows have often targeted its economic hinterland to the north. As a result, Hong Kong has become the largest source of FDI outflows in Asia, significantly outperforming Singapore and other developing countries in the world (Table 9.3).

Table 9.3 FDI Outflows from Hong Kong (Unit: US$ million)

	1997	1998	1999	2000	2001	2002	2003	2004	2005
Hong Kong	24,407	16,985	19,358	59,375	11,345	17,463	5,492	45,716	32,560
Singapore	8,955	380	5,397	6,061	9,548	4,095	3,143	8,512	5,519
China	2,563	2,634	1,775	916	6,884	2,518	−152	1,805	11,306

Source: UNCTAD, 2003: 255; 2005: 306; 2006: 301–2.

UNCTAD also publishes an "Outward FDI Performance Index," where performance is calculated by the share of an economy's outward FDI in world FDI as a ratio of its share in world GDP, reflecting factors determining FDI outflows by specific economy. Driven by the competitive pressures of economic globalization, firms have been increasing their investments abroad by establishing foreign affiliates. Statistics show that most of Hong Kong's outward direct investment has gone to the PRD region of Mainland China, helping the PRD to emerge as one of the most important manufacturing centres in the world. This provides an explanation for the rise of Hong Kong's ranking in the Outward FDI Performance Index, from thirteenth place in 1990 and to first place after 2000 (Table 9.4).

Table 9.4 Ranking in the Outward FDI Performance Index, 1990–2005

Economy	1990	2000	2004	2005
Hong Kong, China	13	1	1	1
Norway	25	2	2	2
Luxembourg	–	–	5	3
Switzerland	4	3	3	4
Netherlands	3	4	4	5
Belgium	–	–	7	6
Singapore	16	5	6	7
Panama	1	8	8	8
United Kingdom	5	7	9	9
Sweden	7	9	10	10

Source: UNCTAD, Country Fact Sheet (2006).

Hong Kong: A Preferred Location for Regional Headquarters/Offices

To foreign businesses, Hong Kong affiliates of multinational corporations (MNCs) play a very special role in organizing regional business activities. Hong Kong serves as a pre-eminent management and coordination centre not only for the Greater China region, but also for the Asia-Pacific region. Studies show that Hong Kong is the regional headquarters/offices[7] (RHQs/ROs) capital of the Asia-Pacific region by a wide and growing margin over Singapore, and that Hong Kong has more than three times the number of regional headquarters as Tokyo, nine times that of Sydney, and roughly twelve times that of Shanghai and Beijing (Enright, Scott and Chang, 2005, pp. 22–23).

Hong Kong's free port benefits all businesses, not only domestic firms, but also foreign investors. While no preferential treatment is given to foreign companies, they are not discriminated against either. Foreign companies from all around the world see Hong Kong as an ideal place to set up their regional headquarters/offices for the purpose of developing and managing their regional business operations, especially those in Mainland China. According to a serial survey, 3,845 overseas companies had established either regional headquarters or regional offices in Hong Kong in 2006, the number having grown from 3,237 in 2001 (Table 9.5).

Hong Kong's attractiveness as a favourable location for regional headquarters/offices can be attributed to its world-class infrastructure and its high degree of integration with Mainland China. We have witnessed a growing trend of foreign companies using Hong Kong as their regional headquarters/office for managing and developing business in Asia or Mainland China. The Hong Kong regional headquarters/office of a firm is often used as a special investment vehicle for the firm's parent company. This has brought inflows of FDI to Hong Kong and outflows of FDI to the Asia-Pacific region and Mainland China in the form of trans-shipments through Hong Kong.

Table 9.5 MNCs' Regional Headquarters and Regional Offices in Hong Kong

	2001	2002	2003	2004	2005	2006
RHQs	944	948	966	1,098	1,167	1,228
ROs	2,293	2,171	2,241	2,511	2,631	2,617
RHQs + ROs	3,237	3,119	3,207	3,609	3,798	3,845

Source: *Invest Hong Kong*, 2007.

Hong Kong and the PRD Region: An Integrated Economy [8]

Since the 1980s, when China began its reforms and open policy, Hong Kong has provided global and local businesses with long-term access to Mainland China. Thanks to its proximity to Hong Kong, the PRD region became a pioneer in the process of opening up to the outside world. In the early 1980s, the Hong Kong manufacturing industry began to move its operations northward, to the PRD region. As a result, over the past 20 years, the PRD has become a major manufacturing base in the world.

During the last decade, however, official statistics have shown that Hong Kong's direct investment in Guangdong has remained at a level of around US$7–9 billion each year, falling from about 80% to 50% of total FDI inflows to Guangdong. But we believe that the size of Hong Kong's investment in the PRD region has been significantly underestimated due to the rise of trans-shipment investments from offshore financial centres (mainly the British Virgin Islands). Data for Hong Kong show that 27% of its outward FDI stock in 2004 was to non-performing offshore financial centres, as this type of trans-shipped investment increased significantly after the handover (UNCTAD, 2006, p. 13). At the same time, FDI in Guangdong from those offshore financial centres has increased rapidly. I argue that official statistics might not reflect the actual picture of Hong Kong's investments in Guangdong. Some adjustments must be made accordingly. Drawing on data related to trans-shipped investments from offshore financial centres, I estimate that Hong Kong's direct investment in Guangdong was about US$1–2 billion more per year than stated by the official statistics.

While the success of the PRD region has been attributable to its proximity to Hong Kong, Hong Kong's economic success has also depended upon its strategic position in globalization and its economic interactions with the PRD region. As Hong Kong's costs were already the highest among the Asian economies in the 1970s, its labour-intensive manufacturing industries would have relocated to other lower-cost areas — if not the PRD region (Sung, 2004). Integration with the PRD region has proven to be the best solution to Hong Kong's structural transformation.

During the 1980s and 1990s, Hong Kong's businesses moved their manufacturing facilities to the PRD region, but retained their management know-how, marketing and value-added product-services at home in Hong Kong. Hong Kong has thus been transformed into a service-dominated economy. After 20 years of development, a "front shop, back factory" model of regional division of labour between Hong Kong and the PRD region has taken shape, highlighting the pattern of trade between the two sides.

Today, the degree of economic integration between the PRD and Hong Kong is, to some extent, greater than that between Guangdong and any other province, in terms of investment activities, trade and the exchange of people. The basic argument of this chapter is that Hong Kong and the PRD region should be considered as a single economy — as one highly integrated region. Only then would we be able to decode the true changes in the business environment in the past decade. Otherwise, when comparing the business environment of Hong Kong with that of other national-level economies, we are simply comparing "apples to oranges."

In this chapter, contrary to many studies that analyze Hong Kong and the PRD separately, Hong Kong is placed in the context of the GPRD region and the business environment is discussed from the perspective of a single economy. If Hong Kong and Guangdong are taken as one economic entity, the collective growth of the GPRD region should be examined. Between 1995 and 2004, the compound annual GDP growth rate of the GPRD region amounted to 6.34%, which was quite impressive considering that the Asian financial crisis and a global economic depression had broken out during those years. The region's GDP reached US$450 billion in 2006, making the size of its economy comparable to that of Switzerland.

Trade between Hong Kong and the PRD region (mostly in the form of re-exports) had been rising rapidly during the last decade. Trade from Hong Kong to the PRD had risen from US$41.2 billion in 1995 to US$123.2 billion in 2004, representing a compound annual growth rate of 12.94%; and trade from the PRD to Hong Kong had risen from US$45.4 billion in 1995 to US$93.9 billion in 2004, for a compound annual growth rate of 8.4% although there had been a relatively high level of volatility during those years.

The GPRD region has become an economic powerhouse in the last decade. Regional integration between Hong Kong and the PRD is largely the natural outcome of historical, cultural and geographical factors. Given that regional economic integration is a constantly changing process, there is a need to redefine the extent and scope of economic integration from time to time. Looking back, the classification of the economic zones of the PRD has undergone three stages, reflecting an expanding interactive economic region. Hong Kong and the PRD rely on each other, and this reliance has grown as the trading activities carried out inside the region further develop. In fact, the establishment of the Pan-PRD grouping gives

Hong Kong the opportunity to integrate with a much larger part of the Mainland than it might otherwise have had.

In recent years, Hong Kong's integration with Mainland China has gone beyond developments in the manufacturing sector. About 250,000 Hong Kong residents now work on the Mainland, almost double the number in 1997. Another survey in 2005 showed that 472,900 Hong Kong residents are living or spending substantial periods of time on the Mainland. The flow of people to the Mainland, seeking work and investment opportunities, matches the trend of growing numbers of Mainland people arriving in Hong Kong, for reasons of tourism, leisure, shopping and business.

Another area of closer integration has been the increasing number of Mainland enterprises securing a listing on the Hong Kong stock market. At the end of 2006, there were 367 Mainland companies listed in Hong Kong, triple the number in 1997. The total market capitalization of Mainland-listed companies reached HK$6,714 billion that year, almost 13 times that of in 1997 (Table 9.6). Today, Mainland-listed companies account for more than half of the Hong Kong stock market's capitalization and over 60% of the daily trading volume of Hong Kong stocks. All of these developments are boosting Hong Kong's aspirations to be Asia's leading international financial centre.

Table 9.6 Mainland Enterprises Listed in Hong Kong

As at year-end	Total market capitalization of Mainland enterprises (HK$ billion)	Mainland enterprises as % of market	Number of Mainland enterprises listed in HK
1997	522.42	16	101
1998	372.81	14	112
1999	1,005.30	21	124
2000	1,308.65	27	142
2001	1,049.17	27	168
2002	982.09	27	214
2003	1,679.69	30	249
2004	2,020.45	30	304
2005	3,192.09	39	335
2006	6,714.46	50	367

Source: *Hong Kong Exchanges and Clearing, 2007.*

Hong Kong's Investment Environment

The capability of an economy to successfully create an attractive business and investment environment, and ultimately to maintain its competitiveness over other economies, is critical for economic growth. There are various international indices that seek to rank the degree of economic freedom, competitiveness and business environment of a place. In this section, we will review Hong Kong's ranking in related international indices published by leading think tanks and research institutions. This will help us to understand Hong Kong business environment from different perspectives.

Ranking of Economic Freedom

There are two leading indices of economic freedom, compiled separately by the Heritage Foundation and the Frasier Institute. Hong Kong has kept its status as the world's freest economy for 13 consecutive years since the Washington-based conservative research firm the Heritage Foundation published its first "Index of Economic Freedom" in 1995. According to its 2007 annual report, Hong Kong scored exceptionally well in almost all of the 10 areas of economic freedom listed by the foundation.[9] Among them, income and corporate tax rates were extremely low, and overall taxation was relatively small as a percentage of GDP. Business regulation has been simple, and the labour market has remained highly flexible. Inflation has been kept low, and investment in Hong Kong is wide open, with virtually no restrictions on foreign capital. Hong Kong is also one of the world's leading financial centres, with an extensive banking and services industry that is regulated non-intrusively and transparently. The judiciary, independent of politics and virtually free of corruption, has an exemplary ability to protect property rights.

Singapore remained in second place in the Heritage Foundation's rankings of economic freedom. However, in its 1999 and 2000 rankings, the conservative think tank warned that Hong Kong might lose the top spot to Singapore because of the government's intervention in the stock market and involvement in the Disneyland theme park project.

The Fraser Institute, another independent think tank based in Vancouver, Canada, has, since 1996, published an annual book entitled *Economic Freedom of the World*. Thirty-eight data points are used to construct a summary index and to measure in five areas the degree of economic freedom of a place.[10] In the report for the year 2006, Hong Kong also retained the highest rating for economic freedom, followed by Singapore, New Zealand, Switzerland and the United States.

Ranking of Competitiveness

The competitiveness of locations — nations, regions or cities — is arguably rooted in the nature of the business environment they offer to firms (Porter, 1998, pp. 7, 155–96). The best known index of global competitiveness is that of the World Economic Forum, which each year publishes a "Global Competitiveness Report." Hong Kong has seen its place in the rankings slip from second in 1997, to thirteenth in 2001, and further to twenty-eighth in 2005. However, the World Economic Forum has often changed its methodology for measuring competitiveness. In its 2006–2007 report, it raised Hong Kong's position to eleventh and revised Hong Hong's position in 2005 to fourteenth (World Economic Forum, 2007). In this most recent report, Hong Kong ranked behind Switzerland, Finland, Sweden, Denmark, Singapore, the United States, Japan, Germany, the Netherlands and the United Kingdom.[11]

Another leading index of competitiveness, compiled by a Swiss business school, International Institute for Management Development (IMD), has provided a quite different picture of Hong Kong's competitiveness. IMD bases its ranking on 20 sub-criteria covering four areas: economic performance, government efficiency, business efficiency and infrastructure. Hong Kong was ranked second overall and Singapore third for three consecutive years, from 2004 to 2006. Hong Kong came first in two of the four areas: business efficiency and government efficiency. By comparison, in the year 2000, Hong Kong had fallen to as low as fourteenth (IMD, 2006).

Ranking for Business Environment

The World Bank's International Financial Corporation has published a "Doing Business Index" since 2004. The index is intended to measure the regulation and protection of property rights in various places, and their effect on businesses, especially small and medium-sized domestic firms. A high ranking on the ease of doing business index means that the regulatory environment of a place is conducive to the operation of business, and that there are better, usually simpler, regulations for businesses and stronger protection of property rights in that place than in a place with low ranking.

According to the 2007 "Doing Business Index," Hong Kong is the fifth easiest place to do business among 175 economies in the world, up from seventh in 2006, and sixth in 2005. This is a reflection of Hong Kong's improvement in "trading across borders," from fourteenth in 2005 to first in 2007. Although Hong Kong achieved a high ranking in many of the 10 categories,[12] for example, second in getting credit, third in protecting investors, and fifth in both starting a business and paying taxes, Hong Kong lagged well behind in dealing with licences (sixty-fourth) and registering properties (sixth). Hong Kong's rival, Singapore, ranked first, and outperformed Hong Kong in 5 out of 10 categories: dealing with licences, employing works, registering properties, protecting investors and closing of businesses (World Bank and IFC, 2007).

Another frequently quoted ranking is the Economist Intelligence Unit's (EIU) "Global Business Environment Index," which measures the quality or attractiveness of the business environment in 82 economies. The EIU's business environment ranking model examines 10 separate criteria,[13] designed to reflect the main criteria used by companies to formulate their global business strategies, and is based not only on historical conditions, but also on expectations prevailing over the next five years.

In the most recent EIU report, Hong Kong ranked eighth in its "Global Business Environment Index" from 2001 to 2005, while Denmark ranked first, Canada second and Singapore third. Hong Kong scored highly in taxes (first), foreign trade and exchange controls (second), and the labour market (second); and poorly in political stability (forty-fourth) and political environment (twenty-sixth). The EIU further predicted that Hong Kong's overall ranking in business environment will drop from eighth to tenth in the period 2006 to 2010, due to a deterioration in Hong Kong's political effectiveness, infrastructure and market opportunities. The EIU also expressed a belief that Hong Kong will maintain its leading position in taxes, foreign trade and exchange controls (EIU, 2006).

Debates and Disputes

There have been different interpretations and, as a result, debates and disputes within academic circles and society at large, about the momentous changes that have taken place in Hong Kong in the first decade after the handover in 1997. With regard to Hong Kong's business environment, the debates and disputes have mainly focused on four areas — first, the role of the government in the economy; second, the future of Hong Kong's business-friendly political environment; third, the possible loss of Hong Kong's competitiveness over its rivals; and fourth, the growing social pressure to protect the natural environment.

Government Economic Policy

One crucial area of debate is the role that the government plays in Hong Kong's economy and the impact of this on the business environment. Generally speaking, there are numerous "players" or "interest groups" in every economy, including businesses, customers and governments. In any economic system, the government does play a role, directly or indirectly, in balancing the interests of different groups in the economy. The issue of how to maintain and how to distribute fiscal resources between different interest groups is also a political decision. In addition, the government itself takes in revenues and spends large amounts of money; it also has to maintain a fiscal balance just as if it were running a business, and formulates economic policies to promote growth.

It is often said the Hong Kong government plays a very limited role in the economy, and that Hong Kong's success in the 1980s and 1990s had never been planned or directed by the government (Chen, 1998, pp. 34–40). However, the debate on the role of the government intensified when the government took a number of measures to intervene in the economy during the last decade, including purchasing shares to counter a speculative attack on the market and its involvement in the Disneyland theme park project to promote Hong Kong's tourism sector. The debate was further fuelled by Chief Executive Donald Tsang himself who, on 18 September 2006, publicly disavowed the policy of "positive non-intervention," and re-defined the Hong Kong style of capitalism as "big market, small government" (Tsang, 2006). Mr Tsang argued that "positive non-intervention" was an ambiguous "slogan" and stated that what he believed was that the government should "respond to the needs of the market and do our best to support and promote economic development within the limits of a small government." He later explained that the role of the government is to "facilitate what the market does" (Kissel, 2007).

One month later, Nobel Laureate Milton Friedman wrote on the *Wall Street Journal* to argue "Hong Kong's policy of 'positive non-interventionism' was too good to last." He stated that "it (positive non-interventionism) provides a lasting model of good economic policy for others who wish to bring similar prosperity to their people." He further predicted that "although the territory may continue to grow, it will no longer be such a shining symbol of economic freedom" (Friedman, 2006). The different perspectives of Mr Tsang and Professor Friedman have led to a heated debate on the role of the government in the economy, both in academic and business quarters.

The belief that Hong Kong has followed an approach of "positive non-interventionism" is, I believe, a big myth; Hong Kong is not, and has never been, a pure *laissez-faire* economy because the government has had a crucial "visible hand" in, for example, the critical areas of land supply and housing supply. I predict that the trend of government involvement in the economy would continue in the future. One indication of this is the Chief Executive's move in September 2006 to convene the Economic Summit on China's Eleventh Five-year Plan — a plan that unequivocally supports Hong Kong as an international financial, trading, logistics, tourism and information centre. Later, the government initiated work on Hong Kong's first strategic action agenda within the broad development plan of Mainland China.

Political Environments

Under colonial rule, Hong Kong was denied the right to develop a democratically elected legislature until the eve of the 1997 handover. Political power was controlled by an alliance between expatriate officials and the business elite, with both parties cooperating to create a pro-business environment and to minimize intervention in social as well as economic affairs (Goodstadt, 2005, pp. vii–viii).

Since 1997, Hong Kong's political environment has gone through dramatic changes. While the political system defined by the Basic Law is widely understood to be an executive-led system, a constitutional design is not equivalent to political reality. The government has been checked and balanced by a legislature with weak policy-making powers, but which is nonetheless endowed with the real power to veto initiatives coming from the government (Lau, 2002, pp. 30–31). After the handover, there has been a new tension in executive-legislative relations and, occasionally, political deadlock. Left with little room to play a constructive role in the making of policies and laws, legislators have turned more and more towards "oppositionist" rhetoric. Political parities and legislators have increasingly acted in an "opposition" role towards the government (Cheung, 2002, p. 42).

Hong Kong's political system is still not well developed. During the last decade, pro-business policy initiatives have faced more and more challenges from political parties and the legislature, and the government has often been blamed for actions that favour business interests at the expense of the public's interests. The controversy over the West Kowloon Cultural District Development in 2004, and over the relocation of the Star Ferry Terminal in 2006, have raised concern among the business community about Hong Kong's political environment. The endless disputes have indeed damaged the image of Hong Kong as a business-friendly place.

The "pro-democracy camp" has pointed to the absence of democratic institutions as root cause of such a political deadlock. Members of this group appear to believe that universal suffrage will provide a solution to all of Hong Kong's political problems. However, for the first time in Hong Kong's history, the Basic Law guarantees the step-by-step introduction of universal suffrage. The issue, therefore, is not the strategic one of "whether or why," but rather the technical one of "how and when."

The Marginalization of Hong Kong

Through economic integration over the past 20 years, a remarkable level of prosperity has been achieved in both Hong Kong and the PRD region. It is increasingly clear that, if Hong Kong had not integrated with the PRD region as China opened up to the outside world, Hong Kong would have lost most of its manufacturing sector to other Asian counties without having made any gains in its service sector (Sung, 2004). However, the previous "front shop, back factory" model of integration between Hong Kong and the PRD region is under threat from rising metropolitan cities in the Mainland, such as Shanghai, Guangzhou and Shenzhen. Hong Kong needs to quickly respond to the new competitive landscape and position itself up along the value chain to offer high-end financing, R&D, logistics and supply chain management.

In 2006, the debate over whether Hong Kong would be marginalized by the rapid development of Mainland cities became heated when the then Hong Kong's Chief Secretary for Administration, Mr Rafael Hui Si-yan, publicly expressed his concern (*Wen Wei Po*, 2006). The fear in Hong Kong is that there are certain internal and somehow hidden causes behind Hong Kong's economic problems that will lead to Hong Kong's marginalization by Mainland China. First, Hong Kong's traditional role as a gateway to Mainland China is rapidly eroding, with the aggressive growth of coastal Mainland cities. Second, excessive political emphasis on "two systems" has led to an isolationist mentality in Hong Kong that has often caused obstacles to be placed to Hong Kong's integration with the Mainland. Third, there has been insufficient progress in government-level collaboration between Hong Kong and Mainland China; delays in building cross-border infrastructure have hampered the flow of goods, and put pressure on Hong Kong's role as an international trade and logistics hub.

The only solution to prevent Hong Kong from becoming marginalized is simply to encourage further integration with Mainland China. In this regard, providing better physical connections between Hong Kong and the PRD is crucial to enhancing Hong Kong's position in relation to the PRD region. However, there are a number of obstacles to doing this. First, the existence of regionalism in Mainland China is impeding the process of integration; second, the existence of a "boundary" between Hong Kong and the PRD region restricts cross-boundary business activities; and third, Guangzhou, Shenzhen are moving ahead, both wanting to surpass Hong Kong as an international financial, trading and logistics centre. Hong Kong is facing fiercer competition than it has ever experienced before.

Natural Environment

Challenges posed by the environment are increasingly having an impact on global businesses. These include air pollution, global warming and the depletion of natural resources. It is crucial for businesses to fully appreciate the cultural values of a society, and to understand the changes in values and attitudes. In Hong Kong, the growing concern with the natural environment among many groups in society is one example of a changing social and cultural environment.

Air quality is one of the vitally important factors within the overall concept of sustainable development and quality of life. With the growing integration of Hong Kong, the PRD region has become a growing concern over air pollution. Hong Kong's air pollution, most of it traceable to the factories and power stations of the neighbouring PRD region, has worsened steadily in the last decade. As a result, Hong Kong's ranking as a desirable place to live for expatriate employees has fallen sharply, according to the "Location Ranking Survey" carried out on an annual basis by ECA International, a human resources consultancy firm. For Asian expatriates, Hong Kong dropped in the rankings in 2006 from twentieth to thirty-second place, due to an increase in the level of air pollution in the city (ECA International, 2006). Hong Kong scored even lower in the rankings for North American and European expatriates, at sixty-sixth place in 2005–

2006 and sixtieth in 2004–2005. Some western expatriates have moved from Hong Kong to Singapore or have returned to their home countries, citing air pollution as one of the factors that persuaded them to leave (Mallet, 2006).

Improving air quality has been a high priority on the government's agenda. Hong Kong and Guangdong policy-makers have been considering cross-border cooperation efforts to alleviate air pollution problems. However, this is an area in which governments, communities and business have to work hard and very closely to resolve the air pollution problems that have been identified.

Conclusion

In this chapter, a number of important issues in Hong Kong's business environment since the handover in 1997 were reviewed. First, while Hong Kong experienced dramatic economic, social and political changes in the last decade, its fundamental capitalist institutions and way of life remain unchanged. Second, Hong Kong has retained its strategic position in the process of globalization, maintaining a favourable location for global FDI inflows and a platform for FDI outflows. Third, the integration between Hong Kong and the PRD, having progressed to a very high level, has created a single economy entity — the GPRD region. The competitiveness of the regional business environment lies in a deeper division of labour within this increasingly integrated region. Fourth, Hong Kong has been given a high ranking in leading international indices complied by different bodies using different methodologies. By and large, the results have confirmed that Hong Kong offers one of the most attractive business environments in the world. Fifth, the ongoing debates and disputes on the role of the government, political development, competitiveness and the natural environment will define the landscape of Hong Kong's business environment in the future.

Notes

1. "Asia's world city," a major programme to create a global brand, was launched by the former Chief Executive, Mr Tung Chee-hwa, at the FORTUNE Global Forum in 2001, to focus international attention on Hong Kong's role as an Asian metropolitan city.
2. For reasons of space, an analysis of this protest will not be included in this chapter. On this incident, readers can refer to other chapters in this book,

although the observations and interpretations there may not necessarily reflect my point of view on this issue.

3. Interestingly, global FDI inflows also reached record high of US$1.4 trillion in 2000. In 2006, global FDI inflows were about US$800 billion, still far below the 2000 peak (UNCTAD, 2007).

4. A preliminary estimate by UNCTAD (2007).

5. The UNCTAD Inward FDI Potential Index is based on 12 economic and structural variables: GDP per capita, the rate of growth of GDP, the share of exports in GDP, telecoms infrastructure (the average number of telephone lines per 1,000 inhabitants, and mobile phones per 1,000 inhabitants), commercial energy use per capita, share of R&D expenditures in gross national income, share of tertiary students in the population, country risk, exports of natural resources as a percentage of the world's total, imports of parts and components of electronics and automobiles as a percentage of the world's total, exports of services as a percentage of the world's total, and inward FDI stock as a percentage of the world's total (UNCTAD, 2006, p. 38).

6. They are: (1) FDI inflows as a percentage of gross fixed capital formation for the past three years; (2) FDI inward stocks as a percentage of GDP; (3) the value added of foreign affiliates as a percentage of GDP; and (4) employment of foreign affiliates as a percentage of total employment.

7. Regional headquarters (RHQs) are organizations that have control over the operation of one or more other offices or subsidiaries in the region without the need to make frequent referrals to, or consult with, the parent companies or headquarters. Regional offices (ROs) are companies that are responsible for general business activities in one or more countries/territories in the region for the parent companies.

8. This section has been revised from an unpublished research paper, which was based on a survey conducted in 2005 by a team of in-house analysts at China Merchants Groups, led by myself and Ding Anhua, Edward.

9. They are: (1) business freedom; (2) trade freedom; (3) fiscal freedom; (4) freedom from government; (5) monetary freedom; (6) investment freedom; (7) financial freedom; (8) property rights; (9) freedom from corruption; and (10) labour freedom (Heritage Foundation, 2007).

10. They are: (1) size of government; (2) legal structure and security of property rights; (3) access to sound money; (4) freedom to trade internationally; and (5) regulation of credit, labour and business (Fraser Institute, 2006).

11. Interestingly, China scored very low in this list for competitiveness, having dropped from fourth-eighth in 2005 to fifty-fourth in 2006, although for the last decade China has been the fastest growing economy in the world. Obviously, the index is of limited utility in explaining the rise of China as an important economic powerhouse in the world.

12. They are: starting a business; dealing with licences; employing workers;

registering property; getting credit; protecting investors; paying taxes; trading across borders; enforcing contracts and closing a business.

13. They are: the political environment, the macroeconomic environment, market opportunities, policy towards free enterprises and competition, policy towards foreign investments, foreign trade and exchange controls, taxes, financing, the labour market and infrastructure.

References

Chen, Edward K. Y. (1998), "The Economic Setting." In David G. Lethbridge and Ng Sek-hong (eds.), *The Business Environment in Hong Kong*. Hong Kong: Oxford University Press.

Cheung, Anthony B. L. (2002), "The Changing Political System: Executive-led Government or 'Disabled' Governance?" In Lau Siu-kai (ed.), *The First Tung Chee-hwa Administration*. Hong Kong: The Chinese University Press.

Deng, Xiaoping (2004), *Deng Xiaoping on "One Country, Two Systems."* Hong Kong: Joint Publishing.

ECA International (2006), "Poor Air Quality in Hong Kong and Kuala Lumpur Cause Fall in Ranking." Press Release, *ECA International*, 3 April.

EIU (Economist Intelligence Unit) (2006), *Global Outlook Report*.

Enright, M. J., E. E. Scott and K. M. Chang (2005), *Regional Powerhouse: The Greater Pearl River Delta and the Rise of China*. Singapore: John Wiley & Sons (Asia).

Fraser Institute (2006), *Economic Freedom of the World: 2006 Annual Report*. Vancouver: the Fraser Institute.

Friedman, Milton (2006), "Hong Kong Wrong: What Would Cowperthwaite Say?" Editorial, *Wall Street Journal*, 6 October.

Goodstadt, Leo F. (2005), *Uneasy Partners: The Conflict between Public Interest and Private Profit in Hong Kong*. Hong Kong: Hong Kong University Press.

Heritage Foundation (2007), *Index of Economic Freedom*. Washington: Heritage Foundation and *Wall Street Journal*, at http://www.heritage.org.

Hong Kong Exchanges and Clearing, *Data and Statistics* (2007), at http://www.hkex.com.hk/data.

International Institute for Management Development (IMD) (2006), *IMD World Competitiveness Yearbook*. Lausanne: International Institute for Management Development.

Invest Hong Kong (2007), "Investment Results," at Invest Hong Kong website: http://www.investhk.gov.hk/pages/1/349.aspx.

Kissel, Mary (2007), "The Journal Interview with Donald Tsang," *Wall Street Journal* (Asia), 26 February, p. 14.

Lau, Siu-kai (2002), "Tung Chee-hwa's Governing Strategy: The Shortfall in

Politics." In Lau Siu-kai (ed.), *The First Tung Chee-hwa Administration*. Hong Kong: The Chinese University Press.

Mallet, Victor (2006), "Hong Kong's Pollution Cuts It Appeal," *Financial Times*.

Porter, Michael E. (1998), *On Competition*. Boston: Harvard Business School Publishing.

Sung, Yun-wing (2004), "Hong Kong's Economic Integration with the Pearl River Delta: Quantifying the Benefits and Costs," at Hong Kong Central Policy Unit website: http://www.cpu.gov.hk.

Tsang, Donald (2006), "Big Market, Small Government," Press Releases, the Government of Hong Kong SAR. Also 2003 and 2005.

United Nations Conference on Trade and Development (UNCTAD) (2006), *World Investment Report 2006*. Geneva: United Nations. Other years also.

Wen Wei Po (2006), "Rafael Hui Si-yan: Hong Kong Has to Face the Risk of Being Marginalised," 3 March.

World Bank and IFC (International Financial Corporation) (2007), *Doing Business in 2007*.

World Economic Forum (2007), *Global Competitiveness Report 2006–2007*. Geneva: World Economic Forum.

Yergin, D. and J. Stanislaw (2000), *The Commanding Height: The Battle for the World Economy*. New York: Simon & Schuster.

10

Hong Kong's Economy and Financial Sector

Yun-wing Sung

Hong Kong's economy has gone through many ups and downs in the first decade since the territory's reversion to China in 1997. In the six short years from mid-1997 to 2003, Hong Kong went through two full-scale economic recessions and one near recession. The first recession, starting in late 1997, was triggered by the Asian financial crisis (AFC). Hong Kong experienced five quarters of negative growth. After the recovery and an economic boom from 1999 to 2000 fuelled by the tech bubble, the economy suffered a second recession from mid-2001 to early 2002. This recession is due to the bursting of the tech bubble and the terrorist attacks of 11 September 2001.

An export-led recovery began in the second half of 2002. This recovery was interrupted by an outbreak of severe acute respiratory syndrome (SARS) in the second quarter of 2003. The economy veered on recession, with one-quarter of negative growth. However, the SARS episode was brief, and the recovery gained momentum in the second half of 2003, helped by a weak U.S. dollar and measures taken by the China's central government to boost Hong Kong's economy.

While the Hong Kong economy has been growing rapidly since mid-2003, it was only at the end of 2006 that Hong Kong's per capita GDP regained the level reached in 1997. Hong Kong has lost close to a decade of economic growth. Its economic performance in the last decade is nearly the worst among the economies of East Asia. Given the breath-taking development of the Mainland's economy, the risk that Hong Kong's economy will become marginalized cannot be discounted. Hong Kong has yet to succeed in its transformation towards a knowledge-based economy.

Despite the stellar performance of Hong Kong's financial sector in

2006, the sector is not immune to marginalization. In March 2007, during his campaign for a second term in office, Mr Donald Tsang, the Chief Executive of the Hong Kong Special Administrative Region (HKSAR), promised to turn Hong Kong into the region's incontestable financial centre. One month later, the market capitalization of the Mainland's stock markets surpassed that of Hong Kong (*Hong Kong Economic Journal*, 12 April 2006).

The rapid economic development in Mainland China has rapidly narrowed the gap between Hong Kong and the Mainland in skills and also in infrastructure. In short, Hong Kong faces a loss of competitiveness. Hong Kong's hitherto unchallenged position as the gateway to China started to erode in the mid-1990s, just before the 1997 handover. For instance, the share of China's trade handled by Hong Kong as entrepôt trade peaked at 41% in 1996, and declined sharply to 19% in 2004 (Sung, 2006a, p. 168).

While the year 1997 appears to be a watershed for the performance of the Hong Kong economy, the seeds of Hong Kong's post-1997 malaise were sown in the heady prosperity of the years leading up to 1997. In the lengthy transitional period from the signing of the Sino-British Declaration in 1984 to the reversion in 1997, the elites of Hong Kong spent their energies on speculation in real estate or in obtaining foreign passports as a hedge against the 1997 handover. Few were worried about the erosion of Hong Kong's competitiveness.

The long period of prosperity before 1997 had generated a huge economic bubble, which was unwittingly exacerbated by a clause in the 1984 Sino-British Declaration restricting the annual leasing of land to 50 ha. The clause was inserted by the Chinese authorities to forestall a possible pre-emptive attempt on the part of the British colonial administration to lease excessive amounts of land, thereby leaving too little land for the post-1997 government. The clause was intended to ensure a smooth transition. Ironically, it led to a huge real estate bubble, which proved to be a very destabilizing factor in Hong Kong's reversion.

In itself, the bursting of the bubble would at most have led to an economic recession. Hong Kong had experienced serious real estate bubbles before, for example, in 1981, and the economy managed to recover in 1984. Hong Kong's prolonged economic malaise in the post-reversion era cannot be accounted for entirely by the bursting of the real estate bubble, by the AFC, or by the slowdown of the U.S. economy in 2001. Hong Kong faces a loss of competitiveness, and an improvement in its economic performance would require a fundamental restructuring of the Hong Kong economy.

Unfortunately, the HKSAR government was ill-equipped to deal with the economic crisis. The Sino-British dispute over Governor Pattern's reform proposals before the reversion led to "elite fragmentation," as both Britain and China tried to win over Hong Kong's elites (Lau, 1999, pp. 51–60). Tung Chee-hwa, the first HKSAR Chief Executive, failed to build a strong coalition because of his limited political experience (Lau 1999, pp. 61–70). The HKSAR government was inexperienced and had a very limited ability to manage the economic crisis. The erratic responses and policies of the Tung Chee-hwa administration compounded Hong Kong's economic malaise.

Relocation of Manufacturing and Competitiveness

The opening of China in 1979 naturally led to the re-integration of Hong Kong's economy with that of its hinterland. There is a huge gap in wages between Hong Kong and the Mainland. As a result, Hong Kong businesses have relocated their operations that do not require a high level of skills and that are relatively labour intensive to the Mainland — first in manufacturing and then in services. Through outsourcing, Hong Kong is benefiting by specializing in relatively skill-intensive processes. The result is a gain in productivity, as the relocation of low-end services frees Hong Kong's manpower for high-end services such as financial services, order-taking, logistics and headquarter functions. As Hong Kong is a developed economy, it should concentrate on the knowledge-intensive part of the production chain, following the example of New York and London.

However, the productivity gained by outsourcing low-value-added activities (whether labour-intensive manufacturing or low-end services) is one-off. The process will eventually lead to the outsourcing of all low-value activities that can be relocated, and outsourcing will then no longer be result in gains in productivity. Sustained growth will require continuous improvements in efficiency and technology. Without such improvements, Hong Kong will not be able to maintain its lead in skills, and outsourcing will only lead to the hollowing out of the Hong Kong economy.

According to the most up-to-date study on improvements in total factor productivity in Hong Kong (or efficiency gain in layman's language), Hong Kong's performance was the best among the Four Little Dragons from 1980 to 1990, but was the worst during the entire decade of the 1990s (Li, Wei and Xie, 2007, pp. 10–11). There was little pressure to improve efficiency during the pre-1997 boom years, as easy money could be made through speculation. This deterioration in the rate of efficiency gain in Hong Kong in the 1990s was an important factor in Hong Kong's long economic malaise starting from late 1997. Fortunately, Hong Kong's efficiency gain recovered in 2000, and Hong Kong's performance was the best among the Asian Four from 2000 to 2004.

Economic Restructuring in Hong Kong

In the early stage in the opening of China, Hong Kong had a near monopoly in producer services (e.g., trading, financing and containerization) due to the Marxist bias against services. Through outsourcing, Hong Kong built a vast manufacturing base in Guangdong that depended on Hong Kong for producer services. The share of China's trade that was re-exported via Hong Kong rose from 4% in 1979 to around 40% in the mid-1990s.

Due to the very rapid expansion of producer services in Hong Kong, economic restructuring in Hong Kong was exceedingly smooth before the mid-1990s. Although manufacturing employment fell from a record of 998,323 in 1981 to 306,400 in 1997, so many new jobs were created in producer services that total employment rose from 2.39 million to 3.17 million in the same period. The unemployment rate was less than 3.5% throughout the period.

However, after Deng Xiaoping's 1992 southern tour in support of economic reforms, the Chinese government liberalized investment in ports and other service sectors. Hong Kong's foremost conglomerate, Hutchison Whampoa, quickly invested in container ports in South China. Since the mid-1990s, Hong Kong has been facing increasing competition from Mainland ports. As mentioned above, the share of China's trade re-exported via Hong Kong has declined sharply since 1996.

The year 1996 can be taken as a watershed in Hong Kong's economic integration with the Mainland: Beginning in the mid-1990s, Hong Kong started to lose its near-monopoly in producer services. Low-end services began to be relocated to the Mainland, and job creation in Hong Kong slowed down. Economic restructuring has become less smooth, and Hong Kong has to upgrade its skills to avoid an economic hollowing-out.

From a "Dragon" Economy to the Laggard of East Asia

As mentioned above, Hong Kong's economic performance in the last decade was the worst in East Asia. Hong Kong, which was once a "dragon" economy, had become the sick man of East Asia. Figure 10.1 shows the per capita GDP index of the Four Little Dragons (in nominal U.S. dollars) from 1997 to 2006, using 1997 as the base year. Although the per capita GDP of South Korea dropped precipitously during the AFC, the South Korean economy rebounded rapidly. By 2006, South Korea's per capita GDP was 60% higher than it had been in 1997. While Singapore and Taiwan also suffered from the AFC and the 11 September terrorist attacks, in 2004 both regained their 1997 level of per capita GDP. Hong Kong did not regain its 1997 level of per capita GDP until 2006. By 2006, the per capita GDPs of Singapore and Taiwan were, respectively, 18% and 12% higher than they had been in 1997, while that of Hong Kong was only 1.5% higher than in 1997. Hong Kong had by far the worst economic performance among the Four Little Dragons.

Figure 10.2 shows the per capita GDP indices (in nominal U.S. dollars) of the Southeast Asian economies of Indonesia, Malaysia, the Philippines, and Thailand from 1997 to 2006. All four economies were hit hard by the AFC, but recovered more quickly than Hong Kong's economy. Indonesia, Malaysia and Thailand regained their 1997 level of per capita GDP in 2004, and the Philippines did the same in 2005. By comparison, Hong Kong had the slowest recovery.

Figure 10.3 shows the absolute levels of per capita GDP (in nominal U.S. dollars) of the Four Little Dragons and the U.S. and U.K. from 1980 to 2006. Hong Kong's per capita GDP surpassed that of the U.K. in 1993.

Figure 10.1 Indices of per capita GDP (in US$) of the Four Little Dragons (1997 = 100)

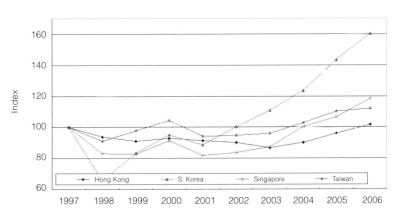

**Figure 10.2 Indices of per capita GDP (in US$) of Selected Southeast Asian
Countries (1997 = 100)**

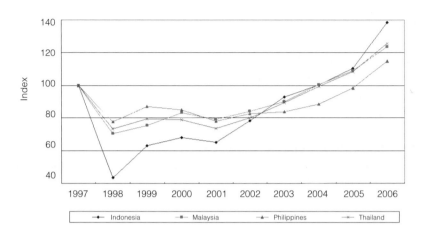

**Figure 10.3 Per capita GDP of the U.S., the U.K. and the Four Little Dragons
(US$)**

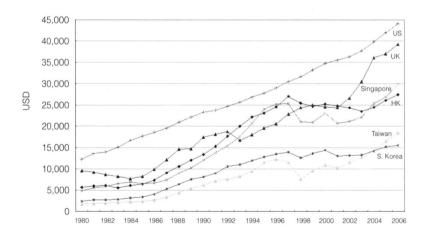

The ratio of Hong Kong's per capita GDP to that of the U.S. rose from 36% in 1985 to 89% in 1997, showing that Hong Kong was rapidly catching up with the U.S. However, this ratio declined rapidly to 62% in 2006, reflecting the poor economic performance of Hong Kong after the reversion. The per capita GDP of the U.K. and Singapore surpassed that of Hong Kong in 2002 and 2004, respectively. By 2006, the per capita GDP of the U.K. and Singapore were, respectively, 43% and 9% higher than that of Hong Kong. These comparisons highlight the need for Hong Kong to undertake fundamental economic restructuring efforts to regain its competitiveness.

Hong Kong's Four Key Industries

In response to Hong Kong's prolonged economic malaise, the Hong Kong government has focused its attention on developing "four key industries":

1. Financial Services,
2. Tourism,
3. Trading and Logistics, and
4. Professional Services and Other Producer Services.

Tables 10.1 and 10.2 show the contributions of the four key industries to GDP and employment in Hong Kong from 1996 to 2005. Trading and Logistics has long been the largest industry. In 2005, its contributions to GDP and employment were nearly 29% and 25%, respectively. The corresponding figures for Tourism were only 3.2% and 4.8%, showing that it is a small industry. Those for Financial Services were 12.7% and 5.3%, showing that the value-added per worker was 2.4 times the average for the economy. For Professional Services and Other Producer Services, the corresponding contributions were 10.6% and 11%.

This chapter will focus on the two industries that are the most important for the future of Hong Kong, namely Trading and Logistics, and Financial Services. Trading and Logistics is the largest industry, and its growth has been very robust in the past. In fact, Trading and Logistics has been Hong Kong's most important engine of growth since the opening of China in 1979. Contrary to popular belief, Trading and Logistics, instead of the Mainland's Individual Visit Scheme (IVS), has been the main factor behind the strong recovery of the Hong Kong economy since mid-2003. The Tourist industry is simply too small to provide a large boost to Hong Kong's economic recovery.

Table 10.1 The Four Key Industries in the Hong Kong Economy — Percentage Share to GDP

Percentage share (%)	1996	1997	1998	1999	2000	2001	2002	2003	2004	2005
(1) Financial services	10.3	10.3	9.8	11.0	11.9	11.3	11.5	12.3	12.2	12.7
(2) Tourism	3.1	2.6	2.1	2.3	2.3	2.2	2.8	2.3	2.9	3.2
(A) Inbound	2.5	2.0	1.5	1.6	1.6	1.5	2.0	1.6	2.2	2.4
(B) Outbound	0.7	0.6	0.6	0.7	0.7	0.7	0.8	0.7	0.8	0.8
(3) Trading and logistics	22.7	21.9	22.4	22.5	23.8	24.3	25.0	26.3	27.6	28.6
(A) Trading	18.7	18.1	18.5	18.3	19.4	20.0	20.5	21.5	22.3	23.4
Wholesale trade	1.2	1.1	1.0	1.1	0.9	1.0	0.9	0.9	1.0	0.9
Import and export trade	17.4	17.0	17.4	17.2	18.5	19.0	19.6	20.6	21.3	22.5
(B) Logistics	4.0	3.8	3.9	4.2	4.5	4.3	4.4	4.9	5.3	5.2
(4) Professional services and other producer services	12.4	13.1	12.3	10.5	10.2	10.4	10.3	10.3	10.5	10.6
(A) Professional services	3.3	3.6	3.5	3.4	3.4	3.3	3.3	3.6	3.7	3.7
(B) Other producer services	9.1	9.5	8.8	7.1	6.8	7.0	7.0	6.8	6.8	6.8
Four key industries = (1)+(2)+(3)+(4)	48.5	47.9	46.5	46.3	48.3	48.2	49.5	51.2	53.3	55.0

Source: Census and Statistics Department, Hong Kong.

Table 10.2 The Four Key Industries in the Hong Kong Economy – Percentage Share to Total Employment

Percentage share (%)	1996	1997	1998	1999	2000	2001	2002	2003	2004	2005
(1) Financial services	4.9	5.4	5.4	5.5	5.3	5.4	5.4	5.2	5.1	5.3
(2) Tourism	NA	NA	3.4	3.2	3.4	3.5	4.2	4.3	4.6	4.8
(A) Inbound	NA	NA	2.7	2.6	2.7	2.8	3.6	3.6	3.9	4.1
(B) Outbound	NA	NA	0.7	0.6	0.7	0.7	0.7	0.7	0.7	0.8
(3) Trading and logistics	NA	NA	24.5	24.0	24.2	23.9	23.4	23.9	24.3	24.7
(A) Trading	18.8	18.7	18.3	18.0	18.1	17.9	17.7	18.0	18.3	18.6
Wholesale trade	2.5	2.5	2.6	2.3	2.3	2.2	2.2	2.1	2.2	2.2
Import and export trade	16.3	16.2	15.7	15.7	15.9	15.7	15.5	15.9	16.1	16.4
(B) Logistics	NA	NA	6.2	6.0	6.1	6.0	5.8	5.9	6.0	6.0
(4) Professional services and other producer services	NA	NA	9.8	9.9	10.5	10.6	10.6	10.9	10.9	11.0
(A) Professional services	3.4	3.6	3.4	3.4	3.8	3.9	3.9	3.9	4.0	4.0
(B) Other producer services	NA	NA	6.4	6.5	6.7	6.7	6.7	7.0	6.9	7.0
Four Key Industries = (1)+(2)+(3)+(4)	NA	NA	43.0	42.7	43.3	43.3	43.7	44.3	44.9	45.8

Source: Census and Statistics Department, Hong Kong.

However, the future of the Trading and Logistics industry is highly uncertain due to the high cost of Hong Kong's port and to the intense competition from ports in the Pearl River Delta. It is widely expected that the container throughput of Shanghai and Shenzhen will surpass Hong Kong's very shortly. In comparison, Hong Kong's competitiveness in Financial Services appears to be more secure, and the Hong Kong government has placed high hopes on the development of Hong Kong as an international financial centre (IFC). However, as mentioned above, the position of Hong Kong as an IFC is not incontestable.

This chapter will also focus on the prospects for the Trading and Logistics industry and the Financial Services industry. The Tourist industry is small. As for Professional Services and Other Producer Services, its share of Hong Kong's GDP declined from 12.4% in 1996 to 10.6% in 2005. Moreover, its direct role in exports is small. In 2005, exports of these services were only $41 billion, or 8.2% of Hong Kong's services exports. In contrast, trade and transportation accounted for, respectively, 33% and 32% of Hong Kong's total services exports in the same year.

Trading and Logistics

The growth of the Trading and Logistics industry is very robust: Its share of Hong Kong's GDP rose rapidly from 21.9% in 1997 to 28.6% in 2005, an increase of 6.7 percentage points. This is largely due to the very rapid expansion in China's trade, especially after China's accession to the WTO in 2001. From 2001 to 2006, the Mainland's trade has grown at the neckbreak pace of 28% per year.

In the years 2001 to 2006, Hong Kong's container throughput grew only at the average annual rate of 5.7%, indicating that a great deal of cargo is being diverted to Shenzhen ports. However, Hong Kong's trade grew at an average annual rate of 11%, showing that Hong Kong has shifted towards handling higher value cargo, e.g., air cargo or high-end cargo that requires intensive logistics support. Moreover, Hong Kong's offshore trade (trade handled by Hong Kong firms but that does not go through Hong Kong) also grew rapidly during the same period. Instead of visible trade, offshore trade appears under the export of services. The best measure of offshore trade is exports of trade-related services, which have grown at an average annual rate of 11% during the period. As offshore trade uses an overseas port (e.g., Shenzhen) rather than Hong Kong, it is not directly affected by the competitiveness of Hong Kong's port.

Table 10.3 compares the average annual rate of growth of the Mainland's trade with that of Hong Kong. From 1979 to 1996, Hong Kong's trade grew at the rate of 19% per year, exceeding the Mainland's growth of 14% per year. This was the period when Hong Kong had a near-monopoly in producer services. From 1996 to 2001, growth in the Mainland's trade slowed slightly to 12% per year as a result of the AFC, while growth in Hong Kong's trade plummeted to a mere 0.8% per year, indicating a severe degree of trade diversion to Mainland ports. From 2001 to 2006, growth in the Mainland's trade accelerated to 28% per year, mainly as a result of WTO entry, and growth in Hong Kong's trade also recovered to 11% per year. Hong Kong's trade growth was still much slower than the Mainland's, indicating the continuing diversion of cargo. Hong Kong is now getting a smaller share of a bigger pie. The size of Hong Kong's slice is growing only because the size of the pie is growing very quickly. If the growth in China's trade should slow down from its current blistering pace of 28% per year to a more normal pre-AFC rate of 14% per year, growth in Hong Kong's trade would likely stagnate.

In the long run, it is highly unlikely that China's trade will continue to grow at the rate of close to 30% per year. China is already the world's third largest trading nation, and is projected to soon surpass the U.S. and Germany to become the largest. Protectionist sentiments in the U.S. and E.U. against China's exports are running high, and the Chinese authorities are taking various measures to slow down the country's export growth, such as cutting export tax rebates. A slowdown in the growth of China's trade is inevitable. Thus, continued high growth in Hong Kong's trade is very unlikely.

Although the Hong Kong government has undertaken various measures to facilitate cross-border trucking, it is about US$300 more expensive to ship a container via Hong Kong's port than via Shenzhen's ports. Sixty percent of that excess cost is due to the higher cost of cross-border trucking,

Table 10.3 Annual Growth Rate of External Trade in the Mainland and Hong Kong

Period	Mainland	Hong Kong
1979–1996	14%	19%
1996–2001	12%	0.8%
2001–2006	28%	11%

Sources: The Mainland data were obtained from *China Customs Statistics* and the Hong Kong data were obtained from *Hong Kong External Trade*, Census and Statistics Department, various issues.

which is monopolized by Hong Kong truckers as Mainland truckers are not allowed to enter Hong Kong. Liberalizing cross-border trucking would be the most effective means of lowering the cost of using Hong Kong's port, but protecting the livelihood of Hong Kong's 12,000 container truck drivers is a high priority to the Hong Kong government. The major political parties in Hong Kong have chosen to protect local truckers even though they know that, without the liberalization of trucking, Hong Kong's container throughput will soon be surpassed by both Shanghai and Shenzhen.

As mentioned above, Hong Kong has had some success in developing higher value cargo such as air freight and goods that require intensive logistics support. As can be seen from Table 10.1, the share of the Logistics industry in GDP has increased from 3.8% from 1997 to 5.2% in 2005. However, in Guangdong's Eleventh Five-year Plan (2006–2010), the development of logistics is being given a high priority, and there will be increasing competition in logistics between Hong Kong and Guangdong. Moreover, Hong Kong's air cargo is also under competitive pressure from Guangzhou's new airport. In the 12 months to March 2007, Hong Kong's air cargo grew by only 2.8%. This is the lowest rate of growth in five years. In May 2007, China and the U.S. agreed to double the number of flights between the two countries in two years. The effect will be to further undercut the status of Hong Kong as China's premier air hub.

Offshore trade is not directly affected by the competitiveness of Hong Kong in shipping and air transportation. However, a slowdown in China's trade will adversely affect the growth of Hong Kong's offshore trade. While the value of Hong Kong's offshore trade is close to that of its re-exports, the contribution of offshore trade to GDP was only 45% of re-exports in 2004 (Sung 2006b, Table 4). Offshore trade does not use Hong Kong's port and its rate of value added is slightly less than half that of re-exports. In a nutshell, the strong boost from trade to Hong Kong's economic growth since 2001 is likely to weaken in the long run.

Financial Services

The Hong Kong government targets Financial Services as the focal point of Hong Kong's development. The performance of Hong Kong is particularly impressive in the area of initial public offerings (IPOs), mainly from Mainland companies. In 2006, Hong Kong surpassed New York to come to a close second to London in terms of total funds raised through

IPOs, and also overtook Toronto and Frankfurt to rank sixth in equity market capitalization (Tse, 2007, p. 2).

In the report of the City of London Corporation in mid-March 2007 on the competitiveness of 46 financial centres in the world, Hong Kong was ranked third after London and New York (City of London Corporation, 2007). According to the report, among Asian cities, Hong Kong is most likely to emerge as a global centre, while Shanghai and Tokyo are unlikely to be global centres. In contrast, an earlier report released by the Corporation two years ago suggested that there was no clear leader among the Asian centres. The prospects for Hong Kong as a financial centre have clearly risen.

It must be emphasized, however, that it is by no means certain that Hong Kong will become a global financial centre. Competition among Asian cities is keen. Singapore is a close competitor, while Shanghai has good long-term potential. In financial services, Hong Kong's global rank is only impressive in IPOs. The size of New York's financial services sector is roughly seven times that of Hong Kong's in terms of value added (Ying, 2006, p. 3). It is clear that Hong Kong has a long way to go if it is to become a true global centre.

Hong Kong's strengths as a financial centre are very uneven. While Hong Kong is strong in the equity market and in IPOs, its debt market is miniscule. In 2006, the size of Hong Kong's debt market was only 2% that of the U.K. and 1% that of the U.S. (Leung, 2007). Despite Hong Kong's efforts to develop its debt market, the growth in this area from 1996 to 2006 was much slower than in the U.K. and the U.S. As for the foreign exchange market, turnover in Hong Kong is just 4% of the world's total and trails Singapore (Leung, 2007). Hong Kong's share of the turnover in global derivatives is also small. Unlike Shanghai, Hong Kong does not offer commodity futures. With the exception of IPOs and equities, Hong Kong's financial markets lack both depth and breadth. Hong Kong is also weak in innovations in financial instruments, such as financial derivatives and asset securitization, due to a lack of financial institutions and talent (Tse, 2007, p. 4). At present, Hong Kong only acts as a regional distribution centre for innovative products developed in London or New York.

The Decline of Banking and the Rise of a Capital Market

In recent years, the demand of Mainland enterprises for loans from Hong Kong banks has fallen greatly because China has ample savings and, with banking reforms, Mainland banks are increasingly capable of catering to the needs of non-state enterprises. From 1997 to 2002, the foreign currency loans of Hong Kong banks fell by 80%. In 1997, Hong Kong ranked first in East Asia in the area of syndicated loans, ahead of Japan and Australasia by a wide margin. However, as China's demand for syndicated loans fell after the AFC, both Japan and Australasia rapidly surpassed Hong Kong in syndicated loans. Hong Kong has become more of a domestic than a regional banking centre (Leung, 2007).

Although levels of fund raising by Mainland enterprises through Hong Kong banks have fallen greatly, Mainland enterprises have flocked to the Hong Kong stock market in recent years to raise equity capital. This is not because the Mainland is short of funds. Through listing in Hong Kong, Mainland enterprises can signal to international and domestic investors that their stocks are of good quality, enabling them to raise more funds in the domestic stock market. Although the Mainland's stock markets have surpassed Hong Kong's since April 2007 in turnover and market capitalization, more Mainland enterprises will continue to list in Hong Kong to acquire a good reputation before listing in the domestic market.

While fund raising by Mainland companies in Hong Kong will decline somewhat after the flood of IPOs by Mainland banks in the Hong Kong market in 2006, Mainland enterprises will continue to list in Hong Kong as long as the *renminbi* is not fully convertible on the capital account. Even when the *renminbi* becomes fully convertible, Mainland enterprises may still want to list in Hong Kong to signal their high quality. This implies that Hong Kong has to maintain the high quality of its market regulation. The 2007 City of London Corporation Report rated Hong Kong highly for the quality of its market regulation.

In serving China's financial needs, Hong Kong has switched from indirect financing (bank loans) to direct financing through the equity market. China's economic reforms have reached a stage in which large state-owned enterprises (SOEs) can securitize and raise capital in the stock market. The primary purpose of securitization is to promote enterprise reforms and economic reforms. Raising capital is secondary, as China is not short of capital. Listing in Hong Kong has the advantage of forcing an enterprise to comply with international accounting standards and to come under the continuous scrutiny of international investors. This is important for improving a company's corporate governance.

The rapid transformation of Hong Kong's financial sector from focusing on indirect financing and banking to focusing on direct equity financing in the decade since 1997 is a testimony to its flexibility and resilience. The decline in the demand for loans led to a great deal of hardship in the banking industry. Besides the 80% decline in foreign currency loans already mentioned, the number of licensed banks also fell from 186 in 1997 to 138 in 2006 (Tse, 2007, p. 3). Many Japanese banks left Hong Kong. The surviving banks have to diversify from traditional lending into becoming financial supermarkets. Despite the consolidation of the banking industry, the share of Financial Services to GDP has risen from 10.3% in 1997 to 12.7% in 2005. This is a tribute to the dynamism of Hong Kong's Financial Services industry.

There has been a tendency for financial systems to evolve from a banking-oriented stage to a stage in which the equity market plays a leading role, and then to a securitization stage (Tse, 2007, p. 4). The U.S. and the U.K. are in the third stage, while Japan is still in the first stage. The rapid transformation of Hong Kong from the first stage towards the third stage since 1997 is a sign of strength.

Hong Kong as a Centre of Wealth Management

In the early years of the opening of China, Hong Kong's main role as a financial centre was to raise funds for the Mainland's development. After nearly three decades of breath-taking economic growth, the Mainland now has the largest foreign exchange reserves in the world — a feat it achieved in 2006. The Mainland has a high and growing savings rate, which reached 45% in 2006. Hong Kong's role as a financial centre will increasingly shift from fund raising to wealth management for the Mainland.

It is no accident that Hong Kong's fund management business has more than trebled in size from 2000 to 2005, growing from HK$1,485 billion to HK$4,526 billion. Hong Kong is fast becoming an important regional fund management centre, especially for China funds. Hong Kong's fund management business is highly international. In 2005, 63% of the business involved non-Hong Kong investors, and the assets under management included very substantial amounts outside Hong Kong/China and also outside Asia (Leung, 2007).

The *renminbi* is likely to be close to full convertibility in a few years. It has often been thought that this will help Shanghai to develop its international financial business and threaten the uniqueness of Hong Kong. While this is true to a certain extent, it must be stressed that the convertibility of the *renminbi* will give a big boost to Hong Kong as a wealth management centre, as Mainland wealth would then be able to flow freely to Hong Kong.

In May 2007, the Chinese authorities announced the relaxation of China's qualified domestic institutional investors (QDII) scheme. The scheme, introduced in April 2006, allowed domestic and foreign banks to invest up to US$14.2 billion for their clients in overseas assets. However, after one year, only US$400 million of the quota was used because the scheme was restricted to bonds and foreign currency products that have low returns. The relaxation in May 2007 allows qualified banks to invest up to half of their QDII funds in stocks. Initially, investment is restricted to Hong Kong–traded stocks as the Mainland has regulatory agreements with Hong Kong, but the scheme is expected to be expanded to other markets. On 15 May 2007, the first trading day after the announcement, Hong Kong stock prices and turnover set new records (*South China Morning Post*, 15 May 2007). This limited liberalization of the outflow of the Mainland's capital shows the great potential benefit of the convertibility of the *renminbi* for Hong Kong.

With regard to wealth management, secure legal protection is of the utmost importance. Moreover, the development of financial markets is highly dependent on a clean, transparent and even-handed regulatory environment. Although Shanghai is rapidly developing its financial institutions, a reputable legal framework and transparent regulatory system takes time to evolve and mature. Given the corrupt and cumbersome bureaucracy in China, it will be difficult to develop an international financial centre and wealth management centre on the Mainland. Political reforms are needed to create a reputable legal and regulatory system on the Mainland, and the process of achieving such reforms is more time-consuming and riskier than economic reforms. Hong Kong has a fundamental edge over other Chinese cities in the goal of becoming an international financial centre, in that it possesses the rule of law, a clean and transparent structure of governance, and has a free flow of information. As long as Hong Kong can maintain a world-class standard in market regulation and in the quality of its Financial Services, the prospects for Hong Kong as an international financial centre are bright.

Conclusion

While Hong Kong has good potential to become a global financial centre, the city should not risk putting all of its eggs into one basket. Moreover, the financial sector generates too little employment: Its share to total employment in 2005 was only 5.3%. A lopsided concentration in Financial Services will undermine social stability. While Hong Kong aspires to be a global financial centre like New York, it should be noted that New York has quite a diverse economy. It is a global centre for creative industries, such as media, publishing, fashion, advertising, film-making and the arts. It has a high quality and growing health-care industry, and dynamic high-tech industries, such as software development, internet services and biomedical research.

It has often been alleged that a major stumbling block to the transformation of Hong Kong into a knowledge-based economy is the low international rank of Hong Kong in education. In the 2006 World Bank dataset on the Knowledge Index, which contains data for 2003 and 2004, Hong Kong ranked 65th out of 128 economies in the area of education. Hong Kong received low scores for secondary school enrolment and tertiary enrolment (Enright, Scott & Associates Ltd., 2006, p. 27). In the Education Index of the United Nation's Human Development Index, Hong Kong also had a low ranking of 71st in 2003, even trailing the Philippines. This is attributable to a low school enrolment ratio (Enright, Scott & Associates Ltd., 2006, p. 55).

However, international rankings of education indices can be misleading because such rankings are not adjusted for the quality of education, which is relatively high in Hong Kong. According to the Programme for International Student Assessment (PISA), Hong Kong students ranked among the top 10 jurisdictions in all four areas of assessment, namely mathematics, science, problem solving and reading. Hong Kong's universities also do well in global rankings. In addition, Hong Kong has a very pluralistic education system, with many international schools. In comparison with other economies, a relatively large number of Hong Kong youths are educated in some of the best schools and universities in the U.S. and the U.K. Moreover, school attendance rates in Hong Kong have increased rapidly in recent years, to a level comparable to that of Singapore in 2005 (TeamOne Economist Ltd., 2006, p. Slide 57).

The crux of Hong Kong's transformation into a knowledge-based economy is the availability of talent. As long as Hong Kong remains an attractive place for talent, the relocation of manufacturing or services will not imply the hollowing out of the Hong Kong economy, as enough new, high value-added activities will develop to sustain economic growth. Despite high costs and poor air quality, Hong Kong remains an attractive place for talent due to its international connectivity, pluralism, diversity and protection of freedom and human rights. Hong Kong universities attract an increasingly large number of gifted Mainland students, and the majority of them prefer to work in Hong Kong after graduation. Prominent Mainland artists, musicians and athletes have acquired Hong Kong residency. The fact that the senior positions in high-tech finance in Hong Kong are dominated by expatriates underlines Hong Kong's openness and international connectivity. Moreover, quite a few of the Hong Kong youths who have been educated overseas are making their way up in the financial markets of London and New York. Hong Kong has access to a diverse range of talent from its diaspora around the world. Hong Kong's prosperity will depend on its ability to tap talent in the Mainland, among its diaspora, and in the international arena.

References

City of London Corporation (2007), "The Global Financial Centres Index," March (http://cityoflondon.gov.U.K./Corporation).

Enright, Scott & Associates Ltd. (2006), "Hong Kong's Competitiveness: A Multidimensional Approach," Bauhinia Foundation Research Centre and Enright, Scott & Associates, Hong Kong, 26 September (http://www.bauhinia.org/publications.htm).

Lau, Siu-kai (1999), "From Elite Unity to Disunity: Political Elite in Post-1997 Hong Kong." In Wang Gungwu and John Wong (eds.), *Hong Kong in China: The Challenges of Transition.* Singapore: Times Academic Press, pp. 47–74.

Leung, George S. K. (2007), "Hong Kong SAR as a Regional and Global Financial Hub," presentation to the Symposium on the Making of China's Hong Kong: Retrospect on Hong Kong SAR's First Decade and Prospects Ahead, organized by the School of Professional and Continuing Education of The University of Hong Kong, Hong Kong, 27–28 April.

Li, Hongyi, Wei Xiangdong, and Xie Danyang (2007), "Competitiveness of the Hong Kong Economy: A Study on Productivity Growth, Unit Labour Costs and Structural Changes in Export Composition," Bauhinia Foundation Research Centre, May (http://www.bauhinia.org/publications.htm).

Sung, Yun-wing, (2006a), "The Evolving Role of Hong Kong as China's Middleman." In Lok Sang Ho and Robert Ash (eds.), *China, Hong Kong and the World Economy.* Palgrave, Basingstoke and New York, pp. 152–69.

—— (2006b), "Economic Contributions of Hong Kong's External Trade Sector: Input-Output Analysis" (mimeograph).

TeamOne Economist Limited (2006), "Review of Hong Kong's Socio-economic

Progress: A Quantitative Assessment," Bauhinia Foundation Research Centre, December (http://www.bauhinia.org/publications.htm).

Tse, Kwok-leung (2007), "Recounting the Development of Hong Kong's Financial Centre in the Past Decade," *Economic Review*, Bank of China (Hong Kong) Ltd., May (http://www.bocHong Kong.com).

Ying, Jian (2006), "Hong Kong Should Focus on Knowledge-based Service Industries," *Economic Review*, Bank of China (Hong Kong) Ltd., May (http://www.bocHong Kong.com).

11

Social Transformation and Cultural Identities*

Wong Siu-lun

Hong Kong has barely emerged from its post-handover blues, 10 years after 1997. The long bout of collective gloom and depression was unexpected. Things first went wrong a decade ago on the economic front, triggered by the Asian financial crisis, even though the political change in sovereignty appeared to have gone smoothly. Property prices plummeted, unemployment rates soared and popular grievances grew. Public discontent reached a climax on 1 July 2003, when an estimated half-a-million people marched on the streets to express their dissatisfaction. Since then, particularly after the resignation of Mr Tung Chee-hwa as Chief Executive in 2005, the popular disgruntlement has somewhat subsided. The election of Mr Donald Tsang as the new Chief Executive in June 2007 has apparently calmed the nerves of the community and restored a cautious sense of optimism.

Why did Hong Kong fall into deep depression so unexpectedly and for so long? What were the main sources of the malaise? With hindsight, I would suggest that the post-handover blues were a combination of the triple transition that the community is going through, the compressed development that preceded the change in sovereignty, and the entangled identities that are embedded in our psyche. Let me provide a quick sketch of these three phenomena before attempting to separately analyze their impact.

What do I mean by the triple transition? First, there is the well-known political transition, with the year 1997 as the watershed. After one-and-a-half centuries of British rule, there was a change in sovereignty on 1 July

* This chapter is partly based on the findings of the Hong Kong Social Indicators Project funded by the Hong Kong Research Grants Council (RGC Ref. No.: HKU7255/03H; PolyU5411/05H).

of that year. Colonial Hong Kong became Chinese Hong Kong under the "one country, two systems" (OCTS) arrangement. But there is a second transition on the economic front, which is occurring with much less fanfare. Hong Kong began its colonial existence as a "fishing village." After the Second World War, it was transformed into an "industrial colony." Then, since the mid-1980s, manufacturing gave way to services as the leading sector of the economy. The weight of manufacturing production in Hong Kong's gross domestic product (GDP) shrank from 22% in 1985 to 8.8% in 1995, while the role of the service sector expanded from 70% to 84% during that period. By 2004, the Hong Kong economy was so thoroughly service-oriented that industrial manufacturing only accounted for 4% of GDP (Maruya, 1998; Tsang, 1998; Hong Kong Information Services Department 2006, p. 46). Within the short span of two to three decades, Hong Kong changed from an industrial society into a financial and service centre. Then there is the third, almost silent, transition on the demographic front. In the 1960s, Hong Kong's population was still youthful in composition. As in many other developing regions, the population pyramid had a broad base that was shaped by high birth rates as well as high death rates. But by 2005, Hong Kong's population pyramid had changed into a diamond shape typical of developed societies marked by low fertility and mortality rates (Council for Sustainable Development, 2006a). If youth is golden, then the golden Hong Kong of the 1960s has rapidly been turning silver after the turn of the century.

Thus, at the handover in 1997, Hong Kong was heading towards the confluence of three currents of change. It had to navigate the turbulent course of a triple transition. Compounding the potential hazards was the fact that events in Hong Kong were happening at high speed. The territory was being propelled by a process of compressed development. The growth of its economy in the post-war period was dizzying. Hong Kong's GDP grew at an average annual rate of 9% in the 1970s. Then, throughout the 1980s and 1990s, the yearly increase remained a robust 6% and 5.2%, respectively. Living standards rose rapidly. Other related social changes followed at break-neck speed. Transformations of the economic and demographic structure that had usually taken more than a century to be accomplished in developed regions of the West were completed in a few decades. Such a process of compressed development through hyper-growth is an unprecedented phenomenon. It has fostered an intense form of exhilaration and disorientation in the Hong Kong way of life that I shall analyze in a later section.

The triple transition and compressed development are two of the major underlying causes of Hong Kong's post-handover woes. The third is the entangled sense of identity ingrained in the community's collective psyche. As the former Chief Secretary Anson Chan pointed out, the transition is not just about sovereignty. The crux of the matter is identity. It is about "hearts and minds," something that is both intangible and complex, and in Hong Kong's case, something fraught with ambivalence. Hong Kong's collective sense of identity is a complicated one, not just because it is shaped by both subjective preferences and objective circumstances, such as immigration policies and family strategies (Zheng and Wong, 2005a; Wong, 1998). It is also because collective identity is multifaceted in its make-up. Even though the issue of national identity has become more salient as Hong Kong confronts the handover, it is inevitably tied with other forms of identity, such as those of class, territory and ethnicity (Wang, 1991). This entanglement is heightened and made more confusing by the processes of triple transition and compressed development that are occurring simultaneously in Hong Kong.

Colonial to Chinese Hong Kong

After identifying the three major phenomena contributing to Hong Kong's post-handover blues, let me now examine their impacts and implications in more detail. As the three processes are in fact tightly interwoven with one another, I shall use the notion of triple transition as a convenient springboard for the following analysis. I shall explore in turn the problems involved in the transitions from Colonial to Chinese Hong Kong, from industrial to financial Hong Kong, and from golden to silvery Hong Kong.

The transition from Colonial to Chinese Hong Kong has attracted much attention. After all, the handover on 1 July 1997 was symbolized by a change in flag, marking the transfer of sovereignty. But what has actually changed more broadly on the social front remains somewhat unclear. For instance, what exactly do we mean by "Colonial Hong Kong?" What precisely are the colonial legacies? I have argued elsewhere that during the colonial period, there occurred a process of "decentring" in China proper. The imperial order sustained by a Confucian cultural centre crumbled, while in Hong Kong itself, a new social order emerged under the protection of British rule. The new order was a form of "network society" with five key features: shared sovereignty, network capital, hybrid identity, creative destruction and fluid disembeddedness (Wong, 2006). The rise of this form of network society has set Hong Kong apart from the Chinese Mainland, which was going through a different and often tumultuous process of social metamorphosis. When Hong Kong reverted to Chinese rule in 1997, it had to reconcile the potential incompatibilities of not just two economic systems — that of capitalism and socialism — but of two social systems as well – that of a network society and an emergent form of market-transitional society.

As Hong Kong's full-blown network society had to assume a new existence under the OCTS framework, two aspects stood out as more problematic than others. They were the characteristics of shared sovereignty and hybrid identity. Both involved tricky issues of loyalty and allegiance: one at the elite level and the other at the popular level.

In colonial times, shared sovereignty in Hong Kong meant a special mode of political governance. The colonial civil service constituted the governing body. Externally, in its relationship with the sovereign power in London, it was not a completely pliant tool. It managed to attain a high level of autonomy, which it jealously guarded. Internally, in its dealings with the business and community elite, it was not an over-powering presence. It maintained effective rule through cooptation and compromise.

As Hong Kong reverted to Chinese rule in 1997, this special mode of political governance ran into difficulties. The colonial style of shared sovereignty was not readily transferable. At least three thorny problems stood out. The first relates to the role of the civil service. Should it remain the kingpin politically? Could it be trusted from Beijing's point of view, given the bitter row provoked by Chris Patten as the last Colonial Governor and the expressed desire of Beijing to set up "a new stove" after the handover? While Tung Chee-hwa was in office from 1997 to 2005 as the new Chief Executive of Hong Kong, he apparently leaned towards answering these questions in the negative. He chose not to adopt the civil service as his surrogate governing party. Instead, he initiated radical reforms soon after he assumed office so as to break the back of the civil service and to bring it under submission. Much of the political paralysis during his tenure can be attributed to this stand-off between himself as Chief Executive and the senior civil servants as represented by the former Chief Secretary Anson Chan.

The second problem concerns the delicate balance between autonomy and unification. A new relationship has to be forged between Hong Kong as a Special Administrative Region (SAR) and Beijing as the sovereign power. The old pattern of maximum autonomy for Hong Kong as a colony and minimal intervention from London as the metropolis cannot simply be replicated. The colonial arrangement of shared sovereignty was worked out at a particular historical juncture when the British Empire was in decline and London was already resigned to accepting the worldwide trend of decolonization. The colonial administration in Hong Kong did not have to push too hard in order to attain a large measure of *de facto* autonomy.

But after the handover, the Hong Kong SAR has been facing a China that is on the rise. Even though Beijing has shown great caution in refraining from intervening in the internal administration of the SAR in the past decade, it has not been shy in insisting on what it regards as the prerogatives of sovereignty. This insistence ignited the two explosive controversies that rocked the territory in the post-handover period. One was the interpretation of the Basic Law by the Standing Committee of the National People's Congress in Beijing that overturned the ruling of the Court of Final Appeal in Hong Kong on the right of abode issue in 1999. The other was the abortive attempt by the Hong Kong SAR government, apparently urged by Beijing, to pass anti-secession legislation to implement Article 23 of the Basic Law, which triggered the massive demonstration on 1 July 2003. Both events indicate that a new balance between autonomy and unification has not yet been found. A fresh formula for shared sovereignty between Hong Kong and Beijing has yet to be worked out and agreed upon.

The third problem relates to the internal sharing of power between the civil service and other members of the elite, most notably the business leaders. The SAR government is clearly aware of the need to forge an effective ruling coalition after the handover. But this is a daunting task, and there are tell-tale signs that the government-business relationship is in considerable trouble. Anti-business sentiment is mounting in the community. Popular accusations about collusion between the government and business interests are getting strident. An opinion poll conducted in 2006 has found that a large majority of the respondents, about 82.4%, believed that such collusion exists. Moreover, the respondents were divided over the issue of whether business leaders can be trusted, with 25.3% expressing distrust, 19.9% avowing trust, and a majority of 54.8% unsure of where they stand on the issue (Zheng and Wong, 2006, pp. 7, 13).

There is some irony in the current popular indignation over government-business collusion. In the colonial days, a close relationship between the government and business interests undoubtedly existed, which was well captured in the common saying that "[p]ower in Hong Kong resides in the Jockey Club, Jardine and Matheson, the Hong Kong and Shanghai Bank, and the Governor — in that order" (Hughes, 1976, p. 23). This close relationship was obviously taken for granted by the community as a fact of life. It was seldom vilified as a form of collusion. Academic research has revealed the existence of well-defined business clusters in the Hong Kong economy in the 1970s and 1980s, with the Hong Kong and Shanghai Bank as the kingpin (Gilbert Wong, 1996). A significant change after the handover is that the former economic kingpin has gone. Part of the role of the Hong Kong and Shanghai Bank was to act as the quasi-central bank of the territory. That function was replaced by the newly created Hong Kong Monetary Authority. But other than that, its position as the economic pillar has not been taken up by a new substitute. The fragmentation of business interests and groupings is thus on the rise, with emergent contenders fighting fiercely to define their turf. Until a new economic order is formed, the political partnership between the SAR government and the business community will remain tentative and unstable.

So much for the problems engendered by shared sovereignty at the elite level. The other key characteristics of Hong Kong as a network society is the hybrid identity embraced by the general populace. This hybrid form of identity flourished in the community after colonial Hong Kong emerged as the main hub of emigration from the Chinese Mainland in the nineteenth century (Sinn, 1995). Such hybridity consisted of several components. One was the heightened significance attached to sub-ethnic affiliations, such as being Cantonese, Fukienese or Hakka, as these social bonds and dialect groupings played an important role in facilitating mutual assistance among the Chinese migrants. The other was the proliferation of hyphenated identities, such as being Indonesian Chinese, Australian Chinese or Canadian Chinese as multicultural experience grew among the migrant Hong Kong population. Emotional attachment to one's native place in the Chinese Mainland steadily weakened, and the notion of "home" became more varied and uncertain (Wang and Wong, 2007). Yet, another element of hybridity was, and is, a pragmatic and instrumental approach towards issues of nationality and passports. The acceptance of dual nationality and the holding of multiple passports are quite common among Hong Kong inhabitants, reflecting the importance they attach to the values of individual autonomy and freedom of movement rather than the primacy of national identification.

The hybrid form of identity arose in Hong Kong under colonial rule, where social networks flourished and the cultural centre in China declined. When Hong Kong was reincorporated into the Chinese polity in 1997, this mixed mode of identity would inevitably create tensions with the demand for allegiance from the centre as represented by Beijing. It was a tussle between an ingrained centrifugal force spinning away from the centre and an emergent centripetal force exerting its pull towards the centre. As a consequence, the study of identity has become a hot topic in Hong Kong, yielding an abundance of survey findings in recent years. Let me just cite the findings from our Hong Kong social indicator surveys (Zheng and Wong, 2005b, p. 11) as an illustration.

As Table 11.1 reveals, national and cultural identities have tended not to change abruptly. Over the past two decades, subjective identification in Hong Kong has undergone a gradual shift. The majority who regard themselves as more Hongkongese than Chinese has shrunk from about 58% in 1990 to around 45% in 2006. Those who put their Chinese identity first remain a minority, rising from about 26% in 1990 to around 30% in 2006. The most significant change seems to have occurred among the ranks of those who embrace both identities equally. They grew from about 14% in 1990 to around 24% in 2006.

The general trend remains one of a collective endorsement of the hybrid form of identity. This tendency is reflected even in the way in which the survey questions were framed. The respondents were asked to choose among identities not in exclusive terms as either Hongkongese or Chinese, but only in a relative sense that accorded with their sentiments. One may well imagine that this mode of questioning would seem odd or even objectionable to respondents in Beijing or other Chinese cities who might uphold a purer and more exclusive form of national identity. Thus, the tension arising out of the clash between different outlooks pertaining to national identity remains unresolved and very much alive in Hong Kong, 10 years after it again became part of China.

Table 11.1 Changing Identities in Hong Kong 1990–2006 (%)

Year	Hongkongese	Chinese	Both	Neither	Total (N)
1990	58.3	26.2	14.3	1.2	100 (1,900)
1993	55.1	29.6	14.5	0.8	100 (1,942)
1995	53.2	32.3	13.1	1.2	100 (2,226)
1997	56.1	28.6	14.6	0.6	100 (2,078)
1999	52.7	27.4	19.1	0.9	100 (3,227)
2001	49.3	30.6	19.2	0.8	100 (4,049)
2004	48.5	31.1	19.5	0.9	100 (3,236)
2006	45.1	29.9	24.1	0.9	100 (3,443)

Source: Hong Kong Social Indicators Survey, various years.

Industrial to Financial Hong Kong

While Colonial Hong Kong was transformed into Chinese Hong Kong with 1997 as the political watershed, a parallel transition was occurring on the economic front. Industrial Hong Kong with manufacturing as its mainstay gave way to financial Hong Kong with services as its core activity. This transition from a reliance on the secondary sector to the predominance of the tertiary sector was accomplished within just a few decades. The speed of change was so breath-taking that it is only appropriate to depict it as a compressed form of economic development. This pattern of compressed development is an unprecedented phenomenon mainly found among the "Four Little Dragons" in Asia. As such, its social consequences and implications are yet to be fully identified and understood. But as far as Hong Kong is concerned, this compressed development has at least created a special social ethos and called into being a distinctive social stratum.

That social ethos is a mixture of high hopes and deep anxieties, commonly known as the "Hong Kong Dream." Industrial take-off in the 1960s and 1970s had lent credence to the popular belief that Hong Kong was a land of opportunity, where individual efforts would be rewarded and social advancement would be within reach even for those of humble and lowly origins. Hopes were so high and so pervasive that they constituted a cohesive force that sustained a long period of prosperity and stability in the territory. However, underneath these high hopes, there had always been an undercurrent of deep anxiety, generated first by the refugee mentality accompanying the influx of migrants in the post-war era, and then by the collective apprehension about an uncertain future associated with the impending change in sovereignty. Yet, on the whole, individual hopes tended to override collective gloom all the way up to 1997. Even when pessimism about the future led to a substantial wave of emigration from Hong Kong in the early 1990s, the paradoxical result was the opening up of opportunities for accelerated advancement for those who had stayed put, thus reinforcing individual hopes for upward mobility (Wong 1992, p. 928).

The ethos of high hopes was buttressed by a robust pattern of upward social mobility as Hong Kong underwent rapid industrialization. Such upward movement called into being a new middle class consisting of administrators, managers and professionals who achieved advancement through the credential route of accumulating educational qualifications. At the same time, there also emerged a thriving group of small factory owners, sometimes referred to as the petty bourgeoisie, who pulled themselves up through the entrepreneurial route of innovation and risk-taking.

This new middle class, broadly defined, has a number of distinctive characteristics. First of all, it represented a class in ascendance during the period of Hong Kong's industrial take-off. Its ascent was smooth and speedy, as it did not threaten the vested interests of the other social classes such as the capitalists or the workers. Its members moved into positions newly created through the structural expansion of the economy. They did not have to push out existing incumbents before they could move ahead. This resulted in the second feature of this middle class, namely its individualistic orientation. They tended to rely on their own resources when they were confronted with problems or obstacles. They were not prone to resorting to collective action to advance their interests. But probably most important of all was its third trait of being a nascent class in formation. The great majority of its members were administrators and professionals of the first generation. They came from diverse and often humble backgrounds. They had yet to cultivate taste, and their lifestyle had yet to take shape. In short, they did not have a ready-made cultural blueprint to guide their action (for a fuller depiction of the Hong Kong middle class, see Lui and Wong, 2003; Lui, 2005).

The Hong Kong Dream and the new middle class had their heyday in the last three decades of the twentieth century. But when the Asian financial crisis hit the territory in 1997 just as Hong Kong was undergoing the handover process, the impact was tremendous. It nearly shattered the dream, and it threw the new middle class into disarray. It exposed the inherent vulnerabilities of Hong Kong's service economy. With the pillar of manufacturing as a source for stable employment gone, the job market became far more fickle. Thus, unemployment soared at an alarming rate. The economic rebound was far more sluggish than before, as the service sector tended to be the first to be hit and the last to recover during a recession. Thus, Hong Kong fell into the deepest economic depression it had ever experienced since the Second World War. It then began to dawn on the Hong Kong community that the good old days might be over, that hyper-growth might have come to an end, and that the prospect of going downhill might be imminent.

This was a rude awakening, and most painful for the vast majority of the populace to accept. The individual optimism that had sustained high hopes in the past became dimmed. One indication of this decline in optimism can be found in the survey data we have collected over the years in the Hong Kong Social Indicator Survey. We classify our respondents into "pessimists," "optimists" and "neutralists" according to their reply to the question: "By your general estimation, do you expect your family's living standards in the next three years to become worse, better, or to remain more or less the same?" As shown in Table 11.2, a large majority of the respondents, about 63.1%, were optimists in 1988.

By 1997, less than half of the respondents were optimists, making up about 42.6% of the total. The ranks of the optimists decreased further to just 30.0% in 2004. Another sign of the dampening of optimism can be detected in the rising suicide rate. In the 1980s and 1990s, the rate of suicide in Hong Kong was relatively low, with an annual average of about 10 per 100,000. But in the last few years, it rose substantially, reaching a rate of 18.6 per 100,000 in 2003, which was 28% higher than the world average of 14.5 per 100,000. (Hong Kong Jockey Club Centre for Suicide Research and Prevention, 2005).

The new middle class was by no means the hardest hit by the prolonged recession and the dimming of hope. For instance, as far as unemployment and growing pessimism were concerned, it was the lower worker class that suffered the most (Lui and Wong, 2003, p. 73; Wong and Zheng, 2005, pp. 294–95). But it is fair to say that members of the new middle class did suffer a heavy blow, at least psychologically. Some of their fundamental beliefs were being undermined. Urgent economic restructuring during the recession brought home to them that they could no longer count on stable bureaucratic careers and long-term employment opportunities. The bursting of the property bubble shattered their assumptions about home-ownership and the purchase of real estate as a safe form of investment. The rapid expansion of tertiary education and radical educational reforms spurred a

Table 11.2 The Composition of Pessimists, Neutralists and Optimists, 1988–2004 (%)

Year	Pessimists	Neutralists	Optimists	% (N)
1988	7.4	29.5	63.1	100 (1,276)
1990	6.7	30.5	62.9	100 (1,602)
1993	15.1	31.7	53.2	100 (1,605)
1995	25.0	40.4	34.6	100 (1,863)
1997	14.3	43.1	42.6	100 (1,861)
1999	18.4	46.0	35.6	100 (2,819)
2001	21.0	46.9	32.1	100 (3,613)
2004	20.1	49.9	30.0	100 (2,880)

Source: Wong and Zheng, 2005, p. 289.

depreciation in the economic worth of credentials and a confusion in the rules of the game for seeking advancement through educational competition. All of these developments disoriented the new middle class. As a nascent class, without a reliable cultural blueprint to fall back on, its members were at a loss as to how best to cope with adversities and unexpected shifts in their economic circumstances. They became agitated and took to the streets in large numbers for the first time in 2003 during the 1 July demonstration. Yet, it would be an exaggeration to say that there has been a sea change in the mentality of the middle class. What is actually happening appears to be an internal fragmentation of this class. As Lui Tak-lok pointed out, "[differences] within the middle class are growing. A higher level of anxiety and uneasiness is found among the lower-middle class. In contrast to the upper-middle class, which continues to be self-assured, the lower-middle class is anxious, uneasy, and restless" (Lui, 2005, p. 196). This tendency has probably been generated more by the economic transition that Hong Kong is undergoing than by the political handover. In any case, it is reasonably clear that the "golden days" of the Hong Kong middle class, glorious as they have been, are basically over (Lui and Wong, 2003, p. 129).

Golden to Silvery Hong Kong

If youth is golden, then the golden days of Hong Kong as a youthful community is also something of the past. Since the 1970s, Hong Kong has undergone a rapid demographic transition. By 2007, its population has become middle-aged. Those in their forties and fifties form the largest age groups, and they are fast approaching retirement. In this demographic transition, three issues are particularly noteworthy for their impact on post-handover developments in general, and on changing identities in particular. They are, respectively, the phenomena of a sharp decline in fertility, a rapidly ageing population and popular ambivalence towards immigrants.

The birth rate in Hong Kong has been in free fall in the past few decades. It dropped below the replacement level of 2,100 children per thousand women in the early 1980s. By 2005, the birth rate had further declined to 966 per thousand, among the lowest in the world (Council for Sustainable Development, 2006a, p. 44). The causes for this sharp decline in fertility are complex, and the subject awaits a detailed investigation. But there are strong indications that this decline in fertility may be closely related to the anxiety of the middle class about its ability to reproduce itself. For example, in our 2004 social indicators survey, "we found that young, local-born, better-educated, high-income, and professional and managerial respondents … generally favour establishing a small family and having few children." This led to the paradoxical finding that "although the high-income respondents have a stronger financial position, they choose to have fewer children; while the low-income respondents, who are in a tighter financial position, prefer to have more" (Zheng and Wong, 2005a, p. 242).

This paradox probably reflects the underlying anxiety of the middle class about the future prospects for their children. Having risen rapidly from humble origins, Hong Kong yuppies are getting less and less confident that their offspring will be able to retain their present class position, let alone to do better than themselves. For their children, such a rapid advancement would be a hard act to follow, particularly when local opportunities are no longer expanding at the same rate, or are even declining. Middle-class parents would have to invest heavily in educating their children to prepare them for the competition that lies ahead, but even so the outcome would not be very promising. Thus, they complain about the high financial costs of raising children and the imperfections in the educational system. Having children is no longer a symbol of hope for them. It has become a psychological burden.

In the social indicators survey, we found a clear trend of pessimism among our respondents about their children's future. From 1988 onwards, "the percentages of those expecting a better future for their children dropped continuously from 88.5% (in 1988) to 79.3% (in 1995), 72.9% (in 1999), and 65.9% (in 2004)" (Zheng and Wong, 2005a, p. 256). When the respondents were asked about their perceptions of the opportunities for achieving success in 2004, an unexpected finding was that "it was the upper- and lower-middle classes that were most critical of this belief in equal opportunity for success (41% and 34.4% disagreed with the statement, respectively). It turned out that, paradoxically, it was the class of manual workers and flexible workers (73.5%) that continued to believe in the dream of low barriers to success in Hong Kong" (Lui, 2005, p. 194).

Therefore, it is quite likely that the sharp decline in fertility is an indicator of the disorientation felt by a Hong Kong middle class that is getting more and more unsure about its collective identity and destiny. Another implication of the decline in fertility is its unsettling impact on the local educational system. With fewer babies being born, the demand for school places will continue to drop. In the past few years, many primary schools have had to close because of a shrinking student intake. The effect of these closures on the morale of primary school teachers has been devastating. But this is just the beginning. In the coming decade, the problem of a shrinking supply of students will spread to the secondary and tertiary educational sectors, putting many professional teaching careers in jeopardy and adding to the woes of the Hong Kong middle class.

Hand in hand with the sharp decline in fertility is a rapidly ageing population. In 1961, the elderly (those aged 65 and above) constituted only 3.2% of the total population. In 2005, they had increased to 12.1%. By 2033, they are projected to reach 26.8% (Council for Sustainable Development, 2006b, p. 17). That means in about two decades' time, Hong Kong will have a silvery population. The implications are far-reaching. The active workforce will contract, fiscal revenues from salary taxes will decline, and public medical expenditures will soar. In addition, the future political landscape will change, as senior citizens become a major voting bloc. Fortunately, these developments are not imminent. Right now, Hong Kong is basking in "a demographic window, which opened up when the overall dependency declined because of the falling fertility rate experienced in the past several decades. However, this window will close in the years ahead (in about 2019) as the overall dependency rises again with an increasingly elderly population" (Council for Sustainable Development, 2006a, p. 47).

This window of opportunity should enable the Hong Kong SAR government and the community to devise measures to cope with the looming demographic challenge. One well-tried measure is the induction of new immigrants. But in adopting such a measure, the government would have to confront at least two main obstacles. The first is the lack of enthusiasm, if not outright opposition, among the general public to the introduction of new immigration schemes. In an opinion poll conducted in 2004, it was found that the majority of the respondents, about 60%, felt that it was not necessary for the government to adopt measures to increase immigration. Roughly the same proportion of them, about 59.7%, felt that even the existing daily quota of admitting 150 new migrants from the Chinese Mainland was excessive (Zheng and Wong, 2004, pp. 23; 28). It seems that the Hong Kong populace, having undergone the transition from a community of migrants in the immediate post-war period to a more settled community of citizens since the 1980s, are reluctant to open their doors again to accept newcomers.

The second obstacle is institutional inertia. In the post-war era, the entire government machinery in Hong Kong was geared up to deal with the "problem of people," i.e., the influx of refugees and illegal immigrants (see, for example, Hambro, 1955). It had to contend with successive waves of refugees from the Chinese Mainland, Vietnam and elsewhere in Southeast Asia. It had to develop defences against these human tidal waves. Therefore, it was quite natural for it to adopt the stance of a passive immigration regime. Institutional memory and accumulated wisdom within the official bureaucracy would counsel against major changes in matters relating to immigration, particularly in the relaxation of controls. It will take a considerable amount of time and much lobbying before the bureaucracy can be turned around to become an active immigration regime that will reach out and search for new blood to sustain Hong Kong's future development.

Conclusion

Hong Kong's post-handover blues, as I have tried to show in this chapter, are not fleeting symptoms that can be simply attributed to the political inexperience of the Tung administration or external shocks brought about by the Asian financial crisis and the SARS epidemic. There are deeper causes involved, which I have identified as the after effects of a triple transition, compressed development and entangled identities. If this diagnosis is not mistaken, then the present economic recovery should be regarded only as a temporary respite. There are many daunting challenges ahead, because the root causes of our post-handover woes are still with us.

At least three major issues will need to be tackled with care by the Hong Kong SAR administration and the community as a whole during the coming decade. They are, respectively, the politics of autonomy, the politics of consolidation and the politics of identity. The tussle between Hong Kong as a network society with inherent "decentring" tendencies and the Chinese Mainland as an emergent market-transitional society with a growing need for a strong centre will be a long-standing one. The tension will express itself in renewed debates about electoral reforms and anti-secession legislation in the future. Thus, the politics of autonomy. The prolonged economic depression in the past decade should have brought home to the Hong Kong community that compressed development and hyper-growth are unlikely to be sustainable. It may well be that Hong Kong is following the footsteps of Japan in entering an economic plateau after a steep ascent, and that the politics of expansion will have to give way to the politics of consolidation. Finally, both Hong Kong and the Chinese Mainland have to come to terms with the territory's entangled identities. The issue is not just one of local versus national identities. Class identification, particularly that of the new middle class, is undergoing transformation. Hong Kong's social identity as a community of migrants or a community of settled citizens is also at the crossroads. The politics of identity will surely be on the rise. With the need to grapple with these myriad challenges, the next decade for Hong Kong should be as interesting, if not more so, than the past one.

References

Council for Sustainable Development (2006a), *Enhancing Population Potential for a Sustainable Future: Invitation and Response Document for the Second Engagement Process*. Hong Kong: The Council.

—— (2006b), "Enhancing Population Potential for a Sustainable Future: PowerPoint Presentation." Hong Kong: The Council.

Hambro, Edvard (1955), *The Problem of Chinese Refugees in Hong Kong: Report Submitted to the United Nations High Commission for Refugees*. Leyden: Sithoff.

Hong Kong Information Services Department (ed.) (2006), *Hong Kong 2005*. Hong Kong: The Department.

Hong Kong Jockey Club Centre for Suicide Research and Prevention (2005), "Suicide Rates by Gender in Hong Kong 1981–2004". http://csrp.hku.hk/WEB/eng/statistics.asp.

Hughes, Richard (1976), *Borrowed Place Borrowed Time: Hong Kong and Its Many Faces*, second revised edition. London: Andre Deutsch.

Lui, Tak-lok and Jimmy Wong (2003), *Xianggang zhongchan jieji chujing guancha* (Situational Observation on the Hong Kong Middle Class). Hong Kong: Joint Publishing.

Lui, Tai-lok (2005), "The Psychology of the Middle Class." In Lau Siu-kai, Lee Ming-kwan, Wan Po-san and Wong Siu-lun (eds.), *Indicators of Social Development: Hong Kong 2004*. Hong Kong: Hong Kong Institute of Asia-Pacific Studies, The Chinese University of Hong Kong, pp. 179–99.

Maruya, Toyojiro (1998), "Tasks for Hong Kong's Economy in the New Era — The Shift to a Service-oriented Economy and the Introduction of a Comprehensive Competition Policy." In Wong Siu-lun and Toyojiro Maruya (eds.), *Hong Kong Economy and Society: Challenges in the New Era*. Hong Kong: Centre of Asian Studies, The University of Hong Kong, pp. 1–14.

Sinn, Elizabeth (1995), "Emigration From Hong Kong Before 1941: General Trends." In Ronald Skeldon (ed.), *Emigration From Hong Kong: Tendencies and Impacts*. Hong Kong: The Chinese University Press, pp. 11–34.

Tsang, Shu-ki (1998), "Changing Structure of Hong Kong's Economy." In Wang Gungwu and John Wong (eds.), *Hong Kong in China: The Challenge of Transition*. Singapore: Times Academic Press, pp. 101–26.

Wang, Cangbai and Wong Siu-lun (2007), "Home as a Circular Process: A Study of the Indonesian Chinese in Hong Kong." In Mette Thunø (ed.), *Beyond Chinatown: New Chinese Migration and the Global Expansion of China*. Copenhagen: NIAS Press, pp. 169–91.

Wang, Gungwu (1991), "The Study of Chinese Identities in Southeast Asia." In Wang Gungwu, *China and the Chinese Overseas*. Singapore: Time Academic Press, pp. 198–221.

Wong, Gilbert (1996), "Business Groups in a Dynamic Environment: Hong Kong 1976–1986." In Gary G. Hamilton (ed.), *Asian Business Networks*. Berlin: Walter de Gruyter, pp. 87–114.

Wong, Siu-lun (1992), "Emigration and Stability in Hong Kong," *Asian Survey*, Vol. 32, No. 10, pp. 918–33.

—— (1998), "Changing Hong Kong Identities." In Wang Gungwu and John Wong (eds.), *Hong Kong in China: The Challenges of Transition*. Singapore: Times Academic Press, pp. 181–202.

—— (2006), "Decentering: The Rise of Hong Kong as a Network Society," *Social Transformations in Chinese Societies*, Vol. 2, pp. 163–87.

Wong, Siu-lun and Victor Zheng (2005), "Social Anticipation and Social Reality." In Lau Siu-kai, Lee Ming-kwan, Wan Po-san and Wong Siu-lun (eds.), *Indicators of Social Development: Hong Kong 2004*. Hong Kong: Hong Kong Institute of Asia-Pacific Studies, The Chinese University of Hong Kong, pp. 285–328.

Zheng, Victor and Wong Siu-lun (2004), "Renkou yu shehui fazhan: 2004 nian Xianggang renkou wenti minyi tiaocha jianbao yu pinglun" (Population and Social Development: A Report and Analysis on the 2004 Opinion Poll about the Population Problem in Hong Kong). Occasional Paper No. 1, Hong Kong Culture and Society Programme. Hong Kong: Centre of Asian Studies, The University of Hong Kong.

—— (2005a), "Subjective Well-being and the Decline in Fertility." In Lau Siu-kai et al. (eds.), *Indicators of Social Development: Hong Kong 2004*, pp. 229–64.

—— (2005b), "Shenfen rentong yu zhengfu jiaose: Xianggang de lizi" (Identities and Government's Role: The Case of Hong Kong), *Ershiyi shiji shuangyuekan* (Twenty-first Century Bimonthly, No. 92, December, pp. 4–15).

—— (2006). "Guanshang goujie? — Xianggang shimin yanzhong de zhengshang guanxi" (Government-Business Collusion? — Government-business Relations as Seen by Hong Kong Citizens). Occasional Paper No. 3, Hong Kong Culture and Society Programme. Hong Kong: Centre of Asian Studies, The University of Hong Kong.

12

Reforming Education beyond Education

Kai-ming Cheng

Introduction

The 10 years since the changeover of sovereignty over Hong Kong have been 10 years of education reform. In these 10 years, a paradigm shift in the basic concepts of education in Hong Kong took place. Also during these 10 years, the most dramatic confrontation erupted between the unions and the government since the teachers' strike in 1973. In this chapter, the reforms are documented, their causes and outcomes are analyzed, their nature highlighted, and speculations are made on the long-term consequences of the reforms.

An attempt is made to shed light on the experiences and lessons of Hong Kong's education reforms that could be of international interest. Here, the writer makes full use of his personal experience as a former insider in the reform process, but also strives to ensure that the analyses presented here are not tarnished by personal biases.

The Reforms

Official documents tend to quote 2000 as the starting point of the education reform process in Hong Kong. However, it could also be justifiably argued that the process began in January 1999, when, before a forum of 800 prominent leaders in the community invited to listen to a presentation entitled: "Questioning Education," the Education Commission declared that reforms were to be launched to the education system in Hong Kong.[1]

The preparation for the reforms actually took place even earlier, in 1996, when Tung Chee-hwa was preparing to run for Chief Executive of Hong Kong. He had a genuine belief that education is crucial to the future of Hong Kong. He formed a small informal group of private advisors to help him chart the path for education in Hong Kong. Tung had also identified Antony Leung as the person to champion the reforms. These efforts were taking place at a time when the word "reform" was almost taboo in Hong Kong, and the advice was that the government should be careful not to "rock the boat."[2]

After the change in sovereignty, Antony Leung was made Chairman of the Education Commission and formally championed the campaign.[3] The campaign was launched at a time when the Education Commission, which had been established in 1986, had produced seven Education Commission Reports, and indeed had addressed all issues of concern to the community. Tsang Wing-kwong, an academic at The Chinese University of Hong Kong, reckoned that in the decade since the establishment of the Education Commission, the seven policy reports had made 297 recommendations, but few of them had truly been implemented and had had an impact (Cheng, 2002). The Education Commission, therefore, decided to redesign the system from the ground up. This plan received the support of Tung Chee-hwa, who charged the Education Commission with carrying out reform tasks on three fronts: structure, curriculum and assessments.

Reform in Structure

The reform in structure is dramatic. Hong Kong's system mirrors that of the United Kingdom (UK), with 3+2 years of secondary school, followed by two years of pre-university schooling leading to the Advanced Level Certificate of Education Examination (abbreviated as A-Levels, as is the case in the U.K.). The reform is to change to a 3+3 junior-senior secondary school system, so that young people will enter higher education a year earlier. This is going to take place in 2012, and the first batch of students in that new system already enrolled in Secondary One in 2006.

The structural reform will mean that the entire school-age population of Hong Kong will attend one more year of formal schooling. At the moment, enrolment is almost universal at Secondary 5. The vast majority of the school-age population in Hong Kong notionally finishes basic education at the age of 17. In the new 3+3 system, all young people are expected to complete senior Secondary 3 at the notional age of 18.

The structural change will also imply that young people who choose to pursue a post-secondary education will enter institutions of higher education one year earlier. In other words, higher education in Hong Kong will start at the notional age of 18 rather than 19. The net effect of that is that an additional year of higher education programmes will be required. As part of the British legacy, degree programmes in Hong Kong are normally three years in duration. This will change to four years. That will fundamentally change the higher education landscape in Hong Kong. It will further facilitate the continuous attempts that are being made to broaden students' learning experience in higher education.

The structural reform, which is often known as "3+3+4", is a necessary move to break away from the tradition of an elite and selective education system. Hong Kong universalized its primary education only in 1971. There was spectacular expansion of secondary education in the 1970s, so that junior secondary education was largely universalized. However, even then, the public school system was designed for an enrolment ratio of 60% in the last two years of secondary schooling. The structure remained almost stagnant until before the launching of reforms in 2000, when less than 40% of Secondary 5 graduates were given places to continue on to Secondary 6 and 7. The latter, similar to the "sixth forms" in the U.K., is basically designed for "matriculation," with university entrance as the sole purpose. With the reform, which makes pre-university education available to the entire population, there should be a much broader participation in higher education. Such an anticipated expansion of education was confirmed in Tung Chee-hwa's Policy Address in 2002, when he set as a 10-year target for a 60% enrolment ratio in higher education.

An important dimension of the reform, or the consequence of the reform, is the rapid expansion of community colleges. There was mention of the possible development of community colleges in the 2001 reform document, but community colleges mushroomed right away without any signal or subsidy from the government. In a short period of four years, the ratio of enrolment in higher education increased sharply from 30% to 65%, due almost totally to the contribution of the community colleges, which offer associate degrees and higher diplomas. Tung's target of 60% has been well exceeded, and well in advance of the target year. The development of community colleges is a very good reminder that, where a need exists, it would be too restrictive to consider the government to be the only driver for reforms in education.

Reform in the Curriculum

Closely related to the structural reform is curriculum reform. The overall idea of curriculum reform is to broaden the learning experience of students, thus providing young people with the learning experience that they deserve. The new curriculum aims to achieve seven Learning Goals: a healthy lifestyle, breadth of knowledge, learning skills, language skills, the habit of reading, consciousness of national identity and responsibility.

The core of the curriculum reform is the change from subject-bound studies to Key Learning Areas. The Key Learning Areas include the Chinese Language, the English Language, Mathematics, Humanities ("Personal, Social and Humanities Education"), Science, Technology, Arts and Physical Education. They are meant to provide learning experiences in five areas: moral and civic education, intellectual development, community services, physical and aesthetics development, and applied learning.

From a broader perspective, reforming the curriculum is a first step to breaking away from the hundred-year-old model where young people learn in "chunks" of knowledge (subjects). The model not only limits the width of knowledge that is learned (as the number of subjects are limited) but also forbids integrated learning and the application of knowledge (which is partitioned by "subject discipline" boundaries).

The new curriculum also allows for a more balanced framework for different learning experiences. Similar to reform exercises in other systems, the traditional subjects that are tested in the public examinations have been compressed in order to leave room for other non-academic learning opportunities.[4] As a consequence, many of the traditional subjects have been combined, or "integrated," in order to form a broader Key Learning Area. Achieving this "integration" entails the major task of preparing teachers who were trained to teach only subjects in the traditional categories.

The repartitioning of "subject knowledge" into Key Learning Areas is only a part of the reform process. The reorganization of the curriculum implies a new approach, where students learn to construct their own knowledge rather than to simply receive knowledge from teachers and textbooks. This approach reflects contemporary theories of learning. Such a fundamental change in the concept of learning is succinctly expressed in *Learning to Learn*, a milestone document published by the Curriculum Development Council in 2001.

It is understandable that the subjects that secondary schools are expected to offer are basically dictated by the admissions requirements of higher education. Hence, the change in admissions requirements is an inevitable yet hidden reform that is crucial to the success of reforming the secondary school curriculum. There have been on-going negotiations between the

Education and Manpower Bureau (EMB) (non restructured as Education Bureau) of the Special Administrative Region (SAR) government and Hong Kong's higher education institutions to redefine the threshold requirements for entrance to such institutions, so that secondary schools will be given more room to offer alternative learning experiences.

Since the turn of the twenty-first century, higher education institutions have been starting to relax their admissions requirements. As part of such efforts, these institutions are now beginning to open their doors to young people with talents other than in academic studies, in particular, those who have excelled in sports and those who have demonstrated qualities of leadership.

A breakthrough was achieved in 2002, when higher education institutions began to admit students after Secondary 6 (rather than Secondary 7), who had, therefore, not undergone the A-Level examinations. In this "Early Admissions Scheme," students are admitted based on their performance in the school-leaving Hong Kong Certificate of Education Examination (which takes place at the end of Secondary 5). The first batches of such students have already graduated. Their often outstanding academic performance was another argument for making admissions requirements to higher education more flexible. Despite some controversies among educators about the disruption to schools from the loss of their best students at Secondary 7, the smooth introduction of the Early Admissions Scheme is a powerful "protest" against the very strict admissions system based on A-Level scores.

Reform in Assessment

Examinations have always been central to education systems in Chinese communities. The strong tradition of the civil examination, which started in the seventh century, has underpinned examination-oriented education systems for centuries, even the modern school system (Cheng, 2000). There are widespread complaints that cramming for examinations is a serious hindrance to genuine learning. However, the holding of examinations and the desire to achieve success in such examinations are deeply rooted in the culture, and have become the major motivation for students to perform well in school.[5] There is a consensus, therefore, that the "reduction of examination pressure" be made a priority in the agenda for education reform.

In particular, the Academic Attainment Test (AAT) that took place at the end of the primary education process had always been a source of undue pressure. The AAT was comprised of three school internal assessment scores running across the last two years of primary schooling. In reality, most schools had sacrificed both Primary 5 and Primary 6 for drilling in mock tests in preparation for the AAT. The immediate removal of the AAT in 2000 at the end of primary schooling met with little opposition.

The major reform in the area of assessments is associated with the structural and curriculum reforms mentioned above. The changes in the school structure and curriculum mean that a new public examination, which has to be compatible with the curriculum reform, will be held at the end of the 12th grade (Senior Secondary 3). Instead of two examinations, held respectively at the end of Secondary 5 and Secondary 7 within a short span of three years, there will be one examination at the end of the new Senior Secondary 3 (or Secondary 6). This new public examination will take place for the first time in 2012. However, the reform is about much more than just the elimination of one examination. The new examination is supposed to be an instrument of "authentic assessment," where the actual competency rather than the relative strength of the students is to be measured. The new examination has to serve the two sometimes contradictory functions of recognizing a student's attainment of universal secondary education on the one hand, and acting as a reliable tool for selecting students for higher education on the other.

In any reform of an education system, it is always an issue to balance the needs of schools that cater to the masses and the needs of selective higher education institutions. The decision has been made to address the secondary curriculum first, and then to negotiate with higher education institutions the issue of how their admissions requirements should be adjusted. This decision has been justified by the rationale that the public examination must, first and foremost, serve the secondary school learning, which caters to the entire school-age population. The large majority of young people do not go into higher education. In the final analysis, reforms to the curriculum and to the manner of assessment are being carried out to build a firm foundation for young people, so that they will have tools to continue learning in the future. This should benefit higher education in the end. Meanwhile, with regard to community colleges, which now enrol a large number of young people, the entrance requirements are much less selective.

Nature of the Reforms

The process of education in the Hong Kong Special Administrative Region

(HKSAR) is among the more comprehensive and conceptually consistent reforms that are taking place on the international level. First, the reform process was prompted by changes in society rather than by needs as perceived within the education system. Second, there is an emphasis on individual needs vis-à-vis societal changes. Third, the reforms are underpinned by a state-of-the-art understanding of human learning, and hence are moving in a clear direction, even at the micro level.

Societal Changes

Hong Kong has been doing very well in international comparisons. This was recognized in a presentation made by Barry McGaw,[6] the former Chief of Education at the Organization for Economic Cooperation and Development (OECD). He noted that Hong Kong students scored among the highest internationally in tests in "mathematics," "reading" and "science literacy," and did very well even in "problem solving."

In addition, ample resources are being poured into Hong Kong's education system. Hong Kong has a qualified and professional teaching force, and there is almost full attendance at the primary and secondary levels. The curriculum has undergone constant revisions, and Hong Kong's public examinations are among the most rigorous and reliable in the world. These could all be fodder for the argument that Hong Kong's education system is close to perfect and deserves no major surgery. Hong Kong, therefore, could have proceeded with simply offering more of what it has had in education and improving upon it.

However, the pressure for reform was tremendous. In the abovementioned gathering in January 1999 where the reform effort was launched, there were heated discussions fuelled by grumbling from parents and the frustrations of employers. Parents complained about the excessive homework and massive pressure on their children, which nevertheless did not lead to any significant gains in learning. Many have chosen to send their children to international schools,[7] but most of the populace have no choice but to put up with the rather traditional approach to education in public schools.

Employers, both from the business sector and among the NGOs, could not find enough graduates who were able to fulfil the demands of the contemporary workplace. They complained that either the language standards of young people were appalling or that they were not prepared to be innovative or to deal with complex situations.

The continuously high levels of unemployment at the end of the last century show that such complaints had substance. The unemployment rate in 1999, at the time the education reforms were launched, was over 6%.

In this context, it is not surprising that the reforms were prompted by demands from outside rather than from within the education system. The championship of the reforms by Antony Leung, a leading banker at the time,[8] symbolized such demands. The general economic outlook of the Tung Chee-hwa administration also contributed to external pressure for reform. Academic advice[9] pointing to the fundamental gap between education and a changed society further reinforced the view that reforms were urgently required.

The unemployment rate escalated to almost 8% in 2003, and stayed at over 4% in 2006, even when the economy had undergone a significant recovery. It would be useful to look into the various attributes of the unemployment situation. In 2002, a survey revealed that 19% of 15–19 years old teenagers in Hong Kong were "doubly disengaged": neither engaged in studies, nor in work (Commission on Youth, 2003). These are young people who would be the most unlikely to get a job in the long run. This is quite understandable when one realizes that a substantial percentage of secondary school graduates do not attain scores good enough to allow them to pursue further education or to find a job. In 2006, a typical year, of all of the candidates who sat for the school-leaving Certificate of Education Examination,[10] 14.7% did not pass any of the subjects, and 22.6% passed in one to four subjects, short of the conventional threshold of a pass in five subjects.

Thirty years ago, such students, who are seen as "failures" in the school system, would have been considered ideal candidates for blue-collar manual work in manufacturing factories. Such factories have simply disappeared from Hong Kong. This is partly because the manufacturing base has shifted from Hong Kong to the Mainland; and partly because there has been a general expansion of the service economy. In a service economy, the front-line workers have to interact directly with clients, face problems and challenges, take risks and venture to make changes, design solutions and make innovations. There is no longer much demand for people to carry out routine, manual and unskilled work.

The fundamental change in society, and the workplace in particular, is illuminated by the change in the nature of the organizations, business firms and NGOs that are found in Hong Kong. In September 2006, 99.3% of the 304,000-odd registered companies in Hong Kong were small and medium-sized enterprises (SMEs) of fewer than 100 employees. Moreover, 94.3% of SMEs had fewer than 20 employees and 87% fewer than 10. These are typical service-sector units, either firms or NGOs, who do not operate with layers of management. Nor are they organized in departments. Employees have to work in teams, and be prepared to interact intensively. There are few rules and regulations to follow, but employees are expected to manage themselves according to the needs of the tasks that need to be tackled.

The above description is only a snapshot of how workplaces in Hong Kong have changed, but it is perhaps sufficient to illustrate the changing expectations of society on our young people.[11]

It is in this context that the Education Commission designed and launched the reforms. An entire chapter in the reform document *Learning for Life, Learning through Life* (Education Commission, 2000) provides a blueprint of the reforms. A summary of the same report was published a year later, after formal endorsement by the Tung Chee-hwa administration, for popular dissemination (Education Commission, 2001). The opening lines in the introduction to both the chapter and the summary of the report are as follows:

> The world is undergoing fundamental changes, and Hong Kong is no exception. Globalisation and a knowledge-based society have brought many opportunities as well as challenges to Hong Kong. In the social environment of the new era, adaptability, creativity, the power of analysis, judgement and the ability to self-learn, communication, organisation and cooperation are prerequisites for one to meet the requirements in life and at the workplace. To cope with these changes, corresponding reforms must be made to the education system to enable students to develop their potential and to lead a rich life in the new century.

In this context, the agenda for education reforms in Hong Kong is not a matter of how to improve the existing system of education. It is not so much about improving the examination scores of students, or about fine-tuning the curriculum and teaching methods. Rather, it is about how education has to be reconstructed in order to better prepare young citizens for a changing reality. This line of thought underpins the Hong Kong reform that started right after the establishment of the SAR.

Individual Needs

In the reform documents, the main theme of societal changes is augmented by the emphasis on individual needs.

All policies on education development around the world face the need to deal with the same issue of the interplay between *societal* (or national) needs and *individual* needs. There were discussions on this issue within the Education Commission when the reform documents were being drawn up. A conscious decision was made to place a strong emphasis on needs of the *individual*.

This is a deviation from the tradition in Chinese societies, where individual needs are subordinated to national needs, and personal development is seen as manpower development as part of economic growth. This deviation from tradition was consciously made. In the initial stage of process of formulating the recommendations, the first few drafts of the document were totally rewritten to reflect the thinking that education should be based on the personal development of the individual.

This fact perhaps counters the criticism that the reforms were prompted solely by the concerns of businesses or employers. The Education Commission was very conscious that the reforms were about helping young citizens face a changing reality, not about moulding individuals to fit the "labour market."

To the Education Commission, the emphasis on individual needs is not so much an ideology as a matter of reality. If the changes that are taking place in the workplace are dramatic, then the challenges to individuals are even more dramatic. People are frequently changing their jobs and, indeed, their careers.[12] Hence, the notion of "preparing young people for jobs" has to be put under serious scrutiny. In other words, young people have to prepare themselves for the possibility of multiple careers, changing environments, as well as uncertainty and insecurity in their lives. If the education of young people is only targeted at particular niches in the labour market, these young individuals will suffer. Hence, the real challenge to the existing education system was to fight against the emphasis on processing students in order to acquire credentials, sacrificing personal development in the process.

New Understanding of Learning

The education reforms in Hong Kong took place alongside the global trend of a refreshed understanding of human learning. The acceptance of the notion of *constructive learning* has coloured the entire reform movement. If one carefully reads the major documents on reforming the education system, it should be evident that most of the documents are about *learning*.

Examples include *Learning for Life, Learning through Life* (2000, 2001), published by the Education Commission; *Learning to Learn: The Way Forward in Curriculum Development* (2002), published by the Curriculum Development Council; and *Towards a Learning Profession: A Teacher Competency Framework and the Continuing Professional Development of Teachers* (2003), published by the Advisory Committee on Teacher Education and Qualifications.

In essence, learning is no longer seen as a matter of transmitting knowledge from teachers (or other sources) to students. Rather, learning is the active construction of knowledge by the learner. People in various disciplines — neuroscientists, psychologists, teacher educators and programme developers — concur that learning is a matter of experience. It is a process in which the human brain develops and hence shapes the individual's understanding of reality (i.e., knowledge). There is an emerging group of researchers, known as learning scientists, who are trying to create a holistic body of knowledge that is useful in practice.

There are a few commonly accepted corollaries to the above view of what constitutes learning. Learning is about activities. The range of activities in which students are engaged dictates their construction of knowledge (i.e., learning). The understanding and application of knowledge are intertwined, and the test for understanding lies in the meaningful application of the knowledge thus developed. Human learning also takes place through mutual learning, hence the importance of collaborative (group) learning. Teachers are facilitators of learning as well as senior co-learners, but they set up "scaffolding" for their students so that their students can benefit from existing human knowledge. Translating these principles about learning into practice in education is one of the major tasks of the reform effort.

Hence, the aim behind the reform of the curriculum is basically to create a platform for learning to take place. First, the focus of attention is on "key-learning areas"[13] rather than on subjects. Second, the "key-learning areas" framework ensures that all students receive the comprehensive spectrum of learning experiences that they deserve. The reform in teacher education is also basically along a framework of professional development as a matter of teachers' learning.

The emphasis on *learning* as the core of the reform effort is what distinguishes the education reforms that are being carried out in Hong Kong from similar reforms in many other jurisdictions. It reminds people that much of what is done in education is not necessarily conducive to genuine learning. Such an emphasis effectively challenges the assumption that the existing system of education always supports genuine learning. It hence carries with it a connotation of criticism if not scepticism about the existing institution of "education." It, therefore, leaves ample room for rethinking the existing system of education and suggests that the system should be reconstructed. In a way, the emphasis on "learning" is itself a symbol of the entire reform effort.

The Ecology of the Reform

The above analyses, however, are only about the intentions or the design of the reforms. The actual implementation and consequences of the reforms depend on many factors, some of which work to contravene the intentions of the reformers. On this matter, a few observations can be made.

Perceptions within and outside the Education System

As stated above, it is mostly people from outside the education system who are emphasizing the necessity and urgency of carrying out reforms to Hong Kong's education system. Such people see the situation from the perspective of an employer or a parent. Employers complain about the poor quality of graduates, believing that they are not able to handle the demands of the job. Parents are frustrated at the misery their children have to go through, with large amounts of homework assigned to them and undue examination pressure. Few feel that the education system should remain the same. These views are reflected in the Hong Kong media on a daily basis.

Teachers, on the other hand, also feel frustrated because of the difficulties they face in teaching students to the standard that is set for them. In many cases, they feel frustrated at the low levels of motivation and achievement shown by the students. They would very much like to improve the situation. However, perhaps it is beyond the teachers' framework of thinking to take a different approach to education. In other words, teachers are also looking for a change, but not for a change in paradigm. Teachers' perceptions are in part a product of their professional training and indeed are part of the professional culture. They feel that their task is to bring the students through the system so that the students will obtain the credentials they will need to have a future. In reality, teachers who work in schools are not in any position to change the larger system. In the final analysis, most teachers undertake teaching as their first and only career, and it would be unfair to expect teachers to understand the overhauling changes outside the education system.

Hence, there is a fundamental gap between the aims of the reformers and the expectations of the teachers, although both feel that major changes should be made to the system. Cheung Kwok-wah, a sociologist, who specializes in education policies, has made the following observation:

> There are two clocks. The education reform is seen as being too slow compared with the clock in the minds of those who are outside the education system. However, the education reform is perceived to be clicking too fast when compared with the educators' clock.[14]

The Education Commission and the EMB have apparently realized the existence of such a gap. They have, therefore, spent a great deal of energy launching various activities aimed at bridging the gap. Such activities promote to teachers a new framework of thinking about education. For example, after the publication in 2001 of the blueprint for the reform effort, over 100 seminars and forums, varying in size from a few hundred to over a thousand participants, were organized to communicate the principles and implications of the reforms to teachers. Other organizations have also hosted similar gatherings for concerned members of the public. In addition, members of the Education Commission and the EMB have had numerous interactions with editors, union leaders, chambers of commerce, professional societies and various associations. Such gatherings have also led to a sharpening of the principles that underpin the reforms.

The conscious move to narrow the gap between intentions behind the reform effort and the expectations of the teachers was further intensified when "retreat" sessions on curriculum reform were organized. Six representatives from about 12 schools were invited to each of these overnight "retreats," which were held in hotels. During the "retreats," the principles and approaches of curriculum reform in schools were discussed and debated. The representatives from the schools included principals, vice-principals and school managers who were not educators. From 2005 to 2006, 45 such "retreat" sessions were organized, involving all secondary schools in Hong Kong. In 2007, similar sessions were organized for middle managers in schools.

Since curriculum reform will affect all schools, and the new senior secondary curriculum will be introduced only in 2009, this gives the reformers in the EMB a rather long lead time to promote the reforms to the teachers and to prepare them for a very different way of organizing student learning in schools.

A Learning Administration

However, the very well-planned and comprehensive efforts of the Administration have been contravened by other shortcomings of the Administration. It is indeed a challenge for the Administration to advance comprehensive reforms on multiple fronts. The Administration seems to have demonstrated a weakness in strategic thinking. Little consideration has apparently been given to timing and sequencing, i.e., which changes should come first, and which would follow; which are urgent and which can wait. There does not seem to be a clear concept of what should be given emphasis and priority, and what can be the subject of give-and-take. All fronts are being pushed at almost the same time with a strong sense of urgency, which is often perceived by teachers as a sign of impatience.

Complicating the picture is the fact that the reform measures are being promoted while earlier policies continue to be implemented. There are administrative measures that are the result of policies formulated earlier, the perpetuation of which is distracting people's attention from the main thrust of the reforms. There are also new measures that have been introduced without careful coordination, and are being perceived by people as yet another "attack" from the reform drive. The gap between the intentions of the reformers and the thinking of the teachers has, therefore, widened, because of various developments unintended by the reformers. Examples include the "benchmarking of language teachers," the introduction of "school-based management," changes to the "medium of instruction" in schools as well as the mandating of an "external school review."

- The Benchmarking of language teachers was an exercise to "re-train" practising language teachers who did not possess the proper qualifications in the English or Chinese language. The requirement was initiated before 1997, but was put into practice only in 2000. It affected about 55% of the language teaching force and aroused huge resentment among teachers. This was followed by a subsequent requirement for language teachers to obtain a remedial language degree if they were to be allowed to keep teaching the language.
- School-based Management is part of a continuous effort to improve school management. In this scheme, the governing bodies of all schools had to be restructured and "incorporated," in accordance with a particular composition and formula. This move has caused opposition from the traditional major school sponsoring bodies,

particularly church bodies. Again, school-based management was a policy that had been launched before 1997, but it took a long time before the policy was actually enforced.

- The Medium of Instruction exercise refers to an earlier policy to ensure that schools use the medium of instruction, English or Chinese, most appropriate for them. In the exercise, first implemented in 1998, only 104 schools were permitted to use English as the medium of instruction, and the others were told to teach in the "mother-tongue" (Cantonese). Subsequently, strict inspections were carried out at schools, to make sure that the "other language" was not used. This has caused resentment among schools as well as among parents, who have interpreted the policy as depriving their children of the chance to learn in English.

- The External School Review is an extrapolation of the quality assurance exercises initiated by the Education Commission before 1997. External teams are sent to schools to carry out a review, in essence a full-scale inspection, of the school. Reports of the reviews are published on the web for public consumption. Teachers often see the reviews as a threat. In addition, a great deal of paperwork is required of teachers in preparing for the visit, and teachers see this as adding to their workload.

Each of these schemes is well intentioned. However, the fact that all of them have been introduced at nearly the same time has placed a great deal of pressure on teachers. Teachers see all of these measures as being part of the reform effort. Hence, their general comment on the "reforms" is that they are "too many, too fast, and too disorganized." Perhaps there is some truth to this criticism.

Both the Administration and the unions are not keen to distinguish these rather uncoordinated efforts at change from the main thrust of the reform effort. The Administration believes that putting these measures under the banner of "reform" will give them some weight in implementation. The unions have been quick to exploit the apparent "chaos" that has thus been created, and to build on the momentum of confrontation against the Administration.

The tension between teachers and the Administration that is promoting the "reforms" has been exacerbated by the sudden realization that the population of school-going age is declining dramatically. The number of children born each year has dropped from around 90,000 in the 1980s to around 50,000 in recent years. There is a significant surplus of teachers and many school face the threat of closure. There is no foreseeable reversal of this demographic decline, and this has caused serious concern among teachers. Unions have been organizing teachers to engage in protests against the government. The confrontations have been disguised as a debate over whether or not Hong Kong should have small classes. The Administration has all along taken a passive and defensive role. It has not managed to take a high moral ground and defend the interests of the public, and positively present solutions to ease the worries of schools and teachers. Rather, it has regarded the opponents to its plans as the sole party with which it has to negotiate, and attempted to cut a deal simply to pacify the opposition.

The change in the administrative structure ("ministerial system") of the government has strengthened the decision-making position of its executive administrators. However, the system of accountability that should accompany such an elevation of power has not been set up. In the end, most of the advisory and consultative organs involved in the education process felt sidelined, because many major decisions did not go through the necessary consultation processes. The rather abrupt abolition of the Board of Education, which had a history of over 50 years, was a critical example of the changed attitude on the part of the government towards advisory bodies. Such organs could be a very good sounding board for the Administration and could help to protect it from criticism and from making mistakes (EMB, 1998). Unfortunately, there has been a general weakening of the functions of such organs.

There is a general lack of intention on the part of the Administration to secure an alliance among different stakeholders. The weakening of the advisory organs has caused the Administration to lose allies that could support and defend the measures it wants to promote. The breakdown of a sincere partnership between the Administration and the school-sponsoring bodies is an unfortunate reflection of this weak sense of alliance. Even with the dialogue between the Administration and the unions has largely been disrupted.

In a way, the Administration of the young SAR is still feeling its way. Despite the colonial legacy of a renowned civil service, the implementation of a comprehensive set of reforms demands a new level of thinking with regard to policy. It has to be borne in mind that Hong Kong's civil service is among the few in the world that has not undergone major reform. In the name of stability, the civil service has managed to evade major reforms both before and immediately after the changeover in sovereignty.

Reform as Ecology

The education reform effort emerged in response to a changing society. It is also underpinned by an emphasis on the future of individuals, informed by contemporary theories on learning.

The reform effort, therefore, does not promise ease and comfort for schools and teachers. It does not follow the teachers' framework of thinking, which is basically one of *improvement* rather than *reform*. Even in the last report of the Education Commission before 1997 (the Education Commission Report No. 7 on "Quality Education"), the main theme was enhancement of the quality of education, with its existing concepts and systems. The reform effort advocates a different way of conceiving and delivering education.

Therefore, all along the way, there have been negotiations between the "reformers" on the one side and the "teachers" on the other.

The Education Commission and the EMB were quite conscious of the need to prepare teachers for a shift in paradigm. This was demonstrated by the massive "perception management" exercises that were launched during the initiation stage. The reform effort started with social appeals on lofty ground. There are also ongoing thorough discussions about the imminent reforms to the curriculum, and these have been organized with sufficient lead time.

Nonetheless, the reform movement in the past 10 years is also a good demonstration of the professionalism of teachers in Hong Kong. There have been many events and incidents where Hong Kong teachers took to the streets in protest against the government, basically to protect their own welfare. However, these same teachers are the ones who have tried very hard to change their paradigm about education and have worked industriously to change their students' learning environments.

Surveys conducted since 2003 have repeatedly confirmed that the overwhelming majority of Hong Kong people support the education reforms. Annual surveys on curriculum reform have been commissioned by the then EMB, and conducted among school heads, teachers and other relevant stakeholders. These include (a) a commissioned Stakeholder Survey conducted among teachers, parents and students in 2003–2004 and 2004–2005; (b) a commissioned Stakeholder Monitoring Survey in 2004 and 2006 of school sponsoring bodies, school management committees, principals, teachers, students, parents, early childhood educators and teacher educators, with a Thematic Household Survey of the public; (c) a commissioned Interim

Survey in 2006 of school heads, middle managers, teachers and students. The results have been very encouraging:

- The Stakeholder Surveys of 2003–2004 and 2004–2005 found that more than 75% of primary students and more than 50% of secondary students liked their school, and 87% of primary parents and 78% of secondary parents were pleased to let their children study at that school.
- In the Thematic Household Surveys of 2004 and 2006, there was very strong public support for the reform tasks and for the five essential learning experiences (76–92%).
- The Stakeholder Monitoring Survey of 2006 indicated that over 50% of the respondents in secondary schools agreed that the new curriculum would result in a widening of learning opportunities to meet the educational needs of Hong Kong, and supported changes to develop the independent learning capability and critical thinking skills of students, e.g., through Liberal Studies.
- In the interim survey of 2006, (a) over 80% of primary and secondary school teachers and heads agreed with the rationale of the reforms and with the seven learning goals; (b) over 85% of primary and secondary school heads felt that the reforms helped students to meet challenges of the twenty-first century, especially given the impact of IT and the rising need to make moral considerations. The level of agreement with various aspects of the reforms was higher in 2006 than it was in 2000.

Overall, there is a marked change in discourse in schools in Hong Kong, and a mushrooming of alternative learning opportunities for students. All of these echo the real intentions of the education reforms, and are where teachers and reformers are finding room for reconciliation.

Beyond the Reforms

The reforms were designed and launched at a time when Closer Economic Partnership Arrangement (CEPA) was not in sight. The CEPA notion, initially confined to economic activities, has initiated a total rethink of the concept of "one country, two systems."

In the realm of education, the reforms that began in 1999 did not foresee the crisis as well as the opportunities for further developments beyond the border. As a metropolitan urban centre, Hong Kong has the responsibility to be not only a financial hub, but also a hub for culture, medicine, research, religion and education. Around the world, this is what a metropolitan city is supposed to be. A simple survey has revealed that there are 51 institutions of higher education in London, 59 in New York City, 54 in Boston and 25 in Tokyo. There is perhaps no such thing as a pure financial centre, as the policies of the Hong Kong government seem to hint that Hong Kong should be. Even within the national scene, there are 75 higher education institutions in Beijing and 57 in Shanghai. It is noticeable that such institutions admit students from all over the nation, if not the world, and that their graduates serve a much wider geographic scope than the city *per se*. This is what higher education in a metropolitan city is about.

Perhaps very much prompted by the accession to the WTO by many countries, the government does indeed have the intention of turning Hong Kong into an education hub. However, most metropolitan cities host their higher education institutions not as a way of generating income, but rather as a responsibility to the region, the nation and the world. In the Hong Kong context, this is particularly significant. Hong Kong has accumulated its wealth from economic activities that extend well beyond its border. It is time for Hong Kong to reciprocate by shouldering responsibilities in the other realms of human activity. Education in Hong Kong, and higher education in particular, has to be conceived in this framework.

Even in the narrower sense of the term "education hub," there exist in China two visible hubs of higher education. The first is the Bo-Huang Hub, which is centred at Beijing, Tianjin, Dalian and Shenyang, where about a dozen leading institutions cover the northern part of China. The second is the Yangtze Hub, which is centred at Shanghai, Nanjing and Hangzhou, and includes another dozen fine institutions in the nearby region. In lieu of a hub in the southern part of China, Hong Kong could well lead a third hub of higher education if it partners with nearby institutions in Guangzhou, Wuhan and other cities. That will be a major contribution to China and bring the Chinese system of higher education to the international arena. It is also the only viable vision for the development of the Hong Kong system of higher education (and, indeed, education in Hong Kong as a whole).

Only then will higher education in Hong Kong have a large enough student base and alumni network to be significant to the nation. Only then will higher education in Hong Kong have the scale and capacity to conduct world-class research and to assume leadership in issues of significance for humankind.

Hong Kong has to think beyond Hong Kong, and education is no exception.

Notes

1. This was a presentation made by Kai-ming Cheng, the writer of this chapter. The 25-minute presentation offered only questions but no answers, about the commonsense expectations of attainment at all levels of education which, however, had not been achieved.
2. A remark made by Tsang Yok-sing, who was also a member of the informal group.
3. Antony Leung was Chairman of the University Grants Committee before he was appointed Chairman of the Education Commission.
4. In their curriculum reform, Japan compressed the formal curriculum by 30% in order to leave room for other learning experiences. Singapore did so by 33%, and for the same reason.
5. Very enlightening discussions about this subject are found in various articles in Watkins and Biggs (1996).
6. Barry McGaw is the former Director for Education for the Organization for Economic Cooperation and Development (OECD) and is currently the Director of the University of Melbourne's Education Research Institute. He has been instrumental in developing and implementing the OECD's Programme for International Student Assessment (PISA). The data here also refers to his earlier presentation in 2004 at an OECD meeting in Paris. See B. McGaw (2006).
7. Over 80% of the students in international schools in Hong Kong are from local families. See Yamato (2003).
8. Antony Leung was the Chief Executive Officer (CEO) of Citigroup in Hong Kong, and later became the CEO of Chase Manhattan before its merger with J. P. Morgan.
9. Among others, such advice is attributable to Kai-ming Cheng, the writer of this chapter, who, in various keynote presentations inside and outside Hong Kong, persistently advocated the need for education reforms to meet the changed needs of "post-industrial" societies. His views are summarized in Cheng (2004), a work that was subsequently translated and published in *Peking University Education Review* (Cheng, 2004); reprinted in a full-page format in *China Education Daily*, and extensively extracted by *New China Abstracts*.
10. This examination is held at the end of Secondary 5 (Grade 11), which marks the end of basic education in Hong Kong.
11. Elaborations of this argument can be found, for example, in other publications by the writer (Cheng, 2007a, 2007b, 2007c, 2007d, forthcoming).
12. Unfortunately, no data has been collected in Hong Kong on the switching of jobs or careers. It is estimated that the average American will make over four career changes in his/her lifetime, while the average number of job-changes in the U.K. is reckoned to be 13. See the presentation made by Chris Humphries (2007), the Director General of City and Guilds, U.K.

13. Remarks made at various seminars in which the subject of education reform was discussed. For example, Cheung (2002), p. 9. Cheung Kwok-wah is an academic at The University of Hong Kong. He was once a member of the Education Commission and chaired the Committee on Home-School Cooperation.

References

Advisory Committee on Teacher Education and Qualifications (2003), *Towards a Learning Profession.* Hong Kong: Hong Kong Government.

Census and Statistics Department (various years), *Quarterly Survey of Employment and Vacancies.* Hong Kong: Hong Kong Government.

Cheng, K. M. (2000), "Education and Development: The Neglected Dimension of Cross-cultural Studies." In R. Alexander, M. Osborn and D. Philips (eds.), *Learning from Comparing: New Directions in Comparative Educational Research, Volume 2.* Oxford: Symposium Books, pp. 81–92.

—— (2002), "Re-inventing the Wheel: Education Reform." In Lau Siu-kai (ed.), *The First Tung Chee-hwa Administration: The First Five Years of the HKSAR.* Hong Kong: The Chinese University Press, pp. 157–74.

—— (2004), *Questioning Education: Learning and Society in a Post-industrial Era.* Professorial Inaugural Lecture, delivered and published on 20 October 2004. The University of Hong Kong. Subsequently translated and published in *Peking University Education Review* 2005 (4): 6–15.

—— (2007a), "Learning Society: The East Asian Perspective." In M. Kuhn (ed.), *New Society Models for a New Millennium: The Learning Society in Europe and Beyond.* New York: Peter Lang, pp. 515–30.

—— (2007b), "Education versus Learning: Challenges of the Post-industrial Era." Inaugural Shanghai Education Forum, 27 January 2007. Published in *Shanghai Education,* March A, 2007.

—— (2007c), *Facing the Knowledge Society: Reforming Secondary Education in Shanghai and Hong Kong.* Washington, D.C.: World Bank.

—— (2007d), "Education for All, But for What?" In J. E. Cohen and M. Malin (eds.), *The Wise Child: International Perspectives on the Goals of Basic and Secondary Education.* American Association of Arts and Sciences/Stanford University.

—— (forthcoming), "The Post-industrial Workplace and Challenges to Education." In Marcelo M. Suárez-Orozco (ed.), *Learning in the Global Era: International Perspectives on Globalization and Education.* California: University of California Press, Chapter 8.

Cheung, K. W. (2002), *Social and Political Conditions of Educational Reform in Hong Kong.* Paper presented at Regional Forum on Educational Reform and Policy Change in East Asian Tigers, City University of Hong Kong, 27 July 2002.

Commission on Youth (2003), *Continuing Development and Employment Opportunities for Youth.* Hong Kong: Hong Kong Government.

Curriculum Development Council (2002), *Learning to Learn: The Way Forward to Curriculum Development.* Hong Kong: Hong Kong Government

Education and Manpower Bureau (1998), *Consultation Document on the Review of the Education-related Executive and Advisory Bodies.* Hong Kong: Hong Kong Government.

────── (2000), *Education Blueprint for the 21st Century Review of Education System: Reform Proposals.* Hong Kong: Hong Kong Government.

Education Bureau (2007), *Progress Report on Systematic Collection of Feedback on Curriculum Reform and Development of New Academic Structure for Secondary Schools.* Report presented to the Education Commission, 4 July 2007.

Education Commission (2000), *Learning for Life, Learning through Life. Reform Proposal for the Education System of Hong Kong.* Hong Kong Government.

────── (2001), *Learning for Life, Learning through Life. Reform Proposal for the Education System of Hong Kong. Summary.* Hong Kong: Hong Kong Government.

Humphries, C. (2007), "Linking Education to the Labor Market: City and Guilds Case Study." Presentation made at the World Bank Institute, Washington, D.C., 15 May 2007.

McGaw, B. (2006), "An International View of Hong Kong's Education Reform." Paper presented at the Education Commission's Reporting Session on Reform, 2 December 2006, Hong Kong.

Watkins, D. A. and J. B. Biggs (eds.) (1996), *The Chinese Learners: Cultural, Psychological and Contextual Influences.* Hong Kong/Melbourne: Comparative Education Research Centre/The Australian Council for Educational Research.

Yamato, Y. (2003), *Education in the Market Place: Hong Kong's International Schools and Their Mode of Operation.* Hong Kong: Comparative Education Research Centre (CERC), The University of Hong Kong.

13

Cross-boundary Integration

Yue-man Yeung and Jianfa Shen

Introduction

Since Hong Kong's reversion to Chinese rule in 1997, one litmus test of
the success or otherwise of the formula of "one country, two systems" is
the extent to which Hong Kong is integrated with the Mainland. The degree
of Hong Kong–Mainland integration can range from minimal change from
pre-handover conditions to full integration between the two jurisdictions
within one country, with all barriers removed. The reality is, of course,
somewhere between these two extremes, and it is a question of how rapidly
and substantively Hong Kong has moved away from the pre-handover state
to full integration. Integration can be measured politically, economically,
socially and even emotionally/psychologically at the personal level.

As a Special Administrative Region (SAR) enjoying a "high degree of
autonomy" and with "Hongkongers ruling Hong Kong," the impetus to
move towards closer integration lies largely with Hong Kong. True to the
spirit of the Basic Law, the central government carefully adopted a hands-
off attitude towards the new SAR, at least in the early years after 1997. The
policy stance of the two governments has been a fundamental factor
influencing the degree and speed of cross-boundary integration. In addition,
regional and international factors have been no less important in that they
have affected the political stability and economic health of Hong Kong and
the Mainland, thereby influencing sentiment towards integration.

Indeed, the past decade since the Hong Kong handover has been
extraordinary. It was a period during which China continued its rapid
economic growth, was admitted to the World Trade Organization (WTO)
in late 2001, and which saw the world rudely shaken by several cataclysmic
events, such as the Asian financial crisis, the 9/11 terrorist attacks and severe

acute respiratory syndrome (SARS). All of these events against the background of a resurgent China have been critical factors that have delayed or accelerated the integration of Hong Kong and the Mainland.

This chapter examines, first, the institutional framework within which cross-boundary integration has been designed to proceed in a changing political milieu. Second, it traces the path of economic integration. In an economic environment in which China has been emerging as a global economic power, Hong Kong has been struggling to adjust to its own changing role. Third, social integration has become stronger than ever. This has brought both challenges and opportunities for people on either side of the boundary, which they have never before encountered. Finally, this chapter concludes with a statement on the future outlook of integration.

Integration within a New Political Context

On 1 July 1997, Hong Kong turned a new political leaf and began life as an SAR of China. No sooner had the Chief Executive, Mr Tung Chee-hwa, and his team sworn allegiance to the central government and to the new SAR government, than they received news that the Thai baht had been floated, ushering a period of unprecedented financial turmoil widely known as the Asian financial crisis, which severely hit most countries in the Asia-Pacific region. While Mr Tung was occupied in the early years with the task of building a new image and vision for the new SAR, the Chief Secretary for Administration, Mrs Anson Chan, was entrusted with setting up the necessary institutional framework to improve and ensure Hong Kong–Mainland integration.

As a follow-up to Mr. Tung's first policy address in 1997, a high-level institutional framework — the Hong Kong/Guangdong Cooperation Joint Conference — was established in March 1998, with Anson Chan in charge on the Hong Kong side. The plan was to hold meetings between the two sides every six months, but this did not happen as Hong Kong became embroiled in a series of economic and political crises. Little progress was achieved in the area of cross-boundary cooperation until 2001. It also has to be admitted that one reason for the lethargy in pushing for more active cross-boundary cooperation was that some government officials and even the general public were adamantly in favour of strict controls on immigration from the Mainland, for fear of a huge influx from that source. A "Hong Kong first" or "Superfortress Hong Kong" mentality prevailed in some quarters (Sung, 2002; Yeung and Shen, forthcoming). Discrimination against Mainlanders remained deeply rooted in society, as was seen in the right of abode saga in 1999 and in allegations that Mainland migrants rely on government welfare benefits (Yeung, 2002). The first interpretation of the Basic Law by the Standing Committee of the National People's Congress focused on two sections of Article 23 relating to the right of abode in Hong Kong.

From his first policy address in 1997, Mr Tung continued to emphasize the need for Hong Kong to establish closer links with the Mainland, which is where the future of Hong Kong lies. Towards this end, the Hong Kong SAR government has been systematically building up its institutional presence on the Mainland to enhance liaison and communication, promote Hong Kong, process applications for the entry of Mainland residents to Hong Kong, and to provide practical assistance to Hong Kong residents in distress. The first Office of the Government of the HKSAR was established in Beijing in March 1999. Later representative offices were oriented more towards trade and related affairs. The HKSAR's Guangdong Economic and Trade Office (GDETO) was opened in July 2002, and later expanded in April 2006 to cover five provinces, including Fujian, Jiangxi, Guangdong, Guangxi and Hainan, in the wake of an increasing need for its services after the establishment of the Pan–Pearl River Delta (Pan-PRD) cooperation framework in June 2004. Similar economic and trade offices were opened in Chengdu and Shanghai in September 2006, to promote exchanges and cooperation between Hong Kong and the eastern and southwestern regions of China, respectively. The SAR's Shanghai Economic and Trade Office (SHETO) covers Shanghai, Jiangsu, Zhejiang, Anhui and Hubei, whereas its Chengdu Economic and Trade Office (CDETO) serves Sichuan, Yunnan, Guizhou, Hunan, Shaanxi and Chongqing. With these representative offices, the bulk of the provincial units in China are covered.

Likewise, several of Hong Kong's quasi-public bodies have either newly established or expanded their institutions to extend their reach and range of services. The Trade Development Council, a traditional and strong institutional promoter of Hong Kong trade and economic interests outside Hong Kong, has now 40 commercial centres worldwide, including 12 offices on the Mainland, namely Beijing, Chengdu, Dalian, Fuzhou, Guangzhou, Hangzhou, Kunming, Qingdao, Shanghai, Shenzhen, Wuhan and Xi'an. The Hong Kong Productivity Council (HKPC), in response to the economic integration between Hong Kong and Guangdong and with the aim of helping Hong Kong companies capture new business opportunities arising from the Closer Economic Partnership Arrangement (CEPA), announced in mid-2003 the extension of its network of services to the Pearl River Delta (PRD) and Guangdong. The HKPC's representative office in Guangzhou has been strengthened by subsidiary consulting companies in Dongguan, Guangzhou and Shenzhen. Finally, the General Chamber of Commerce has set up a China Committee and the Federation of Hong Kong Industries has established a Pearl River Delta Council to serve their member firms in the PRD and beyond.

In his 1999 policy address, the Chief Executive placed the emphasis on Hong Kong's economic future, duly recognizing that the SAR's largest contribution to the motherland would come from its increased integration and co-development with its hinterland in Guangdong and in its emerging role as China's world city (HKSAR net, www.info.gov.hk, accessed 14 April 2007). However, progress towards cross-border integration continued to be slow until 2001. As the protracted negotiations over China's entry to the WTO came to a successful conclusion, many in Hong Kong and elsewhere began to question the viability of Hong Kong's traditional role of middleman between China and the world. Early discussions began in 2001 on the process of fashioning a "new-style" free trade area (FTA) link between Hong Kong and the Mainland. The process was a long-drawn-out one, with many doubts and challenges raised along the way. However, an agreement was reached and, in June 2003, CEPA was promulgated by the central government (Sung, 2002, 2003). CEPA was a major institutional breakthrough in integrating Hong Kong with the Mainland, two separate customs areas within the same country. It gave Hong Kong privileged access to the China market ahead of other WTO countries during the first five years after China's admission to the WTO. CEPA was announced at a time when Hong Kong's societal morale and economic health were at unprecedentedly low levels. It gave the SAR a major boost towards its present economic and social recovery.

The nagging doubts about cross-boundary integration persisted for years after the handover. In a telephone poll carried out by the Hong Kong Institute of Asia-Pacific Studies in September 2002, only 54.2% of the respondents endorsed the idea of a 24-hour border crossing for people, as opposed to much higher support for cooperation in developing infrastructure, controlling environmental pollution, building a new bridge to the western part of the PRD, and selecting immigrants through an investment scheme (Sung, 2003). In any event, the Lok Ma Chau/Huanggang border crossing was finally open around the clock for people on 27 January 2003, marking a historical step in facilitating the flow of people across the Shenzhen border. Another catalyst for economic and social recovery came in mid-2003, with the announcement of the Individual Visit Scheme, which allowed Mainland visitors to come to Hong Kong on individual visits rather than on group tours, which until then had been the requirement. The arrangement, which began in July 2003, originally covered only four cities in the PRD; by January 2007, it had been vastly extended to include a total of 49 cities across China. By March 2007, 18 million Mainland visitors had visited Hong Kong on this scheme, which has contributed greatly to the revival of Hong Kong's retail market and overall economy (Xinhuanet.com, accessed 19 March 2007).

Another milestone in furthering cross-border integration was the Hong Kong/Guangdong Cooperation Joint Conference. Its Sixth Meeting, on 5 August 2003, was led by Chief Executive Tung Chee-hwa and Guangdong Governor Huang Huahua, indicating the importance of the occasion. For the first time, consensus was reached on the economic division of labour between Hong Kong and Guangdong, with the former to serve as a service centre and the latter as a manufacturing base. Fifteen subjects that required cooperation and further work on both sides were followed up after the meeting. This meeting set the pattern of closer and more concrete cooperation and integration between Hong Kong and Guangdong across many spheres of activity. Enhanced cross-border cooperation and integration, in fact, began with the early retirement of Anson Chan as Chief Secretary for Administration in May 2001. With her succession by Donald Tsang and with the appointment of Antony Leung as Financial Secretary, the pace of integration accelerated, leading to several critical institutional breakthroughs as outlined earlier.

In June 2004, the establishment of the Pan-PRD grouping provided another push for integration, this time beyond Hong Kong's immediate hinterland in the PRD and Guangdong. As a member of the new 9+2 regional grouping, Hong Kong has entered a new era of cooperation and integration with a hugely enlarged area of China (Yeung, 2003, 2005). The opportunities are immense for Hong Kong to play a positive role in bringing to the new grouping the influences of globalization, where its own strengths and experiences lie (Yeung, 2006a). Hong Kong has already become the largest outside investor in many of the provinces, which have also used Hong Kong as their major export market (Yeung and Shen, forthcoming). Finally, the opening in Hong Kong on 12 September 2005 of a new mass entertainment institution with a global brand name, Hong Kong Disneyland, will bring

Mainland visitors to its shores, thereby promoting mutual understanding and integration.

Measured progress has been made in cross-boundary integration since 1997, but the passage to the end of the first decade has been bumpy. The year 2003 was a special year. In addition to earlier-mentioned developments, that year saw the attempted introduction of a bill on Article 23, which prompted half a million people to go on a peaceful march on 1 July of that year. It was a wake-up call for Beijing, which since then has taken a more proactive approach to the handling of Hong Kong affairs. Mr Tung was made to step down as Chief Executive in March 2005 and, after an uncontested election, Donald Tsang was appointed to replace him in June 2005. Cross-boundary relations thereupon improved further. This is reflected in opinion poll figures. In December 2003, only 45.7% of Hong Kong people trusted the central government versus 30% who trusted the Hong Kong government (*SCMP*, 23 April 2007, A15); in April 2007, the corresponding figures were 78% and 58% (*Ming Pao*, 27 April 2007, A12). The degree of trust that Hong Kong people have in the central government has climbed to a historic high since the handover, a fact that speaks loudly of greatly improved cross-boundary relations as the tenth anniversary of Hong Kong's return to Chinese sovereignty approaches.

In the decade following the handover, Hong Kong's economy is much stronger, despite early setbacks from a series of internal administrative fumbles and equally sudden and violent external shocks. As the tenth anniversary of the handover approaches, the economic data sheet looks impressive. Bilateral trade between Hong Kong and the Mainland saw a twofold increase from $1.116 trillion in 1997 to $2.349 trillion in 2006. Hong Kong's re-export trade, including goods transferred from overseas via Hong Kong then enter the Mainland, has recorded double-digit growth since 2003. Mainland enterprises listed in the Hong Kong Stock Exchange grew from 101 in 1997 to 367 in end-2006, accounting for 16% and 50%, respectively, of the stock exchange's total market capitalization. During the same period, the total market capitalization of Mainland enterprises increased 13 times to $6.714 trillion (*SCMP*, 23 April 2007, A15). By early 2007, Hong Kong had become the sixth largest stock market in the world by total market capitalization from its previous ninth-place ranking.

The close symbiotic relationship between Hong Kong and the Mainland is reflected in foreign direct investment (FDI) flows. Mainland China is the most important destination for FDI from Hong Kong, accounting for 40.3% of cumulative FDI from Hong Kong. Conversely, as the recipient of

31.4% of Mainland China's FDI, Hong Kong is the most important destination for FDI from Mainland China. At the regional level, Hong Kong is the single largest source of FDI in Guangdong, Shanghai, Jiangsu and Zhejiang. At the end of 2005, 65% of Guangdong's total cumulative FDI, or US$105.4 billion, was derived from Hong Kong. Similarly, 31% of the total cumulative FDI invested in the Greater Yangtze River Delta region, or US$61 billion, came from Hong Kong. In 2005, 237,500 Hong Kong employees worked on the Mainland, a huge increase from 52,300 in 1988 (FHKI, 2007).

As a neighbouring city, Shenzhen has loomed large in Hong Kong's efforts to integrate with the Mainland since 1997. Even before the handover, proposals for closer cooperation and integration had been floated, specifically from Shenzhen, but no concrete plans appear to be forthcoming. In August 2005, the Hong Kong Institute of Asia-Pacific Studies conducted the first Hong Kong–wide telephone poll aimed at determining how Hong Kong people stand in matters of mutual interest in Shenzhen and on the development of that city. The survey uncovered many aspects of how Hong Kong people felt about Shenzhen as a dimension, if any, of their lives. A majority of the residents expressed support for closer cooperation with that city (Yeung, 2006b). Indeed, the governments of both Shenzhen and Hong Kong have apparently since been working behind the scenes to find feasible ways of moving forward on the issue of cooperation. A recent research report undertaken by us also contains some proposals relating to opportunities and challenges for Hong Kong with the release of the Eleventh Five-year Plan (11th FYP) (2006–2010) (Yeung et al., 2006).

Economic Integration

Economic Relations between Hong Kong and Mainland China before 1997

To a large extent, the economic relationship between Hong Kong and the Mainland is a continuation of the relationship that existed between them in the period 1978–1997. It is one that builds mainly on market-led, cross-boundary business investments and population movements, with minimal input from the Hong Kong government. The emerging institutional arrangement at the government level for economic cooperation between Hong Kong and Mainland China mentioned in the previous section did not have a major impact on economic integration until 2003.

There have been close economic and trade relations between Hong Kong and the Mainland from the beginning. From 1841 to the early 1950s, Hong Kong's economy benefited from the entrepôt trade with Mainland China. After 1950, Hong Kong's economic links with the Mainland were largely severed as a result of the embargo on China imposed by the United Nations. Economic growth was based on industrialization within Hong Kong in the period 1950–1980. In 1978, Hong Kong was largely an industrial city, with 47.8% of the labour force employed in manufacturing (Sung and Wong, 2000, p. 211). Before 1978, there was little movement of population and goods across the border.

The open-door policy followed by China since 1978 has greatly facilitated and enhanced cross-border investment and development. Due to the economic complementarities and comparative advantages of Hong Kong and the Mainland, a spatial division of labour has been established across the border, which has generally been called the "front shop, back factory" model (Sit, 1989). Hong Kong has relocated the majority of its manufacturing operations to the PRD and has itself become a prominent service centre, specializing in design, marketing, coordination, trading, transport, communication and financial services. By 1996, the share of the labour force employed in manufacturing had fallen to only 18.9% (CSD, 1997, p. 94). Manufacturing as a share of GDP declined to 6.0% in 1997 (CSD, 2007a, p. 88).

However, the amount of manufactured products "made by Hong Kong" has increased significantly, as a labour force of over 11 million is employed by Hong Kong investors in various enterprises in the PRD region (FHKI, 2007). The re-export trade in Hong Kong grew dramatically in the 1980s and 1990s, due mainly to large-scale outward processing in the PRD region (Shen, 2003). Re-export trading activities with Mainland China have brought huge profits to the business community in Hong Kong. Sung and Wong (2000, p. 225) estimated that the income generated by China-related trade and investment accounted for 24.4% of Hong Kong's GDP in 1996. With a large amount of investment in the Mainland, Hong Kong has also contributed significantly to rapid economic development in Mainland China.

During the period 1979–1997, Hong Kong emerged to become a world city in Asia. The service sector's share of total GDP increased from 68.5% in 1981 to 85.9% in 1997 (CSD, 2007a, p. 88). The share of the labour force employed in the tertiary sector increased to 76.4% in 1997 (CSD, 2001a, p. 25). In 1997, Hong Kong was the ninth largest exporter in the world (CSD, 2001b, p. 126). Its GNP (Gross National Product) per capita was US$24,540 after adjusting for purchasing power, ranking Hong Kong fourth in the world (World Bank, 1998, p. 90).

Impact of the 1997 Handover

The return of Hong Kong to China in July 1997 was widely expected to affect cross-border development between Hong Kong and the Mainland. There have been many questions and doubts about whether Hong Kong would become just another city in China after 1997, while many Mainland cities aspire to learn from Hong Kong and to themselves become international cities (Skeldon, 1997).

The boundary between Hong Kong and Mainland China continues to function and each remains an independent economic entity as before. Overall, the handover in 1997 did not alter the configuration of the boundary in a practical sense, and its impact on cross-boundary development was far less significant than the effect of the open-door policy introduced by China in 1978. The closed boundary area on the Hong Kong side continues to exist. In practical terms, the cross-boundary regional integration has continued in Hong Kong and Mainland China under "two systems," as in the period 1978–1997. However, with the rapid growth of the economy and major cities of the Mainland, the previous "front shop, back factory" model is also being challenged — an indication of changing economic relations between Hong Kong and the Mainland. Such changes are occurring as a result of the growth of the Mainland economy, rather than because of the handover in 1997.

Trade between Hong Kong and Mainland China

One important role that Hong Kong plays is that of a middleman — especially for Mainland China — who imports from, and exports to, the rest of the world. Hong Kong's trading and re-exporting activities with the Mainland were trivial in the 1960s and 1970s, before the boom in cross-border activities. During the period 1959–1987, Hong Kong's domestic exports exceeded its re-exports (Table 13.1). Since 1978, re-exports have grown faster than domestic exports, which were overtaken by re-exports in 1988. Re-exports grew from HK$182.8 billion in 1987 to a peak of HK$1,244.5 billion in 1997. Due to the Asian financial crisis, re-exports declined slightly to HK$1,159.2 billion in 1998, and then picked up again to hit HK$1,391.7 billion in 2000 and a new peak of HK$2,326.5 billion in

Table 13.1 Hong Kong's Imports and Exports, 1959–2006 (HK$ billion)

Year	Imports	Domestic imports	Re-exports	Domestic exports	Total exports	Re-exports share of imports (%)	Re-exports share of exports (%)
1959	4.9	4.0	1.0	2.3	3.3	20.1	30.4
1961	6.0	5.0	1.0	2.9	3.9	16.6	25.2
1971	20.3	16.8	3.4	13.8	17.2	16.9	19.9
1981	138.4	96.6	41.7	80.4	122.2	30.2	34.2
1987	377.9	195.2	182.8	195.3	378.0	48.4	48.4
1991	779.0	244.2	534.8	231.0	765.8	68.7	69.8
1996	1,535.6	349.8	1,185.8	212.2	1,397.9	77.2	84.8
1997	1,615.1	370.6	1,244.5	211.4	1,455.9	77.1	85.5
1998	1,429.1	269.9	1,159.2	188.5	1,347.6	81.1	86.0
1999	1,392.7	214.3	1,178.4	170.6	1,349.0	84.6	87.4
2000	1,658.0	266.3	1,391.7	181.0	1,572.7	83.9	88.5
2001	1,568.2	240.7	1,327.5	153.5	1,481.0	84.7	89.6
2002	1,619.4	189.8	1,429.6	130.9	1,560.5	88.3	91.6
2003	1,805.8	185.1	1,620.7	121.7	1,742.4	89.7	93.0
2004	2,111.1	218.0	1,893.1	126.0	2,019.1	89.7	93.8
2005	2,329.5	215.4	2,114.1	136.0	2,250.2	90.8	94.0
2006	2,599.8	273.3	2,326.5	134.5	2,461.0	89.5	94.5

Sources: Holmes (1965, p. 1); CSD (2006a, 2007b, p. 46).

2006. Clearly, the pre-1997 growth pattern in the re-export trade continued in the period 1999–2006.

In the period 1991–2006, Mainland China was Hong Kong's largest trading partner, although the U.S. was the largest destination for domestic exports in 1991, 1999, and 2002. The Mainland's share of Hong Kong's total imports and re-exports increased significantly in the period 1997–2006, indicating the development of a closer economic relationship between Hong Kong and Mainland China (Table 13.2). The relevant figure on total imports was an increase from 37.7% to 45.9% and on re-exports an increase from 35.7% to 48.0%. In terms of the domestic export of products made in Hong Kong, Mainland China's remained at 30% during that same period. In the period 1991–2006, the U.S. was the first or second most important destination for domestic exports. In the same period, it was also the second most important destination for re-exports, after the Mainland. Japan and Taiwan were the second and third most important origins for imports by Hong Kong in the period of 1991–2006, with the exception of the years 1997 and 1998.

Table 13.2 Hong Kong's Main Trading Partners, 1991–2006 (HK$ billion)

Type of trade/Main country/Territory	1991	1997	1999	2006
Imports	779.0	1,615.1	1,392.7	2,599.8
Mainland China	293.4	608.4	607.5	1,193.0
Share of Mainland China (%)	37.7	37.7	43.6	45.9
Japan	127.4	221.6	162.7	268.1
Taiwan	74.6	124.6	100.4	194.9
U.S.	58.8	125.4	98.6	123.6
Domestic exports	231.0	211.4	170.6	134.5
Mainland China	54.4	63.9	50.4	40.3
Share of Mainland China (%)	23.5	30.2	29.5	30.0
U.S.	62.9	55.1	51.4	33.2
United Kingdom	13.7	10.7	10.4	7.9
Germany	19.3	10.3	8.5	4.9
Re-exports	534.8	1,244.5	1,178.4	2,326.5
Mainland China	153.3	443.9	399.2	1,115.9
Share of Mainland China (%)	28.7	35.7	33.9	48.0
U.S.	110.8	261.4	269.4	338.0
Japan	29.6	77.7	67.5	115.5
Germany	32.1	46.3	44.1	70.8

Sources: CSD (2001a, p. 52, 2007b, pp. 46–49).

Note: U.K. ranked fourth in 1999 as a destination for Hong Kong's re-exports. Singapore ranked fourth in 2006 as a source of imports to Hong Kong. Japan ranked fourth in 1997 as a destination for Hong Kong's domestic exports; the Netherlands ranked third and the U.K. ranked fourth in 2006.

It is important to note that Hong Kong does not just play the simple role of trade agent between Mainland China and the world. Much of the trade between Hong Kong and Mainland China is related to outward processing activities by Hong Kong investors. Table 13.3 shows that 44.7% of the Mainland's imports via Hong Kong and 81.2% of the Mainland's exports to Hong Kong resulted from such outward processing activities by Hong Kong investors in 1997. There were no major changes in this situation during 1997–2001. After 2001, the percentages declined to reach 35.0% and 64.0%, respectively, in 2006, indicating the rising importance of general trade between Hong Kong and Mainland China. It is significant that in 1991–2005, about 95% of the total exports from the Mainland involving outward processing to Hong Kong actually originated in Guangdong. The nature of Hong Kong as a trading hub has been transformed with the emergence of a regional production system (Shen, 2003). Large amounts of trade and re-exports have arisen from FDI activities. However, general trade has also been growing in importance in recent years.

**Table 13.3 The Outward Processing Trade and Its Share of the Total Trade
between Mainland China and Hong Kong, 1991–2006 (HK$ billion)**

	1991	1997	2005	2006
Mainland China's direct imports from Hong Kong	40.4	47.1	25.1	20.7
(percentage share in total)	(76.5)	(76.1)	(56.3)	(52.0)
Mainland China's imports via Hong Kong	73.6	197.81	363.4	389.2
(percentage share in total)	(48.2)	(44.7)	(37.6)	(34.9)
Subtotal	113.9	244.9	388.5	409.9
(percentage share in total)	(55.5)	(48.6)	(38.4)	(35.0)
Mainland China's exports to Hong Kong	197.4	491.1	692.0	769.3
(percentage share in total)	(67.6)	(81.2)	(65.9)	(64.5)
Guangdong's exports to Hong Kong	186.6	430.8	657.1	753.7
(percentage share in total exports involving	(94.5)	(95.1)	(95.0)	98.0
outward processing from the Mainland)				

Sources: CSD (1992, 1998, 2006b, pp. 206, 212, 2007c).

While Mainland China is still Hong Kong's most important trading partner, the relative importance of Hong Kong in the international trade of Mainland China has declined since 1997. Although exports to Hong Kong from Mainland China have increased over time, from US$43.8 billion in 1997 to US$124.5 billion in 2005, Hong Kong's share in the Mainland's total exports declined from 24.0% in 1997 to 16.3% in 2005 (NBS, 2006, pp. 735 and 740; SSB, 1998, p. 626).

Growth of Ports and Airports for Logistics Services

As mentioned before, many re-exports are related to outward processing activities in the PRD region arising from direct investments by Hong Kong businessmen in Mainland China. Re-export activities are driving the dramatic growth in air cargo and container throughput in Hong Kong. Much freight and many containers are transported across the Hong Kong–Mainland boundary to and from the PRD by road and river, and to and from the world by air and sea. The number of vehicle crossings between Hong Kong and Shenzhen increased from 1.66 million in 1985 to 9.51 million in 1997. Such growth continued unabated after 1997 to 14.99 million in 2006 (CSD, 2001a, p. 165, 2007b, pp. 110–11).

The port of Hong Kong recorded a double-digit growth in throughput from 1986 to 1996. Container throughput in Hong Kong increased from 5.1 million TEUs (twenty-foot equivalent units) in 1990 to 14.6 million in

1997. Hong Kong was the busiest container port in the world in the period 1993–2004, with the exception of the year 1998 (Port, Maritime and Logistics Development Unit, 2006; Port Development Council, 2007a; Hong Kong SAR Government, 1998). It was overtaken by Singapore in 1998 and 2005–2006. Container throughput in Hong Kong was 23.3 million TEUs in 2006, ranking Hong Kong second in the world (website of Shenzhen Port, 2007). Clearly, the growth of Hong Kong's container throughput has slowed since 2000 due to high costs in Hong Kong and the rapid growth of the port of Shenzhen. But Hong Kong remains an important container hub, providing some 500 container liner services per week connecting to over 500 destinations worldwide (Port Development Council, 2007b).

Hong Kong has one of the world's best international airports. Due to an increasing demand in the PRD region for logistics services, the amount of cargo handled by the airport increased from 1.79 million tonnes in 1997 to 3.58 million tonnes in 2006. The number of passengers also increased from 28.3 million in 1997 to 43.3 million in 2006. Except for a temporary slowdown in 1998 due to the Asian financial crisis, there was a clear trend of growth in air services during the period 1997–2006. Hong Kong ranked second in the world in 2006 in the handling of air cargo and fourteenth in passenger throughput (Civil Aviation Department, 2007; Port Development Council 2007a; *Ming Pao*, 9 March 2007).

Air cargo service is an important part of the airport's business. By weight, air cargo accounted for 1.2% of all cargo handled by Hong Kong in 2004 (CSD, 2007d, p. 125). By value, however, its share was as high as 21.3% in 1997. This further increased to 34.5% in 2006 (CSD 1999, p. 104, 2001b, pp. 1, 104, 2007b, p. 46, 2007d, p. 104). The air industry contributed 11.3% of the total service exports of Hong Kong in 2005.

Cross-boundary Passengers and Tourists from Mainland China

A high percentage of Hong Kong's population originated from Guangdong. According to the 2001 census (CSD, 2002), over 33.74% of Hong Kong's population, or 2.26 million, were born in Mainland China or Macao. During the period 1949–1978, there was little interaction among the populations of Hong Kong and the Mainland. Exchanges and interactions in population between Hong Kong and the Mainland accelerated after 1978. The number of passenger crossings between Hong Kong and Shenzhen reached 64.9 million in 1997. This figure continued to soar in the period 1997–2006, to

150.8 million in 2006, more than double the 1997 figure (CSD, 2001a, p. 183, 2007b, pp. 123–24). This is a strong evidence of ever-closer social and economic relations between Hong Kong and Mainland China after 1997.

As mentioned in the previous section, since 2002 there have been important policy changes to make it easier for Mainland visitors to travel to Hong Kong. The quota on the number of tourists from Mainland China permitted to visit Hong Kong, 2,000 a day, was abolished on 1 January 2002. Since 28 July 2003, individual tourists from an increasing number of cities have been allowed to apply for travel permits to visit Hong Kong.

The above arrangement for more Mainland people to travel to Hong Kong benefits Hong Kong's tourism industry and businesses, as many Mainland visitors also go shopping in Hong Kong and use various professional services such as financial services, life insurance and hospital services. The number of tourists from Mainland China increased from 2.4 million in 1997 to 8.5 million in 2003 and 13.6 million in 2006. Although Mainland China was already the largest source of tourists in 1997, its share of total tourists to Hong Kong increased further from 18.4% in 1997 to 53.8% in 2006. As a result, the total number of tourists coming to Hong Kong increased from 13.0 million in 1997 to 25.3 million in 2006 (CSD 2001a, p. 184, 2006c, p. 216, 2007b, p. 126).

Social Integration

Given the sharply different and separate legal, political and administrative systems in Hong Kong and the Mainland as provided for in the Basic Law, social integration can only proceed at a considered and measured pace. After all, life as usual and as before was promised for Hong Kong as part and parcel of the handover plan. Nevertheless, as the overwhelming majority of Hong Kong people have their roots in the Mainland, especially in the PRD region, they are predisposed towards easier cross-border social integration, given the fact that they share a common ethnicity, language and culture with people across the border.

Viewed in a broader context, regional economic integration is an outcome of social and economic globalization. "One country, two systems" and economic integration in the Guangdong–Hong Kong region is the result of two different social systems that are adapting to and challenging each other during a period of economic transition and development in the region, as each place attempts to maintain its overall advantages in the region (Ma, 2006, p. 389). Indeed, social integration can be seen against the background of the economic transition that both Hong Kong and the Mainland are going through under the Basic Law, and under the macro processes of globalization.

Cross-boundary social integration has to do largely with people. The vast increases in the flow of people between Hong Kong and the Mainland have been highlighted in the last section. Conceptually, four types of cross-boundary sojourners have been identified: cross-boundary shoppers, Hong Kong residents working on the Mainland, buyers of homes across the border, and elderly people from Hong Kong who have chosen to retire in Guangdong (Tse and Lin, 2006, p. 185). These are some of the people who are drawing the populations on both sides of the border ever closer together.

The cost differentials between Hong Kong and cities in the PRD soon encouraged Hong Kong residents to travel frequently across the border. The number of Hong Kong residents who travelled to the Mainland for leisure for at least once a week almost doubled from about 85,000 in 1999 to 148,000 in 2001 (HKPD, 2002, p. 111). Cross-boundary travellers for leisure can be further divided into two types. First are those who undertake the trip to get value for money, with females from the ages of 26 to 45 especially numerous. They travel in order to purchase clothing, shoes, electronic products, books, food and a variety of services at much lower prices than in Hong Kong. The other group consists of those who travel to engage in recreational activities in the delta area and beyond, such as playing golf, enjoying massage or spa sessions, and the like. They consist largely of males aged from 30 to 40, who frequently visit Shenzhen, Dongguan and Guangzhou (Tse and Lin, 2006, p. 186). Hong Kong retailers have had some misgivings about such travellers, especially the first group, fearing that their business will be adversely affected if people spend their money outside of Hong Kong. The ambivalence of some Hong Kong residents towards the proposal to establish a 24-hour border crossing partly arose from this fear. A February 2002 survey showed a dead split among Hong Kong residents on the issue of whether or not the government should implement a round-the-clock boundary crossing, at 38% each (Yeung and Wong, 2002, p. 5). However, with the implementation of the Individual Visit Scheme in mid-2003, reverse-direction travel has increased by leaps and bounds. The number of Mainlanders travelling to Hong Kong for leisure and shopping increased from 2.36 million in 1997 to 13.59 million (including 6.67 million who came on the Individual Visit Scheme) in 2006. Mainland visitors are generally big spenders. In 1997, each spent an average of HK$6,782 per visit, although this fell to HK$4,799 in 2006. They contributed a total of HK$15.5 billion to the Hong Kong economy in 1997 and HK$47.6 billion in 2006 (*Ming Pao*, 25 April 2007, A12).

As the Hong Kong and Mainland economies have become further integrated, the number of Hong Kong people working on the Mainland has increased apace. According to surveys on cross-boundary travel, in 2001 about half a million people travelled at least once a week between Hong Kong and the Mainland, especially Guangdong. This number increased by 20% to 600,000 in 2003, as economic conditions worsened in Hong Kong and drove many northwards in search of jobs. Of these Hong Kong people, some 30,000 travelled for work on a daily basis (Cheung, 2006, p. 453). Another study reported a dramatic three-fold increase in the number of Hong Kong residents working on the Mainland, from 52,000 in 1988 to 190,000 in 2001. The latter figure represented 5.6% of Hong Kong's labour force. More than 90% of cross-boundary workers are from Hong Kong, and are predominantly male (Tse and Lin, 2006, p. 187). A more recent survey sponsored by the Central Policy Unit showed that in 2005, 290,900 Hong Kong residents took up residence on the Mainland, with 45.8% of them doing so for reasons of work, and 42.3% having made the move to the Mainland between 2002 and 2004. Only occasionally do they make use of Hong Kong services (27.2%) (CPU, 2005). Still another survey has ascertained that 69.3% of those Hong Kong residents who work on the Mainland do so simply because of the much better economic opportunities there and 22.6% because of inadequate employment opportunities in Hong Kong. Shanghai led in the cities where Hong Kong residents were interested in finding jobs (22.6%), followed by Shenzhen (16.1%), Guangzhou (8.0%) and Beijing (6.6%) (Yeung and Wong, 2002). It is clear from the survey figures presented here that the increasing integration of the Hong Kong and Mainland economies has been spurred above all by China's sustained rapid growth and many attendant opportunities for investment, the creative exercise of one's abilities, and jobs. The recent implementation of CEPA since early 2004 has also provided a new window of opportunity for Hong Kong professionals to enter the Mainland market. The Mainland market will, in all probability, continue to grow in attractiveness for Hong Kong people and vice versa. Thus, in both quantity and quality, the scope of Hong Kong–Mainland cooperation and integration from the viewpoint of employment and work is poised to grow.

The purchasing of homes across the border is another aspect that critically relates to the integration between Hong Kong and the Mainland. The purchase of a home is a significant indicator of the intention to stay in a place, and is tied to a bundle of decisions associated with life cycle, personal finances, a sense of belongings and future plans. Many Hong Kong people purchase property in Guangdong and elsewhere for work and for family reunion, out of a desire for more spacious and comfortable living conditions that they would not be able to afford in Hong Kong, and as an investment in hopes of appreciation. Consequently, many people from Hong Kong have bought holiday or second homes at very affordable prices. In fact, since the development of commodity housing in an emerging housing market in China, many developers have targeted Hong Kong buyers. Hong Kong–style housing complexes have sprung up in cities in the PRD, complete with hospitals and schools, and the Hong Kong model of home security. Every year new housing projects in major coastal cities in China are advertised prominently in Hong Kong. Indeed, some of these projects have been financed and developed by Hong Kong entrepreneurs.

More and more Mainland properties are being purchased by Hong Kong people. A 2002 survey revealed that of the 1,023 Hong Kong residents polled, fully a quarter of them or their family members owned properties in the Mainland. Over 70% owned one property, but one-fifth of the respondents owned two properties. More than 60% of the properties cost less than half a million Hong Kong dollars to purchase, with half of them ranging in size from 500 to 1,000 sq ft. Close to 90% of the properties were for personal or holiday use, with only 13% being rented out. The most popular cities for Hong Kong buyers were Shenzhen (23.9%), Guangzhou (12.7%) and other places within Guangdong (53.3%), with Shanghai (1.4%) and Beijing (0.4%) hardly coming into the picture (Yeung and Wong, 2002). It is clear from such survey data that proximity to Hong Kong figured prominently as a choice of location and that, despite the growth in such investments, there has been little direct impact on the Hong Kong property market, which is a different market.

For some years now, Hong Kong has had to grapple with the problem of an ageing population, the result of low birth rates and longer life expectancies. The issue of how to care for the elderly remains unresolved. By 2031, the elderly population is expected to reach 2.12 million, or a quarter of the total population. As part of preparations for the handover, the government took early steps to deal with the problem, thinking that many elderly Hong Kong people would wish to retire in the PRD. In March 1997, the Social Welfare Department launched the Portable Comprehensive Social Security Assistance (PCSSA) Scheme, which allows elderly people to take their Hong Kong welfare benefits and retire in their hometowns or villages in Guangdong. The response to this scheme has been favourable, with the take-up rate having increased from 700 in 1997 to 2,200 in 2001, and many indicating in surveys that they would seriously consider retiring in Guangdong. This scheme has led to a corresponding growth in the number of residential institutions for the elderly in Guangdong, which have spread from initial clusters in Shenzhen, Panyu and Dongguan to more peripheral cities such as Shaoguan, Yangjiang and Jieyang (Tse and Lin, 2006, pp. 194–95). Since 2005, the scheme has been extended to include Fujian.

The PCSSA scheme has highlighted a crucial issue of the portability of benefits for many Hong Kong residents who have relocated or who intend to relocate themselves and their families to the Mainland. The CPU 2005 survey showed that of the 290,900 Hong Kong people who had taken up residence on the Mainland, 27.2% only used Hong Kong services, mainly in the areas of health care and services for the elderly. The survey also revealed that 39.6% of those interviewed lived in public rental housing in Hong Kong, proportionately higher than the 30.8% of the total population (CPU, 2005). In the 1990s, the Hong Kong Housing Society floated the suggestion of building public housing for Hong Kong residents in Shenzhen but the reaction of the public was decidedly negative. Nevertheless, the issue of whether or not social benefits, notably those relating to housing and medical care, should be made portable is one that will continue to divide the Hong Kong community. It is also one that will critically influence the pace and substance of cross-boundary integration.

As Hong Kong and the Mainland have become increasingly integrated since 1997, the number and range of the social issues that are confronting the Hong Kong community, including some that have never before arisen, have continued to grow rapidly. Fears of an epidemic of avian influenza, traced to the H5N1 virus, gripped Hong Kong in December 1997. Only the decisive decision by the administration to cull more than one million chickens saved Hong Kong from suffering an actual epidemic. There have been persistent problems relating to the safety of food, whether vegetables, meat, fish, chicken or processed food. Hong Kong residents have often succumbed to a siege mentality, since the bulk of Hong Kong's food supply is imported from the Mainland. However, the most serious social and economic catastrophe triggered from developments in the Mainland occurred during the period from March to June 2003, when an outbreak of SARS brought Hong Kong to its knees. The community came to a standstill, economically and socially. Some 300 Hong Kong people lost their lives. The degree of mistrust expressed by Hong Kong people of their government climbed to a historic high of 41.7% in April 2003, according to surveys conducted by the Hong Kong Institute of Asia-Pacific Studies. In April 1998 and October 2006, the corresponding figures were 14.6% and 9.8%, respectively (*Ming Pao*, 16 April 2007, A14). The novelty of the problems relating to social integration continues to catch the attention of Hong Kong people. The latest involves the problem of Mainland mothers giving birth in Hong Kong, thereby putting considerable pressure on local medical services. In 2006, some 26,000 babies were born in Hong Kong of Mainland mothers, who did not always pay their hospital bills. New measures were introduced in February 2007 to address the problem.

Despite its complexity and growing intensity, the social integration that is occurring between Hong Kong and the Mainland is a major dimension of the application of "one country, two systems." With every episode, people on either side are increasing their understanding of each other and moving another step towards nation building.

Conclusion

This chapter has traced the subject of cross-boundary integration from three perspectives. From an institutional point of view, the Hong Kong SAR was from the start fully aware of the need to establish new mechanisms to enable integration and cooperation between the Hong Kong and Mainland governments to proceed smoothly under the regime of "one country, two systems." However, the new government's good intentions were soon overwhelmed by negative internal and external developments that shook Hong Kong. The first few years after 1997 were indeed very challenging for the government and people of the SAR. Fortunately, the tide began to turn in Hong Kong's favour in 2001, with China's accession to the WTO. More important progress was made in mid-2003 when, with the SARS nightmare barely behind the community, several policies favourable to Hong Kong were announced by the Mainland government. CEPA, the Individual Visit Scheme, the Pan-PRD cooperation framework and the 11th FYP, all gave Hong Kong a new dynamism and opportunities to play out its unique role in an emerging China.

Economic integration over the past decade has unfolded in ways that have confirmed Hong Kong's importance and special position, as the Chinese economy further integrated with the global economy and as many coastal cities continued to flourish. The statistics that have been presented in this chapter fully demonstrate the spectacular growth that has occurred in economic relations, trade, logistics, and passenger and visitor traffic, to the mutual benefit of Hong Kong and the Mainland. Recent economic developments have fully justified the faith that has been placed on Hong Kong as the leading international financial centre, not just in China but in the entire Asia-Pacific region. In further enhancing Hong Kong's economic role and strengths in the future growth of China, the continued symbiotic relationship between Hong Kong and Guangdong is vital to both places.

Social integration between Hong Kong and the Mainland has proceeded in tandem with economic integration. As has been shown, much of this has been driven by economic factors. Cost differentials have attracted Hong Kong shoppers to PRD cities, and Mainlander shoppers have flocked to Hong Kong. Other factors that have drawn people across the boundary closer since 1997, notably work and other opportunities on the Mainland, and property purchases and plans for retirement, especially in Guangdong. Other issues relating to cross-boundary social integration have drawn headlines and will require innovative measures to address. Health problems arising from avian flu and SARS have left indelible impressions in the memory of Hong Kong people during the past decade. The recurrent problem of food safety and, most recently, of Mainland mothers coming to Hong Kong to give birth continues to arose controversy.

All in all, despite some initial difficulties, cross-boundary integration has generally progressed well since 1997. As Hong Kong and Mainland China become increasingly convinced that they have a shared future that they can collectively shape, integration will accelerate and take new forms for the benefit of both sides.

References

Census and Statistics Department (CSD) (1992) *Hong Kong External Trade*, March issue. Hong Kong: The Government of Hong Kong SAR, pp. 170, 173.

—— (1997), *1996 Population By-census Main Report*. The Government of Hong Kong SAR.

—— (1998), *Hong Kong External Trade*, March issue. The Government of Hong Kong SAR, pp. 203, 207.

—— (1999), *Annual Review of Hong Kong External Trade 1998*. The Government of Hong Kong SAR.

—— (2001a), *Hong Kong Annual Digest of Statistics 2001*. The Government of Hong Kong SAR.

—— (2001b), *Annual Review of Hong Kong External Trade 2000*. Hong Kong: The Government of Hong Kong SAR.

—— (2002), *Population Census 2001: Main Tables*. Hong Kong: The Government of Hong Kong SAR.

—— (2006a), *Hong Kong External Merchandise Trade*, December issue. Hong Kong: The Government of Hong Kong SAR.

—— (2006b), *Hong Kong External Merchandise Trade*, March issue. Hong Kong: The Government of Hong Kong SAR, pp. 206, 212.

—— (2006c), *Hong Kong Annual Digest of Statistics 2006*. Hong Kong: The Government of Hong Kong SAR.

—— (2007a), 2006 *Gross Domestic Product*. Hong Kong: The Government of Hong Kong SAR.

—— (2007b), *Monthly Digest of Statistics*, February issue. Hong Kong: The Government of Hong Kong SAR.

—— (2007c), *Hong Kong External Merchandise Trade*, March issue. Hong Kong: The Government of Hong Kong SAR, pp. 206, 212.

—— (2007d), *Annual Review of Hong Kong External Merchandise Trade 2006*. The Government of Hong Kong SAR.

Central Policy Unit (CPU), HKSAR Government (2005), "Thematic Household Survey in 4th Quarter of 2004: Characteristics of Hong Kong Residents or Long Staying Residents on the Mainland." October (unpublished).

Cheung, Peter T. Y. (2006), "Cross-boundary Cooperation in South China: Perspectives, Mechanisms and Challenges." In Anthony Gar-on Yeh et al. (eds.), *Developing a Competitive Pearl River Delta in South China under One Country-Two Systems*. Hong Kong: Hong Kong University Press, pp. 449 79.

Civil Aviation Department (2007), "Hong Kong International Airport Civil International Air Transport Movements of Aircraft, Passenger and Freight (1998–2006)." http://www.info.gov.hk/cad/english/p-through.htm, accessed on 14 March. Hong Kong: The Government of Hong Kong SAR.

Federation of Hong Kong Industries (FHKI) (2007), *Made in PRD: Challenges and Opportunities for Hong Kong Industry*. Hong Kong: FHKI.

Hong Kong Planning Department (HKPD) (2002), *Northbound, Southbound: Cross Boundary Travel Survey 2001*. Hong Kong: Planning Department.

Holmes, D. R. (1965), *Hong Kong Review of Overseas Trade in 1964*. Hong Kong: The Government of Hong Kong SAR.

Hong Kong SAR Government (1998), *Hong Kong 1997*, http://www.yearbook.gov.hk/1997/econtent.htm, accessed on 6 April 2007.

Ma, Xiaoling (2006), "Economic Integration and the Environmental Legal System for Hong Kong-Guangdong Region." In Anthony Gar-on Yeh et al. (eds.), *Developing a Competitive Pearl River Delta in South China under One Country-Two Systems*. Hong Kong: Hong Kong University Press, pp. 383–98.

National Bureau of Statistics (NBS) (2006), *China Statistical Yearbook 2006*. Beijing: China Statistics Press, pp. 752–53.

Port Development Council (2007a), "Container Throughput of Hong Kong Port (Estimates)." http://www.pdc.gov.hk/eng/statistics/docs/Hkport.pdf, accessed on 14 March. Hong Kong.

—— (2007b), "The Port of Hong Kong." http://www.pdc.gov.hk/eng/facilities/port.htm, accessed on 6 April.

Port, Maritime and Logistics Development Unit (2006), "Summary Statistics on Port Traffic of Hong Kong." September 2003. http://www.pdc.gov.hk/eng/statistics/summary.htm#, accessed on 14 March, 2007. Hong Kong: Economic Development and Labour Bureau, the Government of Hong Kong SAR.

Shen, Jianfa (2003), "Cross-border Connection between Hong Kong and Mainland China under 'Two Systems' Before and Beyond 1997," *Geografiska Annaler Series B, Human Geography*, 85B (1): 1–17.

Sit, V. F. S. (1989), "Hong Kong's New Industrial Partnership with the Pearl River Delta," *Asian Geographer*, 8: 103–15.

Skeldon, R. (1997), "Hong Kong: Colonial City to Global City to Provincial City?" *Cities*, 14 (5): 265–71.

State Statistical Bureau (SSB) (1998), *China Statistical Yearbook 1998*. Beijing: China Statistics Press.

Sung, Yun-wing (2002), "Economic Integration of Hong Kong and the Zhujiang Delta." In Kwan-yiu Wong and Jianfa Shen (eds.), *Resource Management, Urbanization and Governance*. Hong Kong: The Chinese University Press, pp. 9–30.

—— (ed.) (2003), "Closer Economic Partnership Arrangement between the Mainland and Hong Kong." Occasional Paper No. 135. Hong Kong: Hong Kong Institute of Asia-Pacific Studies, The Chinese University of Hong Kong (in Chinese).

Sung, Yun-wing and K. Wong (2000), "Growth of Hong Kong Before and After Its Reversion to China: The China Factor," *Pacific Economic Review*, 5 (2): 201–28.

Tse, Pauline H. M. and George C. S. Lin (2006), "Flexible Sojourners? The Cross-border Flow of People from Hong Kong to Guangdong Province, China." In Anthony Gar-on Yeh et al. (eds.), *Developing a Competitive Pearl River Delta in South China under One Country-Two Systems*. Hong Kong: Hong Kong University Press, pp. 175–200.

Yeung, Chris (2002), "Separation and Integration: Hong Kong-Mainland Relations in a Flux." In Lau Siu-kai (ed.), *The First Tung Chee-hwa Administration: The First Five Years of the Hong Kong Special Administrative Region*. Hong Kong: The Chinese University Press, pp. 237–65.

Yeung, Yue-man (2003), "Integration of the Pearl River Delta," *International Development Planning Review*, 25 (3): iii–viii.

—— (2005), "Emergence of the Pan-Pearl River Delta," *Geografiska Annaler*, 87(b)(1): 75–79.

────── (2006a), "The Pan-PRD and ASEAN-China FTA as Agents of Regional Integration in Pacific Asia." Occasional Paper No. 13. Hong Kong: Shanghai-Hong Kong Development Institute, The Chinese University of Hong Kong.

────── (2006b), "Hong Kong–Shenzhen Cooperative Development: The Search for Forward-looking Ideas." Occasional Paper No. 166. Hong Kong: Hong Kong Institute of Asia-Pacific Studies, The Chinese University of Hong Kong (in Chinese).

Yeung, Yue-man and Shen Jianfa (forthcoming), "Hong Kong." In Yeung and Shen (eds.), *The Pan-Pearl River Delta: Emergence of a Regional Economy in Globalizing China*. Hong Kong: The Chinese University Press.

Yeung, Yue-man, Shen Jianfa and Zhang Li (2006), *China's 11th Five-year Plan: Challenges and Opportunities for Hong Kong*. Unpublished research report for the Bauhinia Foundation. Hong Kong: Hong Kong Institute of Asia-Pacific Studies, The Chinese University of Hong Kong.

Yeung, Yue-man and Timothy Ka-ying Wong (2002), "Hong Kong People's Attitudes towards Living, Working and Purchasing Property in Mainland China: The Impact of Mainland-Hong Kong Integration." Occasional Paper No. 126. Hong Kong: Hong Kong Institute of Asia-Pacific Studies, The Chinese University of Hong Kong (in Chinese).

World Bank (1998), *World Development Report 1998/99*. Washington.

Website of Shenzhen Port (2007), "The Top 20 Container Port in the World 2006," *Port and Shipping Information*, No. 2 (Total No, 48), http://www.szport. net:8080/pop/pop.jsp?page=2&ID=741, accessed on 14 March 2007.

14

Planning for the World City

Joanna Lee and Mee-kam Ng

World City Formation in Hong Kong: An Overview

Historical events have raised Hong Kong, once an obscure fishing village, into a recognized world city. Its status as a British colony since the nineteenth century and its strategic location as a gateway to China have facilitated its entrepôt trade, its key position in the networks of overseas Chinese capital and its connection with the rest of the world (Meyer, 2000). With "transferred industrialization" from the Mainland after the establishment of the People's Republic of China in 1949, Hong Kong succeeded in turning its shattered post–World War II economy into an industrial powerhouse. The further restructuring of the city's manufacturing economy to a service economy with intensified connections with China accelerated after the adoption of the open-door policy in China in 1978 and the designation of Special Economic Zones (SEZs) in the 1980s. Confronted with escalating production costs and stiff competition from other producers in Southeast Asia, many labour-intensive industries in Hong Kong were relocated to the Pearl River Delta (PRD) region, where there is plenty of land and an almost inexhaustible supply of cheap labour.

Hong Kong has also benefited from the rise of China as the world's fastest growing economy, a development that occurred after Chinese leader Deng Xiaoping's southern tour of the SEZs in 1992. Facilitated by a favourable economic environment, Hong Kong has gradually transformed itself into an international financial centre. The number of firms with regional headquarters in Hong Kong rose from 602 in 1991 to 1,228 in 2006.[1] The number of banks with representative offices in the territory[2] also reached a peak in the early 1990s. According to a survey of multinational firms in the Asia-Pacific region,[3] Hong Kong is the most important city in

Pacific Asia for regional coordination and finance (Enright, Scott and Chang, 2005).

In spite of the fact that Hong Kong has played an important role in the global economy for decades, it was only after 1997 that the government formally started the drive to build Hong Kong into Asia's world city. Similar to other cities, the government functions as an urban manager in providing the necessary infrastructure to facilitate the restructuring of the economy. As Yeung and Lo (1998, p. 145) pointed out, "[i]n order to be effective in the new global and regional economies, world cities ... have been preparing themselves in different ways in a process that may be called world city formation." It seems that the government has shifted in the pre-1997 period from playing the role of a "silent facilitator" to becoming a more "proactive advocate" in the late 1990s and the early 2000s in branding Hong Kong as Asia's world city. Indeed, the return of Hong Kong to China in 1997 that redefined its relationship with China under the "one country, two systems" arrangement has moved Hong Kong into a new and interesting phase of world city formation.

This phase in world city formation is embedded within a rapidly changing multi-scalar socioeconomic and political environment. Therefore, the aim in this chapter is to review the major government planning initiatives to turn Hong Kong into Asia's world city at the global, regional and local levels. In the following section, the existing literature on the development and planning of world cities is reviewed. Then, the branding of Hong Kong as Asia's world city amidst a decade-long economic downturn and social movements taking place during that period is discussed. Against this backdrop, planning initiatives to build Hong Kong into Asia's world city at different geographical scales are examined, followed by some concluding remarks.

Planning for the World City

World City: Major Nodes in the Global Economic Network

According to Abbot (1997, p. 31), the term "world city" probably emerged with J. F. Geothe's description of Rome and Paris as *weltstadte*. In his book, *Cities in Evolution* (1915), Patrick Geddes described world cities as national capitals and industrial centres that play a dominant role in trading and communications networks. The term world city was popularized after the publication in 1966 of Peter Hall's book *The World Cities*. In it, he argued that "world cities were essentially the climax product of the single economic system of European industrial capitalism and its offspring in Japan and North America" (Abbot, 1997, p. 31). However, it was John Friedmann's "World City Hypothesis" (Friedmann, 1986) that was the trigger for numerous studies on how to understand cities in the world economy (Beaverstock et al., 1999; Godfrey and Zhou, 1999; Knox and Taylor, 1995; Sassen, 1991; 1994; Smith and Timberlake, 1993; Taylor, 2004). Friedmann's world city hypothesis concerns "the spatial organization of the new international division of labour" (Friedmann, 1986, p. 69). In her seminal book, S. Sassen (1991) argued that New York, London and Tokyo "dominate the global urban hierarchy in terms of transnational corporate ownership and control" (Smith and Timberlake, 1993, p. 193) as socially polarized sites providing "highly specialized technical and financial 'producer services'," but are also "disproportionately staffed by isolated and politically marginalized immigrants and racial and ethnic minorities" (ibid., 1993, p. 193).

However, there has been little work on the planning of world cities. Friedmann (1988, pp. 83–84) has embedded planning implications in his world city hypothesis. As the formation of a world city involves economic, social and physical restructuring, political conflicts are inevitable. When Friedmann revisited the world city concept in the late 1990s, he reiterated that "our hierarchy of cities is not in a stable equilibrium, and cities may rise or fall in their economic standing as 'basing points' and 'control centres' of global capital" (1997, p. 15). He argued that there are four major factors that can affect a city's future (1998, pp. 32–36): changes in exogenous political circumstances; the economic creativity to respond to exogenous change; intercity competition; and socially and environmentally unsustainable growth.

In other words, Friedmann is warning city governments to focus not only on the maintenance of economic spaces — that is, spaces produced by firms and corporations with profit-maximization as their primary concern. This is because economic spaces often end up being "superposed over [the] life spaces of individuals and communities" (Friedmann, 1998, p. 97), which are "typically bounded territorial spaces" — places with history and culture that address the needs of local communities and bestow them with meaning. Hence, the government needs to address the multi-scalar political, social and environmental dimensions of world city development.

Ng and Hills (2003, p. 155) have similarly argued that world cities need to be sustainable, and have suggested the notion of a great city that inspires aspirations for cities to go beyond the status of exerting economic dominance, to pursue an enlightened mode of governance — a city in which innovative technology and economic activities that further sustainable global and local development abound; and one in which human, social, cultural and environmental capital are valued. In other words, the planning of world cities is not just about climbing up the global economic hierarchy through the production and maintenance of "economic spaces." It should also be about showing concern for meeting social needs and achieving environmental protection at different geographical scales in specific and unique places where the drama of life blossoms in various forms and intensities.

The Branding of "Asia's World City"

The Vision: "Asia's World City"

The branding of Hong Kong as "Asia's world city" began with the first Chief Executive, Tung Chee-hwa, who in 1997 appointed a Commission on Strategic Development to map out the city's future role. To Mr Tung, Hong Kong had the potential to become not only a major Chinese city, "but also the most cosmopolitan city in Asia, enjoying a status similar to that of New York in America and London in Europe" (Tung, 1998). He further developed this vision in his 1999 Policy Address:

> [Hong Kong] already possesses many of the key features common to New York and London.... [W]e are already an international centre of finance and a popular tourist destination, and hold leading position in trade and transportation ... if we can consolidate our existing economic pillars and continue to build on our strengths, we should be able to become world class. Then, like New York and London, we will play a pivotal role in the global economy, be home to a host of multi-national companies and provide services to the entire region (Tung, 1999, p. 15).

In the same Policy Address, Mr Tung promised to spend $30 billion[4] to improve air quality in four years, and to start to work with officials from the Mainland to mitigate environmental issues, especially those concerning air and water quality (Stewart, 1999, p. 1). Four months after the first Chief Executive's 1999 Policy Address, the report on the Commission on Strategic Development (2000, pp. vi–vii) was published. The following broad vision was outlined:

> [The pursuit of] a number of over-arching goals, including enhancing income

and living standards for all members of society; ensuring that Hong Kong becomes the most attractive major city in Asia in which to live and work; developing a socially cohesive and stable society that recognizes that the community's diversity strengthens its cosmopolitan outlook; contributing to the modernization of China while also supporting Hong Kong's long-term development; and ensuring that a process of political development is put in place that meets community aspirations and is in line with the pace and provisions of the Basic Law.... The Commission believes that achieving these goals will enable Hong Kong to become Asia's world city and to maintain its position as a major city in China, which are interrelated.

The Commission further discussed its interpretation of world cities and what makes them successful:

[They have] a distinctive economic structure and a level of influence far greater than their size might suggest. They tend to have great strengths in internationally oriented service infrastructure, both "hard" (e.g., transport and telecommunications) and "soft" (e.g., education and training, R&D, urban planning) and a recognition of the need to integrate economic, social and environmental development in a balanced way.... (ibid, 2000, pp. vi–vii).

While these visionary statements go beyond economic growth to address the social and environmental dimensions of world cities, they have little to say on issues of politics and governance. The development of this vision by the first Chief Executive and his appointed Commission took place when the Hong Kong Special Administrative Region (HKSAR) was facing an economic depression, followed by a series of controversial events on social issues and on issues concerning the built and natural environments.

Economic Downturn

Affected by the Asian financial crisis in 1997 and 1998, the economy of Hong Kong has gone through a "roller coaster" decade of development. Gross Domestic Production in the city was in a trough for most of the decade following 1997. On 28 October 1997, the Hang Seng Index dropped about 40% from its peak in August (*FEER*, 1998, p. 118). The economic gloom lasted for about eight years, and the economy did not pick up again until 2003.

While 1997 and 1998 were marked by the completion of significant mega-infrastructure projects, such as Chek Lap Kok Airport and the 1.4 km Tsing Ma Bridge, the world's longest suspension bridge that accommodates both roads and a railway, the HKSAR was also grappling with new challenges. The chaos that marred the opening of Chek Lap Kok Airport damaged Hong Kong's international image. The property and stock markets collapsed a few months later, which in turn caused shops and businesses to fail, leading to unemployment problems. The economic downturn after 1997 was followed by a series of socially and politically controversial events.

Controversial Social Events

The numerous socially controversial incidents that broke out in the decade following 1997 reveal the emergence of a maturing and vocal civil society, where people are demanding a stronger say in determining the future directions for the development of the city. Table 14.1 lists the major events that had been debated heatedly in the first decade of the existence of the HKSAR, vividly marking the end of the colonial era when people used to behave passively to social developments directed by the government.

Debates directly related to the making of a world city include opposition to reclamation as a means of creating more land to accommodate urban growth and to the proposed modes developing the various mega projects launched to facilitate the restructuring of Hong Kong's economy, such as Cyberport, the Disney theme park and the West Kowloon Cultural District (WKCD). The debates also encompassed issues relating to Hong Kong's natural and built heritage, including the success of green groups in forcing the Kowloon Canton Railway Corporation to turn part of the Lok Ma Chau Spur Line into a tunnel to protect a man-made wetland in Long Valley; the preservation of the Hunghom Peninsula, a newly built but unoccupied public home-ownership complex on the waterfront; the failure of the local community to conserve the unique character of Lee Tung Street (Wedding Card Street) in Wanchai; and the demolition of the Star Ferry and its clock tower, "Hong Kong's Big Ben," which were part of the deep collective memory of generations of Hongkongers who had grown up with the chimes of the clock tower as the city became transformed from an industrial powerhouse to an international financial centre.

It was in the midst of such economic and social distress that the government launched its campaign to build Hong Kong into Asia's world city. While the government has undertaken many projects to enhance the role of Hong Kong as a world city, it should be noted that they have not formulated any overarching strategic plan to coordinate the various efforts that are being made to that end in different policy areas.

Table 14.1 Major Controversial Events in the First Decade of the HKSAR

Year	Controversial events
1998	• Chaotic opening of Chek Lap Kok Airport
	• Bird flu (6 people died and 1.4 million chickens were slaughtered)
	• Strong objections to the central Harbour reclamation
1999	• The Court of Final Appeal's ruling in favour of the right of abode for Mainland children with at least one Hong Kong parent was overturned by the National People's Congress. This led to much debate
	• The reintroduction of appointed members in District Councils — some viewed this as a major retrogressive step
	• The awarding of development rights for Cyberport (a hi-tech cum real estate development project) was regarded as an act of favouritism by the first Chief Executive
	• Secretive talks resulted in the development of a Disneyland theme park
2000	• Short piling scandals in the construction of public housing
	• Continued controversy over reclamation
2001	• Continued objections to reclamation
	• The Long Valley/Lok Ma Chau Spur Line controversy: Green groups objected to the construction of a commuter railway that would cut through an ecologically sensitive artificial wetland
2002	• Debate on proposals to implement Article 23 (on an anti-sedition law) of the Basic Law
2003	• The SARS crisis
	• Half a million people marched to oppose Article 23 on 1 July, the date that marked the sixth anniversary of Hong Kong's return to Chinese rule
2004	• The general public and green groups succeeded in stopping the demolition of the Hunghom Peninsula, a public home-ownership complex that had been sold to a private developer who wanted to redevelop the seven blocks into up-market luxurious waterfront properties
	• Rallies against the Central reclamation
	• Controversy over the WKCD development
2005	• Continued debates over the mode of achieving the WKCD development
	• Controversy over the redevelopment of Wedding Card Street
	• WTO protests
2006	• The WKCD development goes back to drawing board
	• Continued controversy over the redevelopment of Wedding Card Street
	• Funding for the construction of the government's headquarters in Tamar was approved
	• Demolition of the Star Ferry, one of 50 must-see sites recommended by the National Geographic

Source: Various newspaper clippings.

A Decade of Plans to Make Hong Kong into a World City

This section discusses various planning initiatives implemented by the government at the global, regional and local levels. The adequacy of these initiatives in planning Hong Kong as a world city is critically assessed so as to highlight directions for future planning.

The Formation and Development of Global Networks?

To realize the vision of developing Hong Kong into the "most cosmopolitan city in Asia comparable to New York and London," one of the main planning objectives put forward in the Hong Kong 2030 Study, which maps out the city's territorial development strategy, is to enhance Hong Kong's hub functions by strengthening its role as a global and regional financial centre. At the beginning of the study, the strategic planning experiences of other leading cities in the world were reviewed to shed light on the implementation of the strategic goal of developing a world city. However, it seems that the government has not followed through on these good initiatives. Although the government has repeatedly emphasized its intention of promoting "Hong Kong as Asia's world city, on par with the role that New York plays in North America and London in Europe" (Tung, 2004, p. 2), no comprehensive planning strategy towards this end has been undertaken beyond the domain of territorial planning.

Through cooperation with the Mainland, it is apparent that Hong Kong has become a platform for China-related companies to solicit funds from international investors. This is reflected in the recent surge in the stock market. As pointed out by *Invest Hong Kong*, "as a world-class capital market, Hong Kong has become a key hub for raising capital for Mainland enterprises of different sizes from different industries. With our outstanding financial services professionals, Hong Kong is able to offer various options for raising funds and pursuing business development for the enterprises. Listing on the Hong Kong stock exchange will also improve their corporate profile and standard of corporate governance. These elements are important for their expansion into regional and international markets."[5] In terms of total equity funds raised, Hong Kong ranked fourth in the world in 2006.[6] The Mainland's share of the Hong Kong market has increased in recent years and is now significant. In 2006, the last full year for which such figures are available, the Mainland accounted for 30.5% of all listed companies and 47.6% of market capitalization in Hong Kong.[7]

Regional Governance: Intercity Networking and Cooperation or Competition?

As the world economy has become increasingly interdependent, the emerging urban form reflects a new territorial division of power by which the governing authority moves from cities to regions as well as multinational territories (Friedmann, 1998). While every state is eager to improve its intercity networking and cooperation efforts, Hong Kong has also become increasingly involved with the PRD region in promoting regional cooperation (Lui and Chiu, 2003). Given Hong Kong's historical and geographical proximity to the PRD region, the Hong Kong government is particularly attracted by the region's unprecedented economic boom. Over 160 "Fortune 500" companies have invested in various sectors in Guangdong (Yeung et al., 2005). These include Toyota and Nissan (automobiles); Siemens (telecommunications) and Wal-Mart (retail). Under the "one country, two systems" arrangement, a new economic partnership between Hong Kong and the PRD region has emerged. Hong Kong has changed from the driver of the PRD region's modernization in the early 1980s to a partner in leveraging its economic power on the Mainland.

At the policy level, economic cooperation with the Mainland has been one of the key directions in territorial planning. As early as the beginning of the 1990s, the PRD/southern China region was included in the Territorial Development Strategy of Hong Kong. Development scenarios (that is, high growth and super-high growth scenarios) were formulated for different degrees of integration with southern China.[8] The subsequent Hong Kong 2030 Study further indicated that "links with the Mainland" were one of the key planning directions for Hong Kong. Cooperation with the Mainland in land use, transport and environmental issues were thus further investigated. These included assessing the development potential of the Hong Kong–Shenzhen boundary area; examining cooperation on port and logistics development; and exploring the potential for providing housing and social facilities in the Mainland for Hong Kong residents. Although the Study has pointed to the right direction of regional cooperation, limited attempts have been made to translate the policy recommendations into concrete local planning strategies.

Under the vision of regional integration with the PRD, the government has, since the late 1990s, launched a series of planning studies to investigate how to increase the capacity of border control points and cross-border transport links to reinforce socioeconomic integration. They include: the

Feasibility Study for Additional Cross-border Links (1997); the *Cross-boundary Travel Surveys* (since 1999) and the *Thematic Household Surveys — Hong Kong Residents' Aspirations and Experience in Taking up Residence in Mainland* (since 2001). In the Seventh Plenary of the Hong Kong/ Guangdong Cooperation Joint Conference, representatives agreed to speed up regional cooperation by launching a *Planning Study on the Co-ordinated Development of the Greater Pearl River Delta Township* in 2006. This represents the first attempt by Guangdong and Hong Kong to jointly undertake a strategic regional study on the town planning front. Under the "one country, two systems" framework, the aim of this study is to formulate a regional development strategy for the Greater PRD region by investigating the development approaches of various PRD cities. In order to be effective, the proposed broad-brush strategy must be translated into concrete plans/ programmes at the local level for implementation. The same applies to the study on *Land Use Planning for the Closed Area* proposed in 2006. Given the increasing cross-border traffic and activities, the Hong Kong government has decided to review the development potential of the closed area, especially the Lok Ma Chau Loop. Currently, land use on both sides of the border is one of contrast, with villages and agricultural pursuits on the Hong Kong side versus two important growth centres (that is, Futian and Lo Wu) in Shenzhen, on the Mainland side. The aim of this study is to formulate a concept plan as well as a detailed development plan that will form the basis for preparing Outline Zoning Plans to facilitate future interactions between the two places.

Apart from establishing key planning directions through a series of planning studies, the Hong Kong government had also invested in hard infrastructure (Figure 14.1 and Figure 14.2). These include the planning and construction in the post-1997 period of different cross-border road links (e.g., the Hong Kong–Zhuhai-Macao Bridge, the Deep Bay Link, etc.) and new railways (e.g., the Regional Express Line and the Sheung Shui to Lok Ma Chau Spur Line, etc.). The Executive Council has recently given the green light to the drawing up of a detailed plan for the Hong Kong section of the Express Rail Line, which will link Hong Kong, Shenzhen and Guangzhou. Moreover, the government is now investigating the possibility of developing an additional crossing point at Liantang and of building an associated new cross-boundary road link (i.e., the Shenzhen Eastern Corridor) in order to expand cross-boundary traffic capacity.

All of these regional initiatives signal the eagerness of the government to turn Hong Kong into a world city with convenient physical connections

Figure 14.1 Existing and Planned Cross-border Road Links in Hong Kong

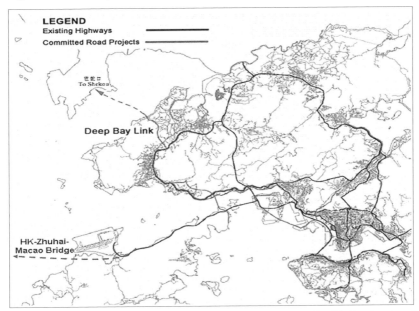

Source: Planning Department: HK2030 Study Working Paper No. 21. *Regional and Hong Kong's Transport Network Planning Framework.* http://www.hk2030.gov. hk/eng/wpapers/pdf/workingPaper_21.pdf.

Remark: The Deep Bay Link, Shenzhen–Western Corridor and the Shenzhen Bay Checkpoint were opened on 1 July 2007.

and close economic ties with the Pan-PRD region. In the course of urban transformation, Hong Kong will be leveraging strategically on the Mainland. Therefore, it is not surprising to find that resources have been directed towards the development of border areas and associated cross-border infrastructure. However, although good proposals have been made for intercity networking, the extent of regional cooperation has been impeded by the different modes of planning governance on the two sides. For example, it will take years to finalize the alignment option for the Hong Kong section of the Guangzhou-Shenzhen–Hong Kong Express Line, while that for the Guangdong section has already been finalized and construction on that section has already begun. Therefore, the different administrative and governance structures have posed a challenge to the implementation of many cross-border infrastructural developments.

Although Hong Kong is keen on regional cooperation and intercity

Figure 14.2 Existing and Planned Cross-border Railways in Hong Kong

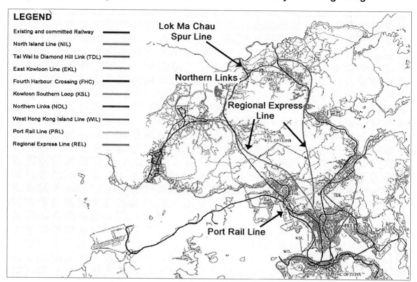

Source: Planning Department: HK2030 Study Working Paper No. 21. *Regional and Hong Kong's Transport Network Planning Framework.* http://www.hk2030.gov. hk/eng/wpapers/pdf/workingPaper_21.pdf.

Remark: The Lok Ma Chau Spur Line was opened on 15 August 2007.

networking efforts, its function as an international hub is being subtly threatened by the unprecedented development of some PRD cities. The building of container ports in Shenzhen and the construction of the Guangzhou Baiyuan International Airport as well as of exhibition facilities in Guangzhou, Shenzhen and Dongguan have all put pressure on the future development of Hong Kong as Asia's world city. These may have some backwash effects on any regional planning measures undertaken by the Hong Kong government, suggesting all the more clearly, the need for regional governance as argued by Friedmann (1998, p. 41).

Planning for Local Sustainability?

In the process of accommodating the additional growth brought by globalization and regionalization, and in their endeavours to upgrade their ranking in the hierarchy of urban areas, many world cities have encountered "world-city syndromes." These syndromes include a high unemployment rate for unskilled labour, growing social disparities, and fiscal problems in the form of a protracted shrinkage in the size of the government. Whether a city can sustain its growth will depend on whether its economic, social and environmental needs can be balanced in the formulation of local spatial planning strategies. During the first decade of the existence of the HKSAR, Hong Kong has witnessed increasing challenges from the population against local development projects. This signifies a growing concern among Hong Kong people about issues of social and environmental sustainability. The Hong Kong government's single-minded pursuit of economic growth has caused it to be criticized for pursuing local spatial planning strategies that are biased towards producing economic space and that direct limited resources to improving the life space of the people.[9]

The Production of "Economic Space"

Increasing the Land Bank for Economic Growth through Reclamation

The vision of developing Hong Kong into a world city with the functions of a financial and logistics hub requires new spaces to accommodate these functions. As a landlord with a vested interest in the land market, the government has focused on the provision of "economic space" so as to facilitate capital accumulation. All along, the government has relied heavily on reclamation as a spatial strategy to acquire additional land for economic growth (Figure 14.3). Guided by a series of planning studies such as the *Study on Harbour Reclamation and Urban Growth (1982)*, the *Territorial Development Strategy (1984)* and the *Quest for Land (1995)*, extensive reclamation projects were completed before Hong Kong reverted to Chinese rule in 1997. These include the Central Reclamation Phases I–II, the Wanchai Reclamation Phase I, the Hunghom Bay Reclamation and the West Kowloon Reclamation. With a development agenda biased towards property development and a voracious demand from overseas companies for office and commercial land in the metropolitan area, most of the reclaimed land is being used for commercial and infrastructural purposes and for residential developments. For example, the International Finance Centre and the extension of the Convention and Exhibition Centre were constructed under the Central Reclamation Phase I (1993–1998) and the Wanchai Reclamation Phase I (1994–1997) projects, respectively.

However, in the post-1997 period, such a "fast-track" development approach has been severely challenged by Hong Kong's fledgling civil

Figure 14.3 Reclamation in Victoria Harbour (Not to scale)

Source: Adapted from Ng (2006), p. 312, Fig. 1.
Notes: Pre-1945: ribbon reclamation along the Victoria Harbour; 1946–1985:
         reclamation to support post-war economic take-off; 1986–1997: Central harbour
         reclamation for the restructuring economy; Post-1997: rising objections to
         massive harbour reclamation.

society. Given the changing social and political climate of Hong Kong after
1997, a more vocal and organized civil society has managed, through a
court case, to overturn the government's reclamation strategy for land
production (Ng, 2006). The economic downturn in the late 1990s and early
2000s caused the public to reflect upon the various social and environmental
issues that lay behind the spatial strategy. The Society for the Protection of
the Harbour Limited openly objected to "the Government using [the spatial
strategy] as an excuse for massive reclamation for the production of land
for sale to private developers as is being proposed in the Wanchai
Reclamation" (Society for Protection of the Harbour Limited, 2003, p. 2).
Friends of the Harbour has taken a similar position. The group has claimed
that "[t]he Government simply chose to meet the demand for land by harbour
reclamation and not by other means, which could have included developing
the New Territories or urban regeneration, because reclamation was
expedient and until 1995, there was no advocate speaking for Victoria
Harbour" (Friends of the Harbour, 2003, p. 4).

The year 1997 is, in a sense, a point of transition because it was in that year that the Protection of the Harbour Ordinance was enacted. The anti-reclamation crusade of the general public in the post-1997 period highlights the need to rethink the current strategy of land production (Ng and Chan, 2005). In 1998, the draft Central District (Extension) Outline Zoning Plan (OZP) No. S/H24/1, covering 38 ha of the Central Reclamation Phase III site, was gazetted. Some 70 objections on the draft OZP were received. The government was eventually persuaded to reduce the total area of reclamation from 38 ha to 23 ha. In the same year, the draft Wanchai North OZP, covering a proposed reclamation area of 24 ha, was gazetted. Some 778 objections were received. The Protection of the Harbour Ordinance has provided a new platform for the people to express their opinions and advance their interests. The Society for the Protection of the Harbour Limited applied for a judicial review and the High Court handed down its judgement in favour of the Society. It ruled that the purpose/extent of reclamation should be assessed by the three tests of overriding need, no viable alternative and minimum impairment to the harbour. The Town Planning Board decided to lodge an appeal against the High Court judgement. In the end, the Court of Final Appeal upheld the High Court's decision, making it necessary for the Town Planning Board to reconsider the relevant plan. While the Central Reclamation Phase III can proceed, the Wanchai Reclamation Phase II and other reclamation projects around Victoria Harbour must be reconsidered by the Planning Department. This signifies the success of civil society in overturning the government's proposals of reclamation.

The Allocation of Land for the Development of Pillar Industries in Hong Kong

The internationalization of Hong Kong into a service hub has caused many industrial buildings in Hong Kong to become obsolete. The government has thus launched a series of planning studies to investigate the possibility of rezoning surplus industrial land into other profitable uses (especially business uses). In 1999, the Planning Department completed *A Study to Review the Planning Framework for the Reservation and Provision of Industrial Land*. As a result of this study, a public consultation on the establishment of a "Business" zone and on guidelines for the rezoning of industrial land was launched in 1999. It was decided that while adequate land should be reserved for production activities, no more than 66 ha of industrial land will be gradually rezoned for non-industrial uses in the coming 10 years. Existing industrial buildings will also be allowed to be adapted for other uses. Recently, the Planning Department conducted the *Commercial and Industrial Floor Space Utilization Survey (2004)* and the *Updated Area Assessments of Industrial Land in the Territory (2006)*. By assessing vacancy rates and predominant uses, recommendations were made to rezone industrial lands in various districts. Given the curtailment of harbour reclamation in land production, the "Business" zone can allow for the flexible use of industrial land in Hong Kong. On the other hand, Hong Kong is moving towards the development of high-tech industries. The Pak Shek Kok Science Park and Cyberport were planned towards this end. However, the Cyberport development has been criticized for being a property development project instead of nurturing high-tech industrial growth.

With the world city formation process having started in earnest in the late 1980s, the government decided to open up new areas of growth. A number of new strategic areas of growth were opened in the Northwest and Southwest New Territories. In the 1990s, Hong Kong's economic relationship with Mainland China (especially in the areas of trade and re-exports) was further strengthened. To achieve closer economic cooperation with the Mainland, the government began investigating options for investing in the cross-border areas, with various proposed cross-border links, such as the Western Corridor, the Sheung Shui to Lok Ma Chau Spur Line, the Deep Bay Link, and others. During the first decade of the existence of the HKSAR, the cross-border areas have become another strategic growth area in Hong Kong. With the opening of the Chek Lap Kok International Airport in 1998 and subsequent completion of the 10 Core Airport Programme Projects,[10] the focus of development has expanded outward and westward.

At the same time, the existing metropolitan area will undergo restructuring in the area of land use, as additional land will be provided for financial and commercial activities to meet both regional and global demands. Notwithstanding the government's interest in developing the border area, the Central business district (CBD) is still its main focus of attention. First, all of the existing/planned strategic transport links have terminals or stops at either Central or Tsim Sha Tsui, such as the Airport Railway; the Sha Tin to Central Link; the MTR Island Line/Tsuen Wan Line/Tseung Kwan O Line, and so forth. Second, the CBD area has long been the focus of the government's planning strategies. Early in 1982, reclamation in Central and Wanchai was proposed to expand the CBD. In the first Territorial Development Strategy announced in 1986, the role of Central and Tsim Sha Tsui as the commercial centres of Hong Kong was reaffirmed. The subsequent Metroplan in 1991 also stated that new commercial offices, hotels and conventional facilities were required in the metropolitan area to sustain the growth of Hong Kong as an international financial centre. This was then taken into consideration in the formulation of development options in the Territorial Development Strategy Review in 1993. In 1999, the Study on the Propensity for Office Decentralization and the Formulation of an Office Land Development Strategy confirmed the need to maintain a strong core CBD through redevelopment and new reclamation, notably, the Central and Wanchai Reclamations.[11] The enhancement of the metropolitan area as an outstanding centre for Asia's world city was reaffirmed in the Stage II Review of the Metroplan in 2001 and, more recently, in the Hong Kong 2030 Study.

In its Eleventh Five-year Plan, China's central government expressed clear support for the development of Hong Kong's logistics industry. As the long-term vision of Hong Kong is to become an international financial and logistics hub that cooperates closely with the Mainland, the Hong Kong government will have to invest heavily in port and airport facilities. The Port Development Strategy and subsequent reviews since 1997 have highlighted a number of strategic development issues that may affect the long-term planning of port facilities in Hong Kong. First, China's accession to the World Trade Organization (WTO) has increased the volume of cargo flowing through Hong Kong's port. Second, the rapid development of the Western PRD region will provide more business opportunities and bring more cargo flow to Hong Kong. Given that the site for a planned container terminal at Penny's Bay has been taken over by the Disneyland theme park, new potential sites (i.e., West Tuen Mun, Northwest Lantau, East Lantau and Southwest Tsing Yi) for the development of container terminals have been investigated in order to cope with future growth needs. Regarding airport development, the plan outlined in the Vision 2025 for Hong Kong International Airport (HKIA 2025) is to position the Hong Kong International Airport as one of the most important gateway hubs in China. The Airport Authority Hong Kong supports the coordinated development of PRD airports in order to optimize runway capacity and airspace. Although Hong Kong has invested heavily in infrastructure in pursuit of its aim to be Asia's world city, competition from the PRD should not be overlooked. It is predicted that, with their double-digit growth, Shenzhen's ports will surpass Hong Kong in the next few years.

The Production of "Life Space"

For a world city to be able to upgrade its ranking in the urban hierarchy, it is important to devise a sustainable planning strategy that enhances not only the economic, but also the social and environmental interests of the community. In fact, in 1997, the government commissioned the *Study on Sustainable Development for the 21st Century in Hong Kong* (SUSDEV 21). In view of the need to enable decision-makers to gain an understanding of the long-term implications of any strategic development decisions, a set of sustainability indicators and a Computer Aided Sustainability Evaluation Tool (CASET) were devised to help government officials evaluate the sustainability implications of strategic policy and project proposals. Although the government has used CASET to screen projects before making decisions, the development projects they announced in the early 2000s have still been criticized for being unsustainable. For example, the Lantau Concept Plan released for public consultation in 2004 was challenged by the community as a plan that would damage natural assets and introduce land-use conflicts. Moreover, the Hong Kong 2030 Study does not include concerns over air, noise, water and solid waste management, despite the identification of sustainability as the overarching principle in the study. Passing a sustainability impact assessment is not a statutory requirement for the launching of any local development projects. It is true that the Sustainable Development Unit (which is responsible for the integration of sustainable development into government programmes) was established under the Government Administration in 2001, followed by the establishment of the Council for Sustainable Development in 2003. Moreover, the government's first Sustainable Development Strategy addresses three discrete policy areas: solid waste management, the sustainable use of energy and urban living space (SDU, 2005, pp. 14–15). However, no explanation is given on the relationships among these three areas and there seem to be no mechanisms for monitoring or evaluating the proposed initiatives recommended by the Strategy. Hence, one can argue that when compared with the production of economic space, unequal amounts of attention and resources have been directed towards the improvement of life spaces in Hong Kong. This is not desirable. As Friedmann (1998) has suggested, the issue of social and environmental sustainability should be "a major policy issue that confronts planners concerned with placing their cities in the top rank of the world hierarchy" (p. 38).

One of the key initiatives proposed under the heading of sustainable urban living, which can be regarded as one of the government's attempts to improve the quality of life space, is the revision of the Urban Renewal Strategy. In his 1999 Policy Address, Mr Tung stated that it was urgent to take a more proactive approach towards urban renewal to bring real improvement to the living conditions of residents in dilapidated buildings. The subsequent Urban Renewal Strategy Study proposed a target area approach to tackling the problem of urban renewal. Four main planning approaches (i.e., redevelopment, rehabilitation, revitalization and preservation) are adopted. However, almost all of the urban renewal projects undertaken in the post-1997 period have come under serious attack by the community, including the redevelopment of Lee Tung Street (Wedding Card Street) and Sham Shui Po. The general public has queried the effectiveness of both the current renewal strategy and the major agent of redevelopment (whether the former Land Development Corporation or the current Urban Renewal Authority). They have been challenged for ignoring the social dimension of redevelopment and public participation. Although the Urban Renewal Strategy is entitled *People First: A Caring Approach to Urban Renewal* (2001), the existing strategy has been criticized for being too dominated by the market and for bringing no real improvement to the life spaces of the people.

Concluding Remarks

When the decision-makers and planners of past decades were investing heavily in infrastructure, they were probably not aware of the fact that they were engaging in the process of building up Hong Kong as a world city. Only later when the concept of world cities became more widely known did Hong Kong officially adopt this concept and begin using it for its publicity campaigns. Since then, the government has changed from a "silent facilitator" to a more "proactive advocate" in branding Hong Kong as Asia's world city.

In the first decade of the existence of the HKSAR, it is clear that various measures have been undertaken to formulate and develop a spatial development strategy. However, the compartmentalization of the bureaucracy, coupled with an absence of a strategy for socioeconomic development, have contributed to the formulation of a spatial plan that replicates interdepartmental discrepancies and conflicts. Strategic (territorial) planning alone without a serious attempt to address environmental and social concerns in an integrated and coherent manner is insufficient to propel Hong Kong into a sustainable world city.

To become a sustainable world city, it is important to improve certain areas of planning. First, it is important to balance the economic, social, environmental and spatial needs of the community. In view of the steady deterioration of life spaces in Hong Kong, planners should look beyond the imperative of maintaining economic spaces and address the dire need to improve life spaces, which have increasingly been superimposed and diminished by the "growth" mentality. As argued by many researchers on world cities (Friedmann, 1998; Knox and Taylor, 1995; Sassen, 1991; Ward, 1995), the economic prosperity of a world city should be guided by the principle of sustainable development. Second, a comprehensive strategy on the development of a world city hinges upon the formulation and implementation of strategic policies at the global, regional and local levels. Issues of regional governance and the "territorial division of power" have to be tackled in a spirit of intercity networking that fosters co-learning and co-development.

In the light of the good initiatives undertaken in the first decade of development, the government should further substantiate its planning policies so as to transform Hong Kong into an example of a sustainable world city in Asia.

Notes

1. Census and Statistics Department, HKSAR *Annual Survey of Regional Representation by Overseas Companies in Hong Kong.* Hong Kong: Hong Kong Government Printer, various years.
2. This refers to banks incorporated in places other than Hong Kong.
3. The survey was undertaken by Enright, Scott and Associates Ltd. This is quoted in Enright, et al. (2005), *Regional Powerhouse.*
4. Unless otherwise indicated, dollars refer to Hong Kong dollars hereafter.
5. Quoted from the website of InvestHK, www.investhk.gov.hk, accessed on 27 September, 2004.
6. Quoted from the website of InvestHK, http://www.investhk.gov.hk/pages/1/335.aspx, accessed on 29 April 2007.
7. Same as note 5.
8. A detailed discussion was included in the Public Consultation Digest of the TDS Review in 1996 and in the Final Report of the TDS Review in 1998. Source: Planning Department (1996), *Territorial Development Strategy Review. Public Consultation Digest.* Hong Kong: Hong Kong Government

Printer; Planning Department (1998), *Territorial Development Strategy Review. Final Report.* Hong Kong: Hong Kong Government Printer.

9. The distinction between "life space" and "economic space" has been discussed in detail by J. Friedmann (1988, pp. 96–97). Life space refers to the improvement of people's quality of life (reproduction), whereas economic space refers to the enhancement of economic growth (production).

10. The 10 Airport Core Programme Projects are Chek Lap Kok Airport, Tung Chung Development Phase I, the North Lantau Expressway, the Airport Railway, the Lantau Fixed Crossing, Route 3, the West Kowloon Reclamation, the Western Harbour Crossing, the West Kowloon Expressway, and the Central and Wanchai Reclamation Phase I.

11. This is stated in the Planning Department's 1999 report entitled, *Final Report of the Study on the Propensity for Office Decentralization and the Formulation of an Office Land Development Strategy.* Hong Kong: Hong Kong Government Printer.

References

Abbot, C. (1997), "The International City Hypothesis: An Approach to the Recent History of U.S. Cities," *Journal of Urban History,* 24 (1) (November): 28–52.

Beaversstock, C. V., P. J. Taylor and R. G. Smith (1999), "A Roster of World Cities," *Cities,* 16 (6): 445–58.

Commission on Strategic Development (2000), *Bringing the Vision to Life: Hong Kong's Long-term Development Needs and Goals.* Hong Kong: The Printing Department.

Enright, J. Michael, Edith E. Scott and Chang Ka-mun (2005), *Regional Powerhouse: The Greater Pearl River Delta and the Rise of China.* England: John Wiley and Sons (Asia) Ltd.

Far Eastern Economic Review (FEER) (1998), *Asia 1998 Yearbook: A Review of Events of 1997.* Hong Kong: Review Publishing Company Ltd.

Friedmann, J. (1986), "The World City Hypothesis," *Development and Change,* 17:69–83.

—— (1988), "World City Formation," *Life Space and Economic Space.* New Jersey: Transaction Books, pp. 57–92.

—— (1997), *World City Futures: The Role of Urban and Regional Policies in the Asia-Pacific Region.* Hong Kong: Hong Kong Institute of Asia-Pacific Studies, The Chinese University of Hong Kong.

—— (1998), "World City Futures: The Role of Urban and Regional Policies in the Asia-Pacific Region." In Y. M. Yeung (ed.), *Urban Development in Asia: Retrospect and Prospect.* Hong Kong: Hong Kong Institute of Asia-Pacific Studies, The Chinese University of Hong Kong, pp. 25–54.

Friends of the Harbour (2003), *The Harbour Premier.* Hong Kong.

Geddes, P. (1915), *Cities in Evolution: An Introduction to the Town Planning Movement and to the Study of Civics.* London: Williams.

Godfrey, B. J. and Y. Zhou (1999), "Ranking World Cities: MNCs and the Global Urban Hierarchy," *Urban Geography,* 20 (3): 268–81.

Hall, P. G. (1966), *The World Cities.* London: Weidenfeld and Nicholson.

Knox, P. L. and P. J. Taylor (eds.) (1995), *World Cities in a World-System.* Cambridge: Cambridge University Press.

Lui, Tai-lok and Stephen W. K. Chiu (2003), *Hong Kong Becoming a Chinese Global City.* Occasional Paper No. 29. Hong Kong: The Centre for China Urban and Regional Studies, Hong Kong Baptist University.

Meyer, David R. (2000), *Hong Kong as a Global Metropolis.* Cambridge: Cambridge University Press.

Ng, M. K. (2006), "World-city Formation under an Executive-led Government: The Politics of Harbour Reclamation in Hong Kong." In M. K. Ng (guest editor), "Special Issue on Planning Asian World Cities in an Age of Globalisation," *Town Planning Review,* pp. 311–37.

Ng, M. K. and P. Hills (2003), "World Cities or Great Cities? A Comparative Study of Five Asian Metropolises," *Cities,* 20 (3): 151–65.

Ng, M. K. and A. Chan (2005), *A Citizen's Guide to Sustainable Planning in Hong Kong: Concepts and Processes.* Hong Kong: Community Participation Unit, Department of Architecture, The Chinese University of Hong Kong and CUPEM, The University of Hong Kong.

Planning and Lands Bureau, The Government of Hong Kong (2001), *Urban Renewal Strategy: People First — A Caring Approach to Urban Renewal.* Hong Kong: Planning and Lands Bureau.

Planning Department (2001), "Regional and Hong Kong's Transport Network Planning Framework, Hong Kong 2030 Study Working Paper No. 21," http://www.hk2030.gov.hk/eng/wpapers/pdf/workingPaper_21.pdf, accessed on 27 April 2007.

Sassen, S. (1991), *The Global City: New York, London, Tokyo.* Princeton: Princeton University Press.

—— (1994), *Cities in a World Economy.* Thousand Oaks: Pine Forge Press.

Smith, D. A. and M. Timberlake (1993), "World Cities: A Political Economy/Global Network Approach," *Urban Sociology in Transition,* 3: 181–207.

Society for Protection of the Harbour Limited (2003), *Position Statement: High Court Decision on Wanchai Reclamation.*

Stewart, A. (1999), "Tung Pledges to reduce Air Pollution within Four Years," *South China Morning Post,* 17 October 1999, p. 1.

Sustainable Development Unit (SDU), the Government of Hong Kong (2005), *A First Sustainable Development Strategy for Hong Kong.* Hong Kong: SDU, The Government of Hong Kong.

Taylor, P. J. (2004), *World City Network: A Global Urban Analysis.* London: Routledge.

Tung, Chee-hwa (1998), *The 1998 Policy Address.* Hong Kong: Government Printing Office.

—— (1999), *The 1999 Policy Address.* Hong Kong: Government Printing Office.

—— (2002), *The 2002 Policy Address.* Hong Kong: Government Printing Office.

—— (2004), *The 2004 Policy Address. Policy Agenda.* Hong Kong: Government Printing Office.

Ward, P. M. (1995), "The Successful Management and Administration of World Cities: Mission Impossible." In P. L. Knox and P. J. Taylor (eds.), *World Cities in a World-System.* Cambridge: Cambridge University Press, pp. 298–316.

Yeung, Yue-man and Fu-chen Lo (1998), "Globalization and World City Formation in Pacific Asia." In Fu-chen Lo and Yue-man Yeung (eds.), *Globalization and the World of Large Cities.* Tokyo: United Nations University Press, pp. 132–54.

Yeung, Yue-man, Joanna Lee and Gordon Kee (2005), *The Pearl River Delta: A Background Study for Assessing Investment Opportunities.* Hong Kong: Hong Kong Institute of Asia-Pacific Studies, The Chinese University of Hong Kong. Unpublished report.

15

Environmental Safeguards and Breakthroughs

Cho-nam Ng and Yok-shiu F. Lee

Introduction

Although some long-term environmental trends in post-1997 Hong Kong are in part the legacy of policies and programmes implemented by the pre-1997 colonial administration, the current state of the Special Administrative Region's (SAR's) environment has largely been shaped by post-handover era policies. Long-term environmental gains have been the most salient, with improvements in the overall quality of beach and river water, and the easing of the noise problem in East Kowloon as a result of the relocation of the city's airport to Chek Lap Kok. In the past 10 years, environmental safeguards in the SAR have been strengthened by the promulgation of one major piece of legislation and several sub-sector oriented policies and programmes: the enactment of the Environmental Impact Assessment Ordinance in 1997, the launching of the Waste Reduction Framework in 1998, the introduction of a comprehensive motor-vehicle emission control programme in 1999, the setting up of the Strategic Sewage Disposal Scheme in 2001, the promulgation of a new Conservation Policy in 2004, and the announcement of the Policy Framework for the Management of Municipal Solid Waste in 2005.

However, the promises of these policies and programmes, and their impact — much of which is not immediately apparent — have been overshadowed by increasing levels of ambient air pollution stemming largely from regional, cross-boundary sources. As a result, an inward-looking perspective focusing on local pollution problems, which was dominant in the pre-1997 era, has gradually been replaced by a regional perspective that calls for intensified cross-boundary cooperation in environmental management. Efforts in forging closer cooperation on transboundary pollution control measures, however, have been hampered by some entrenched institutional constraints emanating from the "one country, two systems" (OCTS) framework of governance. Moreover, concerns have been raised in recent years, by environmental as well as neighbourhood community groups, about the importance of examining the ramifications of town planning practices, such as outdated urban design schemes, on air quality at the neighbourhood level.

A detailed review of the basic parameters of the environment sector as well as a critical examination of the key events that have defined the changing domain of the environment in the past 10 years are presented here. We argue that, despite the introduction of some major initiatives to safeguard the quality of the city's environment, the post-handover government has still failed to formulate an integrated framework of environmental policies. Moreover, in spite of some major breakthroughs achieved by adopting some innovative ideas on the overall approach to managing the environment, the Hong Kong SAR government has yet to produce a badly needed strategy for sustainable development. As such, despite increased investments in the environment sector, several problems have persisted and progress in some key areas has been unduly compromised.

This chapter is organized into the following four parts. Part one provides a historical perspective on the origin, major characteristics and constraints of the dominant approach to managing Hong Kong's environment in the pre-1997 era. The repertoire of policy instruments, the institutional infrastructure and the philosophy underlying this dominant approach, which has continued to influence the post-1997 administration, are delineated and assessed. In part two, the key events recorded in the 1997–2007 period are discussed in accordance with the dynamics associated with each of the basic parameters of the environment sector. The successes and limitations of the management of each of these key sub-sectors in the past 10 years are highlighted to help illustrate the problem of an absence of a comprehensive and integrated policy framework. Part three singles out the problem of ambient air pollution from these key sub-sectors. The discussion here is intertwined with that of cross-boundary cooperation on issues relating to the environment. The institutional constraints barring closer linkages between and among jurisdictions in the region are then identified and examined. Part four concludes the review of the past 10 years with an overall assessment of the major challenges still lying ahead for the SAR in its quest to achieve an improved and sustainable environment.

Managing the Environment in Pre-1997 Hong Kong

Systematic efforts to address Hong Kong's environmental problems were first made by the colonial government in the 1980s. After establishing the requisite institutional framework and introducing an initial set of environmental laws and regulations, the first policy document in the form of a White Paper, entitled *Pollution in Hong Kong — A Time to Act*, was then published in 1989 (HKG, 1989). The White Paper set out a 10-year programme to tackle the territory's environmental problems. Throughout the 1980s and the early 1990s, the first-generation legislation and policies achieved some success in terms of controlling industrial pollution, improving the quality of inland waterways and provisioning some well-functioning waste management facilities.

However, with a booming economy and a rapid construction programme involving large-scale infrastructure projects, notably the new international airport at Chek Lap Kok and its associated core projects, Hong Kong's environment was placed under tremendous pressure in the 1990s. The conclusion from critical assessments of the state of the city's environment in anticipation of the changeover in 1997 was that, by the mid-1990s, Hong Kong was suffering from poor air quality, as measured by concentrations of total suspended particulates (TSPs) and respirable suspended particulates (RSPs) in densely built-up urban areas at the street level, pervasive noise pollution and an increasingly unmanageable waste disposal problem (Hills, 1997). The water quality in Victoria Harbour remained sub-standard because of a major delay in the implementation of the Strategic Sewage Disposal Scheme, Phase I of which was originally scheduled to be completed in 1997. A 1999 study of Hong Kong's sustainability indicators concluded that at the end of 1990s, the territory was heading away from rather than towards a sustainable future (Barron and Steinbrecher, 1999).

The persistence of some decades-old environmental problems into the 1990s (such as marine water pollution), as well as the emergence of some new environmental troubles at the turn of the century (such as impaired visibility), points to the failure of the city's dominant approach to managing the environment. This approach had prevailed for decades in the pre-1997 era and still lingers on after the handover. It was dominated by the conventional "command and control" management model (Hills, 1997, 2002). Critics have repeatedly pointed out the limitations of such an approach: The symptoms rather than the causes of problems were tackled; and there was a failure to formulate a comprehensive environmental policy integrating land-use planning and nature conservation with environmental protection (Hills and Barron, 1997).

While a considerable number of environmental laws have been passed since the early 1980s, critics have argued that Hong Kong has never formulated a clearly defined and unambiguous environmental policy. Environmental laws and mitigation measures were, therefore, introduced within a policy vacuum. In addition, they focused primarily on controlling pollution. Moreover, the proposed measures embodied in the city's first White Paper were largely directed at grappling with the symptoms but not the causes of problems. No integrated thinking on policy formulation was apparent. Besides pollution control, matters with an immediate impact on the environment, such as land-use planning and nature conservation, were not taken into consideration to enable a comprehensive environmental protection policy to be designed (Hills and Barron, 1997). The failure to produce an integrated and comprehensive policy framework meant that the government was taking action on the environment without the benefit of a set of clear and consistent priorities.

The lack of an integrated environmental policy *per se* was compounded by the constraints of a horizontally fragmented government structure, which was functionally organized to address key policy concerns but was not designed to handle trans-sectoral issues such as the environment. As such, the government as a whole was all too often seen as being pulled into different or even opposite directions, with different policy branches and departments pursuing their own, sometimes conflicting, agendas. For instance, while the Transport Department's actions might have a profound impact on the local environment, the policy bureau overseeing transportation matters did not consider the environment to be part of its remit. Indeed, a number of government departments, along with much of the private sector, had always perceived the Environmental Protection Department (EPD) in a negative light and considered its environmental standards unrealistically high and its activities anti-growth and anti-development (Hills and Barron, 1997).

The third major characteristic of the pre-1997 model of environmental management stems from the government's pervasive "top-down" approach to formulating and implementing mitigation measures targeting the sources of pollution. For reasons not yet fully understood, at least up until the early 1990s the community at large did not put pressure on the government to take action to tackle environmental problems (Barron, 1996). Environmental NGOs, a power to be reckoned with in the West, were considered peripheral to the process of environmental policy-making and evaluation in Hong Kong for much of the 1980s. By the 1990s, primarily as a result of a change in the government's tactics, almost all of the leading environmental NGOs were absorbed into the formal consultative process on policy development through appointments of their members to the Advisory Council on the Environment. Given "insider" status, they have largely stopped taking a confrontational stance and have increasingly assumed a professional and consultative role in the overall policy deliberation process. The absence of a vocal, critical voice from the environmental NGO community has thus reinforced the "top-down" pattern in the formulation and implementation of environmental policies.

In short, up until 1997, environmental management in Hong Kong was characterized for the most part by a pre-occupation with pollution control. Environmental managers favoured "end-of-pipe" technical solutions that were fashioned within a largely command-and-control framework. Efforts to tackle environmental challenges were frustrated by the lack of an integrated and comprehensive policy, the fragmentation of the structure of government into sector-oriented units, and a top-down approach that precluded useful input and support from the larger community.

In the years immediately following the handover, there was a hint that the newly formed Hong Kong SAR government was going to give a higher priority to the environment than the colonial administration ever had. In his first ever Policy Address after the founding of the SAR, delivered in 1997, the Chief Executive stated clearly that improving the quality of the environment was as vital as economic growth to improving the city's quality of life. He promised that the government would ensure that consideration of how to sustain and enhance the environment would be built into strategic planning and policymaking (Tung, 1997). In the following year, he further promised that the then Secretary for Planning, Environment and Lands would soon issue a Green Paper on environmental policy (Tung, 1998). This latter commitment was supposedly a timely move to continue and step up efforts to protect the environment after the conclusion in 1999 of the 10-year programme laid down in the 1989 White Paper. However, despite several years of organized deliberation among government officials, academics and environmental NGOs, the SAR government has yet, as of early 2007, to promulgate the Green Paper. The glaring failure to produce the Green Paper begs the question of the degree to which the SAR government is committed to the environment. As we review the key events marking the development of each major sub-sector in the field of environmental management in the past 10 years, it is apparent that the limitations of the environmental initiatives introduced in these 10 years could more or less be traced to the lack of a comprehensive and integrated policy framework in this field.

Major Events in the 1997–2007 Period

In the 10 years since the changeover in 1997, there have been a number of milestones in the environment sector. The most important of these with regard to environmental policy are summarized in Table 15.1. It should be noted at the outset that the policy bureau responsible for the environment sector has been restructured four times in the past 10 years. Whether this has had any major impact on policy continuity is a question that might require further study. Nevertheless, within the environment sector, one of the most salient achievements, and also the earliest, was the enactment of the Environmental Impact Assessment Ordinance (EIAO) in 1997. This Ordinance has since had an unprecedented, and lasting, impact on the SAR's environmental assessment process. In the following, the development of each key parameter of the environment sector is systematically reviewed and discussed with regard to the successes and limitations associated with the policies and programmes of each parameter. Given the significance of the impact of the EIAO on the overall domain of environmental policy, it is reviewed first. Attention is then turned to water, waste and nature conservation. Next, the issue of air pollution is analyzed in conjunction with the government's efforts to forge a closer working relationship with neighbouring jurisdictions to enhance cross-boundary cooperation in environmental management.

Development of the EIA Process

As far as the field of environmental management is concerned, the first major event in the post-1997 era was the implementation of the EIAO in April 1998. The need to institute a formal EIA process in the city was advocated by the Conservancy Association as early as the 1970s (CA, 2003). It was also suggested at around the same time by a government-commissioned study (EPD, 2007a). However, systematic impact assessment procedures were not introduced until 1986, when the government issued an administrative directive to set out the screening process and EIA requirements for public work projects. Being an administrative process, it

Table 15.1 Major Events in the 1997–2007 Period

	Air	Water	Waste	Nature conservation	EIA	Others
1997					EIA Ordinance enacted	
1998			Waste Reduction Framework introduced		EIA Ordinance implemented	Opening of Chek Lap Kok Airport
1999	– Programme for improving ambient air quality announced – A joint study on cross-boundary air pollution commissioned					Emphasis on "Quality People, Quality Home" and sustainable development in the CE's Policy Address
2000	LPG taxi subsidies scheme launched	International Review Panel set up to review SSDS			EIA report on KCRC's Spur Line Project rejected by DEP	Restructuring of PELB to EFB
2001		– SSDS Phase 1 commissioned – SSDS renamed HATS	Review of Waste Reduction Plan		KCRC lost appeal of rejection of Spur Line's EIA report	SDU founded
2002						Restructuring of EFB to ETWB
2003	Regional Air Quality Management Plan for the PRD Region endorsed					SDC founded
2004	New Conservation Policy published					
2005		CE announced that HATS Stage 2 would proceed in phases	– Policy Framework for Management of Municipal Solid Waste published – Construction Waste Disposal Charging Scheme became operational	3 pilot MA projects funded		Merger of EPD and the environmental bureau of ETWB
2006	– "Action Blue Sky" campaign launched – "Clean Air Charter" launched					
2007						Restructuring of ETWB to EB

Keys:
CE   Chief Executive
CPI   Continuous Public Involvement
DEP   Director of Environmental Protection
EB   Environment Bureau
EFB   Environment and Food Bureau
EIA   Environmental Impact Assessment
EPD   Environmental Protection Department
ETWB Environment, Transport and Works Bureau

HATS Harbour Area Treatment Scheme
KCRC Kowloon-Canton Railway Corporation
MA   Management Agreement
PELB Planning, Environment and Lands Bureau
PRD   Pearl River Delta
SDC   Sustainable Development Council
SDU   Sustainable Development Unit
SSDS Strategic Sewage Disposal Scheme

rendered the authority (i.e., the Director of Environmental Protection [DEP]) powerless to enforce the mitigation measures recommended by the EIA reports. In addition, there were no formal and statutory requirements to conduct post-decision environmental monitoring and auditing work to track the actual environmental performance of development projects.

To resolve the plight of the administrative-based EIA system, the Environmental Impact Assessment Bill was introduced in early 1996. The EIAO was subsequently enacted on 4 February 1997 and became effective on 1 April 1998. Under the Ordinance, all designated projects are required to undergo the statutory EIA process and be approved by the DEP before construction work can begin. Approved projects are issued with Environmental Permits and the DEP could attach conditions to them. There is a statutory public consultation procedure before the decision to approve is made — the authority is required to consult the Advisory Council on the Environment (ACE), which is comprised of representatives from the private sector as well as environmental NGOs. The EIAO also stipulates that environmental monitoring and auditing procedures need to be followed once the projects commence.

The EIA process in Hong Kong has been praised for its openness and transparency. The EPD has introduced some pioneering concepts for public engagement, some of which represent international best practices. For example, major documents of the EIA process, including the study briefs, EIA reports and the Environmental Monitoring and Audit reports, are accessible by the public via the EIAO website. Since 2003, on-site webcams have been required for some projects to enable the public to have 24-hour visual access to monitor on-going work. In addition, in 2004 the EPD developed a 3-D computerized tool to facilitate the public engagement process.

The EIAO has undoubtedly resulted in improvements to the environmental performance of major development projects. It has led to a general increase in public awareness of the impact assessment process as well as to increased levels of professionalism on the part of project proponents and their consultants. Nonetheless, problems remain. These problems are largely institutional and are related to the failure, primarily on the part of project proponents, to undertake EIA processes at an early enough stage to seriously consider other alternatives to the proposed projects. Concerns have also been raised on the issue of the enforcement of the Environmental Permit conditions, which rely largely on self-monitoring. Their efficacy, therefore, is questionable (Leverett et al., 2007).

In 2000, public attention to the EIA process reached a new high when the EIA report on the Kowloon-Canton Railway Corporation's Sheung Shui–Lok Ma Chau Spur Line project was rejected by the DEP on the grounds that it would have an unacceptable impact on the wetland in Long Valley. A total of 225 formal objections against the case were submitted by the public to the authority, the highest number ever recorded at the time. The DEP's decision to reject the EIA report was largely based on concerns raised and submitted by the public and the ACE. The authority's decision was unprecedented in Hong Kong's recent history of environmentalism, where a major infrastructure project proposed by a powerful, semi-public corporation was stopped by the public on environmental grounds.[1] The proponent of the project immediately lodged an appeal against the DEP's decision, but the Appeal Board rejected the case in 2001. The Board reasoned that it was not proper for it to approve the application via the appeal process because this would circumvent the statutory public engagement process and nullify the proper role played by the public and the ACE in the overall EIA process (EIA Appeal Board, 2001).

The case shows the need for public consultation, especially at the early planning stage of a project. In response to this, in 2003 the EPD introduced the concept of continuous public involvement (CPI) to allow on-going public consultation in the EIA process. Under the stipulations of the CPI concept, proponents are encouraged to consult the public, in particular, the stakeholders, throughout the entire EIA process. The case also highlights the importance of avoiding having an impact, especially on ecologically sensitive sites. If alternative alignments or designs had been seriously considered at an early stage in the planning of the project, many of the conflicts that arose could have been avoided or resolved. As a matter of fact, the Strategic Environmental Assessment of the Second Railway Development Study 2000, carried out at around the same time as the Spur Line's EIA, suggested that the Long Valley was a "no-go" zone for any future railway development due to its ecological importance (MVA and Maunsell, 2000).

Controversial projects continue to arouse much public concern. For example, during the thirty-day public consultation period in December 2006 for the EIA report on the proposed Liquefied Natural Gas Terminal Project at Soko Island, the EPD received about 16,000 public submissions, although the majority of them were in the form of standard letters of objection (Ng, 2007). So far, most applications for environmental permits have been approved with/without conditions. Very few cases have been rejected by the authority in the past 10 years. The Lantau North-South Link road project was one of those being rejected. By the end of April 2007, a total of 132 EIA reports had been received by the DEP, of which 106 were approved. So far, projects with a total estimated cost of approximately HK$340 billion covering approximately 150 km of roads, 80 km of railways, 670 ha of development project sites, 100 km of drainage works, 20 km of power lines, 1 power station and 164 ha of airport decommissioning space have gone through the statutory EIA process. In the 106 EIAs approved under the EIAO, over 1.5 million people and more than 1,000 ha of ecologically important areas have been protected from excessive environmental impact (EPD, 2007a).

Water Pollution and Sewage Treatment

Whereas the quality of inland water bodies, such as rivers and streams, has continued to improve from the early 1990s to the present moment (EPD, 2007b), the overall water quality of Victoria Harbour remains a problem. This issue has been placed on the back burner at times because the public's attention has turned to the more visible problem of impaired visibility. Nonetheless, it has been raised periodically by concerned parties, such as green groups. The lack of progress in enhancing the Harbour's water quality was primarily the result of a major delay in the completion of the first phase of the hugely expensive Strategic Sewage Disposal Scheme (SSDS).

The SSDS was first put forward by the government in the 1989 White Paper on the Environment as an overall strategy to tackle the problem of water pollution in the Harbour (HKG, 1989). Conceived as a four-phase programme and originally expected to be completed by 2003, it was primarily an engineering-dominated infrastructure scheme. The first phase, scheduled for completion by 1997, encompassed the construction of a very deep tunnel sewage collection system across Kowloon and East Hong Kong Island, the construction of a sewage treatment works at Stonecutters Island, as well as an interim outfall at the western Harbour area. The second phase consisted of the construction of a submarine oceanic outfall through which treated effluent would be discharged into the deep ocean outside Hong Kong's maritime boundary. Phases 3 and 4 included the planning and construction of a collection and treatment system for the rest of the urban areas immediately fronting the Harbour. Phases 2, 3 and 4 were originally scheduled for completion by 2003 (PELB, 1993).

The construction work for all of the Phase 1 projects started in 1994.

The sewage treatment facility at Stonecutters Island was completed, on schedule, and was ready for operation in 1997. However, the digging of the deep tunnel system, which was supposed to collect and feed waste-water to the sewage treatment facility, encountered some major unexpected technical difficulties and its completion was unduly and substantially delayed. The tunnel system was finally completed in 2001. When all of the Phase 1 projects were fully commissioned, they were already four years behind schedule.

The long delay in the commissioning of the Phase 1 projects, plus the fact that their price tag came to the staggering sum of HK$8.2 billion, led to an uproar among the public, especially the green groups. Questions were immediately raised by sceptics about the cost-effectiveness of the entire treatment system, informed by the SSDS approach. In response to the public outcry, the Chief Executive announced in his 1999 Policy Address that an independent review of the remaining components of the SSDS would be conducted. Subsequently, an International Review Panel (IRP) was set up in 2000 to conduct a review through a process of open consultation (ACE, 2000).

In their report, submitted to the government in 2001, the IRP recommended that consideration be given to upgrading the level of treatment to tertiary standard and discharging the effluent within Victoria Harbour. Panel members also put forward four alternative plans for the further development of SSDS (ACE, 2001). The SSDS was subsequently renamed the Harbour Area Treatment Scheme (HATS) in 2001. With the Stage 1 projects of HATS fully commissioned in 2001, about 75% of the sewage treated at Stonecutters Island received a chemically enhanced primary treatment before being discharged into Victoria Harbour. This achievement has resulted in a significant improvement in the water quality in the eastern part of the Harbour. However, the water quality of the beaches near Tsuen Wan, in terms of concentrations of *e coli*, has been adversely affected by the discharges from the Stonecutters treatment works (EPD, 2007b).

In 2004, given that HATS Stage 2 had received major support from the public during the public consultation period, the government decided to proceed with the implementation of Stage 2 in two phases: Stage 2A will consist of the construction of a deep tunnel system to convey currently untreated sewage from Hong Kong Island to the Stonecutters Island Treatment Works. The latter will be expanded and new disinfection facilities will be added by 2009. Stage 2A has been scheduled for completion by 2013–2014. Stage 2B will see the addition of biological treatment to the facilities at Stonecutters Island. The timing of this will depend upon a review of water quality trends, increases in population and sewage flow build-up figures, to be undertaken in 2010–2011. While the government has said that it will shoulder the capital cost of Stage 2, it has clearly indicated that the full operational costs of the treatment system will be recovered through the collection of sewage charges from all users in the city, as a way to begin to apply the "polluter pays principle" in managing the SAR's waste.

Municipal Solid Waste Management

The strategy for managing municipal solid waste (MSW) was first spelled out in the Waste Disposal Plan published in the 1989 White Paper (HKG, 1989). The final disposal of the city's waste relies primarily on three strategic landfills sited in the New Territories, supported by a network of refuse transfer stations located near the urban areas where most of the waste originates. As a consequence of rapid economic development in the 1990s, and the failure to enforce the construction waste charging scheme in 1995, the amount of MSW that needed to be disposed of increased from 12,500 tonnes/day in 1989 to 16,000 tonnes/day in 1997. Given that the original projections for that year had been greatly exceeded, the government became extremely concerned. The government calculated that if that trend should continue, the three strategic landfills would be completely filled up by 2015, five years earlier than planned (PELB, 1998).

In an attempt to reverse the trend of increasing volumes of municipal waste, in 1998 the government unveiled the Waste Reduction Framework Plan (PELB, 1998). This Plan set out various initiatives for waste reduction, but not much progress was made in the ensuing years. The Plan was hence reviewed in 2001. The review resulted in a list of recommended measures that included the promotion of domestic waste separation and recovery, as well as the establishment of various targets for overall MSW waste recovery rates and domestic waste recovery rates. In addition, the construction industry was targeted with the aim of reducing the amount of construction and demolition waste going into the landfills by 25% by 2004, when measured against the base year of 1999.

In 2002, about 1.96 million tonnes of MSW (36% of the total) were recovered through an informal, voluntary waste recovery system. Of that amount, only 11% was recycled locally and 89% was exported to the Mainland and other countries for recycling (EPD, 2003a). Critics have cited the lack of affordable space and infrastructure support, ostensibly a function expected of the government, as the major reason for the low rate of recycling activities performed locally. The lack of an overall MSW charging scheme has also limited the achievement of waste reduction efforts, as there is little incentive for waste producers to reduce and recycle their waste. The amount of waste that is generated has thus continued to climb.

In 2004, the city's households produced over 5.7 million tonnes of MSW. It was estimated then that the remaining landfill space would only last for another 6 to 10 years if the waste levels continued to increase at the prevailing rates of growth. It was also suggested at that time that the city would need to identify about 400 ha of land (10 times the area reserved for the West Kowloon Cultural District) to construct new landfills to serve the needs of MSW management up to 2030 (EPD, 2005). Confronted with these figures, the government finally reckoned that relying solely on landfills for waste disposal was clearly not going to be a sustainable solution.

Recognizing the scale of the waste problem facing Hong Kong, in 2004 the Sustainable Development Council chose solid waste management as one of three pilot areas, along with renewable energy and urban living space, for inclusion in a process of engagement to obtain stakeholders' views on what could be done to promote sustainable practices in all three selected areas. The recommendations generated from this engagement process were included by the EPD in a policy framework stretching to 2014 (EPD, 2005). The Policy Framework set out an overall strategy and specific measures to address the MSW problem in Hong Kong for the said period. One major element of the strategy was the implementation of the polluter-pays principle through the introduction of an MSW charging scheme and the producer responsibility scheme (PRS). In addition, the strategy recommended the establishment of an EcoPark to provide land on a long-term basis for environmentally friendly and recycling businesses, as well as an Integrated Waste Management Facility for the reduction of bulk waste (EPD, 2005). Moreover, the long overdue Construction Waste Disposal Charging Scheme was finally put into operation on 1 December 2005, 10 years behind the original schedule (LegCo, 2007). By the end of 2006, the volume of construction waste disposed of at the three landfills had been reduced from 6,600 tonnes per day (tpd), the daily average figure recorded prior to the implementation of the charging scheme, to 4,000 tpd, equivalent to a reduction of almost 40% (LegCo, 2007).

Nature Conservation

Under the government's nature conservation policy, ecologically important conservation areas are protected through the country park system and by planning controls such as the designation of Sites of Special Scientific Interest and Conservation Area zoning. In addition, a mechanism has been set up, as required by the EIAO, to compensate for areas that merit conservation but that have, nonetheless, been lost to accommodate important development projects. In Hong Kong, as an indication of the city's commitment to nature conservation, about 43% of the city's land area has been placed under some kind of statutory protection — not a small achievement for a city with a large population and high development pressure (ACE, 2004). The Wetland Park at Tin Shui Wai and the KCRC's Lok Ma Chau wetland are two successful examples of the recreation of critical wildlife habitats through the compensation principle under the EIAO process.

However, there is growing evidence to suggest that the existing conservation measures are not effective at protecting privately-owned sites of high ecological importance from harmful human activities such as changing agricultural practices and the filling in of land. The failure to stop war games and off-road driving activities at Sha Lo Tung and the conversion of wet agricultural land into a golf course range at Sham Chung are two typical examples of incompatible human activities infringing on ecologically important areas. In addition, the Sheung Shui–Lok Ma Chau Spur Line railway project, launched in 1999, highlights the limitations of the present EIA system. This system helped to stop an ecologically unacceptable development project from damaging the Long Valley wetland, but cannot ensure the long-term conservation of the site because it falls under private ownership. The government finally recognized this limitation and attempted to address this issue through the New Conservation Policy (NCP) promulgated in November 2004 (ACE, 2004).

In the new policy document, a more comprehensive policy statement was made to replace the earlier one, which had been announced and published in 1993 in association with the 2nd Review of the 1989 White Paper on the environment. A scoring system for assessing the ecological value of potential conservation sites as well as two pilot schemes, namely the Management Agreement (MA) and Public Private Partnership (PPP) schemes, were introduced to help address the issue of the conservation of ecologically important sites owned by private entities. Under the MA pilot scheme, NGOs are encouraged to enter into Management Agreements with the landowners concerned, either with government subsidies or through their own financial resources, to manage privately-owned but ecologically important land areas to meet the city's overall nature conservation objectives. Under the PPP pilot scheme, an individual who owns an ecologically important site is allowed to develop a less sensitive section of his site provided that he undertakes long-term obligations to manage and conserve the ecologically more sensitive portion of the site (ACE, 2004).

By early 2007, a total of 12 priority sites had been identified by the scoring system for enhanced conservation. In 2005, a fund of about HK$4.6 million from the Environmental and Conservation Fund was granted to support three pilot MA projects led by three NGOs at Fung Yuen and Long Valley. By early 2007, six applications had been submitted by developers under the PPP pilot scheme but little progress has been made thus far on these applications. On the other hand, the early results of the three pilot MA projects suggest that this scheme is quite effective in conserving and enhancing the biodiversity of ecologically important sites (NCSC, 2007).

Several other outstanding issues were identified during the public consultation exercise for the NCP but have not been addressed in the new policy document. These issues include marine conservation, conservation plans for rare and endemic species, and the restoration of degraded habitats such as lowland streams and wetlands. In addition, there are calls for the formulation of a biodiversity strategy and an action plan for Hong Kong in line with the requirements of the Convention on Biological Diversity (ACE, 2004).

Air Pollution and Cross-boundary Cooperation

Since the early 1990s, there has been increasing concern in Hong Kong about cross-boundary pollution resulting from rapid urbanization and industrialization taking place in the Pearl River Delta (PRD) region (Lee, 2002b). Although institutional structures have been put in place since then to facilitate cross-boundary cooperation on environmental management, effective policy actions on regional-level environmental planning and management are still few and far between. In spite of the rapid and sustained deterioration of region's air quality, for instance, the progress made through cross-boundary collaborative efforts to tackle air pollution has been extremely limited.

The issue of air pollution is singled out here for in-depth discussion alongside the problem of cross-boundary cooperation because it has topped the agenda of cross-boundary negotiations on the environment since the late 1990s. In the past several years, the cooperative efforts in environmental management across jurisdictional boundaries between Hong Kong and Guangdong have been driven primarily by the public's heightened concern over regional air pollution problems such as smog (as perceived in the Hong Kong SAR) and acid precipitation (as conceded in Guangdong). However, very little progress has been made in alleviating these region-wide air pollution problems, despite the fact that they have been ostensibly given a high priority by authorities on both sides of the boundary.

This begs the question of why cross-boundary cooperative efforts on the environment sector, as exemplified by actions to mitigate air pollution at the regional scale, have been less than satisfactory. Studies have identified several factors accounting for that limited progress: a lack of detailed scientific data to inform policies; a lack of political commitment on the part of government officials on both sides of the boundary to take action; and the presence of some entrenched institutional barriers towards cross-boundary cooperation. Before we examine the root causes of such barriers to closer cooperative efforts, it is instructive to review the early efforts and the ensuing changing dynamics of cross-boundary cooperation on environmental management.

Early Efforts in Cross-boundary Cooperation

In the early 1990s, the most visible cross-boundary pollution problem observed in Hong Kong was marine water pollution in Deep Bay. Regarded as the second most polluted body of water after Victoria Harbour, Deep Bay, which is located in the north-western part of Hong Kong at the mouth of the Shenzhen River, lies between Hong Kong and Shenzhen and was receiving pollutants draining from both cities (Hills and Barron, 1990; Lee, 2002a). Concern was also raised at about the same time about widespread transboundary marine pollution problems in the Pearl River estuary (Hills et al., 1998) and Mirs Bay (Liu and Hills, 1998). Since 1997, however, environmental scientists in Hong Kong have been asserting that, as far as cross-boundary environmental problems are concerned, the worst could be yet to come from air pollution. They predicted, rightly, that air quality in Hong Kong would worsen significantly because increased local efforts to tackle vehicular emissions would be greatly undermined by rapidly expanding volumes of emissions from the explosive growth of motor vehicles in cities in the PRD region, as well as a rapid industrial growth there.

Indeed, since the mid-1990s, the air quality in Hong Kong has been deteriorating steadily and significantly, particularly in terms of ambient concentrations of RSP and TSP. The decline in air quality has in part been attributed to road traffic emissions generated within Hong Kong, most notably those from diesel vehicles. Major episodes of pollution marked by impaired visibility and elevated levels of the Air Pollution Index (API) have, however, been found to be linked to the effects of wind direction (Planning Department, 1998). Days with high ambient concentrations of RSP have been associated with northerly and north-easterly winds blowing from jurisdictions north of the city's boundary (ERM-Hong Kong, 1997).

Although marine water pollution has remained a serious concern, the precipitous and continuous drop in air quality has captured the attention of both government officials and the general public, and heightened their awareness of cross-boundary pollution issues. Compared with polluted bodies of marine water, the haze that now envelops Hong Kong for much of the winter is highly visible and constantly reminds the public of the decline in air quality. This direct personal observation is then reinforced on a daily basis by the official release of API readings extensively reported in the mass media. The significance of this problem has been further amplified by several episodes of pollution that have been widely publicized in the international media since early 1998, arousing much concern among the elite about their impact on Hong Kong's reputation as an international financial centre and major tourist destination.

Both prior to and after the 1997 handover, major stakeholder groups such as environmental NGOs, politicians and the corporate sector have urged the Hong Kong government to strengthen cooperative ties with Mainland jurisdictions to address cross-boundary environmental issues. Although some mechanisms were established, as far back as 1990, to help coordinate such issues, progress since then has remained slow and accomplishments limited. The first bilateral cross-boundary coordinating body focusing on environmental matters, the Hong Kong–Guangdong Environmental Protection Liaison Group, was formed in July 1990. This group was comprised of high-ranking government officials in charge of the environment portfolio on both sides of the boundary. It was given a clearly defined mandate to enhance cross-boundary cooperation and coordination on environmental management and pollution-control efforts.

Reflecting the primary concern at that time, the Liaison Group was supported by a technical sub-group that met quite frequently — once every two months — and focused on the problem of establishing common standards and objectives for protecting the ecosystem in Deep Bay (EPD, 1998).

Given that the Liaison Group was never given the authority to develop policy or to ensure the effective implementation of policies and programmes, it had remained largely a formal forum for discussion between officials from the SAR and Guangdong. In addition, the Liaison Group's agenda was defined by issues and its purview excluded the development of a comprehensive framework for the environmental management of the larger PRD region, of which Hong Kong is a major stakeholder. Thus, the Liaison Group's major achievements pertain to a freer exchange of information between the two governments of the Hong Kong SAR and Guangdong. But it could not effect policy actions tackling environmental problems originating in the latter or impacting on the former, and vice versa (Hills and Roberts, 2001).

In 1999, the HKSAR's Chief Executive, for the first time in the post-1997 era, highlighted the importance of tackling cross-boundary environmental problems in his annual policy address:

> Hong Kong cannot possibly solve all its environmental problems single-handedly. We need to work closely with the Mainland authorities.... We also need the cooperation of our neighbours, for example, to protect our air and water quality. They in turn need our support since some of their pollution problems originate from our economic activities (Tung, 1999, p. 39).

In line with the words and spirit of the Policy Address, the Liaison Group was replaced and its functions taken over by the Hong Kong–Guangdong Joint Working Group on Sustainable Development and Environmental Protection established in the same year. Led by the SAR's Secretary for Environment and Food and by the Director of the Guangdong Environmental Protection Bureau, the scope of the Joint Working Group's agenda was much broader than that of the Liaison Group. Six areas of priority were identified: improving air quality in the region; improving water quality in their respective jurisdictions; exchanging experiences in urban planning and sustainable development; improving the water quality in the Dongjiang; strengthening nature conservation; and examining the feasibility of unifying diesel fuel standards in the region.

Out of these six areas of priority, regional air quality quickly became the focal point of cross-boundary environmental cooperation because of the intense publicity brought about by the several major episodes of pollution alluded to earlier. This focus on regional air quality has, in turn, helped to intensify cooperative activities between the two neighbouring jurisdictions. Since then, the efforts to address Hong Kong's air pollution problem have been increasingly characterized by a two-pronged approach: While attention was increasingly being diverted to regional sources of air pollutants after a sharp increase in the number of hazy days in the city since the turn of the century, the persistently high concentrations of air pollutants found at the street level in densely populated districts have caused the public to continue to prod the Hong Kong SAR government to find a way to tackle local sources of air pollutants. By now, the issue of whether priority should be given to tackling regional or local sources of air pollutants has, in itself, turned into a policy debate as well as the subject of scientific inquiry in Hong Kong. Therefore, it is instructive to review how the local sources have been dealt with before we examine the impact of intensified cross-boundary cooperation on both local and regional sources of the SAR's air pollution.

Deteriorating Street-level Air Quality and Local Mitigation Measures

Hong Kong experienced a number of serious episodes of air pollution towards the end of the 1990s that attracted considerable attention from the local and international media. Since then, the government has undertaken a proactive programme to improve the city's ambient air quality, especially with regard to controlling emissions from diesel-powered vehicles. The aim of the programme, launched in 1999, was to reduce particulate emissions coming from vehicles by 80% and nitrogen dioxide emissions by 30% by the end of 2005. The main elements of the programme included the tightening of fuel and vehicle emission standards, the adoption of cleaner alternative fuels wherever practicable, the reduction of emissions from the remaining diesel engines by the installation of catalytic converters or particulate traps, and the strengthening of vehicle emission inspections and enforcement activities (EPD, 2007b).

The programme relied heavily on direct financial subsidies. For example, in order to encourage the rapid conversion of the 18,000 diesel-powered taxis to liquefied petroleum gas (LPG) vehicles, the government provided a one-off grant of HK$40,000 per vehicle for taxi owners in a subsidy programme that commenced in 2000. A similar scheme was offered to owners of 6,000 diesel-powered public light buses — a one-off grant of HK$60,000 and HK$80,000 was offered for each diesel-powered light bus replaced with, respectively, an LPG-driven or electric vehicle. The excise duty for LPG-powered light buses was also waived and, in order to encourage the timely provision of associated infrastructure, operators of dedicated LPG filling stations were granted sites for no land premium. By the end of 2003, when the programme was completed, almost all (99.8%) of the taxis in Hong Kong had been converted to LPG-based vehicles, and nearly 80% of newly registered public light buses were LPG-driven (EPD, 2007b).

By the end of 2005, in the urban areas, the overall RSPs and nitrogen oxide (NOx) emissions from vehicles had been reduced by about 80% and 40%, respectively, when compared with the emission levels of 1999. Since 1999, RSPs and NOx levels recorded at roadside stations had also been reduced by 14% and 17%, respectively, despite a rapid increase in regional air pollution affecting Hong Kong. During this period, the number of smoky vehicles had also been reduced by about 80% (EPD, 2007b).

Despite all of the effort and investment put into improving the city's air quality, the gains that have been made from 1993 to 2002 in reducing the concentrations of major types of air pollutants have been compromised by the increasingly potent impact of transboundary air pollution, manifested locally as the sharply rising number of days of impaired visibility between 2000 and 2005 (Figure 15.1). In fact, a series of actions were triggered as early as 1998, just one year before the cross-boundary dimension of the city's air pollution problem was formally acknowledged, for the first time since the handover, by the Chief Executive in his 1999 Policy Address (Tung, 1999). In late 1998, for instance, the two governments of the Hong Kong SAR and Guangdong had already agreed to conduct a joint consultancy study on the problem of regional air quality in the PRD region.

This represented a major step forward in cross-boundary cooperation on environmental matters because the study was fully funded by Hong Kong's EPD, but its geographical scope extended far beyond Hong Kong's jurisdiction. As the first major collaborative regional transboundary analysis involving environmental officials from both governments, it explicitly acknowledged that region-wide problems could only be tackled effectively by a response structured at the regional level, scientifically and institutionally speaking. Moreover, the tacit recognition on the part of Hong Kong's government officials of the need to bring in a regional context to address at least some of Hong Kong's environmental problems signified the beginning

Figure 15.1 Air Pollutants Emitted in Hong Kong, 1990–2005

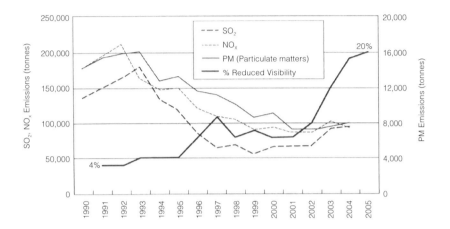

Source: EPD, 2007b.

of a new phase of policy-making in the field of environmental management in the SAR government (Hills, 2002). This joint study, prompted largely by increasing concern over the impact of a highly visible regional smog problem, laid the foundation for an intensified phase of cross-boundary cooperation on the environment sector.

Regional Smog and Intensified Cross-boundary Cooperation

The joint study was completed in April 2002. In their Final Report, the consultants asserted that the region's air pollution problem was similar in nature to that faced by other cities in China and was caused primarily by ozone, respirable suspended particulates and nitrogen oxides (CH2M HILL [China] Limited, 2002). In addition, the Report concluded that poor air quality at the street level in Hong Kong was caused by high volumes of traffic and that this problem could, therefore, be controlled by independent actions within the SAR. Controlling the problem of region-wide air pollution, however, would require the concerted effort of both the Hong Kong SAR and Guangdong provincial governments.

The consultants anticipated that, with the increase in population and economic activities, the emissions of sulfur dioxide (SO_2), NO_x, RSPs and volatile organic compounds (VOCs) in the region would increase by 53%, 34%, 34% and 25%, respectively, in 2010 when compared with the base year of 1997. What was alarming to the two governments was that the consultants also stated that, even with committed measures by the two governments to control air pollution, regional emissions of SO_2, NO_x, RSPs and VOCs would be expected to increase from 1997 to 2015 by 75%, 40%, 45% and 36%, respectively (CH2M HILL [China] Limited, 2002, p. ES-6).

The verdict was clear: Additional control measures would have to be introduced as soon as possible to substantially reduce emissions of these four key pollutants by 2010 at the earliest. And such measures would have to be supported by extensive inter-governmental cooperation. Fully accepting the recommendations made in the Report, in April 2002 the two governments agreed to take immediate action to aim at reducing by 2010, on a best endeavour basis, the regional emissions of SO_2, NO_x, RSPs and VOCs by 40%, 20%, 55% and 55%, respectively, using 1997 as the base year (Government Information Centre, 2002). The SAR government claimed that achieving these targets would not only enable Hong Kong to meet its current Air Quality Objectives, but also significantly improve the region's air quality and hence alleviate the regional smog problem (EPD, 2007b).

In December 2003, as one of the follow-up actions pertaining to the 2002 joint study Final Report, the two governments jointly drew up the PRD region Air Quality Management Plan to formulate specific measures to meet the above emission reduction targets (EPD, 2003b). The following tasks were set out in the Management Plan:

-   implementing a set of measures to enhance the potential of the air pollution control measures;
-   setting up a reliable monitoring system for providing quick and accurate data on regional air quality;
-   compiling a regional atmospheric emissions inventory for the two governments to evaluate the progress and effectiveness of the air pollution control measures;
-   strengthening technical exchanges and training programmes to officers of the region with a view to enhancing their knowledge of regional air quality issues and to upgrade their scientific and technological capabilities for more effective management and monitoring work; and
-   collecting local and overseas information on new technologies and

management practices on controlling air pollution and to study the feasibility of introducing them into the region.

Meaningful and useful data to gauge the actual impact of these regional-level actions have not yet been made available to researchers. Nevertheless, the Hong Kong SAR government has kept up the momentum to tackle the local sources of air pollutants. In part driven and informed by the Management Plan, it has implemented a number of emission reduction measures, such as tightening up the quality of motor petrol to Euro IV standards with effect from 1 January 2005, providing a one-off grant totalling HK$3.2 billion to encourage the owners of 74,000 diesel-powered commercial vehicles to replace their worn-out trucks, and negotiating with the power companies to further reduce emissions from their power plants (EPD, 2007b). As a result of the various emission reduction measures that have been implemented in recent years, some progress has been made in achieving the emission reduction targets. With the exception of SO_2, the amount of emissions of the other three major pollutants has been substantially reduced (Table 15.2). The failure to reduce SO_2 emissions has been attributed to the recent increase in emissions from Hong Kong's own power plants.

Notwithstanding the substantial reduction in local emissions recorded between 1997 and 2004, concerns among the general public as well as the private sector about the problem of air pollution have continued to grow as the city's visibility continued to deteriorate over the same period. In response to the public outcry on the matter, the government launched the "Action Blue Sky" campaign on 25 July 2006 to show its determination to improve Hong Kong's overall air quality. The Hong Kong SAR government also has plans to commission a comprehensive study in 2007 to review the city's two-decade old Air Quality Objectives and to develop a long-term air quality management strategy (EPD, 2007b).

Table 15.2 Progress Made in Achieving the 2010 Emissions Reduction Targets

	1997 Emission (tonnes)	2004 Emission (tonnes)	Changes 1997–2004	2010 Emission targets
SO_2	64,500	94,800	+47%	−40%
NO_x	110,000	92,500	−16%	−20%
RSPs	11,200	8,040	−28%	−55%
VOCs	54,400	41,900	−23%	−55%

Source: EPD, 2007b.

Cho-nam Ng and Yok-shiu F. Lee

Perhaps due to a growing awareness of their shared responsibility for the problem of regional air quality, the Hong Kong–Guangdong Business Coalition on the Environment launched the "Clean Air Charter" initiative in 2006. This was a voluntary scheme that encouraged businesses to adopt a number of air quality management measures, driven by a commitment "to operate to a recognized world class standard on emission of air pollutants, even if it is not a requirement to do so here" (HKGCC, 2006).

Entrenched Institutional Barriers to Closer Cooperation

In the early years of the post-1997 era, many critics attributed the lack of substantial progress on cross-boundary environmental cooperation to three major institutional constraints that have been impeding the application of more effective and persuasive efforts to address region-wide pollution problems (Lee, 2002b). First, under the OCTS framework, which was designed to preserve and protect Hong Kong's autonomy, any major cross-boundary initiatives at cooperation would need to originate from the Hong Kong SAR government in order to be considered viable by the central authorities. One unintended consequence of such an institutional arrangement has been that Mainland environmental officials have found it very difficult to liaise effectively with their counterparts in Hong Kong. Given the accepted, though hidden, understanding of the provisions of the OCTS framework, the SAR government has often been blamed for its unwillingness to exercise its prerogative to initiate cooperative projects with its neighbouring jurisdictions (Hills and Roberts, 2001). In addition, the importance attached in the Basic Law to preserving the SAR's high degree of autonomy has stifled rather than encouraged the development of institutions dedicated to strengthening cross-boundary cooperation.

Second, some government officials within the Hong Kong SAR administration are concerned about the cost of compromising their autonomy in any cross-boundary cooperative accord. Observers have detected little enthusiasm among Hong Kong civil servants for any substantial form of collaboration with their Mainland counterparts that might lead to undue influence on their own policy formulation process. Some Hong Kong government officials have continued to express reservations about the provision of financial support to Mainland-based pollution-abatement schemes, even if such projects would lead to direct or indirect benefits to Hong Kong's environment and were proven to be more cost-effective than local clean-up initiatives. In addition, many sceptics were also fearful that even a handful of assistance projects could mushroom into an overwhelming number of requests from a multitude of jurisdictions from across the boundary for joint funding ventures (Lee, 2002b).

Third, despite the creation of a succession of cross-boundary coordination committees devoted to cooperative efforts in cleaning up the environment, critics have argued that Hong Kong's current mode of cooperation with its neighbouring jurisdictions is still very much ad hoc and reactive in nature. In addition, there is a glaring lack of a unified policy on cross-boundary issues on the part of the Hong Kong SAR administration. In fact, with the membership of cross-boundary coordinating bodies invariably comprised of officials drawn from various computations of policy bureaus and departments, responsibilities on cross-boundary issues, including the environment sector, are diffused and diluted in bureaucracy. Such an inter-departmental committee approach also helps to reinforce the notion of a lack of an institutional home base and an incoherent strategy for cross-boundary cooperation initiatives.

To be fair, the Hong Kong SAR administration has become more proactive in recent years about approaching the Guangdong provincial government and inviting the latter to undertake joint projects to mitigate cross-boundary environmental problems. For instance, the Hong Kong SAR government has raised the proposal of emissions trading to devise and introduce, in partnership with the Guangdong provincial authorities, a voluntary tool to encourage power plants in the region to meet reduction targets in a cost-effective manner. An implementation framework for an emissions trading pilot scheme was announced on 30 January 2007. However, this proposal has received a lukewarm response from the local power sector as well as the Guangdong provincial government. Critics have argued that the rather subdued response of the latter stems from the fact that the authorities in Guangdong are even more pro-growth than the SAR government and, therefore, are less than enthusiastic about placing any restrictions on the development of their power sector.

Conclusion

Similar to its colonial predecessor, the post-handover government has failed to promulgate a comprehensive and integrated environmental policy. Despite the strengthening of environmental safeguards through the adoption of some new initiatives, the SAR government has yet to produce a badly needed sustainable development strategy and a globally oriented, regionally focused Local Agenda 21. Notwithstanding such limitations, the post-1997 approach has made a number of important breakthroughs. The practices of environmental management, for instance, have become vastly different from those of the colonial era in two major aspects. First, primarily due to the newly introduced legislation on the EIA process, public engagement has been fully legitimized and formalized as a policy tool. A high degree of transparency and ready access to environmental information associated with the EIA process have allowed the larger community to play a more active and influential role in the processes of deliberating and formulating environmental measures. Stakeholders, along with the general public, are frequently invited to voice their opinions, and are capable of commenting intelligently at public forums on proposed policies and programmes. As such, the public's view now carries substantial weight that could, at times, directly affect the outcome of environmental debates.

Second, overcoming bureaucratic inertia, scepticism and political opposition, the repertoire of policy tools at the disposal of the environmental managers has been enlarged in the last 10 years to include some economic instruments. The financial subsidy scheme of the year 2000, to encourage owners of diesel-powered taxis to switch to LPG vehicles, has been generally regarded as a success: road-side air quality has improved measurably and markedly as a consequence. After being delayed for years because of resistance from vested interests, the successful launch of the Construction Waste Disposal Charging Scheme in 2005 signalled the reinforcement of the public's acceptance of the merits of putting the polluter-pays principle into practice. The proposition of a charging scheme for the use of plastic shopping bags in 2007 provides further evidence of this trend. While the command-and-control method has remained the dominant approach, the adoption of such economic instruments hints at a gradual shift away from the practices of the pre-1997 colonial government.

Despite the breakthroughs made in the overall approach to managing the environment and the introduction of some major initiatives, serious challenges remain. At the neighbourhood level, for instance, concerns have been raised by environmental and community groups about the need to critically examine the ramifications of town-planning practices, such as outdated urban design schemes, on district-level ventilation and air quality. These concerns, in fact, remind the government of the need to incorporate environmental factors into land-use planning and urban design schemes to improve street-level air quality. At the city-wide scale, highly visible environmental problems such as impaired visibility will very likely persist into the 2010s, even when all of the local emission control programmes have been fully implemented, because emissions from the PRD region will definitely continue to increase and negate the impact of local efforts. Nonetheless, the increasing frequency of smoggy days will weigh on the government, and force it to re-think the need to integrate energy policy with environmental policy to improve energy-use efficiency and reduce local emissions. In terms of cross-boundary environmental cooperation, substantial progress has indeed been made on the problem of regional air pollution. But it is only one of six areas of priority in which neighbouring jurisdictions need to take cooperative action. And such actions have thus far been few and far between because of some entrenched institutional constraints that keep Hong Kong from forging a closer form of cooperation on transboundary environmental matters. All indications thus point to an uphill and protracted battle to achieve improvements in the environment in and around the SAR.

Note

1.   The unprecedented nature of this case earned it a place on *Time* Magazine's five best environmental news items in the world in the year 2000 (*Time*, 18 December 2000).

References

Advisory Council on the Environment (ACE) (2000), Review of the Strategic Sewage Disposal Scheme, ACE Paper 07/2000.

—— (2001), The Way Forward for Sewage Treatment for the Harbour Area, ACE Paper 08/2001.

—— (2004), New Conservation Policy, ACE Paper 37/2004.

Barron, William (1996), "Environment and the Political Economy of Hong Kong." In D. Mole (ed.), *Managing the New Hong Kong Economy*. Hong Kong: Oxford University Press, pp. 127–49.

Barron, William and Neil Steinbrecher (1999) (eds.), *Heading Towards Sustainability? Practical Indicators of Sustainability for Hong Kong*. Hong Kong: Centre of Urban Planning and Environmental Management, The University of Hong Kong.

Conservancy Association (CA) (2003), *Environmental Campaign from 1968 to 2003*. The Conservancy Association.

CH2M HILL (China) Limited (2002), *Final Report: Study of Air Quality in the*

Pearl River Delta Region. Agreement No CE. 106/98. Hong Kong: CH2M HILL (China) Limited.

EIA Appeal Board (2001), *Judgement of Appeal for Sheung Shui to Lok Ma Chau Spurline,* No. 2 of 2000, 30 July. http://www.epd.gov.hk/eia/board/decision. html.

Environmental Protection Department (EPD) (1998), *Environment Hong Kong 1998.* Hong Kong SAR Government.

—— (2003a), *Environment Hong Kong 2003.* Hong Kong: Environmental Protection Department.

—— (2003b), *Key Points of the Pearl River Delta Regional Air Quality Management Plan.* Hong Kong: Environmental Protection Department.

—— (2005), *A Policy Framework for Municipal Solid Waste in Hong Kong (2005–2014).* Hong Kong: Environmental Protection Department, December.

—— (2007a), EIAO website. 2007a. http://www.epd.gov.hk/eia/english/images/general/topbar01.gif

—— (2007b), EPD website. 2007b. http://www.epd.gov.hk/epd/eindex.html

ERM-Hong Kong (1997), *Territory-wide Air Quality Modelling Systems: Proposed Modelling Events and Scenarios.* Hong Kong: ERM-Hong Kong.

Government Information Centre (2002), *Consensus Reached to Improve Regional Air Quality.* Hong Kong: Government Information Centre of the Hong Kong SAR Government, April 29.

Hong Kong Government (HKG) (1989), *White Paper: Pollution in Hong Kong — A Time to Act.* Hong Kong: Hong Kong Government Printer.

Hong Kong General Chamber of Commence (HKGCC) (2006), *The Clean Air Charter — A Business Guidebook.* HKGCC.

Hills, Peter (1990), "Can the Dragon Clean Its Nest?" *Environment* 32: 16–20, 39–45.

—— (1997), "The Environmental Agenda in Post-Colonial Hong Kong," *Local Environment,* 2.2: 203–7.

—— (2002), "Environmental Policy and Planning in Hong Kong: An Emerging Regional Agenda," *Sustainable Development,* 10.3: 171–78.

Hills, Peter and William Barron (1997), "Hong Kong: The Challenge of Sustainability," *Land Use Policy,* 14.1: 41–53.

Hills, Peter and Peter Roberts (2001), "Political Integration, Transboundary Pollution and Sustainability: Challenges for Environmental Policy in the Pearl River Delta Region," *Journal of Environmental Planning and Management,* 44.4: 455–73.

Hills, Peter and Peter Roberts, Zhang Lei and Liu Jianhua (1998), "Transboundary Pollution Between Guangdong Province and Hong Kong: Threats to Water Quality in the Pearl River Estuary and Their Implications for Environmental Policy and Planning," *Journal of Environmental Planning and Management,* 41.3:375–96.

Lee, Yok-shiu F. (2002a), "Towards Effective Regional Environmental Governance for the Hong Kong-Pearl River Delta Border Zone: The Relevance of Some International Experiences." In Anthony Gar-on Yeh, Yok-shiu F. Lee, Tunney Lee and Nien Dak Sze (eds.), *Building a Competitive Pearl River Delta Region: Cooperation, Coordination and Planning.* Hong Kong: Centre of Urban Planning and Environmental Management, The University of Hong Kong, pp. 205–33.

―――― (2002b), "Tackling Cross-border Environmental Problems in Hong Kong: Initial Responses and Institutional Constraints," *The China Quarterly*, 172: 986–1009.

Legislative Council (LegCo) (2007), *Progress Report on Construction Waste Disposal Charging Scheme.* Legislative Council Panel on Environmental Affairs Paper CB(1) 1182/06-07(04).

Leverett, Bill, Lisa Hopkinson, Christine Loh and Kate Trumbull (2007), *Idling Engine: Hong Kong's Environmental Policy in a Ten-year Stall, 1997–2007.* Hong Kong: Civic Exchange.

Liu, Jianhua and Peter Hills (1998), "Sustainability and Coastal Zone Management in Hong Kong: The Case of Mirs Bay," *International Journal of Sustainable Development and World Ecology*, 5:11–26.

MVA and Maunsell (2000), *The Second Railway Develop Strategy — Final Strategic Environmental Assessment Report.* http://www.info.gov.hk/epd/eia/content/index.htm.

Nature Conservation Sub-committee (NCSC), Advisory Council on the Environment (2007), *Review of Pilot Conservation Management Agreement Projects*, NCSC Paper 1/07.

Ng, Cho-nam (2007), Personal research file on EIA in Hong Kong.

Planning, Environment and Lands Branch (PELB) (1993), *Second Review of Progress of the 1989 White Paper: Pollution in Hong Kong — A Time to Act.* Hong Kong: Hong Kong Government, 1993.

―――― (1998), *Waste Reduction Framework.* Hong Kong: Hong Kong Government.

Planning Department (1998), *Development Trends in the Pearl River Delta and Related Transboundary Issues. Topic Report 3, Study on Sustainable Development for the 21st Century.* Hong Kong: Planning Department.

Tung, Chee-hwa (1997), *A Future of Excellence and Prosperity for All.* Address by the Chief Executive at the Legislative Council Meeting. Hong Kong: Printing Department, Government of the HKSAR.

―――― (1998), *From Adversity to Opportunity.* Address by the Chief Executive at the Legislative Council Meeting. Hong Kong: Printing Department, Government of the HKSAR.

―――― (1999), *Quality People — Quality Home: Positioning Hong Kong for the 21st Century.* Address by the Chief Executive at the Legislative Council Meeting on 6 October. Hong Kong: Printing Department, Government of the HKSAR.

16

Public Health Challenges and Reform

Lee Shiu-hung and Wong Tze-wai

Introduction

Over the past decades, public health in Hong Kong has gone through an exciting period of development. In the old days, public health was viewed as a matter of environmental hygiene and sanitation. Public health is now defined as the science and art of promoting health, preventing diseases and prolonging life through the organized efforts of society. In the twenty-first century, public health covers a much wider area than ever before, as described below (Lee, 1994).

New Challenges in Public Health

Emergence of New Infectious Diseases

In Hong Kong today, it is increasingly common for people to move around. Destruction, pollution and the overcrowding of our living environment are the direct results of urbanization. Urban development also increases human contact with reservoirs for infectious agents such as insect vectors and animals. Furthermore, the indiscriminate use of anti-microbial agents and insecticides encourages the microbial agents and disease vectors to develop a resistance to antibiotics and pesticides. It is, therefore, no surprise that new or re-emerging infectious diseases, often caused by drug-resistant strains, will continue to pose a serious threat to human health in the future.

Socially Related Health Problems

Hong Kong's social environment is undergoing rapid changes. Changes in lifestyle and human behaviour have led to a rise in many socially related public health problems such as smoking, drug abuse, obesity, accidents and injuries, and mental illness. Many such problems have been found in children and young people. Chronic diseases have begun to occur even in the young. There is, therefore, an urgent need to conduct vigorous health promotion activities covering the physical, mental and social aspects of health among the young, so that they will have the wisdom, confidence and competence to make wise choices regarding their health. To address this growing problem, the World Health Organization (WHO) is actively promoting the practice of healthy lifestyles, and encouraging community participation in tackling the social determinants of health.

Chronic Non-communicable Diseases

With an ageing population, chronic non-communicable diseases have become the major causes of death and ill health in society. This trend is likely to continue. The burden on existing treatment and rehabilitation services will become increasingly heavy. However, many chronic diseases or disabling conditions can be prevented and the effects can be minimized through primary, secondary or tertiary prevention. Being old does not mean being ill. The crux is to improve the quality of life of elderly people and to minimize the onset of disabling conditions and diseases — the "compression of morbidity." Many activities to promote "healthy living" and "active ageing" have been organized in Hong Kong through government departments, NGOs, the community, District Councils and the Commission for the Elderly. The Department of Health has also established a task force to work out a comprehensive plan for the prevention and control of chronic non-communicable diseases. It is expected that more vigorous health promotion programmes and campaigns will be conducted in the future to tackle the major causes of ill health.

Healthcare System

Hong Kong's healthcare system has been hailed by overseas experts as being equitable, easily accessible and offered at a cost that the community can afford. But in the past decade, Hong Kong's healthcare system has come under heavy strain. In order to maintain the quality and scope of our public health service, it is necessary to introduce further healthcare reforms and to explore alternative ways of financing the healthcare system. The healthcare system of the future will need to focus on four important areas, namely cost effectiveness, long-term financial viability, an efficient public health system and quality assurance.

Globalization

Globalization brings with it many new challenges to public health. On the positive side, globalization offers opportunities for access and the transfer of knowledge, which is one of the major determinants of health. Globalization makes it easier to achieve efficient transport, communication and trade systems. It also provides good opportunities for economic transitions, the production of goods and marketing on an international basis.

On the other hand, globalization has brought significant threats to public health. For example, globalization via trade and economic agreements has facilitated the movement of tobacco and alcohol products to developing countries, providing a lucrative market for the tobacco industry. Through a variety of complex factors, such as advertising, promotion and sponsorship, trade liberalization and foreign direct investment, multi-national tobacco companies have intensified their marketing practices to promote their products in developing countries. This will also mean that national governments in developing countries will find it more difficult to introduce effective policies to control the sale of tobacco products.

Massive movements of people, migrant workers and tourists have created multiple new challenges for the promotion of health and prevention of diseases. It has created a complex environment within which different types of health threats and risks can spread with enormous speed, such as HIV/AIDS, sexually transmitted infections and infectious diseases like severe acute respiratory syndrome (SARS). Globalization has also led to an increase in non-communicable diseases, such as through the marketing of the fast-food culture, consumerism and the glorification of a highly stressful lifestyle as symbolic of social success.

Cross-boundary Integration between Hong Kong and the Mainland

There are special factors that make Hong Kong particularly vulnerable to outbreaks of infectious diseases. First is the increase in the number of local residents travelling to countries and areas outside Hong Kong and the large number of visitors coming to Hong Kong from other countries and from neighbouring areas. The second factor is the globalization of the food supply. A considerable amount of vegetables and other fresh foods is imported to Hong Kong from neighbouring countries and areas. There is a need to ensure the quality and safety of food products imported from outside, in view of the increasing problem of environmental pollution in neighbouring countries and areas. Third, Hong Kong is adjacent to many countries and areas where endemic and epidemic diseases are prevalent.

As early as 1989, the WHO's Regional Office for the Western Pacific had established a surveillance system for important infectious diseases prevalent in the Pearl River Delta (PRD) region in Mainland China, Hong Kong and Macao. After the SARS outbreak in 2003, the surveillance system for infectious diseases was greatly strengthened. There are now regular meetings and exchanges of epidemiological information among the health authorities in these areas. With the establishment of the Centre for Health Protection (CHP) within the Department of Health in Hong Kong in 2004, it is anticipated that there will be greater collaboration, coordination and communication between Hong Kong and Mainland China in the prevention and control of infectious diseases.

Mainland Mothers

The phenomenon of expectant mothers from Mainland China coming to Hong Kong to give birth started to become a public issue in 2006 when the Audit Commission found that many of them failed to pay the fees and charges required by the Hospital Authority (HA) after delivery. The problem later escalated as it became apparent that not only is the practice of Mainland mothers coming to Hong Kong to give birth having a significant impact on the quality of health care, but that it could have wide-ranging social and economic ramifications, including on housing, education, welfare and the right of abode in Hong Kong.

According to the Department of Census and Statistics, in the past five years there has been a rapid and marked increase in the number of babies delivered in Hong Kong from pregnant mothers from the Mainland, from 620 in 2001 to 9,273 in 2005 and 12,398 in 2006 (first 10 months). The immediate impact of this has been on the quality of health care in Hong Kong and its availability to pregnant local mothers. The latter have raised many complaints and protests to the HA about the inadequacy of maternity beds, the overcrowding of maternity wards, and long waits for antenatal care and diagnostic investigations in public hospitals (*Wen Wei Po*, 7 December 2006).

At the same time, healthcare workers in Hong Kong's public hospitals are under great strain because of their increased workload from caring for the mothers and their newborn babies. These nursing professionals have taken their protests to the streets. In recent years, there had been a great reduction in staffing levels and hospital beds for maternity cases because of the decline in the fertility rate of local females. The sudden surge in their workload coming from Mainland mothers has obviously had an unfavourable impact on the quality of care received by local mothers and adversely affected the morale of healthcare workers.

In response to this challenge, the government, together with the HA, took immediate action to cope with the situation. Their first priority was to ensure that local mothers have easy access to all health services and receive quality health care throughout the entire period of their pregnancy and delivery in hospital. Their second action was to review the need to increase resources, particularly maternity beds and manpower, including midwives and obstetric specialists in public hospitals. Subsequently, the HA recruited more nurses, including those working in intensive neonatal care, and midwives.

Their third action was to introduce a plan to stop Mainland mothers from abusing the obstetric services of the public hospitals, while ensuring that those in real need have access to such services before giving birth. The plan involved establishing an appointment system for obstetric care in the HA for Mainland mothers. Fees and charges for delivering the babies of non-local residents have also been further increased. On 1 February 2007, a new measure was introduced at entry points at the border. Women who are at least seven months pregnant must give evidence that they have registered with the HA for delivery before being allowed to enter Hong Kong. Staff from the Department of Health in collaboration with the Immigration Department are responsible for screening such women (Press Release, HKSAR Government, 14 December 2006).

Since the introduction of the new procedure at the border, there has been a notable reduction in the number of expectant mothers coming to Hong Kong for delivery (*Ming Pao*, 21 December 2006). However, in the long run, a solution will need to be worked out in consultation with the China's central government. The rush of pregnant mothers coming to Hong Kong to give birth also has an impact on the Mainland's family planning policy. With the spectacular economic development in the Mainland and the attraction of the right of abode for children born in Hong Kong, many families in the Mainland can well afford to have their babies delivered in Hong Kong. Furthermore, the allocation of resources to increase the number of maternity beds and to recruit more staff and specialists in obstetric care in public hospitals is not in accordance with the prevailing sentiment in Hong Kong about what area of health care should be given priority in the allocation of scarce resources for the development of healthcare services in Hong Kong. With its ageing population and a rise in the number of people suffering from chronic diseases, Hong Kong needs to allocate more resources for the care of the elderly. The issue of Mainland mothers is a complex one that will take time to resolve. In the end, its resolution may require a review of the Basic Law after consultation with all sectors concerned.

Challenges in the Last Decade

Avian Influenza (H5N1)

Before the occurrence in May 1997 of the first case in which a human contracted a form of avian influenza, there were reports of large numbers of chickens dying in the chicken farms in Lau Fou Shan in the New Territories (NT) of Hong Kong. Upon examination, the H5N1 virus was detected in these chickens. In the following months, more deaths of chickens were reported at other chicken farms, wholesale markets and market stalls. In all, a total of 18 people fell ill with avian influenza during the 1997/1998 outbreak, 6 of whom died. An epidemiological investigation revealed that 7 of the 18 had come into contact with poultry. A laboratory investigation of 502 people who had contact with poultry showed that 9 of them had positive antibodies to the H5N1 virus. The highest positive rate, at 17.2%, was found among poultry workers, compared with an overall positive rate of 1.8%.

In the years since 1997, there have been numerous reports of the H5N1 virus being detected among chickens in Mainland China and in other countries in Southeast Asia, including Vietnam, Thailand and Indonesia. Human cases of avian influenza have also been reported in these countries.

As of 1 March 2004, the WHO has recorded a total of 33 confirmed human cases of avian influenza in Vietnam (23) and Thailand (10), and 22 deaths. The avian influenza virus has been detected in more than 10 provinces in Mainland China and more countries and areas in Southeast Asia have reported infections, including the Republic of Korea, Japan, Cambodia, Laos and Taiwan.

In view of the increasing global threat posed by avian influenza, on

30 January 2004 the Department of Health ordered that Influenza A (H5) be added to the first schedule of the Quarantine and Prevention of Disease Ordinance, Cap. 141, making the disease a statutorily notifiable one. The Department of Health has introduced a series of measures to prevent the disease. These include:

- Monitoring the situation through epidemiological surveillance, laboratory surveillance and the investigation of outbreaks of influenza-like-illnesses
- Vaccinating poultry workers against influenza for personal protection
- Launching publicity efforts to educate the public about to protect them against avian influenza
- Advising travellers to take precautionary measures when visiting places where outbreaks of avian influenza are reported to have occurred, including the practice of washing their hands and avoiding contact with seasonal birds.
- Putting a stop to the importation of poultry from areas affected with the disease.

Since late December 2003 and up to 12 January 2007, the WHO has recorded a total of 265 confirmed human cases of avian influenza A (H5N1). The countries and areas that have reported such cases include Taiwan, Cambodia, China, Pakistan, Canada, Indonesia, Laos, Thailand, the Republic of Korea and Vietnam.

The outbreaks of avian influenza (H5N1) have not only posed a threat to the health of people around the world, they have also had a significant impact on the security and economy of the countries affected. During the outbreak of avian influenza in Hong Kong, the tourism industry was hit hard. In an outbreak of H5N1, the greatest threat is the probability of a genetic reassortment between the avian and human influenza viruses. In reassortment with the exchange of genetic materials, the risk is that a highly pathogenic form of human influenza virus will evolve. Among the human cases of avian influenza that have been confirmed so far, there is epidemiological evidence that most contracted the infection through close proximity with poultry farms or close contact with chickens. If a highly pathogenic form of human influenza virus capable of airborne transmission were to be produced as a result of the reassortment of the two viruses, the result could be disastrous. Instead of a chicken-to-human route of transmission, the infection would be directly transmitted among the human population.

Since the outbreak of avian influenza, Hong Kong has taken an active role in partnering with the WHO and the health authorities of other countries to deal with the possibility of a global influenza pandemic. Within the Special Administrative Region (SAR) itself, strategies and plans have been worked out to tackle an influenza pandemic in Hong Kong. The plans cover three phases of a pandemic. The first phase is the period before the occurrence of a pandemic, the second concerns the emergency response during a pandemic and the last is the phase of recovery. The government's plan to introduce the central slaughtering of poultry so as to minimize the contact between humans and chickens is a step in the right direction.

In conclusion, the occurrence of an influenza pandemic is unpredictable and yet inevitable. Only those who are well prepared can respond well. Everybody in the community has an important role to play in its prevention and control. It is necessary for the health authority and the general public to maintain a high level of vigilance against the disease in the years to come.

Seasonal Migratory Birds

In November 2004, a dead seasonal bird in the Mai Po wetland in the NT was found to contain the H5N1 virus. In the following years, an increasing number of the local birds in the NT and in Hong Kong's urban districts that have been found dead have been discovered to harbour the H5N1 virus. This has caused concern among local residents, as bird droppings are often found in homes or on goods being sold in the markets.

There have also been reports that the avian influenza (H5N1) virus has been found in chickens and birds in other countries in the Asia-Pacific region and in areas of Europe. It has been postulated that avian influenza (H5N1) has established a foothold in the Asia-Pacific region and has become an endemic disease. Seasonal migratory birds may have played an important role in this respect, as these birds have long flying range over countries and even continents. The Mai Po wetland in the NT is a well-known stopover for seasonal birds from the northeastern part of Mainland China that migrate to the south during the winter. The presence of seasonal migratory birds will thus pose a threat to public health, as they could pass on the virus to local chickens and birds.

More research will need to be conducted on the impact of seasonal migratory birds on public health. The WHO has stated that there is a need to strengthen collaboration, coordination and communication between the public health sector and the agricultural and veterinary sectors to prevent and control avian influenza.

Severe Acute Respiratory Syndrome (SARS)

The first epidemic of SARS in the twenty-first century started to strike Hong Kong in March 2003. From 11 March and up to 6 June 2003, a total of 1,750 SARS cases were identified and 299 people had died from the disease. Prior to its outbreak in Hong Kong, a severe outbreak of atypical pneumonia had been reported in Guangdong.

Epidemiological investigations revealed that the SARS epidemic in Hong Kong went through three phases. The first phase was heralded by an explosive outbreak of the disease in a teaching hospital. The source of infection was a visiting professor from Guangdong. He developed SARS in Hong Kong and died in a Hong Kong hospital. The second phase was the spread of the disease to other hospitals and to the community. The third phase began in early May. It was characterized by continuing outbreaks in some hospitals and in a large number of housing estates. This situation had improved considerably by the beginning of June 2003.

Prevention and Control

As a first step, when the first few cases of SARS were identified, the Department of Health in Hong Kong passed legislation to include SARS as a notifiable infectious disease, making the provisions of the Ordinance and Regulations of the Quarantine and Prevention of Disease Cap. 141 applicable to SARS. SARS patients were isolated in the hospitals. Family members or those who had come into close contact with these patients were initially kept under surveillance at home, but were later transferred to isolated centres for observation for 10 days. It was during this early phase that researchers in The University of Hong Kong first identified the nature of the virus that causes SARS (a new coronavirus) and the animal reservoirs (civets and raccoon dog) of this new disease.

Public health workers undertook to investigate the source of the infection and to trace contacts. They also encouraged the application of control measures, including promoting personal protection through the wearing of masks, encouraging strict adherence to personal hygiene, and seeing to the disinfection and cleansing of affected households and housing estates. Strict port health measures were introduced to screen incoming or outgoing travellers with a fever exceeding 38°C, and those entering Hong Kong were required to complete health declaration forms. These measures were generally effective in that they raised the awareness of the public about the highly infectious nature of SARS, and about the need to take prompt preventive measures.

In the middle of May 2003 when the epidemic started to peter out, the government announced further measures to tackle the problems resulting from the epidemic. Three committees headed by top senior government officials were established. One committee was responsible for launching an overall cleansing campaign and for making environmental improvements to the housing estates in the city. The second committee was responsible for drawing up plans and programmes to revitalize the city's economy, including the areas of tourism, trade and employment. The third committee was charged with drawing up strategies and plans to promote community involvement and partnership in improving the physical, social and economic environments of the city. Additional funds were approved to support research on the treatment of SARS, on the development of vaccines for SARS and on the various clinical and diagnostic aspects of the disease. A Centre for Health Protection and Prevention was established within the Department of Health to strengthen surveillance, research, training and collaboration efforts with other health authorities, both regional and international.

At the end of May 2003, the Hong Kong SAR appointed a nine-member Committee to review the SARS epidemic in Hong Kong and to make recommendations on preventing and controlling the disease in the future. The expert team consisted of international experts from the U.S., the United Kingdom (U.K.), Australia, Mainland China and Hong Kong (HKSAR Government, 2003).

Conclusion

The epidemic not only severely affected the health of the people of Hong Kong, but also revealed the shortcomings of its public health system, including its public hospitals, with regard to infection control preparedness. It also produced many related social, economic and humanitarian problems, particularly in the areas of tourism, international travel and trade, and highlighted the importance of public health in the overall economic and social well-being of an urban community (Lee, 2003; 2005).

Hong Kong will continue to face the challenges posed by infectious diseases because of the emergence of new infections and the changing lifestyles and behaviour of the population. The epidemic, however, created a strong sense of unity that had not been experienced before, among all sectors of the population, the government, NGOs, and the medical and nursing personnel, as all joined in the effort to fight the epidemic.

Diverse Responses

The Chinese University of Hong Kong Jockey Club School of Public Health

Throughout the past few decades, most of Hong Kong's remarkable gains in health were achieved through the application of sound public health principles and practices. Despite these gains, there are still many challenges in public health, many of them new. A School of Public Health became urgently required in Hong Kong because of the need to provide full-time training to the healthcare professionals who are to staff the various health projects that are in the pipeline, to learn about new approaches to dealing with public health problems, and to discover new solutions and develop new services for Hong Kong to tackle its many new public health problems.

On 2 June 2001, a School of Public Health was officially opened with policy and funding support from The Chinese University of Hong Kong, the Hong Kong SAR, the Hong Kong Jockey Club Charities Trust, and many other organizations, local and overseas, including the World Health Organization for the Western Pacific, and the Shaw Foundation. The mission of the School of Public Health is to contribute locally, nationally and internationally to the health of the Hong Kong population through excellence in research, teaching and training in public health, by working in collaboration with partners from all relevant disciplines and institutions. Since opening, the School has offered many courses and degrees across all areas of public health practice, including a Master of Public Health programme, and courses in epidemiology, occupational health, health promotion and health management.

Other Academic Institutions and NGOs

The responses in the past decade of other academic institutions and NGOs to the new challenges in public health have also been most encouraging.

Many research projects have been undertaken. The SARS-related research includes a wide range of disciplines in the medical and environmental sciences, including infectious diseases, virology, molecular biology, epidemiology, mathematical modelling, geographical information systems, architecture and building design, ventilation engineering, occupational hygiene and the invention of innovative personal protective devices for healthcare workers and patients. Social, economic and media research also abound. Academic activities including seminars and congresses in various subjects such as smoking, emerging infectious diseases, community health, the elderly and health systems have taken place.

Not only have the staff of academic institutions responded well to the changes in the public health scene in the past decade, medical students from The Chinese University of Hong Kong and The University of Hong Kong have also taken an active role in promoting health and health education in the community. The conference on tobacco organized by the Federation of the Asia-Pacific Medical Students Association held in Hong Kong in 2006 was another good example of universities jointly working together to promote health.

NGOs in Hong Kong have also responded tremendously well in tackling the major public health problems in Hong Kong. These organizations include many professional associations such as the medical and dental associations; voluntary organizations, such as the Centre for Health Promotion and Disease Prevention of the Hong Kong Tuberculosis, Chest and Heart Diseases Association; and statutory organizations, including the Health Zone of the HA, the Drug Information and Resource Centre of the Action Committee Against Narcotics, and the Council on Smoking and Health. The contributions from these organizations whether government, academic, professional, voluntary or NGOs are invaluable. The aim is to achieve unity for health for the good of the community.

Community

The responses from the community in the last decade to improving people's health are best reflected in the "Healthy Settings" approach to health promotion.

The publication of the **Ottawa Charter for Health Promotion** in 1986 was a critical point in the development of a settings approach to health promotion. It recognizes that health goes beyond the boundaries of medical intervention. Rather, it is an interplay of social, political, economic, environmental, genetic and behavioural factors. The Ottawa Charter states that:

> Health is created and lived by people within the settings of their everyday life: where they learn, work, play and love. Health is created by caring for oneself and others, by being able to take decisions and have control over one's life circumstances, and by ensuring that the society one lives in creates conditions that allow the attainment of health by all its members.

The Experience of a Setting-based Approach to Health Promotion in Hong Kong

• *Healthy Cities*

In Hong Kong, three districts launched a "healthy cities" project in the beginning of 2000. They were Tseung Kwan O, Wan Chai, and the Central and Western Districts of Hong Kong Island. By 2007, 13 out of a total of 18 districts in Hong Kong had joined the movement. Steering Committees have been established in these districts. Seven principles of the healthy city project have been set out: international collaboration, community participation, equity on health, health promotion, primary health care, an evidence-based approach and international cooperation.

• *Alliance for Healthy Cities*

In 2004, a conference on the Alliance for Healthy Cities and the First General Assembly was held in Kuching, Malaysia. The objective was to establish a link among healthy cities in the Western Pacific Region. Representatives from the Tseung Kwan O and Kwai Ching Districts of Hong Kong attended the Conference and they became founding members of the Alliance.

• *The 2nd General Assembly and Conference of the Alliance for Healthy Cities*

In 2006, the 2nd General Assembly and Conference of the Alliance for Healthy Cities was held in Suzhou, China. The Hong Kong delegation was led by Dr P. Y. Lam, the Director of Health, and included representatives from several districts participating in the healthy cities movement in Hong Kong.

- *Healthy and Safe Housing Estates and Healthy Workplaces*

Within the healthy cities movement, healthy and safe housing estates have
also been promoted. This is a good example of the healthy settings approach
to health promotion for groups of people. Projects to promote healthy
workplaces have been organized in collaboration with the Occupational
Health and Safety Council, the HA, the Department of Health, and the
Recreation and Sports Department.

- *Health Promoting Universities*

At The Chinese University of Hong Kong, a Health Promotion on Campus
Project was launched at the end of 2000. A Steering Committee was also
formed within the University campus, comprising representatives from
various colleges, unit heads, departments, and staff and student associations.
The Steering Committee's role is to advise on policy, to plan, coordinate
and monitor progress, and to later carry out an evaluation of the activities.
In 2006, a Committee on Health Promotion and Health Protection was also
established by the University administration, and given overall responsibility
for health promotion and health protection activities on campus. An Advisory
Committee on Health Promotion and Health Protection was set up as well,
to advise on the formulation of strategies and policies on health promotion
and health protection on campus.

The 1st Asia-Pacific Conference on Healthy Universities, organized
by the School of Public Health of The Chinese University of Hong Kong,
was held in March 2007. The Conference received strong support from the
WHO Regional Office for the Western Pacific, the health and hospital
authorities of the government, and other universities in Hong Kong and
Mainland China. A declaration to form a network of health promoting
universities in the Asia-Pacific region was signed by the vice-chancellors
of all of the universities in Hong Kong. Such an activity will no doubt pave
the way for greater collaboration among universities in the region, and
provide a platform for the exchange of information and experiences on
new directions and strategies in public health education, training and
research.

- *Health Promoting Schools*

The Health Promoting Schools project was launched in 1999. The objective
is to make the school environment conducive to learning, educating and

living, with the involvement of teachers, students, parents, schools and the community. Schools that participate in the "health promoting schools" project are recognized by the "Healthy Schools Award Scheme" if they fulfil the criteria of the scheme. The activities in the "health promoting schools" project include: the training of teachers in health education and health promotion, the establishment of a district-based task force to promote school health, surveillance on the health status of school children, the publication of health education and health promotion materials, and the conduct of health promotion activities in partnership with the schools and parents, such as "the video conference on environmental air pollution" and "health promotion carnivals."

Traditional Chinese Medicine (TCM)

The Preparatory Phase

TCM has been widely used in the community and has made significant contributions to health care. In August 1989, the government established a working group in TCM to review the traditional practice of Chinese medicine in Hong Kong. In October 1994, the working group published its report, in which a number of recommendations were made on promoting, developing and regulating the practice of TCM in Hong Kong. The recommendations were accepted by the government, and a Preparatory Committee on Chinese Medicine (the Committee) was established on 1 April 1995 to advise the government on how to promote, develop and regulate TCM. In March 1997, the Committee submitted a report to the government (HWFB, 1997).

The Regulatory Framework

The objectives of the Regulatory Framework are to protect the health of the public and the rights of consumers, and to ensure that professional standards are upheld in the practice of TCM through "self-regulation" within the profession.

The organizational structure of the framework consists of a Traditional Medicine Council, supported by two Boards, namely the Chinese Medicine Practitioners Board and the Chinese Medicine Board. Under the two Boards are sub-committees responsible for the registration, examination and disciplining of TCM practitioners and the registration of Chinese Medicine traders.

The functions of the Traditional Medicine Council are to ensure the effective implementation of the legislation for regulating TCM, to supervise and coordinate the operation of the Chinese Medicine Practitioners Board and the Chinese Medicine Board, to examine the recommendations of the two Boards and to handle any appeals against their decisions. It also has the responsibility of making recommendations to the government on improvements to, or amendments of, any prevailing legislative provisions covering TCM. The members of the Council include TCM practitioners, TCM educators, government representatives and lay members.

The Implementation Phase

It has taken several years and a series of legislative sessions to implement the recommendations of the Preparatory Committee on Chinese Medicine in the following steps:

	Year
Establishment of the Traditional Chinese Medicine Council	1998/1999 Legislative session
Enactment of subsidiary legislations for the registration of TCM practitioners, the registration of Chinese Medicines and the Chinese Medicine trade	1999/2000 Legislative session
Regulation of TCM practitioners	From 2000 onwards
Registration of Chinese Medicines and the regulation of the TCM trade	To be implemented in phases from 2000

Long-term Development

The establishment of a sound regulatory system has gone a long way to lay a solid foundation for the future development of TCM. TCM has an important role to play in healthcare services in Hong Kong, in both the public and private sectors. Hong Kong has the potential to develop over time into an international centre for the manufacturing and trading of Chinese medicine; for research, information and training in the use of Chinese medicine; and for the promotion of this alternative approach to health care. With more trained and qualified TCM practitioners and science professionals graduating from local educational institutions, and through partnership and collaboration with Mainland China and other countries and areas, it is expected that TCM in Hong Kong will develop more rapidly in the years to come.

Broader Perspectives in Public Health

The broader perspectives in public health must take into account the following new factors:

International Collaboration and Cooperation

Hong Kong is a global centre for trade, finance, business and communications. Hong Kong has significant economic links with the Mainland, especially with the PRD region.

Communicable diseases do not respect geographical boundaries, as the SARS epidemic has clearly demonstrated. Good systems of communication at the regional and international levels are vital if the rapid spread of disease is to be prevented and outbreaks brought quickly under control.

Because of rapid modes of transportation, the world is getting smaller. There is a need to adapt to the new "normals" in disease control, namely, that "local threats have a global impact" and "global threats have a local impact." It is necessary for international health authorities to jointly observe and implement the four "Es" in infectious diseases control:

- "Early detection"
- "Early reporting"
- "Early communication"
- "Early action"

Since the SARS epidemic, there has been much closer collaboration between Guangdong and Hong Kong and between Hong Kong and the international community. This spirit and practice of collaboration within the PRD region and with the international community will be further developed and strengthened, following the establishment of the CHP in Hong Kong.

Greater Development of Public Health Efforts in the Government

The twenty-first century offers golden opportunities in the field of public health. The government has committed itself to implementing the recommendations of the report of the SARS Expert Committee by devising appropriate policies, providing funds, and devoting the requisite human resources. One year after the SARS epidemic, there has been considerable progress in the further development of public health, including the following activities:

- Establishing the CHP
- Developing emergency preparedness plans
- Improving information and data management in infectious diseases
- Strengthening cross-boundary and international cooperation efforts
- Enhancing isolation facilities in public hospitals
- Strengthening the training of healthcare workers in infection control
- Encouraging research and development
- Supporting community involvement in promoting health

Greater Development of Public Health Laboratory Services

Public health laboratory services serve as the eyes and ears of public health practitioners. The Department of Health's Public Health Laboratory in Sham Shui Po is playing an important role in the laboratory surveillance of infectious diseases. It maintains close liaison with other public health laboratories in the Asia-Pacific region and with international reference laboratories in the U.S. and Europe in the global surveillance of infectious diseases, especially the influenza virus. The Laboratory has recently been designated as a Supra-national Reference Centre for Tuberculosis by the WHO Regional Office for the Western Pacific.

Healthcare Reforms

In the past 10 years, the government has undertaken a series of reviews on Hong Kong's healthcare system. It is generally accepted that there is a need to introduce reforms to meet the new challenges and to solve the long-term problems in the delivery of health care, especially with regard to the financing of health care.

In November 1997, the government commissioned a team of economists, physicians, epidemiologists and public health specialists from Harvard University to conduct a study on Hong Kong's healthcare system. The aim of the study was to make a comprehensive assessment of the current system and to come up with a proposal for alternative options to improve the financing and delivery of health care in Hong Kong.

The Harvard Team (Team) produced a report known as "Improving

Hong Kong's Health Care System: Why and for Whom?" (Harvard Team, 1999). Following a period of public discussion of the Harvard Report after its publication in 1999, in 2000 the government published a consultation document on healthcare reform known as "Lifelong Investment in Health" (Government Secretariat 2000). The key health reform proposals consisted of three main pillars, namely, the Heathcare Delivery System, the Quality of Health Care and Healthcare Financing.

Following the SARS epidemic in 2003, the government's Health and Medical Development Advisory Committee issued a consultation document entitled Building a Healthy Tomorrow in July 2005, seeking comments from the public about the future development of healthcare services in Hong Kong. Another consultation document on healthcare financing is expected to be issued in late 2007. With the support of the government, the public, the healthcare professionals and the private business sector, and a determined effort to move ahead, the years 2007 and 2008 will be a golden opportunity to introduce major healthcare reforms for the long-term development of Hong Kong's healthcare system.

Conclusion

New Directions for Public Health in Hong Kong

New directions for public health in Hong Kong should focus on the following areas:

- Giving more emphasis to health promotion and disease prevention
- Developing a new approach to the physical and psycho-social aspects of health
- Taking into account the total determinants of health, including economic, political and social factors
- Applying a multi-sector and multi-disciplinary approach
- Providing both patient-based and community-oriented care
- Promoting the development of community health programmes
- Reforming the healthcare and health financing systems
- Education, training and research in public health
- Linkages with Mainland China
- Building partnerships on health at the national, regional and international levels

In order to achieve the above objectives, the following actions must be undertaken:

- Developing leadership in public health at the local, regional and international levels
- Fostering partnerships and cooperation with all sectors
- Serving as health advocates in securing support from the government, policy and decision-makers, and the community in collective action for sustained improvements in public health.

Reviewing the Past

Over the past 10 years, public health in Hong Kong has entered a golden age of development. Significant achievements have been made in many areas of the field. Hong Kong has never before made such great strides in the development of public health, despite the limited period of time involved, the emergence of new threats, and constraints of manpower and financial resources.

The story that emerges during the SARS epidemic is one of great courage and dignity. The contributions made by healthcare workers, community organizations, NGOs and professional groups represent enormous efforts made by many individuals and the community in struggling against a new disease. It is important that community networks be maintained and their support sought in the further development of public health in Hong Kong.

Looking into the Future

Looking ahead, the further development of public health in Hong Kong is expected to build upon the solid foundation that has been established in the past 10 years. For example, it is encouraging to note that the Department of Health has recently published *The Centre for Health Protection's Strategic Plan on the Prevention and Control of Communicable Diseases* (Department of Health, 2007–2009). The new plan will carry forward from the achievements of the CHP's first three years of operation (2004–2006). The strategy is to concentrate the efforts of the CHP in three strategic directions, summed up as the three "Rs," to prevent and control communicable diseases:

- Real-time surveillance
- Rapid intervention
- Responsive risk communication

It is also encouraging to see that the HA is taking concrete steps towards developing family medicine and preventive care, enhancing community healthcare networks in collaboration with district elderly and rehabilitation care agencies to encourage the provision of home care for patients; and towards establishing specialized tertiary centres for catastrophic illnesses.

Hong Kong's academic institutions have responded actively by carrying out research, education and training efforts on public health and on infectious diseases, and by developing vaccines. Further developments are expected to be made by these institutions.

With the continued support of the government, the community, the academic institutions, the professional organizations and NGOs, the private sector and public-spirited individuals, we are confident that the Hong Kong SAR will continue to succeed in meeting the daunting health challenges it faces, and to sustaining the high quality of health care in the years to come.

References

Government Secretariat, HKSAR (2000), *Lifelong Investment in Health, Consultation Document on Health Care Reform, Health and Welfare Bureau.*

Harvard Team (1999), *Improving Hong Kong's Health Care System: Why and for Whom* (Executive Summary).

Health and Welfare Bureau, Government Secretariat (HWFB) (1997), *Consultation Document on the Development of Traditional Chinese Medicine in the Hong Kong SAR.* Hong Kong: Government Printer.

Hong Kong SAR Government (2003), *SARS in Hong Kong: From Experience to Action.* Report of the SARS Expert Committee.

Lee, S. H. (1994), *Prevention and Council of Communicable Disease in Hong Kong.* Hong Kong: Government Printer.

—— (2003), "The SARS Epidemic in Hong Kong — What Lessons Have We Learnt?" *Journal of the Royal Society of Medicine.*

—— (2005), *The SARS Epidemic in Hong Kong — A Human Calamity in the 21st Century.* Hong Kong: Centre for Health Education and Health Promotion, School of Public Health, The Chinese University of Hong Kong.

"Neidifu Gang chanying wunian zeng shijiu bei" (Mainland Mothers to Give Birth in Hong Kong Increased 19 Times in 5 Years), *Wen Wei Po,* 7 December 2006.

"Weisheng fuli siwu ju juzhang he baoanju juzhang tan neidi yunfu laigang chanzi" (HWFB & SB Secretaries on the Issue of Mainland Mothers to Give Birth in Hong Kong), Press Release, HKSAR Government, 14 December 2006.

"Yiguanju xin cuoshi yingfu neidi yunfu" (Hospital Authority New Measures on Mainland Pregnant Mothers), *Ming Pao* Instant News, 21 December 2006.

PART III

❖ ❖ ❖

Summary and Conclusions

17

Summary and Conclusions: From the First Decade to the Next

Yue-man Yeung

> July 1, 1997, was a day of paramount importance in the history of Hong Kong and a cause for celebration for all Chinese people. After 156 years of separation, Hong Kong was eventually reunited with China to become part of one nation. The destiny of Hong Kong people is now in their own hands. With dignity and pride, we chart our future (HKSAR, 1997, p. 1).

> A decade after its return to China in 1997, Hong Kong is more vibrant and spectacular than ever. But as the city looks to the future, it faces a critical question: How can it be both a part of the motherland — and the world? (*Time*, 18 June 2007, p. 33).

The above two quotations — one taken from the first annual report of the new Hong Kong Special Administrative Region (HKSAR) poignantly stating the historical and political meanings of a new era for Hong Kong, and the other from a leading magazine projecting a buoyant mood in Hong Kong at the end of the first 10 years of the existence of the SAR — represent significant statements capturing the beginning and end points of a decade. The statements, however, have left unsaid what has transpired in Hong Kong between these two junctures in time. This is precisely what this book has purported to accomplish within its own constraints and limitations. The preceding chapters have dealt with a variety of subjects from the broad division of how Hong Kong can be looked at from without and within.

This chapter attempts to piece together the major strands of thought and empirical evidence on the subject, based largely on the materials presented in the earlier chapters. These will be supplemented by some additional materials, to present a picture of the first decade that can stand on its own. Moreover, as the "one country, two systems" (OCTS) design is to last for 50 years, this chapter will conclude with some comments on what the second decade promises to bring to Hong Kong, which will at the same time answer the question raised in the second quotation.

Outside-in Perspectives

For any change of regime, the first decade is a standard yet crucial milestone at which to measure the success or otherwise of the new administration's existence. For Hong Kong, the decade since 1997 means even more, in that the successful implementation of OCTS basically substantiates the far-sighted prescription of the former paramount Chinese leader Deng Xiaoping, who has been credited with presenting this creative solution to the return of Hong Kong to China. Hong Kong's continued prosperity and stability has also settled the minds of Western entrepreneurs who have cherished Hong Kong as the freest economy in the world to conduct business. Not so straightforward is the demonstration effect of the Hong Kong model to Taiwan, the peaceful unification with the Mainland of which is the ultimate target for the OCTS model in Deng's original conceptualization.

Historically, Hong Kong has always been part of China. Only the Opium War and the ensuing Treaty of Nanking led to the ceding of Hong Kong to Britain. That state of separation between Hong Kong and the Mainland lasted for one-and-a-half centuries. During this period, Hong Kong gradually rose in importance as a trading centre and became a thriving city. Its rapid transformation only began after World War II, notably since the 1970s.

In the latter half of the twentieth century, Hong Kong people could be considered the most fortunate people in China. The Chinese Communist Party was prepared to put aside its dogmas and duly recognized the unique value of Hong Kong as a bridge to the outside world during the Cold War period (Goodstadt, 2005, p. vii). Hong Kong's worth to the motherland sharply increased when, with the launching in 1978 of economic reforms in China and the pursuit of a policy of greater openness to the outside world, the Mainland depended even more on Hong Kong to lead China on the way to capitalism and worldliness.

More specific to the historical background of the handover, Wang Gungwu (Chapter 1) has posed some hypothetical questions relating the handover to the Cultural Revolution. The 1982–1984 Sino-British negotiations on the future of Hong Kong was protracted and at times difficult, but it was China's firm stance on the issue of sovereignty that won the day. An agreement on the handover in 1997 was finally struck, leaving a long period of 13 years for the transition and the chance that disruptions would be kept to a minimum. The Tiananmen incident in 1989, nevertheless, threw a spanner in the works, almost derailing the agreed-upon plans. Mr Lu Ping, the then Director of the State Council's Hong Kong and Macau Affairs Office, revealed that Beijing had debated the idea of delaying the handover of Hong Kong (*SCMP*, 27 June 2007, A1). In any event, the Tiananmen incident pushed Hong Kong's authorities into a decision to build the replacement airport at Chek Lap Kok and to embark on a vast expansion of tertiary education. Both of these developments are decidedly positive for Hong Kong's long-term future. However, the same incident led to the replacement of the governor, David Wilson. The last governor, Chris Patten, arrived in 1992. During his term of office, Mr Patten introduced Hong Kong to a new style of democratic governance. Furthermore, his last hurrah on the structural change of political participation was at variance with the previously agreed-upon timetable and substance of democratic reforms. As Sino-British verbal skirmishes escalated in intensity and frequency day by day, they disrupted a through-train arrangement for the Legislature.

As Wang Gungwu has elucidated, the roots of some of the problems encountered in the Hong Kong SAR in its first decade were traceable to the previous decade and earlier. Whether the tests came in the form of a banking crisis, the bursting of the property bubble, chicken flu, severe acute respiratory syndrome (SARS) or education reform, the respective roles of Hong Kong and the Mainland had to be played out if they were to be resolved. From this viewpoint, OCTS worked surprisingly well. In fact, what had been a major concern of the community and of people in Hong Kong prior to 1997 turned out so well that it was beyond their expectations. The division of labour and responsibilities between Hong Kong and Beijing was clear, and Beijing was there more to assist than intervene in Hong Kong's affairs. In a true sense, the promise of Hong Kong people ruling Hong Kong was amply realized. Meanwhile, a new China has emerged and Hong Kong has adjusted in tandem. A more important role is envisaged for Hong Kong, with Beijing leaders keeping their eyes on the larger national agenda. Hong Kong is but a small yet critical part of an emerging, strong and modern China. Wang is supremely confident that the expected convergence between China and Hong Kong under OCTS will eventually materialize, spearheaded particularly by the younger generation on either side who appear to share common goals, values in life and future aspirations.

How would Britain, the long-time colonial masters of Hong Kong, regard the first decade of the SAR's existence? Michael Yahuda (Chapter 2) has made it plain that, even during the colonial period, Hong Kong never much mattered in British domestic politics. Since 1997, the Foreign and Commonwealth Office (FCO) has steadfastly produced for the British Parliament 20 six-monthly reports on Hong Kong. The conclusion is that OCTS has generally worked well, apart from the occasional note of outright disapproval of specific instances of Chinese intervention in the judicial and political affairs of Hong Kong.

After a decade of Hong Kong in new guise, Britain still has important economic and social relations with Hong Kong, but their significance has declined for both sides. Britain's legacy continues in Hong Kong in two important ways: as progenitor of the rule of law, of an apolitical and impartial civil service and of basic freedoms; and as one source of the distrust towards the democratization of Hong Kong felt by many in the Chinese leadership. The British position on the new Hong Kong can be seen from the fact that during his visit to Hong Kong in July 2003, British Prime Minister Tony Blair focused more on his larger agenda with China's leaders regarding Iraq and the European Union than on Hong Kong. According to an FCO report, the British view is crystal clear that the future of Hong Kong depends on the people of Hong Kong. It is noteworthy that, when Hong Kong was returned to China in 1997, it was the only crown colony in Britain's imperial history to be more prosperous than Britain, as measured by the fact that, by the end of British rule, Hong Kong's per capita GDP exceeded that of the United Kingdom (U.K.) (Goodstadt, 2005, p. 1). In 1997, the per capita GDP in Hong Kong reached US$25,280, ranking the territory thirteenth in the world.

In an independent study of the first 10 years of Hong Kong under Chinese rule from a British perspective, Forder (2007) gave full marks to the OCTS experiment, judging it to be almost completely successful. Hong Kong remains remarkably separate in terms of its economic organizations and institutional structure, with extensive political and economic freedoms and a high degree of independence. He concluded that Hong Kong is blessed with just the right kind of separateness from China to maintain its strikingly superior institutions and to play out its unique role.

The view from North America is important in any assessment of the efficacy of Hong Kong under OCTS. We are mindful of the fact that in the lead-up to 1997, most of the doomsayers of the future of Hong Kong originated from North America. Towards this end, Janet Salaff and Arent Greve (Chapter 3) undertook a meticulous analysis of articles about Hong

Kong that appeared in two leading newspapers in Canada (*The Globe & Mail*) and the United States (U.S.) (*The New York Times*). Prior to 1997, Canada was one of the most popular destinations for Hong Kong emigrants. A content analysis of 131 articles about Hong Kong during the said decade revealed that, initially a doomsday scenario was predicted for Hong Kong. Louis Kraar's infamous article, which appeared in a 1995 issue of *Fortune* magazine, entitled "The Death of Hong Kong," cast a long shadow on most of these articles. It was not until late 2003 that the press reported that China seemed to be fulfilling its political assurances on Hong Kong. By 2005, Hong Kong was deemed to be free of the threat that Kraar had foreseen. Towards the latter part of the decade, there was a distinct shift in frames — a shift of attribution from finding fault with the entire leadership to a focus on the people of Hong Kong. The emphasis was on how ordinary people could innovate and how the Chief Executive was able to handle crises. All of the articles that were analyzed focused overwhelmingly on politics and economics, with the former clearly in the majority.

The official American view of the Hong Kong SAR during the decade after 1997 is that it has remained "sufficiently autonomous" from China, taking into account the trends of political, economic and social development. The recommendations formulated for the U.S. Congress were based on cautious optimism in the years ahead (Martin, 2007).

After reviewing the perspectives from Britain and North America, it is crucial to see the view from Beijing. Jia Qingguo's analysis (Chapter 4) begins with the criteria that he would use to undertake an assessment of events in Hong Kong in the decade following the handover. He mentions six criteria: 1) no room for flexibility on the question of sovereignty; 2) the transfer of the administration of Hong Kong to Hong Kong people; 3) the smooth transfer of sovereignty; 4) strengthen Hong Kong; not letting it be used as a base for anti-China activities; 5) helping Hong Kong to be commercially viable and politically stable; and 6) progress on achieving the bigger and larger target of peaceful unification with Taiwan. Based on his examination of these issues, Jia has come to the conclusion that Hong Kong's return to China under the OCTS principle is a success beyond previous expectations. He noted that sovereignty was recovered on schedule; the transfer of administration was smooth and it was proven that Hong Kong people could perform just as well in administering Hong Kong as their erstwhile colonial masters; Hong Kong has not been used as a base for hostile forces to sabotage the Chinese government; and Hong Kong is economically viable and politically stable.

Specifically, OCTS has been successfully applied. From Beijing's side, the policy of respecting Hong Kong's autonomy has been faithfully adhered to. At the same time, the central government has been firm in defending its authority and responsibilities. Beijing is committed to a gradual process of democratization, ever mindful of the "colour revolutions" that have led to instability and regime changes in some of the former territories of the Soviet Union. In addition, Beijing has adopted the proactive approach of helping Hong Kong to maintain the vitality of its economy, such as by introducing Closer Economic Partnership Arrangement (CEPA) and the Individual Visit Scheme. The other side of the coin is that the Hong Kong SAR has strictly adhered to the Basic Law, with a high degree of autonomy, thereby maintaining the trust and confidence of Beijing. It is, therefore, not surprising that Hong Kong people now feel more respect and trust towards Beijing, as shown by recent polls. Viewed from Beijing, the future of Hong Kong is more promising than ever before.

Even from Beijing, there are sceptics of OCTS. Yan Xuetong, of Tsinghua University, for example, has been quoted as saying: "The return of Hong Kong to China is just half achieved. Hong Kong is still regarded as a special place of China, still regarded as a foreign country. Hong Kong has returned in name, but not in substance" (*Time*, 18 June 2007, p. 34). This is almost certainly a minority view, because at the time of the anniversary of the handover, almost every province in China had organized large-scale celebrations. More telling is the fact that President Hu Jintao purposely came to Hong Kong to take part in the official celebration to mark the tenth anniversary of Hong Kong as an SAR and declared OCTS a success.

With Hong Kong's retrocession to China in 1997, a key question was whether Hong Kong–Taiwan relations would undergo any changes. Timothy K. Y. Wong (Chapter 5) has traced and analyzed the shifts and turns in this relationship during the first decade. To begin with, Hong Kong–Taiwan relations were closely linked with Mainland–Taiwan relations, under which Hong Kong–Taiwan relations are subsumed. Beijing's policy towards Taiwan was enunciated in detail in 1995 by the then Vice-Premier and Foreign Minister Qian Qichen in a high-profile seven-point statement to regulate Hong Kong–Taiwan relations after 1997. There are extensive and specific provisions in this statement, but the overarching clause is that the "one China" policy must and cannot be compromised. Since Taiwanese President Lee Teng-hui's visit to the United States and his "two states" proposition in the late 1990s, and the rise to power of the Democratic

Progressive Party in 2000, Mainland-Taiwan relations have continued to deteriorate. In this politically charged situation, the Hong Kong authorities have had to tread gingerly and have adopted a pragmatic approach. Hong Kong–Taiwan relations have typically been depoliticized. Under the SAR government, Hong Kong–Taiwan relations have undergone subtle changes. When the HKSAR was established, Yip Kwok-wah was appointed by the Chief Executive to be his Special Advisor on Taiwan. In June 2002, the Taiwan portfolio came under the ambit of the Constitutional Affairs Bureau, signalling the institutionalization of the work on Hong Kong–Taiwan relations. It can be concluded that until and unless the issue of reunification is settled, there can be no genuine solution to the problem of Hong Kong–Taiwan relations.

Given Hong Kong's historical and deep-rooted social and economic ties with Southeast Asia, Henry Yeung (Chapter 6) examines the changing economic relations between Hong Kong and that region, especially with the five founding members of the Association of Southeast Asian Nations (ASEAN). On the basis of time-series trade investment data, the changing economic relations between Hong Kong and these ASEAN countries are shown to be significant. Prior to 1997, Hong Kong was a fairly important investor in ASEAN, with Hong Kong–ASEAN trade growing rapidly to the mid-1990s. Southeast Asian investment in Hong Kong, notably from Singapore and Thailand, was modest. Two-way economic relations were strong. However, since 1997, several marked changes in Hong Kong–ASEAN economic relations have occurred. First, Hong Kong is not contributing as much as before to the development of Southeast Asia. The Asian financial crisis has weakened both Hong Kong's economy and the economies of some Southeast Asian countries, thereby slowing the flow of Hong Kong investment funds into Southeast Asia. Second, the rise of China as a "global factory" has absorbed foreign direct investment (FDI) from both Hong Kong and, to a lesser extent, ASEAN, to their mutual detriment. Third, the reconfiguration of global production networks has been in China's favour, with possibly fewer locations being needed in the emerging global supply chain. In this respect, it has been argued that Hong Kong investment in ASEAN can be deployed as a strategic counterbalance to excessive exposure to China. Moreover, the "twinning" of Hong Kong and Singapore, traditional cities often paired for their competitiveness and similar socio-economic backgrounds, should be maintained, despite the fact that the former's future lies clearly in China. Finally, Hong Kong can develop a new and pivotal role as a gateway for China-bound investment from

ASEAN. In all, notwithstanding the changes surrounding Hong Kong–
ASEAN economic relations since 1997, the future looks bright for both,
given China's continued resurgence and Hong Kong as an SAR within it.

At another level and from an international standpoint, the Hong Kong
SAR has fared well, if not better than it did under colonial rule. From all
that could be gathered, the Hong Kong SAR has continued to operate well
in all international bodies since 1997. What is more, the fact that Hong
Kong is once again a part of China has bolstered Hong Kong's international
standing. Three examples will bring home this viewpoint. First, Hong Kong
will play host to the Equestrian Competition portion of the Summer
Olympics that will be held in 2008 in Beijing. On its own, Hong Kong
could never dream of having the privilege of hosting even a small portion
of this prestigious world event, but with China hosting the grand show,
having the Equestrian Competition take place in Hong Kong would allow
maximum use to be made of Hong Kong's valuable and professional
experience in horse racing, coupled with its first-rate management skills.
Second, Margaret Chan, a former Health Director in Hong Kong, was
elected, with China's full backing and encouragement, the Director-General
of the World Health Organization (WHO) in 2006, a rare feat for a Hong
Kong professional. Third, the worldwide recognition of the Hong Kong
SAR is growing, as shown by the ever greater number of eligible foreigners
who have exhibited their confidence in taking out its passport, now
recognized by 134 countries for visa-free entry. In the period 1997–2006, a
total of 4.2 million HKSAR passports were issued. In 1997, 30 foreigners
applied for this passport, as opposed to 1,840 in 2006, a huge increase of
60 times (*Wen Wei Po*, 20 June 2007, A01).

Inside-out Reviews

The State of the Economy

In the years leading to 1997, Hong Kong's economy was growing strongly.
It reached its peak at about the time of the handover. Most people thought
that the economy would be one of the least of their worries after the
resumption of sovereignty in Hong Kong. After all, Hong Kong has
traditionally been absolved from the need to spend heavily on defence. The
arrangement for Hong Kong after the handover is that, unlike other Chinese
cities, it is free from the burden of delivering tax to the central government.
Even the stationing of the People's Liberation Army in Hong Kong does

not pose any financial burden on the Hong Kong SAR government, in contrast to the situation during the colonial period, when the local government had to share the expenses of the British military presence in the territory. Little was Hong Kong prepared for what it would go through in the decade that was to follow.

Economically speaking, it was a decade of wild economic fluctuations, punctuated by the Asian financial crisis, the dotcom boom, the deflating of the technology bubble, an attack on Hong Kong's stock market and currency, a global recession in the wake of the 9/11 terrorist attacks, and outbreaks of avian flu and SARS, each producing successive shocks. In mid-August 1998, the Hang Seng Index plunged to 6,600 points, down 60% from its high 12 months before. The government intervened in the stock market, buying billions dollars worth of shares to drive away speculators and boosting the Index by 18%. In the period 1997–2003 alone, Yun-wing Sung (Chapter 10) counted Hong Kong as having gone through two full-scale economic recessions and one near-recession.

Indeed, Hong Kong grew rapidly in the run up to 1997. By 1993, its per capita GDP had surpassed that of the U.K. However, after 1997, when Hong Kong was grappling with many economic difficulties, the U.K. grew rapidly. By 2002, its per capita GDP had overtaken Hong Kong's. In other words, Hong Kong lost a decade of economic growth. While Hong Kong's economic performance was the best among the Four Little Dragons from 1980 to 1990, it trailed all others in the 1990s, due largely to its worsening efficiency gains. Since 2000, Hong Kong has recovered some of its losses. Between 2002 and 2004, its performance again outshone that of the other Asian Dragons.

The strong economic growth in Hong Kong since 2000 has been derived primarily from trading and logistics (28.6%), financial services (12.7%), professional services (10.6%) and tourism (2.4%) in 2005. These four industries account for 55% of Hong Kong's GDP. Meanwhile, Hong Kong has undergone a structural change, with the growth in importance of the service industry, which now accounts for approximately 90% of Hong Kong's GDP and employment. With the relative decline of banking services, Hong Kong has emerged as a centre of wealth management. The recent relaxation of the rules on the QDII (qualified domestic institutional investors) scheme, through which personal funds from the Mainland may be invested in Hong Kong, will likely elevate the city's importance as a capital market. In fact, in his recent election campaign, Donald Tsang articulated his vision to make Hong Kong the global financial centre of

Asia, on a par with London and New York. This vision is shared by Lee Yeh-kwong, the former Chairman of the Hong Kong Stock Exchange (*Hong Kong Economic Journal*, 3 July 2007, p. 17). Hong Kong's economy has come full circle. By the end of the first decade of the existence of the HKSAR in July 2007, Hong Kong's economy had fully recovered and has exceeded previous highs. For example, the stock market has repeatedly broken records and has benefited vastly from the inflow of investment funds from the Mainland and elsewhere. It is, therefore, not surprising that in 2006 Hong Kong was listed third in the world after London and New York in the City of London's global financial centres index. Reinforcing Hong Kong's claim to be a global metropolis, Meyer's (2002) recent research has shown that Hong Kong's recent considerable investment in telematics (that is, the integration of telecommunications and computer technologies that permit the instantaneous transmission of information) has strengthened its aspirations to be a pivotal hub in global telematics. This will enable Hong Kong to raise its profile in global and regional exchanges of capital.

In a related study, Qin Xiao (Chapter 9) examines Hong Kong's strengths as a business centre. In its first decade as an SAR, Hong Kong has reaped large profits from the globalization of finance. In FDI inflows, Hong Kong ranked second in Asia in 2006, behind only China. In FDI outflows, Hong Kong ranked among the world leaders, with, in 2005, funds almost three times that of China and five times that of Singapore. Hong Kong has become a preferred location for regional headquarters/offices. By this measure, its gateway function between China and the world has hardly diminished. Hong Kong's economic strengths are being extended and expanded as Hong Kong continues to integrate with its hinterland in the Pearl River Delta (PRD) and far beyond. In a survey conducted in 2000 by the Economist Intelligence Unit, some 35% of the firms surveyed indicated that Hong Kong was the best location for the regional headquarters of multinationals in East Asia (Sung, 2002, p. 137). Hong Kong's attractiveness as a business centre is time and again ascertained by global surveys, which confirm that the city ranks highly in competitiveness, in economic freedoms, in the ease of doing business and in the favourableness of its business environment. Recent studies have rated Hong Kong as the most competitive city in China (Ni, 2007) and in the world (JCER, 2006; also Yeung et al., 2006). On the basis of these indicators, Qin concludes that Hong Kong offers the most attractive business environment in the world.

Since trading and logistics accounted for the lion's share of Hong Kong's GDP (28.6%) and employment (24.7%) in 2005, Yue-man Yeung and Jianfa

Shen (Chapter 13) reviewed the progress in these sectors over the first decade. Indeed, two-way trade between Hong Kong and the Mainland has continued to grow rapidly since 1988, when, for the first time, the re-export trade overtook the domestic trade in importance. With the further deepening of integration between Hong Kong and the Mainland after 1997, bilateral trade has continued to soar. Total exports leaped from HK$1,255.9 billion in 1997 to HK$2,461 billion in 2006, when re-exports accounted for 94.5% of exports. Similarly, between 1997 and 2006, the number of cross-boundary vehicles increased from 9.52 million to 14.99 million, the number of containers twenty-foot equivalent units (TEUs) handled by the port rose from 14.6 million to 22.3 million, the amount of air cargo handled expanded from 1.79 million tonnes to 3.58 million tonnes, the number of air passengers rose from 28.3 million to 43.3 million, the number of passengers passing through Shenzhen exploded from 64.7 million to 150.8 million, and the number of tourists visiting Hong Kong almost doubled from 13.0 million to 25.3 million. Beyond these actual movements of goods and people, Hong Kong has become a hub of global trade. Advances in logistics have allowed Hong Kong to become a pivot of "borderless manufacturing." The Li & Fung Group is famous for its mastery of supply chain management. The company oversees 73 sourcing offices in 41 countries, and taps into over 8,000 factories making anything from carpets to dog brushes (*Time*, 29 January 2007, p. 47). All of these developments fully show the very significant progress that the HKSAR has made in all aspects of the logistics industry in its first decade.

The Political and Legal Landscape

Where a roller-coaster is a good analogy for the economic changes that have occurred in the HKSAR during is first decade, a perpetual depression is probably an apt description of the political landscape. During the 10 years, a succession of political storms broke out, almost without respite. OCTS was a novel and untried formula, but most Hong Kong people were unprepared for the controversies and the constant wrangling that took place over its implementation. Certainly, the political, legal and administrative systems of Hong Kong and the Mainland are separate from each other, and are sharply different, but after 10 years the governments and the people of both places are still searching for the right formula to achieve a balance between one country and two systems.

During the decade after 1997, many episodes have shaken and divided the community, and some have had deleterious economic and social consequences that are still being felt. These include the controversies over the three interpretations of the Basic Law, the right of abode issue, the housing policy, the abolition of the Regional Councils, Cyberport project, West Kowloon Cultural District, the issue of what to do with site of the former Kai Tak airport, the Central and Wanchai reclamations, the failed proposal to broaden political participation in the 2007/2008 elections, the aborted national security legislation, massive demonstrations, and so on. Some of these controversies are over development projects, which have caused political feathers to be ruffled and have, therefore, been left in limbo. Perhaps the most high profile of these is the West Kowloon project. It consists of 40 ha of prime property along Victoria Harbour, and involves possibly some of the most expensive real estate on earth. After years of preparation, including the holding of an international design competition and the selection of a winning concept, in the face of virulent objections the project had to be scrapped and started afresh. This is a classic case of what former Premier Zhu Rongji described in 2001 as being Hong Kong's style of governance in the early years after 1997: "discussing without making a decision; making a decision without executing it." As a consequence, Hong Kong has suffered. Moreover, even as it is constantly bogged down in endless political squabbles, Mainland cities have roared ahead in infrastructure and development projects. The threat of Hong Kong being marginalized was raised when the National's Eleventh Five-year Plan (2006–2010) was released in early 2006 (Yeung et al., 2006).

Many analysts have advanced different reasons for the political quagmire in which HKSAR found itself after 1997. Former Secretary for Security, Regina Ip Lau Suk-yee, has placed the blame on four aspects of governance. One was the civil service, which sadly had not been adequately trained to deal with life after the handover. Another difficulty was related to the awkwardness of the government at Legislative Council (LegCo), where controversial policies and bills would face uphill battles to be passed because the government simply did not have any votes. Third, the long-standing and purposeful advisory committees that were the cornerstones of the efficient colonial Hong Kong administration, have been undermined by populist politics. The last is the fact that more people are ready to take the government to court over the legality of various political measures (*SCMP*, 16 April 2007, A18).

In his overview of the first five years of political change in the HKSAR, Lau Siu-kai (2002) made the following assessments:

... the executive-led government of Hong Kong exists solely in the constitutional sense. It becomes a political reality only after it has obtained political and ideological preeminence in society. Therefore, the executive-led system of Hong Kong is a highly messy and unwieldy system. It can only function well with a politically astute and skillful Chief Executive at the helm (pp. 30–31).

At the end of Tung's first five-year term, the popularity of Tung is at a nadir. Hongkongers lack confidence in Tung's leadership. Public goodwill towards Tung has by and large dissipated. Fairly or not, Tung is blamed for almost everything that has gone wrong in Hong Kong (p. 2).

Tung stood down from the post of Chief Executive in March 2005 and, after an uncontested election, Donald Tsang was appointed to serve the remainder of the former's second term of office. Things appear to have taken a turn for the better, due no doubt in part to the strong economic recovery that has been taking place since mid-2003. The turning point in Hong Kong–Beijing relations was the massive demonstration of 500,000 people on 1 July 2003, airing their pent-up grievances, including their objections to the proposed legislation of Article 23. Hitherto, Beijing had been leaving Hong Kong affairs largely to local administrators, faithfully adhering to its part of the agreement on OCTS. With so many people taking to the streets, Beijing took this as a wake-up call to begin taking a more proactive stance. All of a sudden, research on Hong Kong affairs took on special significance in many universities and research institutes on the Mainland.

In providing an overview on the political changes that have taken place in the first decade of the HKSAR, Lau Siu-kai (Chapter 7) has submitted that the gradual emergence of a new political order (NPO) in an embryonic form can be perceived. Anti–new order forces (ANOF) are still at loggerheads with pro–new order forces (PNOF). He has pointed out eight basic contradictions in relation to OCTS in the post-1997 situation. These can be regrouped as the need to build the NPO and the marginalization of the PNOF; the need for ideological decolonization and the lack of will to carry out such a task; and the need for a political coalition that can sustain Beijing's OCTS framework and the lukewarm attempts that have been made so far to bring about such a coalition. In addition, there is the discrepancy between the democratic aspirations of Hongkongers and the initial requirements of OCTS, and between the intention behind OTCS to maintain the status quo and a fast-changing society. Also, there is an incompatibility between Beijing's inactive approach towards Hong Kong and the requirements for building the NPO, and an inconsistency between the promise to maintain Hong Kong's pre-1997 status quo and the need to create the NPO. Finally, according to the design of OCTS, the Chief Executive is responsible to both the central government and the people of Hong Kong, hence putting him in the delicate and unenviable position of having to practise allegiance to two different parties. For all the political travail that came with a new government, at the end of the first decade, Lau notes that the popularity of the government has surpassed that of the opposition. With the people-oriented approach that the new government has adopted as a new strategy, the prospects for forging an NPO in the future look promising.

In terms of legal developments in the decade after 1997, Albert H. Y. Chen (Chapter 8) has systematically divided Hong Kong's constitutional and legal history into four periods. In the first period, 1997–1999, the interpretation of the Basic Law in 1999 was the most controversial issue, as it focused on the right of abode. As the ruling affected the life of many would-be abode seekers, it provoked violent actions from some concerned families and individuals. While this interpretation was initiated by the Hong Kong SAR government, later interpretations in 2004 and 2005, relating to issues of political reform and democratization in Hong Kong, were initiated by Beijing. In the second period, 2000–2002, legal disputes centred on the elaboration and consolidation of the regime of rights. They arose out of the controversy over the defacing of the national flag and the election of village representatives serving indigenous inhabitants and other villagers. The third period, 2003–2004, revolved around the Article 23 saga. The bone of contention was whether the legislation curtailed human rights. The fourth and final period, 2005–2007, focused on the continued active exercise of judicial power, with cases involving the right to hold demonstrations, to wire-tap phones and to intercept postal communications brought before the courts.

On the basis of his careful and meticulous analysis, Albert Chen has concluded that in the period under review, the rule of law, human rights and civil liberties have been successfully practised in HKSAR under the constitutional framework of OCTS and in accordance with the Basic Law. Without doubt, the three interpretations of the Basic Law by the National People's Congress Standing Subcommittee and the legislative exercise to implement Article 23 were the most significant legal events. In general, it can be said that during the post-1997 era, the courts of Hong Kong flourished. The delicate balance of judicial, executive and legislative powers was maintained. Finally, the linkages between the legal systems of Hong Kong and the Mainland remained weak and loose. However, there have been some recent and promising signs of increasing linkages, which can only bode well for OCTS and its future.

Societal and Social Panorama

The term "10 years" calls to mind two Chinese sayings that are often associated with that time span. Paraphrased in my own words, one can say that it would take 10 years to grow a tree, but within 10 years, personnel changes could occur several times over. In terms of this chapter, this means that it can take a long time to bring about changes to the physical environment of a society, but within the social environment, which involves people, many changes can occur within that period.

Over the past 10 years in Hong Kong, societal concern over the environment has indeed greatly deepened, as people can literally feel the change for the worse and are clamouring for improvements. In Chapter 15, Cho-nam Ng and Yok-shiu Lee have taken pains to show that since 1997, the SAR government has indeed made progress on a range of environmental safeguards and has finally achieved some breakthroughs. After 1997, several major milestones in the environment sector are worth noting: the enactment of the Environmental Impact Assessment (EIA) Ordinance (1998), the launching of a Waste Reduction Framework (1998), the introduction of a comprehensive motor vehicle emissions control programme (1998), the commissioning of the Strategic Sewage Disposal Scheme (2001), the announcement of the new Conservation Policy (2004), and the setting up of the Policy Framework for the Management of Municipal Solid Waste (2005).

In 1999, not long after Tung Chee-hwa took office, he made it a priority of his government to protect the quality of Hong Kong's air and water. He was concerned about the deteriorating quality of air at the street level and the problem of regional smog. As far as research on air pollution is concerned, the findings are somewhat divided. According to a study by the Hong Kong University of Science and Technology and Civic Exchange, 53% of the 324 polluted days in 2006 were due to emissions from roadside and marine traffic within Hong Kong's borders. By contrast, a study by the Environmental Protection Department released in 2002 found that over 80% of the polluting emissions came from the region, especially during the period of November to March (*SCMP*, 22 March 2007, A2). Cross-boundary cooperation is thus imperative if the cities concerned are to alleviate the problem of pollution. Consequently, the Hong Kong and Guangdong governments agreed to reduce emissions of sulfur dioxide, nitrous oxide and respirable suspended particulates by 40%, 20% and 55%, respectively, by 2010 from 1997 levels (*SCMP*, 25 January 2007, A3). Air pollution has become so serious that it has deterred professionals from coming to work in Hong Kong, or is evidently inducing some of those who have come here to leave.

In Ng and Lee's appraisal, Hong Kong has achieved environmental breakthroughs in two ways. First through the EIA process, public engagement has been legitimized and favourable results have been produced. Second, the repertoire of policy tools for environmental managers has grown, with tellingly positive outcomes. However, Hong Kong still suffers from the lack of a local Agenda 21, and there is a need to rethink how to integrate energy policy with environmental policy.

Another societal change in Hong Kong relates to how urban planning has brought about positive transformations. After 1997, the SAR government started formal efforts to build Hong Kong into Asia's world city. From a "silent facilitator" in the pre-1997 period, the government has since 1999 assumed the role of a "proactive advocate" in branding Hong Kong as Asia's world city. Personally, I have strongly supported the official approach, which has rightly affirmed Hong Kong's standing among cities in Asia and beyond. As a matter of fact, a study comparing cities around the world has found Hong Kong to be one of three alpha world cities (the other two are Tokyo and Singapore) among a dozen world cities in Asia (Beaverstock et al., 1999). A fine distinction is that Hong Kong is truly a first-class world city, not just a world-class city, which is a somewhat belittling appellation for Hong Kong. Towards this end, Joanna Lee and Mee-kam Ng (Chapter 14) have traced major urban developments in Hong Kong in a decade of world city formation. Some of the development projects are within Hong Kong, but many others involve issues of regional governance and touch on intercity networking. What is noteworthy in the past decade is an increasing awareness of planning for local sustainability. Equally, the traditional "fast-track" development approach has been successfully challenged after 1997 by a fledgling civil society. The "save the harbour" campaign has acted as a catalyst to rally diverse civic society groups, initially to focus on planning around the waterfront areas, but eventually spilling over to other urban planning issues. These groups have highlighted the fact that, while economic spaces in the decade in question have improved, life spaces have deteriorated and shrunk.

As we shift focus to the social domain, in Chapter 11 Wong Siu-lun has provided a survey of social transformation and cultural identity in the first 10 years after 1997. Socially, it was a decade soured by a succession of economic woes and riven by acrimonious political bickering among the civil service, politicians and the citizenry at large, who were unprepared for what hit them. Wong has called this a litany of post-handover blues caused by three powerful social forces, namely triple transitions, compressed development and entangled identities. The triple transitions refer to the political change from Colonial Hong Kong to Chinese Hong Kong, the economic restructuring from Industrial Hong Kong to Financial Hong Kong, and the demographic transition from Golden Hong Kong to Silvery Hong Kong. These are fundamental transitions that have shaken the foundation upon which Hong Kong has been constructed. Under OCTS, Hong Kong people were suddenly thrust into the situation of having to tread a thin line between showing loyalty to Hong Kong and to Beijing. Moreover, in an age of globalization and the information society, Hong Kong people have had to manage change coming from without. Under such internal and external pressures, Hong Kong identity has evolved into hybrid and changing entity, a far cry from a solely national identity. Hong Kong identity, or more broadly citizenship, has been made and remade, with notions of participation, rights, membership, belonging and differences no longer abstract concepts but sites of intense contestation. Tensions and struggles between state and society play out in the political and social arenas (Ku and Pun, 2004, p. 12). Wong concludes on a cautious note, emphasizing that the post-handover blues are not fleeting problems. Rather, they are deeply embedded in our fast-changing social milieu, and their resolution will depend on the ingenuity and resources of the new administration.

In the decade after 1997, if any one sector can be said to have grabbed the largest number of media headlines and the most societal attention, it must be that of education. As Kai-ming Cheng (Chapter 12) has elucidated, it has been a difficult and momentous decade, during which major reforms to the education system were pushed through, with long-term implications for society and our future generations. Indeed, there was paradigm shift, one that was brought about by forces outside the education sector, primarily employers and parents. They argued for the need to reform the education system, to make it possible for students to develop themselves as individuals and to prepare them for the flexibility that they will need in order to be able to work in multiple jobs/careers and meet the challenges of an increasingly globalized economy. On the other hand, teachers did not feel the same urgency for change, as students from Hong Kong have consistently performed at the forefront in international scholastic competitions. Consequently, there was a fundamental gap between the intentions of the reformers and the expectations of the teachers in reforms to the education system. A major change involves a revamp of the number of years of study at the secondary level from 5+2 to 3+3 years, scheduled to commence in 2012. I can say that a sufficient amount of discussion on this issue has been held among the community for almost two decades, as I was personally involved in the debate when I was Registrar of The Chinese University of Hong Kong in the late 1980s. Other reforms were apparently implemented too quickly and without careful coordination, whether it was the benchmarking of language teachers, the implementation of school-based management, changes to the medium of instruction, or the requirement to conduct an external review of the schools. When advocates of reform tried to promote a different way of conceiving and delivering education, teachers naturally put up strenuous resistance.

One of the most vocal critics of education reforms throughout the past decade has been Cheung Man-kwong, the President of the Professional Teachers' Union and the Democrat legislator for the education sector. In his words, the past decade has been like a bad dream for Hong Kong's education sector. The competition between schools has introduced a sense of fear that has overshadowed everything that principals and teachers do. Once a school is forced to focus only on survival, its teachers can no longer spare any effort on teaching and learning (*SCMP*, 14 May 2007, A18).

Another sector that has had its share of media attention since 1997 is public health. In Chapter 16, Lee Shiu-hung and Wong Tze-wai have highlighted the fact that the outbreak of avian flu and especially the outbreak of SARS brought grief and economic/social devastation to Hong Kong. These painful outbreaks of new infectious diseases were the result of such socially related problems as dietary habits, the state of the healthcare system, the condition of seasonal migratory birds, cross-boundary integration and globalization. Hong Kong has responded proactively, by setting up the Public Health School at The Chinese University of Hong Kong and many related NGOs. A community setting-based approach to health promotion has been fostered. Traditional Chinese medicine has also been tapped to combat public health problems. It is recognized that international collaboration and cooperation is crucial to improving public health in Hong

Kong. Financing health care has also become a societal concern, as the problem of how to keep providing high-quality health care to the population at an affordable cost is a real challenge, given Hong Kong's rapidly ageing population. The Harvard Report was an initial effort in this direction, but the search for a solution continues. Healthcare reforms will be one of the Chief Executive's toughest battles in his new term. There is a need to find a formula for sustainable long-term funding. Health care already accounts for 15% of government expenditure and people should be prepared to pay more for health care (*SCMP*, 16 June 2007, A15).

As briefly mentioned above, cross-boundary integration has facilitated the spread of new infectious diseases, but there are many important and positive effects of further integration with the Mainland. Yue-man Yeung and Jianfa Shen (Chapter 13) have elaborated on the mechanisms that have been progressively established to further integration and cooperation between governments on either side of the boundary. It is pertinent to note that the "Hong Kong first" mindset that prevailed in the early years after the handover has by degrees been supplanted by an approach that favours more proactive cooperation and collaboration at all levels of government. The year 2001 was an important year for improving the atmosphere for cooperation, with the early retirement of Anson Chan in May and China's accession to the WTO in November. The elevation of the Hong Kong/ Guangdong Cooperative Joint Conference in August 2003 was another landmark in accelerating cross-boundary integration. The purpose of integration has been summed up well by Ma (2006), as follows:

> One country-two systems and economic integration in the Guangdong–Hong Kong region is the result of two different social systems that are adapting to and challenging each other during the process of regional economic transition and development to sustain overall institutional advantages in the region (p. 389).

In fact, Hong Kong has progressively become integrated with an ever larger part of the Mainland. CEPA, the Individual Visit Scheme, and regional designs for integration such as the Pan–Pearl River Delta Cooperation Framework have greatly helped Hong Kong to recover economically since 2003 and opened new opportunities for development.

More specific to the Hong Kong people, Yeung and Shen have also touched on how people across the boundary have changed and availed themselves of the new opportunities that have presented themselves with increasing integration. People on either side are now travelling a great deal more often for shopping and leisure/recreational purposes, because of the price differentials and differences between what Hong Kong and Mainland cities have to offer. The vast increases in the flow of people across the boundary have been mentioned before. A recent study has shown that in 2005, 237,500 Hong Kong people worked in China, a huge increase from the 52,300 in 1988 (FHKI, 2007, p. 22). Property has also attracted people on either side, with Hong Kong investors particularly interested in purchasing property in Shenzhen, Dongguan, Guangzhou and other PRD cities, with Shanghai and Beijing also attracting some attention. Finally, the PRD appeals to many elderly people in Hong Kong who are interested in retiring to where they came from, enjoying at the same time much more affordable living expenses. The Hong Kong SAR government has established a scheme to make social security benefits portable to Guangdong and Fujian. All in all, people in Hong Kong and the Mainland have been drawing closer together over the past decade, economically, socially and culturally.

Towards the Second Decade

Ten years after the handover, Hong Kong is in a much better position to face the future than it was a decade ago. Although the past decade has had its ups and downs, OCTS has proven to be successful and more benefits can be expected from the arrangement in the future. Needless to say, there is still a long way to go before the experiment of OCTS reaches completion.

Notwithstanding the challenges that lie ahead, the second decade should be easier than the last. While it has become irrefutably clear that Hong Kong's future will have to fall squarely within the orbit of China's development, one challenge that Hong Kong must face up to is how to manage change under OCTS against the background of the resurgent world power that China has become, at the same time moving with the broader external trends of globalization and technological change.

On the home front, much remains uncompleted from the first decade. Undoubtedly, ranking foremost is the need to find a way forward in the sphere of electoral reforms, specifically in determining how to meet mass demands for universal suffrage in electing the Chief Executive and LegCo members. The third cabinet under Donald Tsang that was formed at the onset of the second decade will surely conduct widespread consultations on the issue, but finding a solution that will please all parties will not be easy, given that various parties hold conflicting philosophies. The eventual outcome is anybody's guess. Ng Hong-man, a seasoned and astute politician with long years of experience as a Hong Kong deputy to the National People's Congress, is not optimistic. He has predicted that Hong Kong will continue to be bogged down in political confrontations, and that the deadlock between the pan-democratic group and mainstream representatives has only a slim chance of being broken. He has suggested that electoral reform will remain an unresolved issue in the next decade, considering the pan-democratic group's stance on the issue, which led to the defeat in 2005 of the LegCo motion to take an initial step towards electoral reform (*Ming Pao*, 4 July 2007, A28).

It is desirable that the unfinished business of the national security legislation related to Article 23 of the Basic Law be addressed, but the new government is unlikely, at this time, to make this a priority. Lau Siu-kai, the Head of the Central Policy Unit, feels that while Hong Kong had physically returned to the motherland in the first decade, as one consequence of OCTS, the hearts of Hong Kong people have not (*SCMP*, 2 April 2007, A18). Another interpretation of why the hearts of the people have remained alienated from the Mainland can be tied to electoral politics. Again, Ng Hong-man has submitted that the "people's heart" issue is not reflected in any poll result, but rather in the majority view at LegCo, which has to take care not to be opposed to communism or challenge the central government (*Ming Pao*, 6 July 2007, A30). More urgent and immediate, in fact, are more mundane issues of business, such as how to deal with the worsening wealth gap between the rich and the underprivileged, the outcry over minimum wage legislation, the financing of health care, education reforms, and so on. An ongoing and important focus of the administration in the next decade will be how to keep Hong Kong from becoming marginalized as a result of developments in China arising from the release of the Eleventh Five-year Plan in early 2006. To tackle the problem of Hong Kong's ageing population, it may be necessary to reconsider the imposition of a sales and services tax in the future. Recently, the Chief Executive even suggested, somewhat provocatively, that Hong Kong's population should increase to 10 million in order to sustain itself as a viable global financial centre (*SCMP*, 16 June 2007, A14). Whether Hong Kong should in fact move in this direction calls for extensive community consultation and certainly research. The list of unfinished tasks from the first decade is long, but with the new cabinet, flush with new blood and filled with able ex-civil servants, and a new mandate, the chances have never been better that the unfinished business from the last decade will be addressed.

As Hong Kong enters its second decade as an SAR, the question raised in the second quotation that introduces this chapter should be revisited: How Hong Kong can position itself to be part of China and the world at the same time? Based on what has been built over the first decade, and on the momentum that has been generated, Hong Kong can be expected to further integrate with the Mainland, to which it is inextricably linked. Under OCTS, Hong Kong is wedded to the motherland, yet it is distinctly separate from it and not subject to China's rules. This allows Hong Kong to have the best of both worlds, in that it is allowed to have the right degree of separateness from China to maintain the strikingly superior institutions that make it possible for it to play its unique role and maintain its strengths. As Forder (2007, p. 18) has observed, the "Chinese takeover" means something so very different from what it sounds like. The much feared "Communist takeover" has simply not happened, and will not happen. Moreover, time is on Hong Kong's side because OCTS has been given a lifespan of 50 years. It has to be expected that the next decade will be another step in the longer journey to 2047, when with many more trials and errors along the way, the practice of OCTS will lead to the realization of full convergence between Hong Kong and the motherland. In the meantime, and certainly in the next decade, the further fine-tuning of OCTS will mean that Hong Kong will change China, and China will change Hong Kong no less. One example of how Hong Kong is silently changing China, in a way that is completely unexpected and perhaps unnoticed, is in the hordes of social workers, NGO representatives and management professionals from Hong Kong who have, through their work on the Mainland, been inculcating a sense of civic mindedness among their Mainland brethren, as the Chinese society has become more capitalist and uncaring (*Asiaweek*, 8 July 2007). On the other hand, China's influence on Hong Kong, both direct and indirect, is on the rise. Its positive impact on the stock market, the rise of trading, the increasing number of cross-boundary marriages, the growing number of Mainland students studying at Hong Kong universities, and so on, are some examples of how societies and people on either side are being interwoven into new patterns that will be as distinctive as they will be strong.

As for Hong Kong's contribution to the global economy, Hong Kong will, as in the past, grow in stature on the strength of its pillar industries, namely financial services, logistics, tourism and professional services. Its growing importance as a global financial centre can be anticipated. Hong Kong will continue as a crucial link in the global network of financial, logistics, tourism and service activities. Its competitiveness will be sustained, even improved, as long as Hong Kong is vigilant about inventing and reinventing itself, taking into account China's continual rise as a global power and the formulation of regionalization schemes with Hong Kong as a player. In other words, with Hong Kong's unique strengths and the OCTS arrangement, Hong Kong will continue to shine as China's and Asia's world city, and prove its worth as the gateway between China and the world, a role that no other Chinese city can ever replicate in the foreseeable future.

To conclude this chapter and this book, and continuing on the theme of how Hong Kong can serve China and the world, I wish to quote a recent statement by Anthony Cheung Bing-leung, a member of the Executive Council, which in my view is a fitting way of rounding off the subject of the first decade and moving on to the next:

> As the mainland moves rapidly into the world, so is the world moving towards it. Between mainland China and the world stands Hong Kong, whose role lies in its connectedness with both. When becoming immersed in China does not amount to "mainlandisation," and maintaining strong links with the western world does not mean a deficit in national identity, then Hong Kong will have found its confidence.
>
> I have a dream. One day outsiders will see China's face through Hong Kong just as much as through other mainland cities like Beijing, Shanghai, Guangzhou and Tianjin. "One country, two systems" will be turned around so that the two organic parts together make one nation (*SCMP*, 2007, p. 6).

References

Beaverstock, J. V., P. J. Taylor and R. G. Smith (1999), "A Roster of World Cities," *Cities*, 16 (6): 445–58.

Federation of Hong Kong Industries (FHKI) (2007), *Made in PRD: Challenges and Opportunities for Hong Kong Industry*. Hong Kong: FHKI.

Forder, James (2007), *Hong Kong 2007: Tens Years On*. London: John Swire & Sons.

Goodstadt, Leo (2005), *Uneasy Partners: The Conflict between Public Interest and Private Profit in Hong Kong*. Hong Kong: Hong Kong University Press.

Hong Kong newspapers and magazines:

Asiaweek

Hong Kong Economic Journal

Ming Pao

South China Morning Post (SCMP)

Times

Wen Wei Po

Hong Kong Special Administrative Region (HKSAR) (1997), *Hong Kong: A Review of 1997*. Hong Kong: Information Services Department.

Japan Centre for Economic Research (JCER) (2006), *Potential Competitiveness Ranking 2006*. From http:www.jcer.or.jp/eng/pdf/kenrep81pdf.

Ku, Agnes S. and Ngai Pun (eds.) (2004), *Remaking Citizenship in Hong Kong: Community, Nation and the Global City*. Oxon: RoutlegeCurzon.

Lau, Siu-kai (ed.) (2002), *The First Tung Chee-hwa Administration: The First Five Years of the Hong Kong Special Administrative Region*. Hong Kong: The Chinese University Press.

Ma, Xiaoling (2006), "Economic Integration and the Environmental Legal System for Hong Kong-Guangdong Region." In Anthony Gar-on Yeh et al. (eds.), *Developing a Competitive Pearl River Delta in South China under One Country-Two Systems*. Hong Kong: Hong Kong University Press, pp. 383–98.

Martin, Michael F. (2007), *Hong Kong: Ten Years After the Handover CRS Report for Congress*. Washington, D.C.: Congressional Research Service.

Meyer, David R. (2002),"Hong Kong: Global Capital Exchange." In Saskia Sassen (ed.), *Global Network, Linked Cities*. New York: Routledge, pp. 249–71.

Ni, Pengfei (ed.) (2007), *Annual Report on Urban Competitiveness, No. 5*. Beijing: Social Science Academic Press.

Sung, Yun-wing (2002), "Hong Kong Economy in Crisis." In Lau (ed.), *The First Tung Chee-hwa Administration*, pp. 123–38.

South China Morning Post (2007), *Ten Years On*, 1 July.

Yeung, Yue-man, Shen Jianfa and Zhang Li (2006), *China's Eleventh Five-year Plan: Opportunities and Challenges for Hong Kong*. Commissioned research report undertaken for the Bauhinia Foundation. Hong Kong: Hong Kong Institute of Asia-Pacific Studies, The Chinese University of Hong Kong.

Select Bibliography of Hong Kong, 1997–2007

Ash, Robert, et al. (ed.) (2003), *Hong Kong in Transition: One Country, Two Systems.* London: RoutledgeCurzon.

Burns, John P. (2004), *Government Capacity and the Hong Kong Civil Service.* New York: Oxford University Press.

Chan, Ming K. and Alvin Y. So (eds.) (2002), *Crisis and Transformation in China's Hong Kong.* Hong Kong: Hong Kong University Press.

Chang, David Wen-wei and Richard Y. Chuang (1998), *The Politics of Hong Kong's Reversion to China.* Basingstoke: Macmillan; New York: St. Martin's Press.

Cheng, Joseph Y. S. (ed.) (1999), *Political Participation in Hong Kong: Theoretical Issues and Historical Legacy.* Hong Kong: City University of Hong Kong Press.

Chiu, Stephen Wing Kai and Lui Tai Lok (eds.) (2000), *The Dynamics of Social Movement in Hong Kong.* Hong Kong: Hong Kong University Press.

Currie, Jan, Carole J. Petersen and Mok Ka Ho (2006), *Academic Freedom in Hong Kong.* Lanham, MD: Lexington Books.

Dodsworth, John and Dubravko Mihaljek (1997), *Hong Kong, China: Growth, Structural Change, and Economic Stability during the Transition.* Washington, DC: International Monetary Fund.

Enright, Michael J., Edith Scott and Edward Leung (1999), *Hong Kong's Competitiveness beyond the Asian Crisis: An Overview.* Hong Kong: Research Department, Hong Kong Trade Development Council.

Enright, Michael J., et al. (2003), *Hong Kong and the Pearl River Delta: The Economic Interaction.* Hong Kong: 2022 Foundation.

Federation of Hong Kong Industries (FHKI) (2003), *Made in PRD: The Changing Face of Hong Kong Manufacturers.* Hong Kong: FHKI.

—— (2007), *Made in PRD: Challenges and Opportunities for Hong Kong Industry.* Hong Kong: FHKI.

Forder, James (2007), *Hong Kong 2007, Ten Years On.* London: John Swire & Sons.

Fosh, Patricia, et al. (eds.) (1999), *Hong Kong Management and Labour: Change and Continuity.* London; New York: Routledge.

Goodstadt, Leo F. (2005), *Uneasy Partners: The Conflict between Public Interest and Private Profit in Hong Kong.* Hong Kong: Hong Kong University Press.

Grant, Colin and Peter Yuen (1998), *The Hong Kong Health Care System.* Sydney,

N.S.W.: School of Health Services Management, University of New South Wales.

Guan Huanfei (2005). *Yiguoliangzhi xia Xianggang jingji zengchang yanjiu* (The Study of Hong Kong's Economic Growth under the One Country, Two Systems). Hong Kong: Joint Publishing Co. Ltd.

Guo Guocan (2007), *Huigui shinian de Xianggang jingji* (The Ten Years Economy after Hong Kong's Return to China). Hong Kong: Joint Publishing Co. Ltd.

Hamilton, Gary G. (ed.) (1999), *Cosmopolitan Capitalists: Hong Kong and the Chinese Diaspora at the End of the 20th Century.* Seattle: University of Washington Press.

Ho, Kwok-leung (2000), *Polite Politics: A Sociological Analysis of an Urban Protest in Hong Kong.* Aldershot, Hants, England: Burlington, Vt.: Ashgate.

Ho, Lok Sang and Robert Ash (eds.) (2006), *China, Hong Kong and the World Economy: Studies on Globalization.* Basingstoke: Palgrave Macmillan.

Hong Kong Economics Journal Monthly (2007). *Yiguoliangzhi yu Xianggang jubian* (One Country, Two Systems and the Great Changes of Hong Kong. July.

Hong Kong–Japan Business Co-operation Committee (2007), *Evolving Hong Kong — Newly Revealed Secrets of Its Competitiveness.* Tokyo (in Japanese).

Horlemann, Ralf (2003), *Hong Kong's Transition to Chinese Rule.* London; New York: RoutledgeCurzon.

Jao, Y. C. (2001), *The Asian Financial Crisis and the Ordeal of Hong Kong.* Westport, Conn.: Quorum Books.

Koh, Tommy, Aileen Plant and Eng Hin Lee (eds.) (2003), *The New Global Threat: Severe Acute Respiratory Syndrome and Its Impacts.* Singapore: World Scientific Pub. Co.

Ku, Agnes S. and Ngai Pun (2004), *Remaking Citizenship in Hong Kong: Community, Nation and the Global City.* Oxon: RoutlegdeCurzon.

Kwok, Joseph and Joseph Y. S. Cheng (eds.) (2000), *Hong Kong and China in Transition: Strategies for a Better Quality of Life.* Chicago: Imprint Publications.

Lam, Jermain T. M. (2000), *The Political Dynamics of Hong Kong under the Chinese Sovereignty.* Huntington, NY: Nova Science Publishers.

Lam, Wai-man, et al. (eds.) (2007), *Contemporary Hong Kong Politics: Governance in the Post-1997 Era.* Hong Kong: Hong Kong University Press.

Lau, Siu-kai (2002), *The First Tung Chee-hwa Administration: The First Five Years of the Hong Kong Special Administrative Region.* Hong Kong: The Chinese University Press.

Law, Kam-yee and Lee Kim-ming (eds.) (2004), *The Economy of Hong Kong in Non-Economic Perspectives.* Hong Kong: Oxford University Press (China) Ltd.

Li, Kui-wai (2006), *The Hong Kong Economy: Recovery and Restructuring.* Singapore: McGraw-Hill Education.

Li, Pang-kwong (ed.) (1997), *Political Order and Power Transition in Hong Kong.* Hong Kong: The Chinese University Press.

Liao Meixiang (2007), *Zhonggang jiaoyu da ronghe* (The Integration of China and Hong Kong's Education). Hong Kong: Yadian wenhua qiye.

Liu Changle (2003), *Zaizao tiantang: Zhenxing Xianggang jingji de sikao* (Remaking Heaven: The Thinking of Reviving Hong Kong's Economy). Hong Kong: Joint Publishing Co. Ltd.

Lo, Shiu-hing (2001), *Governing Hong Kong: Legitimacy, Communication and Political Decay.* New York: Nova Science Publishers.

Lu Zhaoxing (Lo Shiu-hing) et al. (2003), *Dong Jianhua zhengfu: Guanzhi weiji yu chulu* (*Tung Chee-hwa's Government: Governance Crisis and the Way Out*). 2nd edition. Hong Kong: Ming Pao Publishing Co.

Ma, Ngok (2007), *Political Development in Hong Kong: State, Political Society, and Civil Society.* Hong Kong: Hong Kong University Press.

Martin, Michael F. (2007), *Hong Kong: Ten Years After the Handover CRS Report for Congress.* Washington, D.C.: Congressional Research Service.

Meyer, David R. (2000), *Hong Kong as a Global Metropolis.* Cambridge, UK: Cambridge University Press.

—— (2002), "Hong Kong: Global Capital Exchange." In Saskia Sassen (ed.), *Global Networks, Linked Cities.* New York: Routledge, pp. 249–71.

Miners, Norman (1998), *The Government and Politics of Hong Kong.* Hong Kong: Oxford University Press. (5th Edition, with post-handover updated by James T. H. Tang.)

Ng, Sek Hong and Carolyn Y. W. Poon (2004), *Business Restructuring in Hong Kong: Strengths and Limits of Post-Industrial Capitalism.* New York: Oxford University Press.

Onishi, Yasuo (ed.) (1997), *One Country, Two Systems: China's Dilemma.* Tokyo: Institute of Developing Economies.

Postiglione, Gerald A. and James T. H. Tang (eds.) (1997), *Hong Kong's Reunion with China: Global Dimensions.* Hong Kong: Hong Kong University Press.

Rioni, S. G. (ed.) (2002), *Hong Kong in Focus: Political and Economic Issues.* New York: Nova Science Publishers.

Scott, Ian (ed.) (1998), *Institutional Change and the Political Transition in Hong Kong.* Basingstoke: Macmillan; New York: St. Martin's Press.

—— (2005), *Public Administration in Hong Kong: Regime Change and Its Impact on the Public Sector.* Singapore: Marshall Cavendish International.

Sing, Ming (ed.) (2003), *Hong Kong Government & Politics.* Hong Kong: Oxford University Press.

So, Alvin Y. (1999), *Hong Kong's Embattled Democracy: A Societal Analysis.* Baltimore: Johns Hopkins University Press.

So, Alvin Y., Nan Lin and Dudley Poston (eds.) (2001), *The Chinese Triangle of*

Mainland China, Taiwan, and Hong Kong: Comparative Institutional Analyses. Westport, Conn.: Greenwood Press.

South China Morning Post (2007), *Ten Years On.* 1 July.

Sung, Yun-wing (2005), *The Emergence of Greater China: The Economic Integration of Mainland China, Taiwan and Hong Kong.* Houndmills, Basingstoke, Hampshire; New York, N.Y.: Palgrave Macmillan.

Tan Huizhu (ed.) (2007), *Jibenfa yu Xianggang huigui shizhounian* (The Basic Law and the Tenth Anniversary of Hong Kong's Return to China). Hong Kong: Geshang chuban gongsi.

The Asia Pacific Journal of Public Administration (2007), Symposium on the First Ten Years of the Hong Kong Special Administrative Region of the People's Republic of China, Vol. 29, No. 1, June.

TIME (2007), Hong Kong, China, issue 18 June 2007.

Wang, Gungwu and John Wong (eds.) (1999), *Hong Kong in China: The Challenges of Transition.* Singapore: Times Academic Press.

Wong, Kwan-yiu and Shen Jianfa (eds.) (2002), *Resource Management, Urbanization and Governance in Hong Kong and the Zhujiang Delta.* Hong Kong: The Chinese University Press.

Wong, Siu-lun and Toyojiro Maruya (eds.) (1998), *Hong Kong Economy and Society: Challenges in the New Era.* Hong Kong: Centre of Asian Studies, The University of Hong Kong.

Wong, Yiu-chung (ed.) (2004), *"One Country, Two Systems" in Crisis: Hong Kong's Transformation since the Handover.* Lanham: Lexington Books.

Wright, Sue and Helen Kelly-Holmes (eds.) (1997), *One Country, Two Systems, Three Languages: A Survey of Changing Language Use in Hong Kong.* Clevedon, England; Philadelphia: Multilingual Matters.

Yang Ruwan (Yeung Yue-man) and Shen Jianfa (eds.) (2005), *Fanzhusanjiao yu Xianggang hudong fazhan* (The Pan-Pearl River Delta and Its Interactive Development with Hong Kong). Hong Kong: Hong Kong Institute of Asia Pacific Studies, The Chinese University of Hong Kong.

Yazhou zhoukan (Asia Weekly) (2007), *Xianggang huigui shizhounian—ni buneng buzhidao de Xianggang* (The Tenth Anniversary of Hong Kong's Return to China: You Cannot Afford Not to Know). 24 June.

—— (2007), *Huigui shizhounian—Xianggang gaibian Zhongguo* (The Tenth Anniversary of Hong Kong's Return to China: Hong Kong Changes China). 8 August.

Yeung, Chris (ed.) (1998), *Hong Kong, China: The Red Dawn.* Sydney: Prentice Hall Australia Pty. Ltd.

Yeung, Yue-man (ed.) (2002), *New Challenges for Development and Modernization: Hong Kong and the Asia-Pacific Region in the New Millennium.* Hong Kong: The Chinese University of Hong Kong.

Yeung, Yue-man, Shen Jianfa and Zhang Li (2006), *China's 11th Five-year Plan:*

Opportunities and Challenges for Hong Kong. Commissioned research report undertaken for the Bauhinia Foundation.

You Anshan (2005), *Yiguoliangzhi yu HuGang jingji* (One Country, Two Systems and the Shanghai–Hong Kong Economy). Hong Kong: Xianggang Wenhui chubanshe.

—— (2005), *HuGang jingji hezuo yu CEPA* (The Cooperation between Shanghai, Hong Kong and CEPA). Hong Kong: Xianggang Wenhui chubanshe.

Yuan Xiaojiang (2006), *ShenGang jingji yitihua* (The Economic Integration of Shenzhen and Hong Kong). Shenzhen: Haitian chubanshe.

Xie Juncai (ed.) (2002), *Women de difang, women de shijian: Xianggang shehui xinbian* (Our Place, Our Time: A New Introduction to Hong Kong Society). Hong Kong: Oxford University Press.

Zhang Dinghuai (ed.) (2007), *Mianxiang 2007 nian de Xianggang zhengzhi fazhan* (Facing the Political Development of Hong Kong in 2007). Hong Kong: Dagong bao chuban youxian gongsi.

Editor and Contributors

YUE-MAN YEUNG (楊汝萬) is Emeritus Professor of Geography, Research Professor of the Hong Kong Institute of Asia-Pacific Studies, and Director of Shanghai–Hong Kong Development Institute, The Chinese University of Hong Kong. His wide-ranging research interests have focused on China's coastal cities, South China, globalization and Asian cities. He has published extensively, including, as editor, co-editor or author, *Globalization and the World of Large Cities* (1998), *Fujian* (2000), *Globalization and Networked Societies* (2000), *New Challenges for Development and Modernization* (2002) and *Developing China's West* (2004).

ALBERT H. Y. CHEN (陳弘毅) is a graduate of The University of Hong Kong and Harvard University. He began his academic career at The University of Hong Kong in 1984. He served as Head of the Department of Law in 1993–1996, and as Dean of the Faculty of Law in 1996–2002. He is currently the Chan Professor in Constitutional Law at the Faculty of Law, The University of Hong Kong.

KAI-MING CHENG (程介明) is Chair Professor in Education and Senior Advisor to the Vice-Chancellor at The University of Hong Kong, and is currently member of the Education Commission. He was Dean of Education and Pro-Vice-Chancellor of The University of Hong Kong and Visiting Professor at the Harvard Graduate School of Education, 1996–2006. He was a school teacher and a school principal. He obtained his Ph.D. from the University of London, Institute of Education.

ARENT GREVE, Dr. Oecon., is Professor of Organization Theory at the Norwegian School of Economics and Business Administration. His main research interests are topics related to social capital. He applies the concept to a variety of theoretical and empirical settings using social network analysis. Greve's research focuses on networks looking at migration and settlement, labour markets for immigrant professionals, and entrepreneurship among other topics. His main theoretical point of departure is institutional theory of organizations.

JIA QINGGUO (賈慶國) is Professor and Associate Dean of the School of International Studies at Peking University. He received his Ph.D. from Cornell University in 1988. He has taught in universities in the United States and Australia before his appointment at Peking University. He was a Research Fellow at the Brookings Institution and a Visiting Professor at the University of Vienna. He has published extensively on U.S.-China relations, relations between the Chinese Mainland and Taiwan, Chinese foreign policy and Chinese politics.

LAU SIU-KAI (劉兆佳) is Head, Central Policy Unit of the Hong Kong Special Administrative Region government and Emeritus Professor of Sociology, The Chinese University of Hong Kong. Professor Lau specializes in comparative politics and the social and political development of Hong Kong. He is the author of *Society and Politics in Hong Kong* (1982) and co-author (with Kuan Hsin-chi) of *The Ethos of the Hong Kong Chinese.*

JOANNA W. Y. LEE (李慧瑩) received her Ph.D. from The Chinese University of Hong Kong. She is an Instructor in the Department of Geography and Resource Management and a Programme Director of the Centre for Environmental Policy and Resource Management at The Chinese University of Hong Kong. She is by profession a chartered town planner. Her research areas include urban planning, globalization and regional development.

LEE SHIU-HUNG (李紹鴻) is Emeritus Professor of Community and Family Medicine at The Chinese University of Hong Kong. He had a distinguished career in the civil service, rising to be Director of Health. His extensive experience in public health extends from local to inter-national levels, with recognitions duly awarded, especially in the Asia-Pacific region.

YOK-SHIU F. LEE (李煜紹) is Associate Professor in the School of Geography at The University of Hong Kong. He holds a B.A. degree from the University of Hawaii at Manoa and a Ph.D. degree in Urban Planning from MIT. His current research projects include water resources management, corporate environmentalism, urban environmental management and cultural heritage management in southern China.

CHO-NAM NG (吳祖南) is Associate Professor in the School of Geography at The University of Hong Kong. He holds a B.Sc. and a Ph.D. degree in Environmental Science from the University of Lancaster, U.K. His research interests include environmental impact assessment and modelling, and time-series analysis. He is a member of the Advisory Council on the Environment, and the Chairman of the Environmental Impact Assessment Sub-committee.

MEE-KAM NG (伍美琴) is Associate Professor at the Centre of Urban Planning and Environmental Management, The University of Hong Kong. She is one of the pioneers in developing "planning for real" workshops in the local planning curriculum. Her research interests include urban planning and sustainability issues. She has published widely in various international refereed journals and has won five Certificate of Merit or Silver Medal Awards of the Hong Kong Institute of Planners.

QIN XIAO (秦曉) is Chairman of China Merchants Group and China Merchants Bank. He is also a member of the Tenth Chinese People's Political Consultative Conference and Chairman of Hong Kong Chinese Enterprises Association. Before joining China Merchants Group, he served as President and Vice-Chairman of China International Trust and Investment Corporation (CITIC), and Chairman of CITIC Industrial Bank. He obtained a Ph.D. in economics from the University of Cambridge. He is a professor and doctorate supervisor at the Graduate School of the People's Bank of China. He has authored several papers and books in the fields of economics and management.

JANET SALAFF attended the University of California, Berkeley, for her Bachelor's, Master's and Doctorate degrees in Sociology. In 1970, she joined the faculty of the Department of Sociology at the University of Toronto, where she is Professor Emeritus. She is Honorary Research Fellow, Centre of Asian Studies, The University of Hong Kong. Her major research interests are applying neo-institutional theory to the sociology of migration from Hong Kong.

JIANFA SHEN (沈建法) is Professor and Head of Graduate Division in the Department of Geography and Resource Management, The Chinese

University of Hong Kong. His research interests focus on urban/regional governance and development, spatial population modelling and migration analysis. He serves in the Editorial Boards of *The China Review*, *Population, Space and Place* and *Applied Spatial Analysis and Planning*.

YUN-WING SUNG (宋恩榮) is Chairman and Professor in the Economics Department, Co-Director of the Institute of Economics, and Associate Director of the Hong Kong Institute of Asia-Pacific Studies at The Chinese University of Hong Kong. He is also Editor of the *Asian Economic Journal*. His research interest covers international trade and economic development in China, Hong Kong and Taiwan.

WANG GUNGWU (王賡武) is Director of the East Asian Institute, Faculty Professor in the Faculty of Arts and Social Sciences, University Professor, National University of Singapore, and Emeritus Professor of the Australian National University. Professor Wang received his B.A. (Hons) and M.A. degrees from the University of Malaya in Singapore, and his Ph.D. at the University of London. His teaching career took him from the University of Malaya to The Australian National University and to The University of Hong Kong, where he was Vice-Chancellor, 1986 to 1995. He is a recognized authority in research on overseas Chinese and has published extensively.

TIMOTHY KA-YING WONG (王家英) is a Research Associate Professor and Associate Director of Public Policy Research Centre of the Hong Kong Institute of Asia-Pacific Studies, The Chinese University of Hong Kong. Professor Wong's major research interests include social and political development in Taiwan and Hong Kong. He has contributed to such academic journals as *Nations and Nationalism*, *Journal of Contemporary China*, *Asian Perspective*, *Social Development Issues*, *Democratization*, *Social Policy and Society*, *International Journal of Social Welfare* and *Social Indicators Research*.

WONG SIU-LUN (黃紹倫) is the Director of Centre of Asian Studies at The University of Hong Kong. His research interests include the study of entrepreneurship, business networks, migration, social indicators and the development of sociology in China. He is the author of *Emigrant Entrepreneurs: Shanghai Industrialists in Hong Kong* (1988), and co-editor of *Indicators of Social Development: Hong Kong 2004* (2006).

WONG TZE-WAI (黃子惠) is Professor in the Department of Community and Family Medicine, School of Public Health, The Chinese University of Hong Kong. A specialist in Community Medicine, he has served on many advisory bodies within the Hong Kong SAR government. A prolific writer, he has acquired professional medical qualifications in Hong Kong, the U.K. and Australasia.

MICHAEL YAHUDA is Professor Emeritus of International Relations, The London School of Economics and Political Science. Currently he is a fellow at the Woodrow Wilson International Center for Scholars, Washington D.C. He has been a Visiting Professor at several universities in Australia and the U.S. He is the author of six books and more than 200 scholarly articles and chapters in books. He is the author of *Hong Kong, China's Challenge* (1996).

HENRY WAI-CHUNG YEUNG (楊偉忠) is Professor of Economic Geography at the National University of Singapore. He is a recipient of several research awards, including Commonwealth Fellowship, Fulbright Foreign Research Award and Rockefeller Foundation's Team Residency in Bellagio. He has three single-authored books, one co-authored textbook, five edited books, 75 papers in refereed journals and 30 chapters in books. He is also Editor of *Environment and Planning A*, *Economic Geography*, and *Review of International Political Economy*, Asia-Pacific Editor of *Global Networks*, and sits on the editorial boards of 10 other international journals.

Name Index

Subject Index